THE ORIGINS OF MONEY IN THE IRON AGE MEDITERRANEAN WORLD

This book shows how money emerged and spread in the eastern Mediterranean, centuries before the invention of coinage. While the invention of coinage in Ancient Lydia around 630 BCE is widely regarded as one of the defining innovations of the ancient world, money itself was never invented. It gained critical weight in the Iron Age (ca. 1200–600 BCE) as a social and economic tool, most dominantly in the form of precious metal bullion. This book is the first study to comprehensively engage with the early history of money in the Iron Age Mediterranean, tracing its development in the Levant and the Aegean. Building on a detailed study of precious metal hoards, Elon D. Heymans deploys a wide range of sources, both textual and material, to rethink money's role and origins in the history of the eastern Mediterranean.

Elon D. Heymans is a scholar of the archaeology and history of both the Greek world and the Levant. His main focus lies on the social, political and historical context of early money use.

THE ORIGINS OF MONEY IN THE IRON AGE MEDITERRANEAN WORLD

ELON D. HEYMANS

CAMBRIDGE
UNIVERSITY PRESS

CAMBRIDGE
UNIVERSITY PRESS

University Printing House, Cambridge CB2 8BS, United Kingdom

One Liberty Plaza, 20th Floor, New York, NY 10006, USA

477 Williamstown Road, Port Melbourne, VIC 3207, Australia

314–321, 3rd Floor, Plot 3, Splendor Forum, Jasola District Centre, New Delhi – 110025, India

103 Penang Road, #05–06/07, Visioncrest Commercial, Singapore 238467

Cambridge University Press is part of the University of Cambridge.

It furthers the University's mission by disseminating knowledge in the pursuit of education, learning, and research at the highest international levels of excellence.

www.cambridge.org
Information on this title: www.cambridge.org/9781108838580
DOI: 10.1017/9781108975322

First published 2021

Printed in the United Kingdom by TJ Books Limited, Padstow Cornwall

A catalogue record for this publication is available from the British Library.

Library of Congress Cataloging-in-Publication Data
NAMES: Heymans, Elon D., author.
TITLE: The origins of money in the Iron Age Mediterranean world / Elon D. Heymans.
DESCRIPTION: New York, NY : Cambridge University Press, 2021. |
Includes bibliographical references and index.
IDENTIFIERS: LCCN 2020046708 (print) | LCCN 2020046709 (ebook) | ISBN 9781108838580 (hardback) | ISBN 9781108971652 (paperback) | ISBN 9781108975322 (epub)
SUBJECTS: LCSH: Money–Mediterranean Region–History–To 1500. |
Iron age–Mediterranean Region.
CLASSIFICATION: LCC HG1200.7 .H37 2021 (print) | LCC HG1200.7 (ebook) |
DDC 332.4/937–dc23
LC record available at https://lccn.loc.gov/2020046708
LC ebook record available at https://lccn.loc.gov/2020046709

ISBN 978-1-108-83858-0 Hardback

CONTENTS

FIGURES

MAPS

TABLES

PREFACE

In 1982, Eric Wolf wrote in the preface of *Europe and the People without History* that he had been motived by a need 'to counter the ascendancy in the human sciences of a formal rationality that no longer inquired into the causes of human action but sought merely technical solutions to problems conceived primarily in technical terms'.[1]

Interest in the historical development of money, whether scholarly or not, is all too often framed in technical or functionalist terms. The emergence of money in the ancient Mediterranean, to name but one example, has been perceived as a fundamental innovation to human livelihood and society, facilitating an increased and more sophisticated redistribution of goods.[2]

Yet how money gained prominence was hardly just a matter of overcoming practical obstacles, such as securing a supply of precious metal or processing it into manageable units for practical use. While money's functional properties might partially explain its significance, another part of the story is that financial instruments are adopted and propagated because they serve the interests and ambitions of certain groups and actors in society.

It was in the aftermath of the 2008 global financial crisis that I became intrigued by the causes of money's emergence in the ancient Mediterranean. It seems I was using the past to make sense of the present. In some ways, this book is the result of that pursuit.

1 Wolf 1982, ix.

2 See, for example, John Boardman (2014, 213–214): 'From the 6th century on the Greeks were able to spread the benefits of a monetary economy. Trade was no longer a matter mainly of barter. Wealth could be accumulated in a form acceptable to the whole Mediterranean.'

ACKNOWLEDGEMENTS

> At the outset, however, I have to confess that in looking over my notebook it struck me that Lord Keynes didn't tell the whole story about the long run. At least as far as Anthropology goes, two things are certain in the long run: one is that we'll all be dead; but another is that we'll all be wrong. Clearly, a good scholarly career is where the first comes before the second.
>
> Sahlins [1993] 2002, 2.

This book touches upon a variety of topics. Some of these have drawn an increasing amount of scholarly attention in recent years. In a few cases, the state of research has changed significantly since I embarked on the project that led to this book. Hence, I might not have written the same book, had I done so today. While this is only obvious, it is important for me to note at the outset when and in what settings this book came about.

This book was originally written as a doctoral thesis at Tel Aviv University and submitted in February 2018. The structure and substance of the thesis are retained in what lies before you. Before submitting the initial manuscript to Cambridge University Press for review in August 2019, I revised the text and updated the content to integrate new insights; in preparing the final manuscript, I limited myself to including new information that pertains to the primary data. I can only hope the final result will prove durable.

I am greatly indebted to my supervisors, Israel Finkelstein, Irad Malkin and Alex Fantalkin, for encouraging me to expand my horizon and for setting an inspiring example to look up to. Additionally, Jack Kroll, David Schaps, Josine Blok and Marleen Termeer read most or all of the manuscript in different phases, providing countless comments that helped me to improve the text.

Over the course of this project, many people have been supportive, whether in offering their suggestions or sharing their time or sometimes unpublished work. I am grateful to Jack Kroll, David Schaps, Haim Gitler, Claus Jurman, Christine Thompson, Gil Davis, Josine Blok, Robin Lane Fox, Jane Goodenough, Konrad Schmid, Karen Radner, Samuel Verdan, John Papadopoulos, Peter Rhodes, Tzilla Eshel, Naama Yahalom-Mack, Mimi Lavi, Nava Panitz-Cohen, Omer Sergi, Nadav Na'aman, Yuval Gadot, Eran Arie, Jack Green, Ze'ev Herzog, Lily Singer-Avitz, Daniel Master, Ernst Pernicka, Joost Crouwel, Mathieu de Bakker, Kristin Kleber, David Wigg-Wolf, Winfred van de Put, Chris Williams, Edward Harris and Selene Psoma.

I am particularly indebted to Benjamin Sass, Ran Zadok and Kees Neeft, who have each been most generous in sharing their time and expertise and in answering my many and often tedious questions.

The detailed study of the material presented in this book was undertaken with the help and support of many. I thank Eran Arie (Israel Museum), Alegre Savariego and Fawzi Ibrahim (Israel Antiquities Authority/Rockefeller Museum), Jack Green, Helen McDonald and Kiersten Neumann (Oriental Institute Museum), Katy Blanchard (Penn Museum) and Alex Pezzati and Eric Schnittke (Penn Museum Archives), Deborah Giannessi (NINO), Regina Hölzl (Kunsthistorisches Museum, Vienna), Joe Greene (Harvard Museum of the Ancient Near East) and Ze'ev Herzog, Assaf Nativ and Ido Koch (Tel Aviv University). The Swiss School of Archaeology in Greece facilitated my research and stay in Eretria, while the help of Samuel Verdan in carrying out the work and Pascal Simon, who took the photographs, made the work infinitely more fun than it would otherwise have been. The support of Petros Themelis was instrumental in granting us permission for the study. Research on the Megiddo A and B hoards in Chicago was made possible through the Collections Research Grant of the Oriental Institute of the University of Chicago and undertaken with the assistance of Erin Hall. Sjanna Besteman sacrificed time during vacation in order to help with the photography of the Beth Shean material from the Rockefeller Museum. Thanks to the help of Dafna Langgut, I was able use the lab of Yuval Sapir at the botanical gardens in Tel Aviv for the weighing and photography of some of the material. Furthermore, Yuval Goren was so kind to carry out p-XRF analyses on a selection of objects. Elisabetta Boaretto (Weizmann Institute) and Gillian Vogelsang-Eastwood and Koen Berghuijs (Textile Research Centre, Leiden) helped with the analysis of the textile fragments in the Arad hoard. The support of Jitte Waagen was instrumental in setting up the project database. Libraries in Tel Aviv, Amsterdam and Athens served as bases for a significant part of the study and writing, and I thank in particular the library staff of the British School at Athens for their help and support during the various stages of the work. The Netherlands Institute at Athens formed a safe haven during many extended visits. Revision of the original manuscript was undertaken as a postdoc at Utrecht University, funded through Anchoring Innovation, the Gravitation Grant research agenda of the National Research School in Classical Studies in the Netherlands (OIKOS). I also wish to thank Trent Hancock, Dhanuja Ragunathan, Katherine Barbaro and Beatrice Rehl for their guidance throughout the publication process.

Moreover, I am grateful to many for providing me with images or giving permission for their use. In addition to those already mentioned, I extend my gratitude to Marina Oganyan, Bahadır Yıldırım, Jean-Christophe Peyssard, Stephanie Boonstra, Daniela Rosenow, Joachim Heiden, Katharina Brandt,

Matthaios Bessios, Athena Athanassiadou, Thierry Theurillat, David Schloen, Ami Mazar, Nava Panitz-Cohen, Ariel Warhaftig, Susan Allison, Willemijn Waal and Carolien van Zoest. Acquiring and processing the illustrations would not have been possible without the generous support of the Netherlands Institute at Athens and the Stichting Nederlandse Penningkabinetten/Royal Dutch Numismatic Society. The illustrations were prepared for publication with the help of Mikko Kriek.

Colleagues and friends in Tel Aviv, Amsterdam and elsewhere – in particular, Assaf Kleiman, Mario Martin, George Mavronanos, Adam Kaplan, Noah Kaye, Jitte Waagen and Marleen Termeer – helped me to map out my course, navigating between disparate cultural and geographical regions, both in work and in life. Gert Jan van Wijngaarden, Vladimir Stissi and Cathy Morgan have offered additional support over the years, for which I remain indebted.

Lastly, it is difficult to imagine how it would have come to this without the dedication of my parents and Sjanna, who have taught and given me much of what I know and value. I hope they can accept the result as a small token of recompense.

AUTHOR'S NOTE

The attentive reader searching for consistency in the transliteration of Greek, Hebrew and other ancient names or terms or the use of place names is likely to be disappointed. My only aim has been not to distract the reader with spellings or renderings that appear unconventional or old-fashioned at best and unfamiliar at worst. I have thus used both Arabic and Hebrew places names, opting for Tell Jemmeh, rather than Tel Gama, and Megiddo, rather than Tell el-Mutesellim. In the case of Greek names, I have tried to follow modern transliteration (Chalkidike and Akanthos, rather than Chalcidice and Acanthus), with the exception of conventional forms, such as Corinth and Plutarch. Abbreviations of classical authors and works, epigraphical corpora, biblical texts etc. follow the conventions in the fields of classical and biblical scholarship. See, for example, the *Oxford Classical Dictionary*, 3rd ed. (Oxford: Oxford University Press, 2003) and *The SBL Handbook of Style*, 2nd ed. (Atlanta: SBL, 2014).

Unless specified otherwise, chronological indications refer to before the common era (BCE). Translations are my own, unless referenced or specified otherwise.

ONE

RETHINKING THE ORIGINS OF MONEY

1.1 ARGONAUTS

'The coastal populations of the South Sea Islands, with very few exceptions, are, or were before their extinction, expert navigators and traders'.[1] These opening lines could have well described the pioneering maritime traders of early Greece and the eastern Mediterranean that set out to explore the coastal regions of the Aegean and beyond in search of valuables and the networks that supplied them. Yet, they refer to the populations of Melanesia, in particular, those of the islands east of Papua New Guinea that were engaged in the complex exchange system known as the *Kula*, which Bronisław Malinowski described in his monumental study, *Argonauts of the Western Pacific*. Published almost a century ago, it famously detailed the adventurous explorations of the Massim men of the Trobriand Islands and their exchange of prestigious shell bracelets and necklaces – the so-called *vaygua* or *veguwa*, or tokens of wealth – along a series of islands and across large distances. Through this intricate system of exchange, the Massim sought not to accumulate some general form of wealth, but rather to enhance their reputation and status.

Although invoking with his title the famous seafarers of Greek mythology, Malinowski nowhere explored the obvious analogy. As Annette Weiner pointed out, 'had Malinowski pursued these links beyond the title he might

[1] Malinowski 1922, 1.

not have been so perplexed about why Trobrianders were dedicated to kula. Like the ancient Greeks, Trobrianders endure hardship of travel, disappointment, and even death in their search not just for immediate fame but to achieve the regeneration of their names'.[2] Anthony Forge also drew on the suggested analogy in his 1971 Malinowski Memorial Lecture, titled *The Golden Fleece*, when asking 'What exactly has been brought back from these distant lands, by Malinowski and by later voyagers – what is the quality of the fleece triumphantly returned to these shores: gold, silver, or mere wool?'[3] This play on the treasure that was the aim of the Argonauts' voyage raises another aspect of the analogy, which, beyond what Malinowski might have intended, is certainly worth exploring.

Alluded to already in the earliest known Greek poetry, Hesiod's *Theogony* and Homer's *Illiad* and *Odyssey*, the legend of the *Argonautica* is among the oldest of the Greek world, likely going back to the Iron Age.[4] Although a popular subject in Greek literature, most early works are now lost, making the third-century BCE epic of Apollonius of Rhodes the earliest extant complete version.[5] It has Iason and the Argonauts sail to distant Aia of King Aietes in Kolchis, on the east coast of the Black Sea, on a near-magical ship, the *Argo*, with a speaking timber donated by the goddess Athena.[6] At Kolchis, aided by Medea's magic, Iason acquires the Golden Fleece, which he takes home to assume the throne of Iolkos. Strabo would later explain the voyage as motivated by the precious metal resources in Kolchis, and he describes how placer gold was won in this region from the riverbeds using sheep fleeces, thus explaining the origin of the myth of the Golden Fleece.[7]

The idea that the legend reflected a quest for Kolchis' gold might only have developed in the fifth century, when exploitation of local gold sources began,[8] and the kingdom of Aietes was presumably not associated with Kolchis before the sixth century.[9] Yet, the association with the Black Sea region can be traced back still earlier. Several of Odysseus' adventures were adapted from an earlier version of the *Argonautica*, and the evidently extraneous geographical knowledge of the Pontus region in these parts of the Odyssey suggests that the

[2] Weiner 1992, 132.
[3] Forge 1972, 527.
[4] West 2011, 113–122; 2014, 30.
[5] Gantz (1993, 340–373) provides a full discussion of the legend and all extant sources, including iconographical sources.
[6] Although lying beyond the purpose of our current discussion, the significance of the Argo and its role within the wider epic brings to mind Malinowski's elaborate description of the Trobriand canoes, their construction and their wider role in the kula (Malinowski 1922, 105–145).
[7] Strab. 1.2.39; 11.2.19.
[8] Tsetskhladze 1994, 114–115; 1995, 307, 323–325.
[9] West 2011, 113; *pace* Vanschoonwinkel 2006, 90.

Argonauts' voyage came to be located in the Black Sea in the middle of the seventh century, following the first Greek colonisation of the region.[10] In the preceding phase, however, Aia, the destination of the legend, had not been a known place but was rather some distant mythical land. The seventh-century poet Mimnermos wrote that in order to bring back the Golden Fleece, Iason had sailed to Aia, 'where swift Helios' rays are stored in a golden chamber/treasury by the edge of Okeanos';[11] and also the evident connection with Aya, the Babylonian goddess of the dawn and the Sun-god's wife, points to a distant mythical land of the rising sun.[12]

As noted, this legendary tale of travelling heroes that explored the edge of the world, and brought back great wealth and moreover undying fame, had first developed at an early stage. Like the stories of the Odyssey,[13] it was inspired by early historical Greek maritime exploration and the wealth and power that had come with this.[14] In the legend, the Golden Fleece arguably signifies royal authority,[15] but this cannot be separated from the significance that gold held in early Greece, symbolising wealth and honour and, as alluded to by Mimnermos, worthy to be stored in a treasury.[16] This pre-eminent association of the Argonauts' treasure with gold reflects the idea that wealth, power and authority were intricately linked to long-distance travel.[17]

In this sense, the analogy with Malinowski's Argonauts is clear: these were adventurous seafarers, whose status and social position were linked to the valuables that they managed to acquire through exchanges on their journeys. Significantly, Malinowski placed the elaborate exchange mechanism – the *kula* – that formed the context and focus of their ambitions and interactions at the centre of his work; and this became the monumental contribution that *Argonauts of the Western Pacific* made to the field of anthropology and beyond.

This book, too, is to some degree a testament to the pioneering travellers who brought back treasures from their voyages. Most importantly, however, it puts centre stage a type of exchange that became the focus of activity in the eastern Mediterranean and the valuables involved in these exchanges.

This particular type of valuable – money – has long been the focus of activity in complex societies, albeit in varying degrees. What money is or can be in different societies will be discussed at length in Chapter 2; it suffices for now to describe it as a conventional and standardised embodiment and store of

10 West 2005; 2014, 119–120.
11 Fr 11–11a W; West 2011, 114.
12 West 1997, 407.
13 Cf. Malkin 1998, 62–119.
14 Cf. Vanschoonwinkel 2006, 101.
15 Lordkipanidze 2001.
16 See Section 5.3.
17 Cf. Helms 1988.

transferable value in a set social and cultural context, used for the purpose of exchange and payment. As such, money has been the focus of human livelihood, ambition, mobility and even violence. Money has long, if not always, been with us, but it certainly wasn't always in its current form or extent. A critical stage in that early history of money took place some three thousand years ago in the eastern Mediterranean when the use of precious metal money increased throughout different spheres of society, leaving a lasting mark on the history of money to the present day. That critical stage in the rise of early money-use is the focus of this book.

1.2 THE EARLY HISTORY OF MONEY

1.2.1 The Rise of Money in the Iron Age Eastern Mediterranean

Coinage appears to have been invented independently in three different regions, Lydia, India and China, around the middle of the first millennium BCE. The coins in these different areas of the world were typologically different, and there is little reason, if any, to suggest that the innovation had a single origin. Although, in that regard, it is of little historical relevance who was first, current evidence for coinage from Lydia and the neighbouring east Greek cities slightly predates that from other regions.[18] Much more significant than the matter of precedence is the fact that Greek coinage, through the cultural influence of Greek and Roman civilisation, left its mark so clearly in Western political and economic self-awareness.

Presumably invented in the ancient kingdom of Lydia around 630 BCE, the first coins were minted in electrum, a natural alloy of gold and silver, native to western Anatolia. Within a short period of time, electrum coinage was adopted by the Greek cities of western Anatolia, and by the end of the Archaic period more than a hundred Greek polities were minting their own coins, this time in silver.

Money, most clearly identifiable in the form of coins, was a characteristic aspect of the ancient Mediterranean and Near Eastern world, forming a prominent part of economic structures and interactions throughout antiquity. It is often understood as having had a revolutionary impact on society, in ways comparable to the introduction of writing or the clock, by recalibrating important aspects of daily life and the way society is structured.[19] Gordon Childe famously argued that 'cheap iron democratized agriculture and industry and warfare',[20] and, similarly, one could see money as having liberalised

[18] Schaps 2004, 232–235; 2007.
[19] E.g., Schaps 2004, 1–2.
[20] Childe 1942, 183.

economic relationships and society and politics. However, whether money in itself can be credited with such profound effects is a complex matter of contention that deserves detailed discussion.[21] While it is likely that the spread of money had far-reaching consequences, it is equally possible that the spread of money is itself reflective of the profound and critical changes that affected ancient society.

Regardless of the way in which this issue is dealt with, this early chapter in the history of money, dealing with the initial rise and spread of money throughout society, has often been equated with the invention and spread of coinage within the Greek world.[22] Although coinage is certainly an iconic form of money, money is not necessarily always coin. In fact, evidence for money transactions ranges widely beyond coinage, taking the form of different goods or materials, variously quantifiable, most notably uncoined precious metal weighed out in standard units. The fast spread of coinage across the Greek world, specifically after silver coinage was introduced before the middle of the sixth century,[23] suggests that the concept of money was already familiar to the Greeks and that money was commonly used and accepted, presumably in the form of precious metal in standard weights.[24]

The use of weighed precious metal as a form of money – suitable for use in transactions and hoarding, but also as a standard of value – had long been known in the Mediterranean and the Ancient Near East, but in the centuries prior to the introduction of coinage something had changed. Evidence for this is preserved in the form of a series of precious metal hoards, containing mostly cut and broken objects – known as *hacksilber* and *-gold*, from the southern Levant dating roughly to the Iron Age (see Table 3.1, Map 3.1).[25] This suggests that by this time its circulation and use in the eastern Mediterranean, and specifically in the southern Levant, increased considerably, providing a basis for the pervasive spread of coinage.

This development is more than a prologue to the known history of money in the Western world; it sets the stage and provides a point of departure, but it also leads to the rise and expansion of money into different spheres of society. The importance of money in the many parts of society, such as public administration, religious life, (international) markets and warfare, is ultimately a result of this development.

21 See Section 2.1.
22 Finley [1973] 1985, 141; Balmuth 1975; Price 1983; Howgego 1995; Weatherford 1997; Kurke 1999; Davies 2002; Osborne 2007, 278. Cf. Osborne [1996] 2009, 245.
23 Wallace 2016.
24 Kim 2001, 13–20; Kroll 2001a; 2008a; 2012; Seaford 2004, 89–95; Von Reden 2010, 19–25; Bresson 2016, 261–264. Cf. Davis 2011. see Chapter 5.
25 Kletter 2003; Thompson 2003. See also Appendix.

Although this chapter in the history of money is of critical importance, much of it is still unknown and unwritten. A possible reason for this is that the topic finds itself on the crossroads between different disciplines and regional discourses. The history of money in the ancient world has traditionally been the domain of numismatists and ancient historians, focusing on coins and written sources, while being less receptive to archaeological evidence.[26] At the same time, among archaeological studies of Early Iron Age Greece, interest in the development of money or its social and economic context has been mostly restricted to incidental finds, most prominently the Eretria hoard,[27] while general studies have paid little, if any, attention to the development of money, a concept so strongly associated with coinage.[28] Alternatively, scholarly focus on money in the societies of the Ancient Near East has been more common, due to the abundance of administrative and financial records,[29] and silver hoards have been increasingly regarded as representing an early form of money, or at least a medium of exchange.[30] However, of these archaeological studies on the monetary significance of pre-coinage silver, few have attempted to explore the potential links in the development of precious metal money across different regions of the eastern Mediterranean.[31]

The understanding that a historically significant development in the use of precious metal as a form of money, indicated by its increase in the archaeological record, took place in the eastern Mediterranean during most of the Iron Age forms the premise underlying this book. Representing the historical rise of money in the region, this development is of great importance to the historical context under study, but at the same time holds a wider relevance to the study of money in general. In order to shed light on this development, a detailed analysis of all currently known precious metal hoards from the Iron Age eastern Mediterranean will be presented, as well as an interpretation of the hoards within a social, political, economic and historical context for the use of money as an exchange mechanism and a value strategy. The analysis and subsequent interpretations are not a straightforward matter of reconstructing economic history but demand a thoroughly interdisciplinary approach, addressing anthropological notions, dealing with the material study of precious metal objects and considering a wide variety of textual and

26 E.g., Howgego 1995; Le Rider 2001; Schaps 2004; Seaford 2004; van Wees 2013; Bresson 2016, 260–285. Cf. Kroll 2001a; 2003; 2008a; 2008b; 2012; 2013a.

27 See Chapter 3; Section 5.4; Appendix.

28 Lemos 2002; Dickinson 2006; Osborne 2007; Morris 2007; 2009; Morgan 2009; Thomas 2009; van Wees 2009, 461–462. Cf. Hall 2007, 249–254.

29 E.g., Dercksen 1999; Hudson 2004; Jursa 2010.

30 Balmuth 1964; 1967; 1975; 1976; 2001a; 2001b; Gitin and Golani 2001; Thompson 2003; 2007; Kroll 2001b; 2013a; Peyronel 2010; Eshel et al. 2018. Cf. Kletter 2003.

31 Notable exceptions are M. Balmuth, C. Thompson and J. Kroll. See Section 3.1.

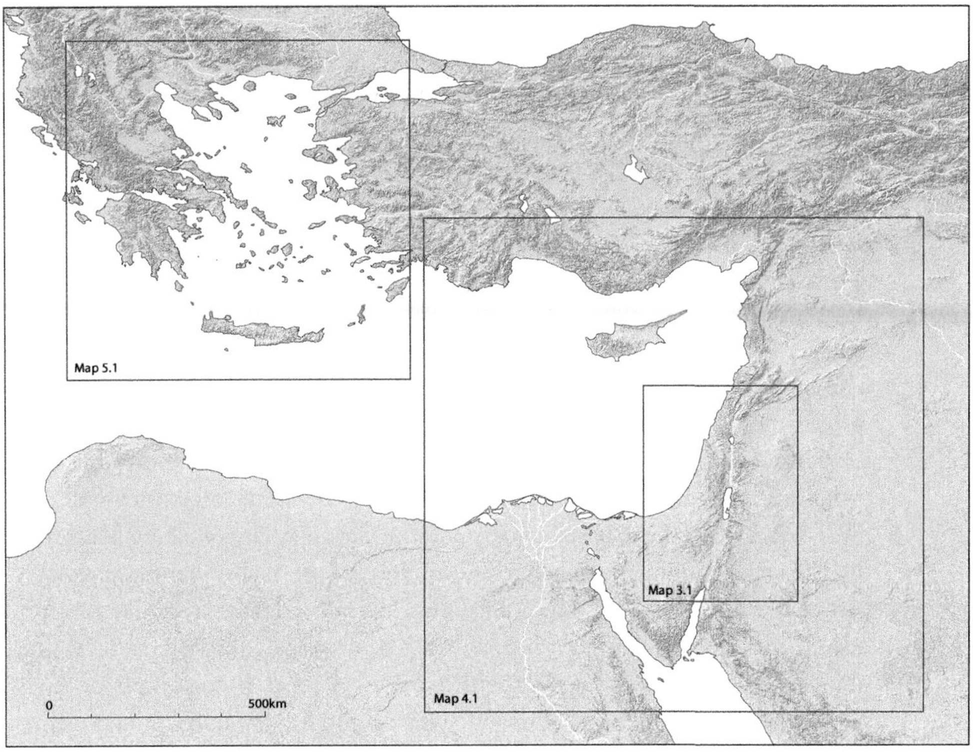

MAP 1.1 The Eastern Mediterranean

archaeological sources from different periods and regions. As a result, the current study does not confine itself to a single scholarly discourse but will navigate across various disciplinary boundaries in the course of the argument presented.

The chronological focus of the study can be broadly defined as the period between the later phase of the Late Bronze Age (the thirteenth century) and the end of the Iron Age in the southern Levant or the early Archaic period in Greece. While the hoards at the core of this study date between the end of the Late Bronze Age (the second half of the twelfth century) and the end of the Iron Age in the southern Levant (early sixth century), the historical scope is slightly broadened, especially on the early end of the time frame, in order to provide a relevant historical context to the hoards, including earlier comparanda.

The eastern Mediterranean provides a broad setting for the development of precious metal money during this time frame (see Map 1.1). Specific focus lies however on two regions, the southern Levant and the Aegean. While evidence from the southern Levant reflects an unprecedented increase in the local use of silver, the Aegean, through periods of intermittent contact with the Levant, came to appropriate precious metal, initially gold and later silver, as a form of money and ultimately in the form of coinage. It is important to emphasise that these forms of money had a local context of use, a local significance, and were appropriated to local needs. Yet interaction in the Mediterranean and the role of precious metals in international trade – the supply of which had to be secured though the maintenance of long-distance contacts – suggest that this development can only be properly appreciated when following an integrated transregional approach.

1.2.2 *The Relevance of Early Money*

The historical rise of money in society does not stand alone as an important development. It was part of long-term dynamics and changes that affected early historical societies in the eastern Mediterranean. Being one of the most profound and striking of these developments, the study of money's rise has direct bearing on the way we understand the various changes taking place from the late second millennium up to the middle of the first millennium BCE. As part of the wider historical and social developments that characterise this time frame, the development of money-use, as a focus of social and political strategies, was intricately tied in with a range of other historical phenomena, such as the development of alphabetic writing and literary traditions, the rise of new religious practices and communities and the rise of territorial states and fiscal institutions. While the development of money-use reflects on many of these historical processes, two should be singled out in particular.

After the collapse of Bronze Age political structures in the course of the twelfth century BCE, the early first millennium witnessed the rise of territorial states around the Mediterranean. In the southern Levant city-states and territorial kingdoms, notably the biblical kingdoms of Israel and Judah, arose and developed complex state institutions mostly during the ninth and eighth century, while city-states or poleis developed in the Aegean during the eighth and seventh century.[32] Although no doubt under their influence, these states were at least initially independent from the large Near Eastern empires (Neo-Assyria, Egypt, Babylonia) that expanded into the southern Levant from the late eighth century onwards. Although territorial polities had already developed in earlier periods as well, these early first-millennium states are often regarded as standing at the basis of Western social and political history, partly due to the fact that their societies developed literary, philosophical and theological traditions passed down to us in writing.

Precious metal money became an important focus of economic and public life in these early states, already before coinage, being used, for example, for

[32] See Section 2.2.

the payment of fines, taxes or religious contributions.[33] Not only did this use affect the significance of money within society, the emerging role of money within interactions under the umbrella of the state also reflects the development of fiscal policies and institutions. Although it is not the case that money can only arise under the authority of an administrative state,[34] its appropriation by state institutions does have a bearing on the character and significance of money. Similarly, although states do not necessarily require elaborate fiscal institutions based on the pervasive spread of money in society, it is fair to say that the character of the territorial states that arose in the early first millennium as well as their subsequent development was profoundly influenced by the historical importance of money in these societies.

A second historical process on which the development of money can shed light is the growth of the Mediterranean economy of the early first millennium. After the relative breakdown of state-sponsored communication and exchange networks in the late second millennium, the first half of the first millennium witnessed an unprecedented growth of the Mediterranean economy and increase in interregional contacts. This was further stimulated by the increasing economic integration of formerly disparate spheres and the rise of interdependent markets.[35] The historic development of precious metal money-use and subsequent spread of coinage were certainly propelled by these developments, but at the same time formed an important stimulating force behind the economic growth. In the Archaic period, this came to expression in the form of trade contacts and economic integration that stretched from Babylonia to central and western Europe and forms of money that were sought after across the Mediterranean and beyond.

Due to the unprecedented spread of money during the Iron Age and its historical impact, the relevance of this study reaches beyond the confines of ancient societies. Money remains one of the most enduring symbols of human society and history, particularly within the Western world. Its development, significance and role in history have been extensively studied and have received considerable attention in recent wide-ranging works on human history, reaching an audience beyond academic readership,[36] not to mention the surge of popular books on money, mostly from an economic perspective, since the start of the 2007–2008 financial crisis. Despite the fact that the topic of money has attracted wide interest, its early development preceding coinage has mostly evaded public but also scholarly attention. However, a thorough

[33] See Sections 4.2 and 5.2–5.4.
[34] See Sections 2.2 and 2.3; Heymans and Termeer 2020a.
[35] E.g., Sherratt and Sherratt 1993; Osborne 1996; Section 5.4.
[36] E.g., Graeber 2011; Harari 2014; Pye 2014; Goetzmann 2016.

understanding of how money came to be so pervasive in life and under what circumstances it conquered its place in society has direct relevance not only to the general history of money but also to the anthropology of money.

This unwritten chapter in the history of money thus offers a valuable opportunity to study the role and significance of money and what can be referred to as 'the politics of value' in society.[37] This case study can help us to understand and scrutinise the general conditions under which money gains importance, the strategies in which it is employed and for what purpose and offers insight into the social and political implications of its spread. These potential insights can contribute to wider historical and anthropological approaches to and understandings of money.

1.2.3 In Search of the Origins of Money

As mentioned, the early development of money in the Iron Age Mediterranean can be regarded as a first chapter in a grand general history of money in the Western world. But more than being a chronological starting point for such a constructed historical narrative, can it offer any insight into the purported origins of money? Does it reveal how money came into being; how, once upon a time, the story of money began?

Histories of money – and there are many – are often and variously troubled by the tendency to describe a single, more or less unified, narrative.[38] Often, such narratives are evolutionist in their approach, meaning that they present money as something that develops along a single line in history, naturally progressing from simple and primitive money in the distant past to sophisticated and complex money in the present.

Such evolutionary histories, as well as definite claims of where and how our money originated, risk encouraging self-congratulatory constructs. They carry with them the danger of looking at ancient society as a fated attempt to become us, bringing to mind Marx's belief in the inevitable results of the laws of capitalist production in noting that 'the country that is more developed industrially only shows, to the less developed, the image of its own future'.[39]

There is not, however, one historical form of money, originating in antiquity and evolving into its present form. Money does not naturally evolve over time, adapting itself gradually to the changing conditions in society, nor can its history be written in one coherent narrative. If such a history would ever be written, we would have to accept that consecutive chapters would not always appear to logically follow from one another. Rather, money is a universal phenomenon

[37] Cf. Appadurai 1986a; Section 2.1.
[38] Cf. Weatherford 1997; Davies 2002; Ferguson 2008.
[39] Marx 1976, 91.

that can be found in different social and cultural settings.[40] It is volatile, subject to the conditions under which it functions and to the regimes of value that happen to carry the upper hand, and its role in society is not necessarily warranted by its previous standing or importance. It can play an important and articulate role in economic interaction or become inarticulate and subsidiary to other exchange mechanisms or value strategies, only to be appropriated again in a different form and under different circumstances. One needs to think only of the hyperinflation that struck the Weimar Republic and Austria in the aftermath of the First World War,[41] or the dominance of barter in post-Soviet Russia,[42] to understand that the use of money in any given society can collapse and subside in a short period of time and without much anticipation.

It seems then that any universal history or universal origin of money has to be constructed from particular histories and particular origins. This requires us to challenge our understandings of what money is before being able to study it in the historical or archaeological record.[43] For now, it suffices to emphasise that money and its significance are particular to a set – social, cultural, political and historical – context.

Aside from these considerations, the origin of money has long attracted general interest on an abstract, non-empirical level. Different theories have gained popularity, emphasising different alleged characteristics of money and becoming engrained in commonly accepted discourses on money.[44] Although these theories will also be addressed in Chapter 2, it is worthwhile to address two opposing theories in passing.

The most commonly accepted origin narrative claims that money developed out of barter, as the ancient predecessor of commercial exchange under capitalism.[45] Although going back to Aristotle,[46] the case was famously stated by Adam Smith, who described the division of labour as a 'consequence of a certain propensity in human nature . . . to truck, barter and exchange one thing for another',[47] and further elaborated by others, notably William Stanley Jevons.[48] Under a division of labour, people would satisfy their needs through bartering, but this would require both sides in the exchange to desire the

40 See Chapter 2.
41 Fergusson [1975] 2010.
42 Humphrey 2000; Seabright 2000.
43 See Chapter 2.
44 For discussions that cover a range of theories, see, e.g., Pryor 1977, 149–183; Graeber 2011, 21–87.
45 For discussions, see, e.g., Pryor 1977, 157–161; Humphrey and Hugh-Jones 1992; Graeber 2011, 21–41.
46 *Pol.* 1.1257a 25–40.
47 Smith 1776, 20, 24–25.
48 Jevons 1875.

product that the other side has to sell. This led to the rise of a marketplace or fairs, where the logistic problem of barter – that one did not always need what the other had to offer – was soon overcome as one object increasingly took on the role of a means of exchange. This became money and gave way to long-distance trade and economic expansion, etc.

This narrative has been subject to extensive criticism[49] but remains the dominant theory on the origin of money within modern economics. A serious problem is that no empirical evidence has even been presented, not from the historical nor the ethnographic record, for the existence of such a society painted by Smith and others, with optimal commoditisation, but no money, and where barter is the dominant mode of exchange. Rather, barter functioned and continues to function alongside other modes of exchange. However, Smith's theory should not be regarded as having historical or anthropological validity but rather as a parable emphasising the efficiency of money within the framework of exchange, by providing logical proof that money reduces transaction costs.[50] This led to its adoption as a creation-myth in classical and neo-classical economics.[51]

An important critique of this narrative was offered by Karl Polanyi, who inverted the purported course of events, suggesting that long-distance trade developed out of political circumstances and the geographical 'division of labour'. Long-distance trade in turn led to markets and barter and allowed people to come into contact with money – emerging as a result – outside the normative confines of society. By coming into contact with money, the inherently socialist nature of human beings would be affected, enabling them to engage in haggling and bargaining and inducing a profit-oriented attitude.[52]

Caroline Humphrey and Stephen Hugh-Jones have carefully pointed out that Polanyi was indebted in his theory to Marx's belief that modes of exchange result from the political economy, rather than human nature. Marx located the origins of barter on the margins between primitive societies, 'on the grounds that only in the absence of communal rights to property was it possible for people to alienate their goods'.[53]

The problem with this principle lies, however, in the fact that the circulation of valuables within a society is not conditioned by the alienation of goods, in the negative sense that people are tempted (and sometimes economically forced) to sell off or give up goods for short-term gain, invoking the term's

49 E.g., Hudson 2004, 108–110; Hart 2005, 161–163; Graeber 2011, 21–41.

50 *Pace* Anderlini and Sabourian 1992.

51 Humphrey and Hugh-Jones 1992, 2.

52 Polanyi 1944, 61–62. For discussions of Polanyi's critique, see Humphrey and Hugh-Jones 1992, 12; Hann and Hart 2011, 60; Hart and Ortiz 2014, 469–470.

53 Humphrey and Hugh-Jones 1992, 12; Marx 1976, 182–183.

association with the gloomy factory products of disenfranchised labourers in industrial Europe. Rather, the circulation of valuables is shaped by strategies to cope with, individualise and appropriate communal property, with the long-term result of upholding the social or cosmic order. Such exchanges, as the *kula* illustrates,[54] can be the focus of communality, allowing individuals to navigate within the community.[55] In this way, the exchange of valuables, from subsistence goods to brass rods and the *vaygua* in the *kula*, is sanctioned by their being encoded in a cultural logic that serves as the basis for normative practice.[56] While modes of exchange indeed result from the political economy, barter and monetary exchange do not stand outside of society but are an essential part of it.

Both these grand narratives are problematic, not in the least due to the absence of empirical substantiation, and perhaps we should be wary towards any abstract origin-theory of money that fails to appreciate the particular variation and heterogeneity of money. That being said, the case presented here can contribute to our understanding of money's origins in the Iron Age Mediterranean world, and thus to our general conception of its role and development in past and present societies.

1.3 A BRIEF OUTLINE

Two lines of argument are pursued in this book. The first is based around the precious metal hoards and argues that the hoards reflect the use of money in exchange and payment, while the second deals with the historical context of money-use and focuses on the historical developments and the social contexts that reflect the changing role and significance of money.

The detailed study of the hoards stands at the centre of the argument presented here and forms a starting point to explore the use and significance of money during the Iron Age in the southern Levant and in the Aegean. Before presenting the material and discussing its implications, we need to examine our framework of reference and explore what it is we mean when we refer to money and what it is we want to refer to, in order to prevent ourselves from employing anachronisms.

In Chapter 2, an elaborate framework is set up for the critical study of money in the past, exploring its characteristics and relations to social, economic, and political contexts of use, based on anthropological and ethnographic scholarship.

54 Cf. Leach 1983, 5–8.

55 This notion can be compared to what Bloch and Parry refer to as the 'long-term transactional order' (1989, 23–28), with the added caveat that individuality and individual competition can be regarded as part of this communality, rather than as being subversive to it.

56 Cf. Brandherm, Heymans and Hofmann 2018.

A determinist approach to money is rejected, arguing instead that there is not one form of money, but rather that the meaning of money depends on the cultural matrix in which it is set (Section 2.1). Also, the various binary distinctions between two types of money, all echoing a distinction between primitive and modern money, are rejected as being not conducive to a better understanding of money in the early Mediterranean (Section 2.2).

Instead, as a suitable approach to the hoard material, an understanding of money as being a commodity and a token at the same time is adopted.[57] The material characteristics of the hoards demonstrate that these aspects are not opposed, but rather interrelated, allowing for an interpretation of the dynamic and transitory physical nature of the hoard material as the basis for its use and appreciation as a form of money (Section 2.3).

This provides a proper basis for the presentation of the hoards in Chapter 3. Here, an analysis and interpretation of the material in the hoards is offered, starting with a discussion of the ways in which these hoards represented value (Section 3.1). The question to what degree the objects in the hoards would have been used as a form of money, and for what this would have been used, is dealt with on the basis of a detailed analysis of the materiality of the hoards. Underlying this approach is the understanding that a consistent pattern of material characteristics reflects a set behavioural practice.

Based on a critique of the ways in which the material has been previously analysed, a methodology is laid out that focuses on the context of the hoards, their internal metrology and the typology of the individual objects (Section 3.2). The comparative analysis that follows (Section 3.3), allows for a diachronic interpretation of the hoard material, demonstrating a dramatic change in the materiality of the hoards between the Late Bronze Age/Iron I transition (ca. twelfth–eleventh century), and the late Iron I (ca. tenth century), reflecting the increasing use and circulation of silver in exchange. These hoards indicate the use of small change in carrying out small-scale transactions. The consistency in the materiality of the hoards until the seventh century (Iron IIC), shows the continuity of this practice, and the comparability with a hoard from late eighth-century Eretria (Greece) indicates a similar use there. After the start of the seventh century, this pattern dissolves, suggesting a change in the circulation of silver during this period. By contextualising the results from the hoard analysis within a historical time frame, it becomes possible to relate changes in the (monetary) use and circulation of silver to historical and social circumstances (Section 3.4).

This preliminary historical reconstruction forms the basis for a more detailed discussion of the historical context that can be offered for the development of

[57] Hart 1986.

money-use in the southern Levant in Chapter 4. In order to gain a proper understanding of the significance of silver and what led to its appropriation as money, the chapter starts with a discussion of the significance of silver in Late Bronze Age Ugarit and Late Bronze Age trade, and subsequently examines the implications of the collapse of Late Bronze Age political hierarchy and the retreat of the Egyptian authority from the southern Levant for trade networks and the modes of exchange employed there. It is argued that the weakening ability of a central authority to secure trade networks stimulated a growing reliance on silver to carry out transactions and maintain a supply of goods (Section 4.1).

The rise of territorial states and the development of fiscal institutions is discussed on the basis of a critical approach to biblical sources documenting the increasing need for collecting silver for tributary payments to overlords, as well as the description of a fiscal procedure for the collection of taxes in the temple (Section 4.2). Next, the effects of Neo-Assyrian involvement in the region on the local circulation of silver starting in the late eighth century are critically examined in light of the claims that the Neo-Assyrian conquest fostered monetisation in the southern Levant. This claim is rejected, demonstrating that the Neo-Assyrians rather depleted the region of its silver. Only following the takeover in the region by the twenty-sixth dynasty of Egypt did fresh silver arrive again to the southern Levant through Mediterranean trade via Egypt (Section 4.3).

Drawing out these Mediterranean connections, Chapter 5 focuses on the different contexts in which money and precious metal resources played a role in the Aegean, in order to better understand the different circumstances under which precious metal became increasingly important as a form of money. Possible forms of money in early Greece preceding the introduction of coinage have attracted considerable attention. However, instead of seeing these as a universal and widespread predecessor of coinage (i.e., *obeloi*) or universal measure of value (i.e., oxen in Homer), the focus is placed here on the specific contexts in which these potential forms of money appear (Section 4.1). This allows us to better understand how valuables and forms of money came to play a role in different spheres of society and through those contexts shaped the development of money. The sphere of cult formed such a context, being a clear focus of value politics starting in the Late Geometric period, with an increasing need for the organisation of expenses through (monetary) fees and contributions (Section 5.2). Also, the sphere of law, through which the state imposed fines and compensation payments, formed a context in which money payments were formalised (Section 5.3).

However, emphasis is placed in this chapter on the increasing importance of precious metal in trade (Section 5.4). Euboian traders likely adopted the use of precious metal money from the Levant, and it is argued that the late eighth-century Eretria hoard reflects the active search of Euboians for precious metal sources, gold specifically, in the area of the Thermaic gulf. Also, the subsequent foundation of colonies in the northern Aegean from the middle of the seventh century is discussed in relation to the exploitation of local precious metal sources. It is argued that the opening up of contacts with Egypt formed an impetus for this development, providing a foreign market for Aegean silver, preceding the production of silver coinage in the Aegean by more than half a century. Aegean maritime traders presumably pioneered this trade, leading by the late seventh century to the integration of formerly disparate economic spheres in the eastern Mediterranean. Silver did not become a focus of their effort because it simply represented a general form of wealth but because its trade and exchange became essential to the maintenance of social networks and the associated status. This stimulated the increasing use of silver in Aegean trade, thereby providing opportunities for the levy of trade taxes by emerging fiscal institutions.

Chapter 6 revisits general questions regarding the way money as a representation of conventional value comes into being and draws out conclusions with regard to the way in which distance plays a role in the construction of value. Although money is constructed as such within a local context, possibilities are suggested for an understanding of an early development of money that lies in the convergence of different valuations or regimes of value within society and across cultural and geographical distance. Finally, I reflect on the implications this study has for our understanding of the introduction of coinage and the historical weight with which it is credited. This can help us re-examine the profound changes that shaped the early Mediterranean and redefine the historical relevance that ancient money has to the present.

TWO

OUTLINE OF AN APPROACH TO MONEY

2.1 TOWARDS A DEFINITION OF MONEY

The nature of money has long been the subject of fascination to a variety of scholarly disciplines. It has proven, however, very difficult, if not virtually impossible, to come up with a single straightforward definition. Some have even raised objections against such an endeavour, commenting that a clear definition would not do justice to the complexities of the concept nor would it prove helpful as a research tool.[1] David Schaps wisely remarked that 'for the historian tracing the beginning of an idea, a definition is a hindrance', which surely applies as much to our case as to his.[2]

In order to find a way around this difficulty, introductions to the topic of money, as well as discussions of its nature, have often found themselves focusing

[1] Jevons 1875, 248; Einzig [1949] 1966, 309–318; Dalton 1965, 61–62; Bloch and Parry 1989; Gregory 1997, 6; Hart and Ortiz 2014, 466. Cf. Einzig [1949] 1966, 6; Pryor 1977, 151–157.

[2] Schaps 2004, 3–4. Note, however, the following (preliminary) definitions. Einzig defines primitive money as 'a unit or an object conforming to a reasonable degree to some standard of uniformity, which is employed for reckoning or for making a large proportion of the payments customary in the community concerned, and which is accepted in payment largely with the intention of employing it for making payments' ([1949] 1966, 317). After having discussed this definition, Davies gives his own preliminary definition: 'Money is anything that is widely used for making payments and accounting for debts and credits' (2002, 23, 29).

on the *functions* performed by money. Although the accounts diverge on details, we can generally identify four basic functions: money is a *means of exchange*, a *means of payment*, a *store of wealth* and a *standard of value*.[3] According to classical and neoclassical economics, a means of exchange enables transactions to take place without being restricted by a 'double coincidence of wants', whereby one wants to give up what the other wants to have and vice versa.[4] A means of payment is different from a means of exchange, since no counterpart is expected in the transaction. Important examples of such transactions are the payment of taxes or fines or perhaps also dedications to a divinity. As a store of wealth, money enables the hoarding of assets. As such, it becomes the focus of strategies to accumulate wealth. A standard of value serves to express the value of commodities under a common denominator; it renders different goods and services commensurable. This means that it can serve as an abstract unit of account in transactions, debts and credits that are not (necessarily) backed up by cash.[5]

However, as to the relative importance of these functions and whether one is essential to the concept of money, different attitudes exist. Economists generally list only three, ignoring money's function as a means of payment, while insisting on the exchange function as money's essential characteristic.[6] By considering payment as a form of exchange, they emphasise the original and continued advantage of monetary exchange over barter, while marginalising the importance of tax extraction and thereby the role of the state in the institution and maintenance of a monetary economy.[7]

Karl Polanyi criticised the primacy accredited to the exchange function. Taking off from the idea that modes of exchange are to be understood in the context of the political economy and that early communities had neither markets nor commercial exchange, he suggested that in primitive societies – defined in contrast to modern industrial society – 'different money-uses [are] institutionalized separately from one another. Insofar as there is interdependence between them, we find use for payment or as a standard or for storing wealth, having precedence over use for exchange'.[8] The sort of payments referred to were seen 'in connection with the institutions of bride-price, blood-money, and fines'.[9]

[3] Polanyi 1968a, 166–169; 1968b, 180–185; Schaps 2004, 12–15; Seaford 2004, 18; Von Reden 2010, 3–4; Guyer 2012, 2214.

[4] See Anderlini and Sabourian 1992, 84; Mankiw 2004, 628; Graeber 2011, 22–23.

[5] Money's function as *unit of account* is sometimes listed separately from its function as *standard of value* (Davies 2002, 27; Maurer 2006, 20), although I see no reason for this.

[6] See, e.g., Goudsmit 2004, 11–12; Mankiw 2004, 628–629; Temin 2006, 147; Ferguson 2008, 24; Graeber 2011, 22–24.

[7] Innes 1913; Hart 1986; Bloch and Parry 1989, 14, 18; Ingham 2004; Graeber 2011, 43–55.

[8] Polanyi 1968a, 157–158, 166–169; 1968b, 178–183, spec. 179.

[9] Polanyi 1968a, spec. 167; 1968b, 181–183; Grierson 1977; Ingham 2004, 90–93; Graeber 2011, e.g., 127–164.

Related to such an understanding of the payment function as a way of cancelling out social and ritual obligations, scholars (mostly from the social and/or historical sciences) have emphasised money's abstract quality as a unit of account, stating that money is essentially a way of determining and recording debt, primordially stemming from such obligations.[10] Philip Grierson, a numismatist and scholar of the early medieval period, searched for the origins of this account function in the context of the institution of *wergeld*, the damages and fines paid in recompense for injury, damage or loss, known from early medieval law codes, such as the *Lex Salica*.[11] An alternative was raised by Bernhard Laum, who identified the origins of the use of oxen as a unit of account in the work of Homer in their sacrifice to the gods.[12] In contrast to the understanding of a unit of account as a way of reckoning social, ritual and religious debts, scholars of the Ancient Near East (and, in particular, ancient Mesopotamia) have long emphasised the use of money of account in organising the production and distribution of agricultural produce.[13] As in many cases where money as a standard of value was used in records, in ancient Mesopotamia, an equivalent in kind, often barley, was commonly used in transactions. In essence, money was an abstraction.

These approaches in scholarship have paid limited attention to money as a means of exchange, to a large extent because its materiality was understood as a consequence of its abstract qualities. Geoffrey Ingham noted that through the 'conceptualisation of money in terms of generalised credit relations', the purpose was to direct the focus 'to the social relations between debtors and creditors' and 'away from money and goods'.[14] He therefore stated that 'as the logical foundation of money is to be found in money of account, it is here that we should attempt to locate its historical origins, not in the excavation and dating of money-stuff'.[15]

However, those who suggest that focusing on money's function as a means of exchange would legitimise and constitute the denial of money as a social relation[16] have been oblivious to certain agendas in social research. In what has been described as the single most influential contribution to current anthropological understandings of value,[17] Arjun Appadurai demonstrated how commodities are constructed through social relations and how their circulation

[10] Innes 1913; Grierson 1977; Hudson 2004; Ingham 2004, 72–75, 90–93; Graeber 2011, 43–71.

[11] Grierson 1977; Ingham 2004; 89–93. Cf. Sections 4.1 and 5.3.

[12] Laum 1924. Cf. Section 5.2.

[13] See Keynes 1982; Dercksen 1999; Powell 1999; Schaps 2004, 34–51; Monroe 2005.

[14] Ingham 2004, 69–73; Gilbert 2005.

[15] Ingham 2004, 89; cf. Grierson 1977, 12. Hudson 2004, 124. Cf. Gilbert 2005, 361: 'What I advocate herein is the necessity for drawing out the paradoxes of money as always a symbolic referent, a social system *and* a material practice.'

[16] Cf. Ingham 2004; Gilbert 2005.

[17] Graeber 2001, 30.

is the subject of politics.[18] The point of departure in his argument was taken from the German sociologist Georg Simmel, who claimed that economic value was not an intrinsic quality of an object, derived from its production (as in Marx's labour theory of value). Rather, the value of an object was constructed through exchange between subjects.[19] Now, if we accept that value is constructed through exchange, then money, in expressing and assessing value, is also intimately related to exchange. Ethnographic studies of primitive currencies have long emphasised that the material objects that feature regularly in these exchanges function in intricate ways in what Appadurai termed 'the politics of value'.[20] It thus appears that the significance of money is shaped to a large degree by the role it has in exchange.

Following this approach, the current study deals with objects of exchange and consequently places an emphasis on the exchange function of money. This does not, however, result from a conviction that one function is necessarily more prominent or essential than the other; as expressed before,[21] the forms in which money and its characteristics appear and develop throughout space and time diverge, and different approaches can prove appropriate and fruitful in different contexts and in dealing with different types of material. Rather, the emphasis placed here on exchange has an empirical basis. As the objects that lie at the core of this study were expressions of material and social value, it is when placed in the context of a transaction (exchange and payment) that we can try to understand their significance as forms of money.

In addition to this, an emphasis is placed here on money's function as a store of value. Likewise, this is mandated by the nature of our evidence. However, anthropological approaches to money have paid little, if any, attention to hoarding, as opposed to archaeological research, which has focused on it for obvious reasons. The conspicuous absence of hoarding or storing of valuables from theoretical and ethnographic studies on primitive valuables and money is noteworthy.[22] Although we know in several cases how the hoarding of valuables was prevented by means of either social restrictions (i.e., sumptuary laws) or conspicuous consumption (like the Kwakiutl potlatch), I have found hardly any ethnographic information on where, how, why and to what extent people hoarded their valuables, if they did so.[23] As to the reasons of the

[18] Appadurai 1986a.

[19] Simmel 1900; Appadurai 1986a, 3–4. For a wider approach to the concept of value, see Graeber 2001, 1–47.

[20] Appadurai 1986a. See also Malinowski 1920; 1922; Douglas 1982a; Leach and Leach 1983; Akin and Robbins 1999.

[21] See Chapter 1.

[22] An exception to this is Graeber 1996; 2001, 91–115.

[23] Concerning the Tiv (see Sections 2.1 and 2.2.1), it is simply noted that 'hoarding of goods' is absent (Bohannan and Bohannan 1968, 225), although it is said elsewhere that '*mere* monetary or subsistence wealth is not sufficient in itself to afford great prestige' (Bohannan 1955, 68–69,

situation, we can only speculate, but perhaps it is a result of the fact that, as hoarding might be considered morally ambiguous in many societies, informants might have been reluctant to share their insights with ethnographers.[24]

It is important to point out that a discussion of money's potential functions can neither lead us to a definition nor necessarily to a proper understanding of its meaning and significance to society.[25] Rather, a preoccupation with money's function would lead to a functionalist explanation of money's development and use, as if it exists and plays a role in societies simply because it performs these basic functions.[26] Additionally and particularly, it invites us to think that the more a specific medium is practically suited for performing these functions, the more likely it is to appear and function successfully as money, or the other way around, to attribute the success of a particular money to its ability to efficiently perform these functions. This reasoning is not strange to us. In fact, the idea that money should meet specific material requirements has become an essential part of the Western economic understanding of money. Presumably, the first economic thinkers to list such requirements were John Stuart Mill (1848) and William Stanley Jevons (1875). Following Mill, Jevons noted that for a commodity to function successfully as money, it would have to be valuable, portable, indestructible, homogenous, divisible, stable in value and cognisable.[27] This list, with slight differences here and there, has been accepted as conventional wisdom,[28] although it applies in fact only to (precious) metal money (specifically coinage) and not to paper money or modern '"dematerialized" credit-money'.[29] Moreover, many famous forms of so-called primitive money, prevalent in non-commercial economies, such as the stone money of the Yap, feathers money, raffia cloth, cowrie shells or butter do not nearly meet the conventional requirements. Although such currencies should appear to the Western economic mind as quite absurd, they nonetheless functioned (and in some cases still do) as acceptable currencies, forms of money, in their respective societies.[30] This shows that the idea of material or

my italics). See also Akiga [1939] 1965, 120ff. Cf. Yellen (1990), who relates the developing practice of hoarding among the !Kung in southern Africa in the 1970s to the transformation to a more sedentary, less mobile and interdependent lifestyle.

24 E.g., Yellen 1990, 102D.

25 Bloch and Parry 1989, 21; Guyer 2012, 2215–2216; Hart and Ortiz 2014, 470. Cf. Thompson 2003, 67, who refers to the four functions as 'Polanyi's ... anthropological definition of money', even though Polanyi himself never qualified them as such.

26 Ingham 2004, 69–70.

27 Jevons 1875, 31. The relevant passage from Mill is quoted by Von Reden 2010, 1–2.

28 Einzig [1949] 1966, 321; Pryor 1977, 153–154; Anderlini and Sabourian 1992, 87; Seaford 2004, 18; Von Reden 2010, 2. Cf. Maurer 2006, 27.

29 Ingham 2001, 312.

30 These, and many more examples, can be found in the two pioneering surveys of 'primitive money' by Einzig and Quiggin, both published in 1949 (Einzig [1949] 1966; Quiggin 1949). Despite having described such examples, Einzig draws attention to the conventional list of

technological requirements, while apparently applicable to precious metal coinage, reflects a kind of technological determinism that is not conducive for understanding the development of money. Money-stuff – the objects or materials that can be used as money – does not necessarily need to possess definite qualities, and a type of money that appears more efficient in this regard is not necessarily always preferred over one that we might consider practically unfit, such as the Yap stones.[31]

Here we reach, however, one of the central dilemmas of this chapter, because one could ask whether we should consider 'primitive money' as money at all. Often these primitive currencies have been disregarded and thought of as something very much unlike *our* money, that is, 'modern money'. Unlike modern money that supposedly serves to buy anything, the use of primitive money is restricted: it does not perform all monetary functions, or it does not buy everything. This forms the basis for the distinction, suggested first by Polanyi and developed further by anthropologist Paul Bohannan, between 'all-purpose money' and 'special-purpose money'. All-purpose or general-purpose money performs all of money's primary functions, while special-purpose or limited-purpose money does not, or, in the rare case that it does, not in all spheres of the economy.[32] This implies that 'our money is "all-purpose" money', and 'early money is ... special-purpose money'.[33] Whether this distinction has any heuristic value to the historical case that currently lies before us is the question that motivates the detailed discussion in Section 2.2.

Relevant for now is that money, and specifically general-purpose money, was long attributed with an inherent power to homogenise, to make all values commensurate. Because of this, Simmel, perhaps the most important thinker in this regard, saw in money a broker of individual freedom and at the same time a dissolver of social cohesion.[34] This perceived capacity to depersonalise social relations was related to an understanding of money as having 'an *intrinsic* power to revolutionise society and culture' and thereby a far-reaching impact on 'traditional' societies.[35]

requirements, while admitting that 'an object need not possess all of them in order to qualify for being regarded as money. After all, even a bad money is undoubtedly money' ([1949] 1966, 321). As explained above, the quality or success of a type of money is not necessarily dependent on its material attributes.

[31] Cf. Dalton 1965, 59–60; Bloch and Parry 1989, 16; Robbins and Akin 1999; Fitzpatrick 2016.

[32] Malinowski 1921, 13; Bohannan 1959, 492; Dalton 1965; Codere 1968, 558; Polanyi 1968a, 166–169; 1968b, 179; Schaps 2004, 14; Seaford 2004, 18; Maurer 2006, 20. Cf. Pryor 1977, 151–156.

[33] Polanyi 1968a, 166–169.

[34] Simmel 1900.

[35] Bloch and Parry 1989, 3; Maurer 2006, 16–22.

This understanding is perhaps best illustrated by Bohannan's famous ethnographic account of the Tiv of Central Nigeria. In two influential articles published in 1955 and 1959, he described how the introduction of Western money led to the disintegration of the traditional Tiv economy. According to Bohannan, the Tiv were an egalitarian society with a non-monetary subsistence economy that consisted of three discrete *spheres of exchange*. The first sphere contained subsistence goods, the second prestige objects, slaves, cattle, brass rods and so-called *tugudu* cloth and the third was reserved for the exchange of rights in human beings, particularly women. Exchange would normally take place within each sphere, referred to by Bohannan as *conveyance*, but could in exceptional cases take place between spheres. These so-called *conversions* were subjected to strong moral judgement: people always aspired to convert up, gaining prestige, while those forced to convert down were met with shame. The introduction of Western money by the British colonial authorities resulted in the breakdown of the system of exchange spheres, as it formed a common denominator for commodities from different spheres that had hitherto been incommensurable. As Bohannan claimed, 'general purpose money was introduced to Tivland, where formerly only special purpose money had been known', subverting their 'multicentric' economy, with dramatic effects on Tiv society.[36] Identifying money as an active, even socially subversive force, he concluded that 'money is one of the shatteringly simplifying ideas of all time, and like any other new and compelling idea, it creates its own revolution'.[37]

Although Bohannan's work has been and remains very influential, it has generated a growing body of scholarship critical of his ethnography as well as his conclusion. His model of the spheres of exchange will be further discussed in Section 2.2; for our current purposes, it is relevant to draw attention to the criticism that has been levelled against his conclusions that money was the cause of the revolutionary change in Tiv society. In what has been termed a 'signal intervention' in the field,[38] Maurice Bloch and Jonathan Parry objected that 'it is not *a priori* obvious that *by itself* money does indeed reduce everything to a common measure, or make it impossible for the Tiv to deny that certain things can be bought for money – as we deny that academic and political honours, marriage partners, sexual favours and so on can legitimately change hands against a money payment'.[39] The changes that occurred in Tiv society,

[36] Bohannan 1959, 500.
[37] Bohannan 1959, 503.
[38] Maurer 2006, 18.
[39] Bloch and Parry 1989, 12–16. See also Melitz 1970, 1037; Hart 2005, 163–165. Cf. Eriksen [1995] 2001, 187. The objections formulated by Bloch and Parry had essentially already been noted by Jacques Melitz in a footnote in 1970. His contribution was mainly overlooked, and he was not credited by Bloch and Parry.

Bloch and Parry argued, were caused not by the advent of an almost mystically empowered money but rather by other factors, such as the growth of markets under the *Pax Britannica*, leading to the introduction of cash crops and the coming of outside traders using cash to buy up Tiv agricultural produce. This resulted in a situation where the Tiv would complain that 'food is less plentiful today than it was in the past, though more land is being farmed'.[40] Another factor was the abolishment of exchange marriage by the colonial authority, thereby dissolving the upper sphere and undermining the position of the Tiv elders who had been in control of these exchanges. Bloch and Parry claimed that, like the Tiv elders, who blamed money for their problems, Bohannan had fallen into the trap of attributing the dramatic changes in Tiv society to the workings of money. True, as they warned from the start, 'money ... is in nearly as much danger of being fetishised by scholars as by stockbrokers'.[41] Thus, rather than money in itself being the cause of change, the increasing integration of regional economies and the rise of interdependent markets, coupled with the appearance of the colonial authority, had created the circumstances under which the traditional Tiv economy was put under pressure, resulting in its purported disintegration.[42]

Bloch and Parry identified the perception of money as naturally opening the gates to unfettered commoditisation of a kind that has been indiscriminately associated with contemporary capitalist society as an integral part of the Western tradition on money.[43] Moreover, anthropologists have shown how in many cases Western general-purpose money has not necessarily smashed traditional economic structures and often continues to exist side by side with traditional currencies.[44] The implication of all this for the current study is that any a priori assumption that money per se must have revolutionised societies in the ancient Mediterranean should be discounted; more so, we should be wary of any suggestion of the sort and remain attentive towards a variety of possible factors (social, political and economic) that could have affected supposed change.[45]

40 Bohannan 1955, 69.

41 Bloch and Parry 1989, 3.

42 However, Bloch and Parry's criticism has not been accepted by everyone: Sillitoe objects to their argument by stating that 'there is an irrefutable logic to the contention that money has a major impact on multicentric orders' (Sillitoe 2006, 20). Cf. Eriksen, who describes Bohannan's analysis as motivated by a 'systemic perspective', emphasising 'exogenous factors', as opposed to an 'actor-centred' one, but does not really offer fundamental objections (Eriksen [1995] 2001, 186–188).

43 Bloch and Parry 1989; Hart 2005, 163–165; Maurer 2006; Hart and Ortiz 2014, 472.

44 Akin and Robbins 1999; Maurer 2006, 20–22; Guyer 2012.

45 Cf. Keynes 1982, 253–254; Morris 1986a, 5–6; Weatherford 1997, 27–30; Schaps 2004, 194–195. In the 1920s, John Maynard Keynes sensibly remarked in the context of early Greece that 'the gradual adaptation of the primitive economy of the tribes to ... individualistic capitalism' should be placed in a context in which 'revolutionary

In the absence of a clear and comprehensive definition, and uncertain as to what impact money has on society, we should abandon the search for an essentialist understanding or unitary theory of money. Money does not have a set meaning nor does it need to have a certain effect on people. Indeed, Bloch and Parry have made this point clear and stress that the meanings attached to it and the symbolism through which it is represented are culturally diverse and result ultimately from the 'cultural matrix into which it is incorporated'.[46] It is not so much intended here that, evidently, different perceptions of value or understandings of exchange within a society and across cultural frontiers can lead to different meanings being attached to money.[47] What is rather meant is that in a set society different notions of wealth, exchange, property etc. give rise to the ways in which money is culturally constructed and viewed. In other words, the ways in which money is incorporated and the meanings attached to it are dependent on the cultural circumstances and can differ from society to society. We should therefore be open to the diversity of forms that money can take, as well as committed to the study of the (social, cultural and political) contexts in which it circulates.

2.2 A DICHOTOMY IN UNDERSTANDING MONEY

While Section 2.1 questioned what money is and the purported impact it has on society, the current section will further investigate the distinction between general-purpose and special-purpose money, introduced to anthropology in the late 1950s following the work of Karl Polanyi and Paul Bohannan. As we saw above, these concepts were put forward as a way to grasp the difference between modern and primitive money. Our purpose here is to critically evaluate this opposition and consider whether it is conducive to a better understanding of money in the historical context with which we are concerned.

Although this opposition applies specifically to the phenomenon of money, it is perhaps rooted in a more fundamental opposition that continues to underline our thinking about exchange and the economy. This concerns the opposition of exchanges considered social and exchanges considered asocial,

innovations of thought' (implying the development of ideas regarding a monetary system), 'coincided with economic contacts strongly tending away from feudalism towards individualistic capitalism' (Keynes 1982, 253–254). Sillitoe (2006, 19) misquoted Keynes by selective use of the above passage, in order to support Bohannan's theory that money had 'smash[ed] the multicentric economy'.

46 Bloch and Parry 1989, 1; Parry and Bloch 1989; Robbins and Akin 1999, 2–3; Hart and Ortiz 2014.

47 See von Reden 1995, 172; Seaford 2004, 3. Cf. Humphrey and Hugh-Jones 1992, 14–15.

meaning that while certain types of exchange are thought to create and maintain social relations on a moral basis, others are considered impersonal, profit-oriented and calculative. Within anthropological discourse, this opposition was manifestly expressed in the perceived dichotomy between 'the spirit of the gift and that of the commodity'.[48] In an intricate discussion, Appadurai noted how these two exchange modalities have been framed as deeply opposed and mutually exclusive as the result of an exaggerated and even ideologically constructed understanding of the contrast between Marx and Mauss. Where Marx emphasised the impersonal and alienating properties of the commodity through its relation to money, Mauss promoted an understanding of the gift as creating personalised and socialised obligations between partners.[49] This contrast has been laid out most explicitly by Chris Gregory, who places these modes of exchange – while coeval – on a continuum of social organisation, with, on one end, pre-industrial clan-based society where the gift is predominant and, on the other end, capitalist class-based society where the commodity dominates exchange.[50] Anthropological focus on primitive and non-capitalist societies paved the way for the dominance of the gift-model with its social and cultural aspects in the discourse.[51]

One of the first to challenge this moral and socialising (i.e., non-economic) notion of the gift was Pierre Bourdieu. Considering the temporal difference between a quid-pro-quo exchange and a gift, equally requiring a return gift, he suggested that 'a rational contract would telescope into an instant a transaction which gift exchange disguises by stretching it out in time'.[52] He asserted that in general, 'contrary to naively idyllic representations of "pre-capitalist" societies ... practice never ceases to conform to economic calculation even when it gives every appearance of disinterestedness by departing from the logic of interested calculation (in the narrow sense) and playing for stakes that are non-material and not easily quantified'.[53] Appadurai and others after him took up these suggestions and rejected the opposition of gift and commodity by drawing attention to the calculative and rational aspects of gift exchange, as well as the cultural logic underlying commodity exchange. As they noted, the dichotomy drawn up between both concepts resulted in part from the heavy emphasis placed on the contrast between small-scale, non-industrial societies

48 Appadurai 1986a, 11.

49 Mauss [1925] 1970; Appadurai 1986a, 10–12.

50 Gregory 1982, spec. 37; 1983. Gregory provided an elaborate response to the criticism levelled against his work, arguing that he intended to do the opposite from what his critics accused him of and emphasising the coexistence of gift and commodity in the colonial economy of Papua New Guinea, see Gregory[1982] 2015, xx; 1997, 41–53. Cf. Sahlins [1972] 2004, 193.

51 Humphrey and Hugh-Jones 1992, 7. Cf. Yan 2005, 253.

52 Bourdieu 1977, 171.

53 Bourdieu 1977, 177; Graeber 2001, 27–29.

and the modern capitalist West, whereby an ideal of the gift was constructed in opposition to market exchange, and the social and cultural dimensions of capitalist economies were ignored.[54] In the end, this can all be traced back to a dichotomy of the economic and the non-economic social/cultural, or what Marshall Sahlins termed 'the sclerotic opposition of economic rationality and culture', typical of the great divide between the West and the Rest.[55]

But the problematic implications of this dichotomy reach beyond our understanding of the concepts of gift and commodity. With barter understood as the predecessor of money,[56] and money tied to commodity exchange in the Marxist sense, barter was long considered the archaic or primitive expression of capitalist commodity exchange.[57] Equated with profit-minded commodity trade in non-monetised, pre-industrial economies, barter was thus considered antisocial and taking place outside the community's borders rather than within.[58] This understanding provides the basis for the persistent misconception in anthropology and the study of the ancient economy alike that barter is restricted to hostile environments of exchange between members of foreign communities.[59]

Humphrey and Hugh-Jones attacked this notion of barter by demonstrating its sociable and non-commercial characteristics. As they pointed out, barter takes place in diverse forms, coexisting with other exchange modalities, such as gift or monetary exchange; it is not likely to take place between pure strangers but demands a level of mutual trust between partners, with the purpose of balancing the exchange; and in some cases it does not involve haggling but rather takes place following customary practice and set exchange rates.[60]

Despite these relatively recent insights, the 'traditional' understandings of these different exchange modalities have shaped the anthropological discourse during the latter half of the twentieth century, also affecting the way money is framed. The attentive reader will have noticed at this point that the opposition underlying 'gift vs. commodity', that between socialising and calculative

[54] Appadurai 1986a, 11–13; Bloch and Parry 1989, 8–12; Davis 1992; Yan 2005, 254–256. Archaeology and ancient history (see also Section 5.3) have been rather slow to take notice of these insights, see, for example, Van Wees 1998, 27; Dillian and White 2010; Earle 2010, 210. Recent exceptions to this are, e.g., Skre 2007 and Kilger 2007, 259.

[55] Bourdieu 1977, 183; Sahlins [1972] 2004, xii; Hann and Hart 2011, 14, 86.

[56] See Section 1.2.

[57] Humphrey and Hugh-Jones 1992.

[58] See Section 1.2; Appadurai 1986a, 10–11; Humphrey and Hugh-Jones 1992, 11–13. Cf. Graeber 2011, 29–34.

[59] Cf. Hart 1986, 648; Graeber 2011, 29–34. Peculiarly, Von Reden wrote that 'anthropologists emphasize that barter is a non-social form of exchange typical of hostile and noncooperative environments rather than harmonious social collectives', while referring to the single contribution that tried to correct this very misunderstanding, Humphrey and Hugh-Jones 1992 (Von Reden 2010, 27–28).

[60] Malinowski 1921, 13–14; Humphrey and Hugh-Jones 1992; Heady 2005.

exchanges, is also reflected in the opposition between special-purpose and general-purpose money.

In Marxist analysis, money was seen as inherently impersonal and capitalist, but this qualification came under pressure when ethnographic research started to provide an increasing body of data on different types of currencies in societies that were most certainly not capitalist.[61] The problem of interpreting primitive valuables in relation to money first arose with Malinowski's assertion that the *vaygua* – 'tokens of wealth', or *kula* valuables – of the Trobriand could not be considered money.[62] Mauss considered money universal to human society and objected to this interpretation by saying that 'in this view ... there is money only when ... tokens of wealth are made into money – when they are named, impersonalised, detached from any relationships with moral, collective or individual persons other than the authority of the state which mints them .... The above definition can only cover a secondary type of money – our own'.[63] Following Mauss' idea that there are historical or ethnographic forms of money that are different from our own, Polanyi saw the need to develop a model of money that would facilitate the existence of *primitive* money in *primitive* or *premodern* society, and this became the concept of special-purpose money.[64] In this way, special-purpose money came to be associated with early clan-based society and social forms of exchange, while general-purpose money came to be associated with modern class-based capitalist society and market exchange.

One of the ways to put these oppositions into perspective is with reference to the wider debate between substantivists and formalists that dominated the field of economic anthropology and had profound influence on the study of the ancient economy.[65] Although there is no need here to provide a full discussion of the debate,[66] it is important to draw attention to the basic principles of the divide. Within anthropology, two different approaches to the study of the economy came into play in the decades after the Second World War, following the work of Karl Polanyi.[67] He propagated a *substantive* understanding of the economy as 'embedded' in society, whereby the

61 Cf. Einzig [1949] 1966, 428–430; Quiggin 1949, 4.

62 Malinowski 1921, 13–14.

63 Mauss [1925] 1970, 93–94; Leach 1983, 4; Hart 2005, 160; Hann and Hart 2011, 42–53.

64 Polanyi 1968a, 166–169.

65 The foremost proponents of substantivism in the study of the old world were Moses Finley for ancient Greece and Leo Oppenheim for the Ancient Near East (Finley 1954; Oppenheim 1957). Both participated in Polanyi's Columbia University seminar, although Finley did not publish a chapter in its final publication, *Trade and Market in the Early Empires* (Polanyi, Arensberg and Pearson 1957).

66 See Isaac 2005; Hann and Hart 2011, 55–71. In the context of the ancient economy, see Morris 1994, 352–354; Tandy 1997, 84–138; Schaps 2004, 18–26.

67 Polanyi 1944; 1968a.

economic livelihood of man results from social determinants. This stood in contrast to *formal* economics, based on the premise that humans make rational decisions towards economising or maximising their resources. According to the substantivists, this formalist approach, leaning heavily on the formal models of neoclassical (i.e., mainstream) economics as the basis for analysis, was only applicable to a market system and not to non-industrial or premodern societies: primitive or premodern economies were thought to be governed by fundamentally different principles than the modern economy.

Substantivists such as Polanyi and his disciples George Dalton and Paul Bohannan introduced and promoted the use of concepts such as reciprocity, redistribution and spheres of exchange to the study of primitive economies, but they were also deterministic, associating particular forms of social organisation with particular modes of exchange, such as industrial class-based society with market exchange. As a result, they marginalised the presence of markets and commodities in archaic societies and were not receptive to the possibility of an interplay or coexistence of diverse forms of exchange within society.[68] The polarising debate with formalism exacerbated substantivism's position on the division between primitive and modern economies and led Dalton, after Polanyi's death in 1964, to concede that its concepts were applicable only to primitive, non-capitalist societies. With the growing importance of the study of contemporary societies from the 1980s onwards, anthropologists developed a concern for commodities and markets.[69] For this, substantivism's tools were inadequate, and its influence waned.[70] In recent years, anthropologists have commented that its long-term influence has been limited, although its influence on the development of the discourse continues to warrant discussion.[71]

By providing a socially integrating alternative for the approach offered by formal economics, substantivism had a profound influence on the study of ancient economies, and Polanyi has been widely credited for this. However, archaeologists, classicists and historians of the classical world or Ancient Near East have sometimes been slow in taking notice of the criticism on substantivism or in adopting alternative or new approaches.[72] It is therefore hardly

68 Cf. Davis 1992.

69 E.g., Gregory 1982; Appadurai 1986b.

70 Isaac 2005, 21.

71 Graeber 2001, 9–12, 22–33; Isaac 2005, 20–21; Hann and Hart 2011, 70–71.

72 See, for example, Tandy 1997; 2012; Gill, Postlethwaite and Seaford 1998; Dillian and White 2010; Seaford 2012; Aubet 2013. However, exceptions are becoming more frequent, see Skre 2008, 9–10; Kilger 2008, 256–259; Bachhuber 2018. Perhaps scholars of the Ancient Near East have been more critical due to the fact that the large amount of documentary evidence is at odds with substantivist orthodoxy (e.g., Warburton 2009; Nam 2012, 29–69). With regard to the field of ancient history, substantivism reinforced an older debate between primitivists and modernists on whether the ancient economy was qualitatively different from the modern economy or only quantitatively. Influenced by substantivism, Finley's work (1954; [1973]

surprising that its concepts and oppositions continue to surface sometimes unaltered.

To return our attention to the issue of money, substantivism's subscription to the division between primitive/non-industrial and modern capitalist society formed a consistent framework for Polanyi's identification of special-purpose money as pre-capitalist, and general-purpose money as modern. Yet, the classical world was accredited a special status, since modern scholars generally did not regard ancient Greek civilisation as 'primitive'. In fact, our modern money, coinage, first flourished in ancient Greece, and ancient coinage was therefore considered modern general-purpose money. This understanding is reflected in one of the basic premises of the study of early money and coinage, that primitive money is money that is not coin.[73]

This premise – the identification of non-coinage money as primitive, and coinage as modern money – has serious implications for the way we look at the development of early money in the historical case with which we are concerned and should be rejected in favour of a more careful consideration of early forms of money within their particular cultural contexts. Moreover, in order to come to a better understanding of the early money that preceded coinage, we need to question the strict distinction between forms of money in functionalist terms of special-purpose and general-purpose. It is not enough to suggest that the distinction is simply rooted in the substantivist opposition between primitive and modern society. In order to properly question the distinction and its value to us, we need to scrutinise the wider social model that provided the flesh on its bones.

2.2.1 *Spheres of Exchange*

As discussed earlier in this chapter, in his 1955 article on Tiv exchange, Paul Bohannan described the spheres of exchange and the disastrous effects that modern money supposedly had on them. Four years later, he redressed his account in terms of Polanyi's distinction between special-purpose (or limited-purpose) and general-purpose money, published two years before. According to Bohannan, the Tiv economy was a multicentric economy – exchangeable goods circulated within three mutually exclusive spheres – that had subverted to a unicentric economy after the introduction of general-purpose money. Currencies in the form of brass rods and *tugudu* cloth had been used in the

1985) reshaped primitivism into the 'new orthodoxy' (Hopkins 1983; see also Austin and Vidal-Naquet [1972] 1977, 3–8; Sherratt and Sherratt 1991, 351–356). In recent years, criticism of Finley has become more widely accepted (see, for example, Von Reden 2002; Morris 2003), although often with no reference to Polanyi's substantivism.

73 Grierson 1977; Kurke 1999, 11; Davies 2002, 23–27; Schaps 2004; Seaford 2004.

multicentric economy, but in principle their use was restricted to the second, prestige sphere. Because the system of spheres placed restrictions on the free circulation of commodities, currencies within this system were naturally restricted in use: they were special-purpose money.[74]

Now, the concept of an economy consisting of separate spheres of exchange was not peculiar to the Tiv. In one form or another, they have been noted widely, most prominently in the western Pacific.[75] Prior to Bohannan, Raymond Firth had described the transactions among the Tikopia in terms of 'three separate series of exchanges, or spheres of exchange'.[76] Although Bohannan had not been the first to note the existence of spheres of exchange, his account was the first to present a more detailed model and became the most influential. Enforced by substantivist thinking, the concept of spheres of exchange, characteristic for primitive economies, thus provided the model in which special-purpose money was framed.

Scholars have generally suggested that these spheres took shape as a way to cope with the difficulty inherent in comparing the value of commodities that are unlike, in absence of a universal means of exchange, a general-purpose money. By creating categories of goods that are roughly accredited the same status (exchanging subsistence goods for subsistence goods or prestige goods for prestige goods), it would become easier to assess their relative value.[77]

Alternatively, other aspects of the model have been emphasised. Noting the fact that valuables are never simply manufactured for the purpose of accumulating wealth, Sillitoe points out that these prestige goods from higher exchange spheres, such as bonito hooks with the Tikopia or *kula* items with

[74] Bohannan 1955; 1959.

[75] Robbins and Akin 1999, 8–9; Sillitoe 2006, 2–6.

[76] Firth [1939] 1965, 340–344; Sillitoe 2006, 5. John Maynard Keynes was possibly the first to come up with the concept, when, in tracing 'the origins of money', he claimed that early Greece had known three 'standards of value', a cow-sheep standard, a corn standard and an iron or bronze standard (Keynes 1982, 259; Gregory 1997, 242; Sillitoe 2006, 5). Written as part of his studies on the history of ancient currencies, a topic that had occupied Keynes between 1920 and 1926, this was published posthumously in 1982 (Keynes 1982). It is not fully evident, however, to what extent Keynes regarded these being incommensurable and belonging to discrete spheres, rather than different standards of valuation. Also, economist Alfred Marshall had noted already in 1890 that consumers tend to rank commodities according to different classes of value (Hart 2005, 164; Hann and Hart 2011, 62).

[77] Kopytoff 1986, 70–72; Hart 2005, 164–165; Graeber 2011, 36–37. This explanation is ultimately based on Marx's labour theory of value, which states that the value of goods is derived from the labour put into their production. 'For all the difficulties that the labor theory of value presents, it at least suggests that while yams and pots can conceivably be compared by the labor required to produce them (even while allowing for the different investment in training that the labor represents in each case), no such common standard is available in comparing yams to ritual offices or pots to wives and offspring. Hence, the immense difficulty, indeed impossibility, of lumping all such disparate items into a single commodity sphere.' (Kopytoff 1986, 71–72).

the Trobriand, are rather 'created' through transactions in order to enter the sphere of social and political exchange. 'The spheres of exchange [thus] intimate restrictions on the supply of objects that circulate in socio-political exchanges, with wealth ideally accessible only through exchanges'.[78]

However, Bohannan's model has also come under criticism. Claiming that it does not fit Melanesian realities, Robbins and Akin pointed out that the model assumes a differentiation of spheres based on goods, while basically ignoring the importance of the relationship between transactors and the exchange modality employed between them.[79] According to them, of these three elements in Melanesian society, the modality is the most resistant to change, and as long as the distinction between modalities is maintained, modern money, like their indigenous special-purpose money, does not dissolve the spheres.[80] Moreover, Bohannan's model was also attacked for failing to appreciate its wider historical and geographical context. The Tiv spheres of exchange did not function in isolation, and regional trading networks through which important goods such as brass rods and *tugudu* cloth were traded served to connect the different spheres. Brass rods for example, like manillas in western Africa, had been imported by English slave traders so that they could tap into local economies with the purpose of extracting slaves.[81] Guyer, incorporating earlier corrections by Dorward and Gregory, noted that 'conversion involved placing oneself on the right routes, with the right goods'.[82]

Concluding from this, it appears that the barriers between the spheres were in no way absolute. We can now re-examine the explanation of the spheres as given above. Kopytoff argues that the number of spheres results from the level of exchange technology, assuming the existence of 'a drive inherent in every exchange system toward optimum commoditisation – the drive to extend the fundamentally seductive idea of exchange to as many items as the existing exchange technology will comfortably allow'.[83] In other words, the more efficient the exchange technology (like general-purpose money), the easier it becomes to compare commodities, and the fewer spheres exist. However, Bloch and Parry have declared themselves 'sceptical of this kind of

78 Sillitoe 2006, 9–14.
79 Robbins and Akin 1999, 8–10.
80 Robbins and Akin 1999, 14–15.
81 Herbert 1984, 123–182; Maurer 2006, 20; Graeber 2011, 151. Europeans were similarly responsible for bringing shells (to be local currencies) into circulation in West Africa or Melanesia (see Hogendorn and Johnson 1986; Robbins and Akin 1999, 21; Graeber 1996; 2001, 91–92).
82 Guyer 2004, 30, 27–31. See Dorward 1976; Gregory 1997, 241–242.
83 Kopytoff 1986, 72.

technological determinism', adding that far-reaching commoditisation and the absence of spheres is more due to the presence of capitalist markets than anything else.[84] Additionally, the criticism of the model suggests that it is not so much the technological capability of the currencies but rather the type of exchange and the distance to and extent of integration with other markets that cause the spheres to take shape.

Indeed, we should wonder whether primitive currencies that feature in economies divided into spheres of exchange are, as suggested by Kopytoff, under any inherent technological constraint warranting their qualification as special-purpose. This can be clarified by looking at the Tiv once more. As mentioned, their primitive currencies, *tugudu* cloth and brass rods, were considered by Bohannan to have been restricted to the prestige sphere and were thus special-purpose. It is remarkable, however, that 'in the old days', before the establishment of the colonial authority, conversions were most commonly performed with these currencies, in particular with brass rods.[85] At the same time, these currencies were the object of external trade linking the spheres.[86] We could therefore conclude that from a technical perspective, the Tiv currencies formed what Dalton described as a 'structural link . . . between the [separate] spheres'. Dalton claimed however that this link could only be formed by a general-purpose money – Western cash – and that without this the spheres would remain discrete.[87]

Although it has been claimed that special-purpose currencies do not function as a standard of value,[88] it is clear that under certain circumstances Tiv currencies could and did function as such. When asked about it, the Tiv might surely have been reluctant to name a price for conversions,[89] because this was subjected to moral evaluations. But the fact that they did not regularly measure food or a wife in terms of brass rods was not because their currencies suffered from any technological, functionalist limitation.

To sum up, the strict distinction between special-purpose and general-purpose money appears problematic and difficult to maintain. Instead of contributing to a better understanding of early forms of money, the technological determinism behind the distinction tends to obscure the social and cultural factors that shape the use and circulation of money.

84 Bloch and Parry 1989, 16.
85 Akiga [1939] 1965, 125–127; Bohannan 1955, 62, 65–67; 1959, 497. Raffia cloth among the Lele in Belgian Congo appears to have functioned in a similar way (Douglas [1958] 1982b, 38–56; Graeber 2011, 137–144).
86 Guyer 2004.
87 Dalton 1965, 61.
88 Eriksen [1995] 2001, 185.
89 Cf. Akiga [1939] 1965, 125–127.

2.2.2 *A Social Understanding of Money*

As implied in Sillitoe's explanation of the spheres, it appears that more than just providing a way to overcome the incommensurability of commodities (through the incommensurability of labour), the spheres of exchange have a social purpose. By separating the circulation of prestige valuables from the sphere of subsistence goods, the system prevents people from accumulating wealth connected with subsistence (e.g., cash-cropping) and in that way sustains the egalitarian order.[90] It is worthwhile to point out that in those societies that have been noted to demonstrate a clear division of spheres of exchange (the Tiv, Melanesia etc.), land is considered communal property and thus inalienable: it cannot be owned as private property or be sold as such.[91] As noted previously, such communal rights to property do not negate the social significance of the circulation of valuables but are rather consistent with it.[92]

Emphasis on the social meaning of primitive exchange systems was also notable in Mary Douglas' approach to primitive valuables. Rejecting the notion that primitive money is restricted while modern money flows freely, by pointing out that modern money is also restricted in many situations (by geographical as well as moral borders), she drew a comparison between primitive valuables and coupons, controlled by an issuing authority.[93] According to her, the main function of such primitive coupons 'is to provide the necessary condition for entry to high-status positions, or for maintaining rank, or for countering attacks on status'.[94] In other words, they have a role in regulating social life.

Likewise, a distinction between primitive and modern valuables based on their social function underlies Appadurai's discussion of the circulation of *kula* valuables.[95] Having pointed out that, despite the absence of monetary valuations, calculated exchange is as much a part of the *kula* as it is of modern commodity exchange, he continues: 'The most important difference between the exchange of these commodities and the exchange of commodities in modern industrial economies is that the increment being sought in kula-type systems is in reputation, name, or fame, with the critical form of capital for producing this profit being people rather than other factors of production'.[96]

[90] Robbins and Akin 1999, 26–27; Sillitoe 2006, 8–9; Graeber 2011, 129–130.

[91] Malinowski 1921, 3–4; Bohannan 1955, 63; Gregory 1982, 116, 162–165; Bloch and Parry 1989, 13; Robbins and Akin 1999, 24. Cf. Bourdieu 1977, 182–183.

[92] See Section 1.2.

[93] Douglas [1967] 1982c.

[94] Douglas [1967] 1982c, 69.

[95] Note that spheres of exchange have been reported among the Trobriand, with the *kula* featuring as the highest sphere (Firth 1957, 218; Isaac 2005, 17–18).

[96] Appadurai 1986a, 19, cf. 32.

David Graeber has attempted to rephrase the distinction between primitive and modern, special- and general-purpose money altogether.[97] The term 'primitive money', he claims, is misleading, because it purports to be a crude version of our modern money. Rather, he argues, 'primitive' currencies are not like modern money at all; they are not used to buy or sell everyday goods but rather function in social and political transactions. Graeber therefore suggests terming them 'social currencies' and the economies in which they function 'human economies', implying that 'they are economic systems primarily concerned not with the accumulation of wealth, but with the creation, destruction, and rearranging of human beings'.[98]

The opposition of two different economies, one concerned with the social order, the other with the accumulation of (monetary) capital, is also implicit in much of the literature on the silver economy of the Viking Age (ca. 800–1050 CE). Here, a distinction is often made between a status or display economy, on the one hand, and a monetary economy, on the other hand. The status economy is indicated by the use and circulation of whole silver objects, mostly jewellery, weapons and other display items, whereby the silver served to express wealth and status through display and gift-giving;[99] the monetary economy, on the other hand, is indicated by the use of silver coinage for the purpose of trade.[100] Additionally, a bullion economy based on ingots and *hacksilber* is thought to represent a transitional stage between the two.[101] Such a contextualisation of the division as part of an evolutionary scheme, whereby the modern/monetary economy naturally develops out of the primitive/social economy, has also been commonly suggested for the development of money in early Greece. There, the introduction of coinage has been regarded as the birth of modern money out of its earlier, primitive predecessors.[102]

Although Graeber's formulation of the division between the human economy and the commercial economy has shed the appearance of substantivist determinism by replacing the special- and general-purpose terminology, and doing away with its insistence on spheres of exchange as a static model,[103] it still reflects a fundamental opposition of the social primitive *Other* and the

97 Graeber 2009; 2011, 125–164.

98 Graeber 2011, 129–130.

99 Precious metal in this context has sometimes been identified as 'special-purpose money' (see, for example, Gaimster 2007, 126–131; Graham-Campbell 2007, 221. Cf. Kilger 2008, 259).

100 It has been acknowledged in recent years though that these are not mutually exclusive and could co-exist (Williams 2007, 181).

101 Hårdh 1996; 2007, 97–99; Gaimster 2007; Graham-Campbell 2007, 215; Graham-Campbell and Williams 2007; Williams 2007, 178–180, 205–207. Cf. Kilger 2007, 259; Metcalf 2007, 1; Sheenan 2007, 160; Sindbæk 2011; Merkel 2016, 46. Cf. Kershaw 2017, 185–187.

102 Balmuth 1975; Price 1983; Weatherford 1997; Kurke 1999, 11; Schaps 2004; Seaford 2004.

103 Graeber 2009.

commercial modern *Same*. Again, whether in the case of historical developments long passed or contemporary non-capitalist societies, we appear to stress the calculative aspects of the economy and currency that we identify with our own, while emphasising the sociality behind a society that uses a type of money that we regard as inherently cultural and therefore primitive.[104]

2.2.3 'Human Economies Exist in the Cracks of Capitalist Societies'

The question arises, though, whether these aspects of 'human economy' are not present throughout modern capitalist economies just as well.[105] In fact, Graeber acknowledges this,[106] and around the same time as he coined the term to describe non-commercial economies, such as the indigenous economies of western Africa in the face of the Atlantic slave trade,[107] another anthropologist, Keith Hart, came up with the idea of the human economy. Hart, though, brought it up not to contrast it with a commercial or capitalist one but to draw attention to the human aspects and institutions present in the contemporary economy; restricting our interest to the dominant economic institutions would cause us to ignore the very fact that 'human economies exist in the cracks of capitalist societies'.[108]

In the same vein, as Appadurai made a point to restore the calculative dimension to primitive economies and the moral dimension to capitalist economies,[109] so has recent scholarship been increasingly attentive towards the social meanings and powers of modern money.[110] Ironically, economist Jacques Melitz already suggested much of this in 1970, by pointing out that our modern money is diverse in form and restricted in use, in addition to the fact that we maintain a variety of economic exchange relations without reference to monetary valuation. He concluded that our money is just as special-purpose as what we consider primitive money and that any distinction along these lines is therefore void.[111] Indeed, we should wonder whether Graeber's distinction between social currencies and our own money and the substantivist distinction

[104] Cf. Kilger 2007, 257.
[105] Hart 2008; 2012.
[106] Graeber 2009.
[107] Graeber 2011, 125–164.
[108] Hart 2008; 2012; Hart, Laville and Cattani 2010. Cf. Davis 1992; Coase 2012.
[109] Appadurai 1986a.
[110] Zelizer 1994; Gilbert 2005; Dodd 2014.
[111] Melitz 1970, 1020–1025; Maurer 2006, 22. 'If the Polanyists ever had bothered to apply the same methods of investigation and criteria of definition to our society as they have to the Tiv and Trobriand Islanders, they could not have espoused their distinction between special-purpose and all-purpose money' (Melitz 1970, 1023). As noted above, Melitz's contribution went largely unnoticed at the time.

between special- and general-purpose money are so different, beyond what they emphasise.

Despite all this, the distinction between two types of money is still upheld by many. Whether a traditional division between primitive and modern, a functionalist division between special- and general-purpose money or a social function-based division between social currencies and modern money, few have made a point out of explicitly rejecting or even criticising these oppositions.[112] The concepts of special- and general-purpose money have been often noted by anthropologists in recent years in relation to substantivist thinking, if noted at all.[113] In historical studies, however, they continue to surface without much reference to recent literature.[114] As to Graeber's concept of social currencies, as opposed to modern money, his social contextual approach certainly enables a better understanding of why and how money is thought of and used and especially applies to the cases he brings up, highlighting a contrast between colonial and indigenous economies.[115] At the same time, it seems doubtful whether a strict division between human and commercial economies can be maintained and, as such, whether this opposition can apply to the early and formative stages of money posed by our historical case. While scholars have pointed out that the distinction between opposite forms of money is gradual, rather than strict,[116] we need to be careful not to think of this as a continuum, like Gregory suggested for gift and commodity, whereby the two ends are represented by ideals that confirm to a set of distinct 'primitive' or 'modern' characteristics.[117] Rather, the reality is one where different aspects, motivations and strategies, such as calculation, sociality or hoarding tend to pervade throughout the system, and appear (perhaps) at random in different contexts, reflecting cultural logic.

Interesting to note is Helen Codere's contribution, published during the heyday of substantivism. While she did not reject the distinction between special- and general-purpose, she claimed that it 'is far too gross to contribute much to the analysis of the historical development of money in any particular society'.[118] According to her, it would be more useful to focus on the factors

112 Maurer 2006; Kilger 2008, 259. Maurer suggests that Bloch and Parry (1989) 'sought to unseat the old distinctions between primitive and modern, special-purpose and general-purpose moneys', which is de facto correct, although they state at the start that their focus lies not on 'so-called "primitive money"', but with state-issued currencies.

113 Isaac 2005; Hann and Hart 2011, 59–61.

114 Kurke 1999, 10–12; Schaps 2004, 14–15; Seaford 2004, 1–9; Von Reden 2010, 22; Haselgrove and Krmnicek 2012, 244–245. Cf. Schaps 2004, 219–220; Kilger 2008, 259.

115 Graeber 2009; 2012.

116 Schaps notes with regard to special- and general-purpose money that the 'distinction ... is one of degree, not one of essence' (Schaps 2004, 219; Weatherford 1997, 12).

117 Cf. Appadurai 1986a, 32.

118 Codere 1968, 558.

that enable money to perform all of its functions, in order to see how it is enforced as a symbolic system. The functioning of money should thus be sought in its interplay with the symbolic sub-systems that are expressed by numbers, amounts and writing. Money is quantified on the basis of numeracy;[119] the conception of amounts in term of weights and measures allows monetary evaluation in specific ratios, calculation and convertibility of monetary value; writing enables accounting and long-term calculation of a complexity that makes monetary exchange consistent and systemic, where it could otherwise be subject to custom or coincidence.[120]

In essence, Codere's model reflects the same technological functionalism and determinism as we have seen before. It does however draw attention to the idea that in complex societies money tends to serve more functions and in a more pervasive way. The set of symbolic systems noted by Codere is often (though not exclusively) associated with one of the most obvious forms of complex social organisation: the state. Not surprisingly, the issue and spread of money in history has often been connected to the state.[121] It is therefore logical that we turn to the distinction between money under or issued by a state and money in stateless society.

2.2.4 *Money and the State*

Ingham notes that 'a money transaction differs from barter in that the burden of trust is removed from the participants in the actual transaction and placed on a third party – the issuer of money'.[122] The underlying understanding of money, not as emerging primarily from exchange but as deliberately issued and functioning by virtue of being guaranteed by an authority, goes back to Georg Friedrich Knapp's *Staatliche Theorie des Geldes*.[123] Its central idea, the 'state theory of money', was that money primarily arose and functioned under authority of the state. Knapp coined the term *chartalism* to give expression to the corresponding position, influential at the time, that in essence money is a token, from the Latin *charta*.[124] In contrast with this stood what he referred to as *metallism*, under which money was essentially conceived as a commodity.[125] As Hart pointed out, this opposition between token and commodity has characterised the discourse on monetary theory for more than a century and

[119] Cf. Netz 2002; Chrisomalis 2010; Everett 2017.
[120] Codere 1968, 561–565; Davis 1992, 81–83.
[121] Hart 1986; Graeber 2011, 46–52; Heymans and Termeer 2020a.
[122] Ingham 2004, 72.
[123] Knapp [1905] 1924.
[124] Knapp [1905] 1924, 25ff, 32–33.
[125] Knapp [1905] 1924, 4–9.

has been much relevant to social and historical sciences.[126] This topic will be dealt with more in depth in Section 2.3.

Echoing a chartalist tenet, Douglas characterised modern money as 'circulating within the control of a sovereign authority',[127] and the distinction between state currencies and indigenous currencies has provided a straightforward way of dealing with money in colonial contexts. In Melanesian contexts, the involvement of state authority serves to distinguish between modern currencies, issued by the state and functioning in the formal economy, and indigenous currencies that are not under mandate of the state but rather of the community and its social codes and structures.[128] Some have also (implicitly) adopted the essentially chartalist position that if not issued by a central authority and enforced as legal tender it cannot in fact be money as we know it. In historical terms this boils down to the understanding that without the active engagement of the state, money cannot come into being.[129]

Again, like in the case of Graeber's division, it seems that this formal political distinction is useful for identifying different economic and social forces in colonial and post-colonial contexts, even though we need to be aware that state currencies are often appropriated in different ways in different cultural contexts and can thus acquire different meanings.[130] However, if applied to the eastern Mediterranean Iron Age, this distinction is prone to lead to problems.

On the surface, two difficulties can be pointed out. First of all, 'the state' is not an obvious matter of fact in the Mediterranean world around the start of the first millennium BCE. Without contemporary historical sources that testify to the existence of a central authority or its institutions, it is difficult to identify statehood, and the question of when a state arose in the early Greek world as well as in the southern Levant has been intensely debated over the last decades.

The appearance of the paradigmatic Greek state of the classical world, the polis, featured prominently on the research agenda during the 1980s and 1990s. Signified by the changes in material culture during the Geometric (in particular, the Late Geometric) period,[131] the 'birth' of the polis was generally assumed to have taken place in the mid-eight century BCE.[132] However, from the nineties on, critical voices arose against the 'adulation of "the state" in early Greece'.[133] The rise of Greek political communities was increasingly

[126] Hart 1986, 644ff; Ingham 2004, 47; Wray 2004; Graeber 2011, 46–52.
[127] Douglas [1967] 1982c, 74.
[128] Robbins and Akin 1999.
[129] Anderlini and Sabourian 1992, 89; Ingham 2004; Graeber 2011, 46–52; *pace* Heymans and Termeer 2020b.
[130] Bloch and Parry 1989.
[131] Snodgrass 1971, 416–436; 1980, 15–84; Coldstream [1977] 2003; Whitley 2001, 98–101.
[132] Hägg 1983a; Morris 1987, 171–210; de Polignac [1984] 1995.
[133] Morris 1992b, xvii.

approached as part of longer-term developments, and additionally, attention was drawn to other, more loosely organised forms of early Greek states or societies.[134] Moreover, beyond its rise, the nature of the Greek state is not obvious in and of itself, although it is certain that Greek states were by no means states in the modern sense of the term.[135]

Scholarly opinion on the rise of statehood in the early first millennium southern Levant has been heavily influenced by two opposing forces: on one side, a (partial) acceptance of the biblical account (in particular, the books of Samuel and the books of Kings), and on the other side, its critical rejection. In recent decades, the archaeological debate has focused on the chronology of Iron Age phases and whether these can be ascribed to King Solomon and as such confirm the historicity of the United Kingdom.[136] Despite today's broad consensus rejecting a large centralised kingdom in the tenth century as an ideologically motivated construct of later monarchic or exilic times, new archaeological data have at times spurred restatements of this traditional view.[137] Alternatively, scholarship has redirected its efforts to the state formation of the two Israelite kingdoms, Israel in the north and Judah in the south, and potential predecessors in the highlands,[138] as well as its neighbours Moab and Edom.[139] These debates have focused more on the chronology and historical development behind the state formation than on the political aspects and institutions of statehood. As in the case of the early Greek state, few have made use of a clear theoretical framework in approaching the issue.[140]

The second problem relates to the supposed interference of the state in the economy. Even if we were able to identify with clarity the appearance of these states, this would not provide a conclusive indication of institutional influence on the economy. Moreover, interference in the economy does not necessarily imply involvement in the issue of money, or in its maintenance as legal tender, whether through trade laws or through taxation. For example, it is known that

134 Morgan 2003.

135 E.g., Hansen 2006; Anderson 2009.

136 Finkelstein 1996; Mazar 1997; Finkelstein and Piasetzky 2011; Mazar 2011.

137 Examples of this are the excavations at Khirbet en-Nahas (Levy et al. 2004. Cf. Finkelstein and Piasetzky 2008; Finkelstein and Singer-Avitz 2009, for summaries of the scholarship), and Khirbet Qeiyafa (Garfinkel and Ganor 2009; cf. Finkelstein and Fantalkin 2012, for a summary of the scholarship).

138 Finkelstein 1999; 2001; 2013; 2019; Master 2001; Herzog and Singer-Avitz 2004; Na'aman 2013.

139 For Moab, see Routledge 2004; for Edom, see Bienkowski and van der Steen 2001; Tebes 2016.

140 *Cf.* Anderson 2009; Master 2001; Hansen and Nielsen 2004, 23–38; Routledge 2004; Hansen 2006, 7–28. Notwithstanding the efforts to identify and date the appearance of historical states, we should note that a state does not develop in a vacuum. Preceding the genesis of a full-fledged state, whatever that might mean, other forms of social organisation that provide the basis for social norms must have been at play.

the Aegean Bronze Age palatial centres were involved in specific parts of the economy, yet, as it seems, did not create nor endorse any general currency.[141] Also, the Roman Republic only started to issue money (struck coinage, cast bronze bars and *aes grave*) around 300 BCE, after it had developed into the dominant political force on the Italic peninsula, and more than two centuries after the Greek cities of Magna Graecia, among which Neapolis, had started to issue coins.[142] In general, the state can influence the use of currency under its authority (e.g., in its harbours or marketplaces) in diverse ways, whether intended or unintended, not only through issue or legal tender. This can be, for example, through control over mining or trade of metals[143] or through the endorsement of a particular medium in payments, such as religious taxes or penalties. This will be explored in Chapters 4 and 5 with reference to various topics, such as the collection of Temple contributions under King Joash of Judah and the laws of Solon of Athens.

However, perhaps more problematic than our difficulty of dating state formation, or assessing its definite implications for monetisation, is our understanding of the concept 'state'. It is a given fact that the historical states in the eastern Mediterranean of the first millennium BCE differed from the state as a Hobbesian construct of Western political philosophy. It was essentially this state – the modern state – that Knapp had in mind in writing his *State Theory of Money*, and it is therefore reasonable to doubt whether a distinction between state-issued money and 'stateless money' with its chartalist undercurrents has a bearing on the conception of money in times of *ancient* state formation.

It seems more relevant to weigh the influence of central authority on money in a more general sense. However, this does not provide a basis for a distinction within our historical framework. After all, whether considered primitive or small-scale, all of the societies in question have some sort of central authority. Even in the Dark Age type-site of Nichoria in Messenia (Greece), for many years the prime example in scholarship of Dark Age weak social hierarchy, there appears to have been some central authority associated with the large apsidal house, Unit IV-1. According to Whitley, it was occupied by a 'big-man'.[144]

It is interesting to point out in this regard that despite their relatively weak power base, such big-men, as we know from Melanesian societies, are able to influence and control economic practice and money in a way that bears basic similarities to the monetary policies of modern states. This can be seen in the

141 E.g., Voutsaki and Killen 2001.
142 Crawford 1985.
143 Bissa 2009.
144 Coulson 1983, 19–42; McDonald and Coulson 1983, 322–328; Whitley 1991, 349; Mazarakis Ainian 1997, 375–381.

case of Rossel Island (Yela) shell money. The exchange economy of the Yela consisted of an ordinal (ranked) system of shells, consisting of some twenty value-classes of *ndap* shells that were used in different types of exchange.[145] The control over the resources for the shells, their transportation and production or 'conversion into *ndap*' traditionally laid with the big-men, whose importance was said to 'rest primarily on the privilege of making *ndap* money'.[146] After the establishment of the colonial regime, when the big-man control over the highest-ranking shells came under pressure, the big-men took these high-rank *ndap* out of circulation by declaring them inalienable from their owners, placing them de facto under their own control. Specific exchanges, such as mortuary payment or marriage exchange, still required these high-ranking valuables, but their use became nominal. This meant the temporary transfer of the valuables (to be replaced afterwards with low-ranking *ndap*), which could only take place with the support of big-men. In this way, the big-men managed to guarantee the functioning of the traditional exchange economy and consolidated their authority over matters of important social and ritual exchange.[147] One could argue that regarding the aspect of central control, state currencies and *ndap* are not so different: both are issued by and through the authority, and their use is demanded and guaranteed by the authority.

The case the Rossel Island *ndap* shells should make us wonder to what extent the concept of legal tender or state-issued or -controlled currency is in fact similar to social normative practices that render a currency acceptable. After all, like sumptuary laws or the power and privileges of big-men or elders, social norms and practices regulating certain payments or exchanges demand, enforce and restrict the use of specific commodities in specific contexts to the effect that they function as money.[148] Perhaps the most notable difference is that legal tender and state currency tend to be formalised through or in relation to law, while social norms enforce practice without formal law. It seems, however, likely that this token quality that the state endows money with, can be based on social conventions in small-scale, primitive or ancient societies as well. This is particularly relevant to our case, because it opens up possibilities for the use and circulation of forms of money in absence of a formal state authority. How this token quality was expressed and on what basis money was used, is the subject of Section 2.3.

[145] For the purpose of clarity, only the *ndap* system is discussed here, while the *kö* shells are left aside. For a full discussion of the system, see Liep 1983.

[146] Armstrong 1928, 60. Cf. Liep 1983, 507.

[147] Liep 1983, 507–511; 1999; Robbins and Akin 1999, 24–25.

[148] Cf. Goldberg 2005.

2.3 HEADS OR TAILS

As noted in Section 2.2, Hart has described how the Western discourse on monetary theory over the last 150 years has been characterised by an opposition between two fundamental understandings of money. On the one side, money is perceived primarily as a token, issued by the state, signifying an obligation or debt between persons in society. On the other side, money is regarded as a commodity, made by the market and invested with definite value. Although Hart focused more on the modern historiography of these opposing approaches in monetary theory, we could say that these are deeply rooted in Western thinking about money. As such, they have been highly influential in the way money is thought of and identified, not only in modern monetary theory but also in dealing with money in ancient contexts. The two strands of thought are even discernible in the different emphases placed on money by Plato and Aristotle. Plato describes that buying and selling in the ideal city is conducted with 'νόμισμα σύμβολον', token money,[149] while Aristotle states that an agreed upon medium of exchange should be useful in itself, such as iron or silver, to the effect of a commodity.[150]

Hart, however, argued that money is neither one nor the other but that they should rather be seen as two sides of the same coin:

> Look at a coin from your pocket. On one side is 'heads' – the symbol of the political authority which minted the coin; on the other side is 'tails' – the precise specification of the amount the coin is worth as payment in exchange. One side reminds us that states underwrite currencies and that money is originally a relation between persons in society, a token perhaps. The other reveals the coin as a thing, capable of entering into definite relations with other things, as a quantitative ratio independent of the persons engaged in any particular transaction. In this latter respect money is like a commodity and its logic is that of anonymous markets. Heads and tails stand for social organisation from the top down and from the bottom up, epitomised in modern theory by the state and the market respectively.[151]

[149] *Resp.* 2.371b. The phrase 'νόμισμα σύμβολον τῆς ἀλλαγῆς ἕνεκα', could also be translated as 'money, a token for the purpose of exchange', where σύμβολον is in apposition to νόμισμα and not an adjective to it. A more elaborate statement of Plato's understanding of money can be found in *Laws*, where he suggests that the possession of gold and silver by private citizens should be abolished, and that 'for the purpose of everyday exchange ... people should possess coinage that is valued/current among themselves, but not current among other people' (ὧν ἕνεκά φαμεν τὸ νόμισμα κτητέον αὐτοῖς μὲν ἔντιμον, τοῖς δὲ ἄλλοις ἀνθρώποις ἀδόκιμον; Pl. *Leg.* 5.742a–b).

[150] *Pol.* 1.1257a 35–38.

[151] Hart 1986, 638.

It should perhaps not come as a surprise that Hart chose the coin as a metaphor for the duality of money; after all, coinage is the historic invention *par example* in which both these elements, token and commodity, were expressed as separate categories in a nearly explicit way. On the one hand, coins were made of precious metal, on the other, they were stamped with a sign of the state. It is perhaps for this reason that the introduction of coinage has often been regarded as the unequivocal start of the history of money.[152]

The observation that money is always both a token and a commodity is of great relevance here. Without preferring one approach to the other, it suggests that money is essentially characterised by the combination and integration of both aspects. This section will demonstrate that this duality is as much characteristic of money preceding coinage, as of coinage itself.[153] We should start off by asking whether money can exist at all without this combination.

The concept of 'commodity money' refers to a commodity that functions as a means of exchange and is accounted for as money but without money actually being at hand.[154] Economies that (partially) function on such transactions in kind have been identified in various regions and periods of history, such as most of Mesopotamian history, or Frankish and Viking Age Europe.[155] We should moreover be aware of the fact that in every monetary economy, including our own, a significant portion of transactions is conducted in kind,[156] and the attempt to distinguish between them has therefore been sometimes referred to as a 'pseudo-dilemma'.[157] However, it is important to point out that commodity money only tends to appear in the context of states and markets, where systemic control was warranted and the concept of money as a standard of value upheld.[158] Without the existence of something truly representing money that in absence would still function as a standard of value, even if only translational, currencies in kind would not commonly feature in the economy. In ancient Mesopotamia, for example, agricultural staple goods, mostly barley, could perform monetary functions, but the silver shekel – a weight unit for precious metal – always hovered in the background as the basic monetary unit, and much the same can be said to some extent for medieval Europe.[159]

152 Weatherford 1998; Kurke 1999, 11–13; Kletter 2003, 149; Seaford 2004, 1–9. Cf. Le Rider 2001; Schaps 2004.
153 See also Heymans 2018a.
154 Skre 2008, 344.
155 E.g., Bloch 1967; Kilger 2008; Skre 2008; Jursa 2010, 500; Von Reden 2010, 93–94; cf. Davis 2012. Such an economy is also referred to as a 'natural economy', opposed to a 'money economy' (Bloch 1967).
156 Cf. Humphrey and Hugh-Jones 1992, 4.
157 Bloch 1967.
158 Graeber 2011, 145.
159 E.g., Bloch 1967; Powell 1996; 1999; Dercksen 1999; Monroe 2005; Skre 2008; Graeber 2011, 39, 48.

We do, however, know that commodities can, under specific circumstances, function as currency without any monetary backing or state enforcement. A favourite example among economists is the use of cigarettes as a kind of currency in POW camps or prisons.[160] It has proven particularly tenacious, because it is understood as confirming one of the basic tenets of monetary theory in the post–Bretton Woods era, that money is and needs to be nothing but a mere commodity, whose value is regulated by the market without interference of the state.[161] The reality is, though, that such a currency can only come into being in a context where people are used to the workings of money and accept it as 'natural', to the extent that having to cope without it leads them to adopt a replacement.[162] As economists would be surprised to hear, no such commodity money could exist in a historical or cultural setting where money itself is not an integral part of daily life.

At the same time, a system based on credit money, whereby money is only a record of debt, an IOU, is similarly unlikely. Cuneiform tables provide ample evidence for credit arrangements in ancient Mesopotamia, even transferable credit, but these are always recorded with reference to current money, commonly silver, and existed under a political authority that could enforce or cancel debt.[163]

Additionally, neoclassical economists generally consider modern money to be fiat money, implying that it has no intrinsic value and is backed only by public trust, and thereby opposing it to commodity money.[164] Because of its centrality to current monetary theory (specifically monetarism),[165] economists have widely felt the need to substantiate the concept of fiat money by claiming the existence of fiat money in primitive societies, such as the stone money of the Yap in Micronesia.[166] However, this projection of the concept of fiat money onto primitive society has been noted to ignore practical, social, cultural and political determinants as a basis for value and should therefore be rejected as a 'myth'.[167] Similarly, so-called fiat money in our economy can and does notably only exist under legal backing of the state.

160 Radford 1945. See, e.g., Mankiw 2004, 629–630.

161 Sweeney and Sweeney (1977) and Krugman (1994) described the imminent difficulties of such a simple money system, and the need for regulation despite its apparent functioning, regarding the so-called Capitol Hill Baby Sitting Co-op Crisis, as a parable to monetary theory.

162 Graeber 2011, 37.

163 Dercksen 1999; Hudson and Van de Mieroop 2002; Van de Mieroop 2002; Hudson 2004.

164 The process to shape this started in 1933 and was completed in 1971, with Nixon terminating the relation between the US dollar and gold, thereby making the dollar a free-floating currency.

165 Hart 1986.

166 E.g., Mankiw 2004, 630–631.

167 Goldberg 2004.

So, not only is our money a token and a commodity at the same time, we can safely assume that money could historically only take shape if it combined both aspects: an object desired for its value and legal tender authorised by the state. But as was hinted at in Section 2.2, a token can be so much more than just a sign of the state. In fact, a token could be seen as a representation and agent of social value. Such tokens are known in stateless societies as well, where they are generally the focus of social activity. This can be seen in Douglas' coupons or Graeber's social currencies and also the Rossel Island *ndap* shells from Section 2.2.4 provide a case in point.

In general, we can suggest that any object, whose use revolves around being commonly accepted with the purpose of being passed on again in a new transaction, is endowed with some kind of iconic status that warrants its acceptability. But it appears that, when looking at primitive or social currencies, the very fact that people sometimes also want to hold on to such an object for a certain period of time forms part of the reason that they can be said to function as a token. David Graeber has drawn attention to the fact that social currencies, and money altogether, develop out of objects that are used to dress, shape or enhance the appearance of human beings. Whether beads, shells, whale teeth, feathers, *raffia* or *tugudu* cloth, most of the objects that served as currency were primarily known as adornment of the human body, thus contributing to its social standing.[168] The brass rods of the Tiv might as such not have been used for adornment but served as raw material for the production of jewellery or manillas, African currency bracelets, and obviously the same applies to precious metals. Because of their function and use, these objects were invested with prestige. Graeber argues that objects of display reflect past achievements, visually endowing the owner with prestige and emphasising their social persona. This causes others to relate and act towards the bearer in a certain way. In contrast to this, money refers to the power to act in the future and is in itself a hidden thing, reflecting the owners' hidden capacities to act on others. As we will see, the precious metal included in this study finds itself in the middle of this, conflating two apparent opposites: its capacity to function as an item of display and its hidden potential for future action. Graeber refers only to the last explicitly as money,[169] although I believe that both sides are to be understood as integral parts of the semantic concept of money, especially when considered in the framework of its early historic development.

In addition to their acceptability as prestige objects, the ways in which these objects are embedded in social practice invoke social and cultural values

168 Graeber 1996; 2001, 91–115; 2011, 144–145.
169 Graeber 1996; 2001, 91–115.

that form the basis for their token quality. After all, in representing social value and powers, such objects are tokens of society and its norms, no less than modern money is a token of the state by virtue of the power invested in it by society. This insight can also be related to the material that will be dealt with in the following chapters. The jewellery in the hoards (or for that matter, many of the votive offerings in Geometric sanctuaries) were most likely used for adornment or enhancement of the owner's prestige, as well as in exchange or payments. Their appearance in the archaeological record as reflecting normative behaviour surely suggests that they were seen as tokens of social value.

2.3.1 *Token and Commodity: Metal Objects in the Iron Age*

The question that presents itself now is how we can approach and attempt to understand the precious metal hoards that stand at the centre of the current study?

The precious metal hoards generally consist of whole objects, mostly jewellery, ingots of different sorts and cut and broken items or scrap metal known as *hacksilber* (Figure 2.1). Although understood in the past as jewellers' hoards, they are now generally regarded as having had an economic or monetary function, whereby the precious metal is considered a commodity, appreciated for the intrinsic value of the material.[170] Simply put, the idea is that precious metal was valued by its weight as bullion, forming the basis for its use in exchange, until, at some point, it was coined by the state and used as legal tender.

In contrast to this singular focus on precious metal as a commodity, scholarship on silver hoards from the Viking Age (Figure 2.2) has drawn attention to the diversity in the composition of the hoards, allowing for a more complex understanding of their use as well as their social and economic significance.[171] As noted, hoards with personal ornaments, mostly rings and bracelets, have been interpreted as belonging to a prestige economy, supported by the fact that a large proportion of them is present in hoards without ingots, *hacksilber* or coins, where their physical integrity appears to have been a normative feature.[172] At the same time, hoards with ingots, *hacksilber* and coins have been understood as indicating a silver weight economy, in which silver is valued as a

[170] E.g., Balmuth 1975; Gitin and Golani 2001; Thompson 2003; Kletter 2003; Kroll 2012. See also Section 3.1.

[171] E.g., Hårdh 1996; Graham-Campbell and Williams 2007; Skre 2008; Graham-Campbell, Sindbæk and Williams 2011. For specific approaches, see Hårdh 1996; Gaimster 2007; Sheehan 2007.

[172] Gaimster 2007, 127–128.

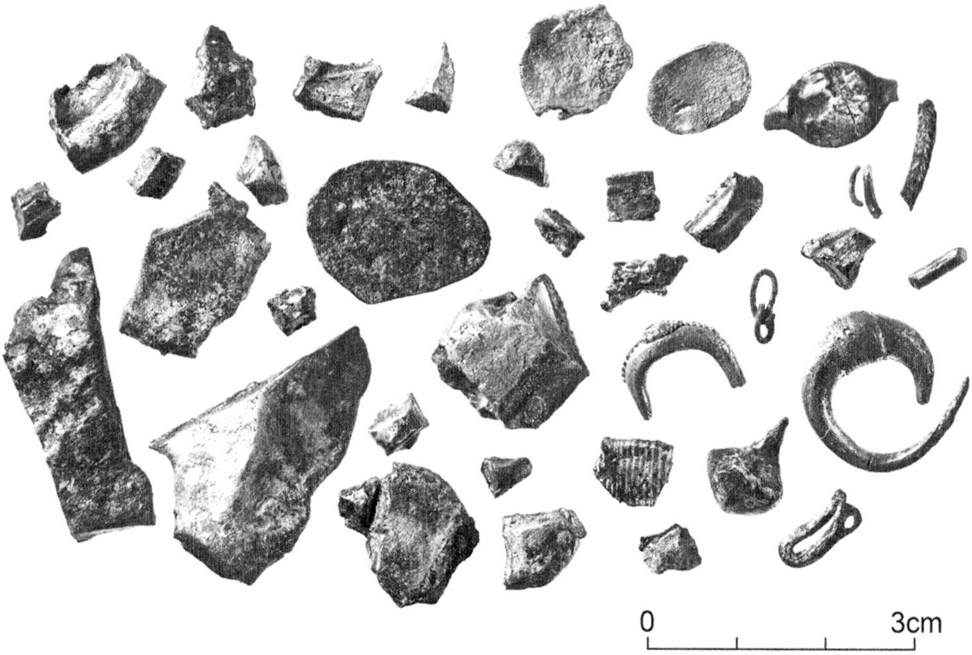

2.1 *Hacksilber*: a selection of objects from the Arad hoard (Courtesy of the Institute of Archaeology, Tel Aviv University [photo by Pavel Shrago])

2.2 Viking hoard from Silverdale, Lancashire (© Ian Richardson / Wikimedia Commons / CC-BY-SA-2.0)

material, regardless of the nature or social meaning of the objects exchanged. This is regarded as a transitional stage towards a full monetary economy.[173]

However, when trying to understand hoards with a mixed composition of jewellery, ingots and *hacksilber*, sometimes hoarded together with types of non-metallic jewellery, one could see how such a distinction misses part of the point. Surely, it seems that certain finished objects, whose completeness was maintained, were valued for their token quality and not only for the material they consisted of. Alternatively, the consistent cutting up of such tokens strongly suggests that their material value as a commodity was central to their meaning and use. Generally, people often refer to this as the 'intrinsic value' of the material, but this should not be understood in an abstract sense. After all, there is no *real* intrinsic value, and any concept of intrinsic value is socially constructed. Now, surely the intrinsic value of metal could be constructed as an abstract quality, but this does not simply seem to be the case in the hoards. Rather, its intrinsic value appears to be perceived as its intrinsic capacity to re-form into prestige objects.

This dynamic quality of the silver in hoards, transforming back and forth from material to object, is reflected in some of the literary evidence that throws light on the use of silver in both the Viking Age and the Iron Age southern Levant. A passage from the *Heimskringla*, composed around 1230 CE by the Icelandic poet Snorri Sturluson, describes the payment presented to the tenth century *skald*, or bard, Eyvindr Skaldaspiller:

> Eyvind composed a poem about the people of Iceland, for which they rewarded him by each bonde giving him three silver pennies, of full weight and white in the fracture. And when the silver was brought together at the General Thing [i.e., the general assembly], the people resolved to have it purified, and made into a shoulder-pin, and after the workmanship of the silver was paid, the shoulder-pin weighed some fifty marks. This they sent to Eyvind; but Eyvind had the shoulder-pin broken into pieces, and with the silver he bought a farmstead for himself.[174]

Despite the late date of the source (the common use of *hacksilber* presumably disappeared in the course of the eleventh century CE), the passage indicates that silver ornamental objects were suitable as a reward or payment and that,

[173] For example, Sheehan shows that of the fifty-three coinless hoards from Viking Age Ireland, 39 per cent contain exclusively complete ornaments, while 29 per cent contain complete ornaments and/or ingots together with *hacksilber* (Sheehan 2007, but see cf. 159–160). Along similar lines, Gaimster demonstrates with regard to south Scandinavia that complete ornaments tend to be present in hoards of low compositional complexity (in which there are few material categories), while *hacksilber* tends to be present in hoards of high compositional complexity (Gaimster 2007).

[174] Quoted and discussed by Graham-Campbell 1982, 32–33; 2007, 216.

if needed, such objects were made from and recycled back into silver pieces that functioned explicitly as silver weight money.

A similar perception of the value of silver can be recognised in Ancient Near Eastern sources. Among others, a letter from Karum-Kanesh, the Old Assyrian trade colony at Kültepe in central Anatolia (ca. 18th century BCE), testifies to the use of bracelets in exchange. It records the complaints of an Assyrian woman, Taram Kubi, to her husband, the merchant Innaya: 'You wrote to me as follows: "Keep the bracelets and the rings that you have, they will be needed to buy you food." It is true that you sent me half a pound of gold through Ili-bani but where are the bracelets that you have left behind? When you left, you didn't leave me one shekel of silver. You cleaned out the house and took everything with you.'[175] It is interesting to note that references to silver money in weight units (shekels) and in standard objects (bracelets) are used here interchangeably. Similarly, there are various sources in which precious metal objects are described in terms of their weight, such as a Neo-Assyrian document from the mid-seventh century, containing the receipt of '29 silver madattu-bowls, 25 mina in weight'.[176] Examples of vessels described with reference to their weight-value are also known from Greek sanctuaries.[177]

Biblical sources make clear that precious metal objects like vessels or rings are sometimes used in payments, such as contributions to the temple.[178] Precious metal vessels were in some cases also used for the payment of tribute, as we know of the tribute paid by Jehu, king of Israel, to the Assyrian king Shalmaneser III, and recorded on the Black Obelisk: 'the tribute of Jehu, of the house of Omri: silver, gold, a golden bowl, a golden goblet, golden cups, golden buckets, tin, a staff of the king's hand, (and) javelins'.[179] Silver used for exchange or payment was also transformed back into finished objects, as is indicated by a passage in 2 Kings. Describing the financial reform of King Joash,[180] it is emphasised that the silver paid to the temple and deposited in the cash-box is designated to pay for maintenance and 'is not be used to *make*[181] silver basins, wick trimmers, sprinkling bowls, trumpets or any other articles of

175 Michel 2001, 466–470; Van de Mieroop 2004, 92.

176 ADD 927* ii, 7–9. See Postgate 1974, 112. Additional examples are the stolen vessels listed in *deben* in the Egyptian *Report of Wenamun* (Wente 2003, 1.12; see Section 4.1) and rings and bracelets listed in the biblical record (Gen 24:22; Jud 8:26).

177 See Section 5.2.

178 Num 7:13–86; Ezra 1:6–11; Job 28:17. For early Mesopotamian 'ring-silver', see Powell 1996, 236, 238. Additionally, the *dbn*, the common measure for weighing metal in Egypt originated from words meaning 'ring' (Monroe 2005, 160, 165).

179 After Younger 2000a, 270.

180 See also Section 4.2.3.

181 Despite the literal meaning of *yēʿāśę̄*, translations and commentaries often incorrectly translate the passage as saying that silver/money is not meant to 'buy' or 'acquire' these objects.

gold or silver for the temple'.[182] Apparently, it was not uncommon for silver in the temple to be used for religious paraphernalia, while, if the need arose, such objects could be used again in tribute payments, as indicated by the example of Jehu, or taken out as loot.[183]

This understanding of precious metal, characterised by its dynamic quality to move back and forth between form and substance, or material and object, clearly applies to hoards. The presence of finished objects alongside *hacksilber* and ingots indicates that these hoards represented prestige and the power to display status, as well as the hidden power to act by economic force. By representing both object and material at the same time, token and commodity were tied up in the hoards in a way that essentially negates the very opposition between them. Specific objects might have represented one or the other in specific contexts, but in general, they were perceived as intrinsically dynamic and appreciated for their ability to move back and forth between different shapes and 'regimes of value'.[184]

Additionally, this approach can also be applied to some extent to the votive deposits in early Greek sanctuaries, as well as the funerary dedications, and specifically the bronze objects. Although these objects, diverse in character, can and have always been regarded as prestige objects or tokens of status, an understanding of them as being appreciated and dedicated *also* for their material value as a commodity seems obvious, considering the relative standardisation of simple objects like pins and rings and their association with or allusion to raw material in spite of their basic form as ornament.[185] Examples of this are coiled objects such as spiral-rings, fibulae and bracelets, or objects that despite their shape are unlikely to have practically functioned as adornment, such as the cast rings, or *krikoi*, that are either too small or too large to be worn.[186] Evidence of physical manipulation or production draws additional attention to the dynamic and transitory element in the perception of votives as objects of display and at the same time as means of economic power. In Chapter 5, I will discuss how the use and value of such objects can be perceived in the context of cult and funerary practices.

A detailed analysis of the hoards from the perspective laid out above – focusing on the object-level within the assemblage posed by the hoard – will be presented in Chapter 3. This is the appropriate way to test and refine our understanding of how this material was used and valued. Furthermore, a

182 2 Kgs 12:14.
183 E.g., 1 Kgs 14:26, 15:18; 2 Kgs 12:19, 14:14, 16:8, 24:13, 25:13–17. See Section 4.2.2.
184 Appadurai 1986a, 14–15; Graeber 2001, 106. Cf. Section 3.4.2.
185 Cf. Rahmstorf 2016a, 32–33.
186 See Section 5.2.

diachronic comparison of the hoard-assemblages will provide the basis for a further analysis of the historical context in which their use should be placed.

2.3.2 *Token and Commodity: An Inherent Opposition?*

As noted above, the way token and commodity were dynamically integrated in the hoards suggests that a simple distinction between them is not always valid or helpful. The appreciation of metal for its ability to form a prestige object and vice versa show that the perceived value of the material as a commodity is not abstract, but consists of its 'tokenability', its ability to function as a token. Similarly, the perceived value of metal prestige objects as tokens cannot be simply seen as a social convention; rather, they are valued as a token because of their quality as a commodity. The opposition between token and commodity as two distinct categories is in our case artificial and, more than being of universal value, it reflects the (Western) historical tradition on money.

Whether from Lydia, India or China,[187] coinage was probably the first historical form of money to give concrete expression to both categories, token and commodity, thereby being accountable to both the state and the market. As such, it partially instigated the opposition between them. Not much later, this was reflected in the different ways in which Plato and Aristotle understood money, which in itself owed much to the institution of coinage.[188] The opposition was further shaped through the historical debate between chartalists and metallists,[189] briefly mentioned above, and has continued to express itself in contemporary debates on monetary policy. One should indeed wonder whether paper money or today's 'dematerialised credit-money' could have taken shape without this opposition characterising our cultural understanding of money. In fact, the conception of money as being shaped between two opposing forces, the state and the market, seems to be an integral part of the contemporary Western (and global) discourse.[190]

However, when dealing with the supposed 'origins' of money, we would do well to acknowledge that these two categories are not independent factors in the development of money systems. Their strict separation in the context of money is perhaps more a modern development that has enabled us to separate them in physical form. As we will see, in the eastern Mediterranean during the centuries preceding the invention of coinage, no clear distinction existed along these lines, and it would therefore be a historical misunderstanding, in fact

187 Cf. Schaps 2007; Scheidel 2010.
188 Cf. Meadows 2009.
189 Hart 1986.
190 Cf. Maurer 2006.

anachronistic, to think that money developed or could have developed in this context as a simple result of either the state or the market. In the remainder of this book, I will try to put forward a more nuanced understanding of the interplay of social and economic factors in the early development of money.

2.4 CONCLUSION

The purpose of this chapter was to 'unpack' the concept of money – to address as much as possible the modern assumptions and understandings that shape and therefore distort our perception of money as a concept in historical and social research and as a heuristic tool. Grounded in a critical appraisal of common ideas from the anthropological discourse on money, I have sought to develop an approach to money that better fits the specific social and political circumstances within our historic case and the nature of the *hacksilber* hoards studied here. This is in contrast to anthropological approaches that generally apply to money in colonial settings or contemporary capitalist economies.

The first important observation is that money does not have to be a particular thing nor does it have to meet material requirements. Not its material features but rather the way it is contextualised in cultural logic determines the meanings attributed to money. Although money can be regarded as serving general functions, these are embedded in different practices and subject to different social and cultural norms in different cultures. Standing in contrast to the long-standing idea that money has an intrinsic (negative) moral bearing on society, this implies that, in itself, money does not have a pre-set effect on society.

By extension, it is argued that an apparent distinction between two types of money is not conducive for creating a better understanding of economic exchange and money in the historical framework addressed here. A distinction along the lines of a primitive/modern divide only serves to attribute a certain significance to those things we identify as money, namely, coinage, while rejecting other forms as economically and historically insignificant. Similarly, an approach to early money with reference to the substantivist opposition between special-purpose and general-purpose money builds on a type of technological determinism that mostly obscures the social and cultural determinants behind economic and social practice. An opposition between social currencies and money in a commercial economy might be suitable for drawing out differences between societies, especially in colonial contexts; however, by glossing over economising behaviour in human economies and the concern for the social order in commercial economies, it encourages mystifications that in the end serve to uphold the divide between a primitive economy and a commercial one, epitomised by coinage. A division between state currencies and indigenous currencies, which makes sense in reference to modern states, is also not applicable to the societies studied here, where the role of a central authority is more ambiguous.

More generally, the idea that some things are money in the modern sense of the word and others simply are not can hardly contribute to a better understanding of the intricacies of money, especially early in its development. This attitude, however, has left its mark, either implicitly or explicitly, on many studies of the topic. As we will see in the following chapters as well, it has served to marginalise the monetary predecessors of coinage and their significance to the effect that it disconnects the discourse on the social and sacred aspects of the economy from that of the historical monetary economy.

An important lesson to draw from this discussion is not that all forms of money are necessarily similar to the type of money that we know, but rather that money is always subjected to restrictions, prescribed by social, cultural and religious norms. At the same time, it is a medium of social and political action and always subject to what Appadurai refers to as 'the politics of value'.[191] As such, it is inherently dynamic and transient.

Another important aspect of money and its development concerns the extent to which it can be related to the market vis-à-vis the state or, in lack thereof, any social structure mandating its use. Following Hart's 1986 seminal contribution to the discourse, the concept of money is regarded here as being always a commodity, constructed by the market, and a token, guaranteed by social convention, at the same time. Even prior to the invention of coinage, its epitome, the combination of token and commodity can be clearly identified in the metal currencies studied here, *hacksilber* in particular. However, these *hacksilber* hoards show that token and commodity are not opposed but rather interrelated qualities, whereby one is based on the other and vice versa. The physical nature of the material as dynamic and transitory should be understood from this perspective, with the objects moving back and forth between being emblems of social prestige and concealed tools of economic action, thereby offering a sophisticated approach to why certain valuables become appreciated as money.

If the invention of coinage was revolutionary in anything, it is in the fact that it brought the opposition between token and commodity as separate categories to physical expression. Possibly because of this, it became the iconic form of money. However, in contrast to the tenacious idea that the advent of a monetary economy should be connected to the coin, the very elements that make up coinage can be seen at work in the centuries before its invention.

191 Appadurai 1986a.

THREE

A STUDY OF IRON AGE PRECIOUS METAL HOARDS

3.1 INTRODUCTION: PRECIOUS METAL HOARDS

Precious metal hoards, predominantly containing silver, have been known from excavations in the southern Levant and the Ancient Near East at large for over a century. From the Achaemenid period onwards, these hoards mostly contain coins;[1] earlier hoards, however, dating prior to the introduction of coinage, can contain a variety of objects, such as ingots of different types, jewellery, all sorts of scrap metal, as well as non-metallic objects. Some of the material in the hoards concerns complete artefacts, but more often objects were broken, bent or cut up before being deposited (see, for example, Figure 2.1).

[1] E.g., Robinson 1937; 1950; Schaeffer 1937, 153; Kraay and Moorey 1968; Reade 1986; Kroll 2001b; Gitler 2006, spec. tab. 1.

The presence of (broken) jewellery and other forms of metal scrap initially led excavators to assume that these were 'metal scraps collected for re-melting', thus suggesting that these hoards had belonged to a metalsmith.[2] A consideration of these hoards in the context of a growing body of parallels has prompted scholars over the past century to reject this interpretation in favour of an understanding of the hoards as metal valued by weight.[3] However, the association of such hoards with metalsmiths has not disappeared from scholarship,[4] nor should it be rejected out of hand.

It is notable, though, that the perception of the hoards has turned around and that over the past thirty years scholarship has gone to mostly understanding the hoards as having a purely economic significance and use. Since the precious metal hoards from the Iron Age southern Levant (ca. 1200–600 BCE) are the main subject of the analysis presented in this chapter, it is important to try to better understand the different ways in which these hoards have been perceived.

3.1.1 Hoards As a Historical Phenomenon

Differences in interpretation of the hoards concern not only the material itself; they relate to the way these particular finds are framed. Whereas the metalsmith-hoard interpretation tends to see and approach the hoard as an isolated find, scholarship presenting an economic understanding has mostly done so with reference to similar material and to the economic context in which the material and its use should be understood. Already in the 1960s, Miriam Balmuth was the first to study and present multiple hoards together, drawing attention to the importance of these hoards in the history and development of money and identifying their contents as 'the monetary forerunners of coinage'.[5] Subsequent research, only following up on Balmuth's earlier work around the turn of the century, has focused on improving our understanding of these hoards and their historical significance, by expanding the corpus of known hoards and exploring their historical and economic context more in detail.[6] The studies of Kletter and Thompson – incidentally appearing both in 2003 – have been particularly important, by providing an extensive survey of the hoards and several of their characteristics, such as archaeological context and weight. It should be pointed out that their work has provided an important basis for any subsequent study of the topic, including the current one. The common ground

[2] E.g., Macalister 1912, 263; Petrie 1928, 10; Schaeffer 1935, 144–145; Loud 1948, pl. 229.

[3] Robinson 1950; Balmuth 1967; 1976; Bivar 1971, 98.

[4] Ogden 1982, 4; Themelis 1983; Bell 1986, 145, 150–151; Knapp, Muhly and Muhly 1988; Sommerfeld 1994; Czichon and Werner 1998, 178–179; Lilyquist 2012, 18.

[5] Balmuth 1964; 1967; 1971; 1975; 1976; 2001a; 2001b.

[6] I.e., Gitin and Golani 2001; 2004; Kletter 2003; 2004; Thompson 2003; 2007; Eshel 2014; Eshel et al. 2018.

for all these studies dealing with the wider context and significance of the hoards is the assumption that they are not actually random finds but represent some sort of historical phenomenon. However, as to what exactly this phenomenon signifies little agreement has been reached.

As noted in Chapter 2, a general consensus currently exists, accepting the metal as being of economic value and emphasising its use as bullion, that is, valued by weight.[7] Whether this value and the metal's use can be considered 'monetary' has been judged differently.

Originally her student and collaborator,[8] Christine Thompson states that 'precious metal of any shape had a value that was fundamentally "monetary" ... during the Iron Age', and follows Balmuth's claim that the Iron Age silver hoards represent a clear development towards coinage, invented in western Anatolia during the late seventh century BCE.[9] Pushing Balmuth's idea, she explores the evidence for the use of sealed bundles (or bags) for the silver and their possible adherence to weight standards in order to show that the silver in the hoards is conceptually related to coinage, in that a coin too is metal of a standard weight, stamped with a device.[10] She thus reiterates Balmuth's identification of the hoards as a precursor to coinage and argues for an understanding of them as the missing link in a linear model between unmarked ingots and coinage.[11]

Although Thompson makes a fair case for the carrying or keeping of silver in bundles with reference to Ancient Near Eastern written sources, the emphasis on sealed bundles as the unit or key characteristic in a uniform or standardised monetary system is questionable. As we will see further in Section 3.3.2, contrary to what has been claimed with regard to the bundles from the Dor hoard (Figure 3.1),[12] the bundles known so far are not of a set weight, and their supposed adherence to a known weight standard is highly speculative. Moreover, although the incidental sealing of these bundles with a figurative stamp likely symbolises a sense of authority, the bullae are of rather random types,[13] making it unlikely that they actually represented any known contemporary authority or were functioning in a standard way.[14] Thompson is right to reject a 'categorical' distinction between coinage and sealed silver as futile; and she is equally right to draw attention to the seal as a token of authority in a

7 E.g., Balmuth 2001a; Dever 2001; Gitin and Golani 2001; Kroll 2001a; 2003; 2008a; 2013a; Stern 2001; Kletter 2003; Thompson 2003; Eshel et al. 2018.

8 Balmuth and Thompson 2000.

9 Thompson 2003, 71.

10 Balmuth 1976; Thompson 2003; Silver 2006; Gitler 2012, 7–8; Haselgrove and Krmnicek 2012, 239; *pace* Eshel et al. 2018, 203–204, 221.

11 Thompson 2003, 87.

12 Stern 1998; 2001; Thompson 2003, 81–83.

13 An example is the Dor bulla with Middle Bronze Age interlocking spirals; see Stern 2001, 23.

14 Cf. Kletter 2003, 146.

3.1 Dor hoard (Courtesy of the Israel Museum, Jerusalem [photo by author])

conceptual sense. However, she assumes that the token quality is a characteristic feature of coinage, rather than of money in general, which is a subtle but important difference. Moreover, the suggestion that the incidental use of seals reflects a clear development towards coinage is wishful thinking. Chapter 2 has provided ample reason why a linear model for the development of money should be met with reluctance; we will see later in this chapter why such a claim is unwarranted in particular for the Iron Age.

Whereas Thompson considers the hoards as evidence for an increase in the monetary use of silver in general during the Iron Age, fuelled by Phoenician maritime expansion,[15] Seymour Gitin and Amir Golani argue more specifically that they testify to the monetisation of the economy in the seventh century BCE. This process, they claim, is a result of the Neo-Assyrian influence in the region and what they refer to as 'the growing fiscal needs of an international

[15] Thompson 2003, 90–95; 2007; Thompson and Skaggs 2013.

economy', causing silver in its turn to develop into a form of money.[16] Gitin and Golani bring up the six silver hoards excavated at Tel Miqne/Ekron from the seventh century as a case in point,[17] implying that they reflect an increase in silver use. Although silver hoards are known from throughout the Iron Age, Gitin and Golani maintain that their chronological focus is informed by a 'historical context provided by the Neo-Assyrian textual evidence of a seventh century silver monetary economy, a context that does not exist for the hoards of previous periods'.[18] It raises the question how this historical context exactly reflects on the use of silver and money and whether a different use of silver can be inferred at all from a lack of the type of written sources we have for the seventh century.[19] Whether the Tel Miqne/Ekron hoards themselves reflect a significant change in relation to earlier hoards – to the effect of a supposed monetisation – will be further discussed in Sections 3.3.3 and 3.4.

Partly in reaction to Gitin and Golani's claim of a seventh-century monetisation, Raz Kletter rejects interpreting the hoards as money altogether. He identifies them as part of a metal-weight economy but speaks only of money in the context of coinage. As silver was used as the dominant means of value in the southern Levant from the Middle Bronze Age onwards, no particular historical or monetary development can be gauged from the Iron Age hoards; the change to a monetary economy only occurs with the introduction of coinage.[20] Like Thompson, Kletter also shows a questionable disposition towards linear or even evolutionary thinking; his persistence to see money only where there is coinage has no analytical value and obscures exactly what we are trying to understand: development and change in the Iron Age economy.[21]

As this short review of recent work shows, there is a clear tendency to regard the metal in the hoards as representing material value in weight. With the emphasis on coinage as the iconic form of economic value and the construction of the hoards in its opposition, this reflects an understanding of the metal as a commodity. In contrast, earlier interpretations of hoards as belonging to a founder or silversmith reflect an emphasis on the object, or at least the material's potential to be an object. This attitude can be seen in the general perception of the material as being used primarily in the production of objects,[22] but also in the focus on specific objects, held as indication for this.[23] The assumption behind the latter approach, ultimately rooted in Marx's labour

16 Gitin and Golani 2001, 40; 2004, 204; Gitin 1995, 69; Golani and Sass 1998, 61–62.
17 See Appendix.
18 Gitin and Golani 2004, 203.
19 See Section 4.3.
20 Kletter 2003; 2004.
21 Cf. Section 2.2.
22 I.e., jewellery; e.g., Marshall 1911, 63–64.
23 E.g., Themelis 1983.

theory of value, undoubtedly was that the (added) value of those objects would have been derived from their production.

It was noted in Chapter 2 how such an approach, seeing the precious metal in the hoards either as material or as object, misses an essential quality of the metal and why it was valued and is restricting in its ability to fathom the hoards and the phenomenon they represent. On a more semantic level, rejecting a qualification of the hoards per se as money by regarding them as a mere commodity and thereby simply ignoring this fundamental duality is equally limited.

A more thorough study of the typology of the hoards would offer a way to deal with this ambiguity, seeing that it would enable a better insight into the prevalence of specific types of objects in relation to the wider corpus. However, the little interest taken so far in the typology of the hoards under discussion here has been of a rather descriptive nature, causing its analytic potential to remain virtually unexplored.[24] Exceptions to this, while methodologically important, have been rare, preliminary and focused on a small set of hoards and are therefore of restricted historical pertinence.[25] All in all, although the fragmentary and scrappy nature of most of the objects in the hoards poses a complication to this effort, there has been no serious attempt to study their composition in a way that would allow comparative analysis, such as known from scholarship on Viking Age hoards.[26]

3.1.2 Towards a New Approach

Hoard scholarship of the past decades has engaged in historical conjecture about the development of money based on broad assumptions regarding the significance of the hoards and (preconceived) projections of the circumstances in which money *should have* developed. This has, in its turn, led to a historical understanding of the hoards that is both limited in scope and questionable in outcome. Alternatively, we are in need of an approach that assesses the hoards at a higher resolution, focusing on the (material) characteristics of the individual objects and the hoards as the basis for appreciating coherence and diversity within the individual hoards and the wider corpus. A comprehensive approach of this type enables us to ask more detailed questions about the use of the metal, its circulation and production, and allows comparison between the hoards on this basis.

Issues of production and circulation have drawn attention in recent years as a result of a growing interest in the metallurgical aspects of the silver. Ongoing research in this field mostly takes the form of compositional analysis by means

[24] See Golani and Sass 1998; Gitin and Golani 2001; Sass 2002a; Thompson 2003; 2009. Cf. Themelis 1983.
[25] Eshel 2014; Shalev, Shechtman and Shilstein 2014; Eshel et al. 2018.
[26] See Sections 2.2.2 and 2.3.1.

of XRF spectrometry and lead isotope analysis (LIA) and is aimed at determining the chemical characteristics, provenience and potential mixing of the metal.[27] Compositional analysis provides a basis for the comparison of hoards, with different metal contents potentially indicating different silver sources, and enables a better insight into the processing of the silver, such as, for example, the possible use of 'native electrum' or the addition of copper.[28] Since silver is not native to the southern Levant, provenance study has the potential to shed light on trade routes and their changing patterns over time. LIA of Iron Age silver hoards has yielded results over the past twenty years,[29] but much of this work has been subject to criticism for failing to address several complexities. As more and more hoard material is sampled and published, and results are debated, we can expect a more complete picture of ancient silver trade to arise in the years to come.[30] Needless to say, while much work still remains to be done, in conjunction with conventional methods, metallurgical research can make a very important contribution to our knowledge of the metal and to our understanding of Iron Age trade systems in the wider Mediterranean.[31] However, as a technological approach to the past, its suitability to confront issues of use and circulation within society, beyond the mixing of silver from different sources or the identification of production processes for primary ingots, is limited. With the current chapter not focusing on the origin of the metal, but rather on how it was possibly handled and used and what behaviour this reflects, I will utilise a different approach to the material in the hoards.

As opposed to metallurgical work on the hoards, the approach adopted here will concentrate on the macroscopic aspects of the material in order to obtain a better insight into the behavioural practice, whether monetary or not, to which it was intricately tied. The focus here will lie on the contextual, metrological and typological data, thereby regarding the precious metal objects as the smallest units, constituting the hoards as larger assemblages.[32]

Likely resulting from the nature and quantity of the material, these smallest units have not always received due attention. With 'diagnostic' objects, mostly

[27] Stos-Gale 2001; Thompson 2007; 2009; Thompson and Skaggs 2013; Eshel 2014; Shalev, Shechtman and Shilstein 2014; Eshel et al. 2018; 2019; Wood, Montero-Ruiz and Martinón-Torres 2019. In general, see Pernicka 2014.

[28] Keyser and Clark 2001; Shalev, Shechtman and Shilstein 2013; Eshel et al. 2018; Wood, Montero-Ruiz and Martinón-Torres 2019.

[29] Stos-Gale 2001; Thompson 2007; 2009; Thompson and Skaggs 2013.

[30] Eshel et al. 2018, 222; 2019; Ben-Yosef 2019; Wood, Montero-Ruiz and Martinón-Torres 2019.

[31] It is important to emphasise that conventional methods, such as typological analysis, remain critical for interpreting the objects themselves and the results of compositional analysis or provenance study. Such methods can, moreover, provide clear insight into the provenance of the objects and matters of circulation and should form the basis for selecting objects for further science-based analysis.

[32] Cf. Eshel 2014; Eshel et al. 2018.

jewellery, often singled out for descriptive purposes, much of the material in these assemblages has in some cases been indiscriminately qualified as *hacksilber*, scrap or fragments.[33] It is important, however, to emphasise that like any form of material culture, such as a house, a work of art or a potsherd, these objects are tied to past human behaviour and therefore relevant to our purpose. Notwithstanding interpretations of the hoards or the value we presume they had, they were in the first place part of a material reality. This reality can be understood as a reflection of past behaviour, but at the same time it is important to understand that material culture enables us to behave in certain ways. Inspired by the work of Goffman and Gombrich on the role and concept of frames (for example, in signalling a work of art), Daniel Miller explains that material objects function as a frame to our behaviour, providing a material setting to our attitudes and actions.[34] Think about the possibility that cutting up prestige objects for use as cash could have constituted a morally degrading act[35] or that the use of silver jewellery fragments as cash could have been a way for certain people in society to defy those traditionally in control of economic resources:[36] the ostensibly mute objects then provide a subtext to human action in a way that most often escapes our awareness. According to Bourdieu, 'it is because subjects do not, strictly speaking, know what they are doing that what they do has more meaning than they know'; as part of what he calls 'the humility of things', Miller extends this understanding to include objects (as opposed to subjects). So, in much the same way as behaviour often *unconsciously* adheres to or emanates from certain cultural and social norms, so does material culture.[37]

The assumption that the hoards represent a single historical phenomenon implies that they would have resulted from a certain behavioural practice. In order to understand whether this is the case and what this practice entailed, we need to check to what extent specific characteristics of the material confirm to a coherent pattern. Often, we do this intuitively, when, for example, we identify an architectural structure as a house, as opposed to a palace, temple or storage space, based on characteristics such as the number of rooms, their size and the type of walls. We do so because the layout of a domestic structure within a certain time and space emanates from and reproduces a certain mental template of what a house should look like; and we therefore consider it logical

33 Golani and Sass 1998; Gitin and Golani 2001; Arie 2013. More rigorous approaches to the hoards, focusing on each object, are Sass 2002a; Kim and Kroll 2008; Thompson 2009; and Eshel 2014.

34 Miller 1987, 100–102; 2010, 48–50. See also Goffman 1975; Gombrich 1979.

35 Compare, for example, the case of Taram Kubi, wife of the merchant Innaya, recorded in the letters from Karum-Kanesh (see Section 2.3.1; Michel 2001, 466; Van de Mieroop 2004, 92).

36 This is what Bloch and Parry imply with regard to the Tiv, when suggesting (without empirical substantiation) that the young men would have had a different attitude to Western money than the elders who were traditionally in control of the highest sphere of exchange, women (1989, 14).

37 Bourdieu 1977, 79; Miller 1987, 85–108; 2010, 50–51.

that it relates to certain norms.[38] Significantly, the metal hoards under study here are still relatively uncharted territory, and it is therefore important that we keep ourselves from being guided by a priori conceptions of bullion or money. We will thus attempt to map out specific material characteristics of the objects in relation to the hoards as a whole, such as weight and type, in order to see to what extent they adhere to specific patterns.

This does not, however, mean that exceptions to such patterns should be necessarily seen as unrelated to the behavioural practice. Deviations from the norm can also be the result of a subject's agency to actively follow alternative practices or strategies, possibly as a means of expression challenging or at least reacting to normative social practice. This might, for example, be by prioritising other modes of exchange or by the deliberate destruction of wealth in defiance of possible money-use. Such potential attitudes and strategies are nearly impossible to project based on the hoard material and is therefore not a focus of the current study. The obvious downside, or rather limitation, to this approach is therefore that it does not relate to the economy as a whole, or even exchange in general, but focuses specifically on the potential role of precious metal in exchange.

Additionally, when assuming trends, we need to be aware of the restrictions of the data and the extent to which they are representative. First of all, the corpus of hoards is in itself rather limited, and as I will further explain in Section 3.2.1, it is for different reasons currently not possible to study and compare all hoards on equal grounds. This limited dataset can only be expanded by disclosure and full publication of known hoards, and by the chance discovery of new ones (see Section 3.2.1, Chapter 4 n. 8 and Appendix). Although about a third of the total number of hoards known to us has been excavated since 1990, making it not unlikely that new hoards will be discovered over the course of the coming years, they remain chance finds in excavation. Even more so, considering the fact that these hoards are generally utilitarian – that is, designated for use,[39] they were presumably left behind by chance as well. It does not seem likely that this would in any way distort our image of the precious metal that was actually in use.

3.2 MATERIAL AND METHOD

For the approach advocated here to be put into practice, I will carefully lay out methods for exploring the material properties of the hoards. As noted, the focus will lie on the contextual, metrological and typological characteristics of the material, with due reference to previous scholarship and several of its assumptions. First, however, a new discussion of the material corpus that stands at the basis of the current chapter is needed.

[38] Bourdieu 1970.

[39] Cf. Knapp, Muhly and Muhly 1988.

3.2.1 A Corpus of Hoards

As described in Section 3.1, the surveys of both Kletter and Thompson have been particularly important in providing a systematic overview of the known hoards,[40] setting the stage for subsequent attempts to understand the material.[41] Despite small differences in the composition of both their catalogues (e.g., Thompson limits herself to silver hoards, whereas Kletter also includes other precious metal hoards), both corpora broadly overlap, covering precious metal hoards from the southern Levant from the final stage of Egyptian rule in the region (Late Bronze Age; ca. twelfth century BCE)[42] to the end of the Iron Age (early sixth century BCE).

A detailed review of their work and the availability of additional evidence allow us now to expand and update this corpus. Additions and corrections can also be made to the catalogues provided by Kletter and Thompson on a detailed level, sometimes concerning the contents of the hoards, their archaeological context or their dating.[43] Where relevant, such changes will be mentioned in the text; additional details and references are included in the updated catalogue (see Appendix).

To start with, several hoards can be added to the corpus, some newly discovered, others overlooked. Two different hoards from Tell Balata/ Shechem were conflated:[44] the first was found by Ernst Sellin in 1913, while the other hoard was excavated by the Drew-McCormick expedition in 1957.[45] A group of ten gold and silver earrings was found by W. F. Petrie at Tell Jemmeh but not included by either Kletter or Thompson.[46] Additionally, some recently excavated hoards can be added to the corpus. A hoard consisting of gold and silver jewellery and *hacksilber* was excavated at Tel Megiddo during the summer of 2010 but only discovered the year after during the pottery restoration;[47] at Abel Beth Maacah (Tell Abil el-Qameḥ), a small silver hoard consisting of jewellery and some scrap pieces was discovered in 2013.[48]

[40] Kletter 2003; Thompson 2003.

[41] E.g., Gitin and Golani 2004; Kletter 2004; 2013; Kletter and De Groot 2007; Thompson 2007; 2009; Vargyas 2007; Thompson and Skaggs 2013; Eshel 2014; Shalev, Shechtman and Shilstein 2014; Eshel et al. 2018; 2019.

[42] This specific period has alternatively been referred to as Late Bronze III, Iron Ia or the period of the twentieth dynasty; see Mazar 2009, 23–24.

[43] Eshel et al. (2018, 200–201) offer an updated catalogue based on Eshel's MA thesis (2014), although also here several additions/corrections can be made.

[44] Balmuth and Thompson 2000; Kletter 2003, 145; Thompson 2003, 100; see Appendix.

[45] Shechem A: Sellin 1914, 38; Shechem B: Kee and Tombs 1957, 105.

[46] Petrie 1928, 10.

[47] Megiddo D: Arie 2013; Arie et al. 2019.

[48] Abel Beth Maacah: Panitz-Cohen, Mullins and Bonfil 2013; Panitz-Cohen et al. 2016; Yahalom-Mack et al. 2019. The Abel Beth Maacah hoard is currently dated to the LB IIB (thirteenth century), falling outside the chronological range of the corpus. However, because it was previously dated 'Late Bronze Age–early Iron Age I', contemporary to the Beth Shean

Moreover, the detailed publication of hoards from Wadi el-Makkuk, Ein Gedi and Beth Shean D has in recent years contributed to the available data.[49] Additionally, hoards from Akko, Dor, Ein Ḥofez and Tell Keisan have been studied by Tzilla Eshel in the framework of her MA thesis at Haifa University.[50]

Regarding the dates assigned to the hoards, several corrections can also be proposed. The dating of the hoards can be complicated by either the lack of conclusive data or the contradiction of different elements. The archaeological context provides in many cases the primary source for dating but also a possible container (a pottery vessel or preserved fragments of textile) and objects in or associated with the hoard can be taken as evidence. However, the archaeological context has not always been (properly) recorded (e.g., Gezer hoards, Shechem A), and in some cases, the context either poses problems of interpretation (e.g., Tawilan) or simply provides no datable clue (e.g., Eshtemoa). The Shechem B hoard, for example, has all likeliness of being an Iron Age hoard but was found in an apparently disturbed context under a Hellenistic house.[51] Pottery vessels are often not closely datable and therefore rarely provide close dates (cf. Arad), and while textile remains can potentially be radiocarbon dated, one of two examples published so far (Megiddo D) turned out to be significantly older than the stratum in which it was found, possibly indicating an '"old textile" effect'.[52] Finally, contents of a hoard or associated objects such as jewellery or scarabs are in some cases well datable but could also be antiques, offering only a *terminus post quem* (e.g., Abel Beth Maacah, Megiddo D).

Although lacking conclusive grounds for assigning a date, we can tentatively exclude several hoards from our dataset on the basis of the available evidence. The contents of the Gezer A and B and Shechem A hoards – only known through photos or drawings – appear to predate the end of the Late Bronze Age; the penannular earrings, open crescent pendants and toggle pins, as well as the scarabs in Gezer B, suggest a MB IIb to LB I date for the hoards.[53] The dates of various other hoards can also be revised on diverse grounds.[54] These revisions lead altogether to an adjusted corpus (Table 3.1).

D hoard (Panitz-Cohen, Mullins and Bonfil 2013, 39), it has been included in the catalogue for the purpose of clarity (see Appendix).

49 Wadi el-Makkuk: Sass 2002a; cf. Kletter 2003, 145; Ein Gedi: Kletter and De Groot 2007; Beth Shean D: Thompson 2009.

50 Eshel 2014. Cf. Eshel et al. 2018; 2019.

51 Campbell 2002, 335; Wright 2002, ill. 40, 42. See Appendix.

52 Toffolo et al. 2014, 228, 233. Cf. Eshel et al. 2018, 210–211, on the textile of the Tell Keisan hoard.

53 See Appendix. Cf. Kletter 2003, 144–145; Thompson 2003, 99–100; Eshel et al. 2018, 200–201.

54 See Appendix.

TABLE 3.1 *Precious metal hoards included in the corpus*

Hoard	Cat. no.	Date	Degree of quantitative analysis (metrology; typology)[a]	Source of data
Abel Beth Maacah[b]	1	LB IIB	Excluded	
Timna	31	End of LBA	Excluded	
Beth Shean D	8	LB III	Metrology; typology	Thompson 2009
Megiddo D	21	LB III–early Iron I	Metrology; typology	First-hand study
Wadi el-Makkuk	32	Iron I	Metrology; typology	Sass 2002a
Ashkelon	4	Iron I	Insufficient object data	
Beth Shean C	7	Iron I	Metrology; typology	First-hand study
Tell Keisan	17	Iron I	Metrology; typology	Eshel 2014
Megiddo A	18	Iron I	Metrology; typology	First-hand study
Megiddo B	19	Iron I	Insufficient object data	First-hand study
Megiddo C	20	Iron I	Excluded	
Tawilan	30	Iron I–early Iron IIA	Excluded	
Shechem B	29	Iron I–IIB	Metrology; limited typology[c]	Balmuth and Thompson 2000, assessment of author
Beth Shean A	5	Early Iron IIA	Insufficient object data	First-hand study
Beth Shean B	6	Early Iron IIA	Metrology; typology	First-hand study
Tel Dor	9	Early Iron IIA	Metrology; typology	Eshel 2014
Akko	2	Iron II	Metrology; typology	Eshel 2014
Ein Ḥofez	11	Late Iron IIA	Metrology; typology	Eshel 2014
Tell Jemmeh	16	(Late?) Iron IIA	Excluded	
Eshtemoa	12	Iron IIB	Insufficient object data	
Arad	3	Iron IIB	Metrology; typology	First-hand study
Eretria (Greece)	33	LG II	Metrology; typology	First-hand study
Tel Miqne/Ekron A	22	Iron IIC	Limited[d]	Gitin and Golani 2001
Tel Miqne/Ekron B	23	Iron IIC	Limited[d]	Gitin and Golani 2001
Tel Miqne/Ekron C	24	Iron IIC	Limited[d]	Gitin and Golani 2001
Tel Miqne/Ekron D	25	Iron IIC	Limited[d]	Gitin and Golani 2001
Tel Miqne/Ekron E	26	Iron IIC	Limited[d]	Gitin and Golani 2001
Tel Miqne/Ekron F	27	Iron IIC	Limited[d]	Gitin and Golani 2001
Ein Gedi	10	Iron IIC	Metrology; typology	First-hand study
Gezer C	15	Iron Age	Insufficient object data	

TABLE 3.1 *(continued)*

Hoard	Cat. no.	Date	Degree of quantitative analysis (metrology; typology)[a]	Source of data
Deselected from the corpus				
Gezer A	13	MB II–LB I	Excluded	
Gezer B	14	MB II	Excluded	
Shechem A	28	MB II–LB I	Excluded	

Source: Based on Thompson 2003 and Kletter 2003), with indication of whether the hoards have been included in the analysis, and, if so, the source of the data used. Catalogue number refers to the Appendix.

[a] For the analyses, see Section 3.3, subsections Metrology and Typology; see Appendix for specific data on the hoards.

[b] Cf. n. 48.

[c] Limited typological data are based on assessment of photographs; hoard was included in Figures 3.28 and 3.30, but not in Figure 3.29 (subdivision of types). See Section 3.3, n. 174 and Appendix.

[d] Individual object weights are not available; hoard not included in detailed metrological analysis. Limited typological data are available; hoard was included in Figures 3.28 and 3.30, but not in Figure 3.29 (subdivision of types). See Section 3.3, nn. 174, 181.

A detailed study of parts of this updated corpus has provided the basis for the analyses presented in the current chapter. However, not all hoards from the updated corpus have been investigated on an equal basis (see Table 3.1). This selection of hoards and the relating data was made on the basis of different criteria, relating to the composition or the availability and suitability of the material for investigation.

As the analysis of the material focuses on the characteristics of the (precious) metal objects, hoards with a deviant composition in this regard have been left out to a large degree. A hoard containing only complete jewellery items (and other objects) might be identified as a hoard in terms of its deposition but can be regarded simultaneously as a collection of jewellery, rather than a metal hoard in the sense of the other hoards. The Megiddo C hoard contains jewellery and other objects such as spindle whorls and zoomorphic weights but no precious metal (cf. Timna),[55] and the Tell Jemmeh and Tawilan hoards consist only of complete gold and silver jewellery and carnelian beads. Although relevant as hoards of valuables no less, detailed comparison with *hacksilber*-scrap hoards would be of little added value due to the obvious material differences.

Alternatively, for several other hoards limited data are available. Some remain unpublished, in other cases selected material has been published, but no or limited quantitative data on the object level are available (Ashkelon; Eshtemoa; Timna, containing no silver); and several other hoards have not, or only partly, been cleaned, thereby restricting their potential for study (in particular Megiddo B).

[55] See also Kletter 2003, 145–146.

Otherwise, part of the remaining hoards have been studied first hand, while others have been processed based on published data (see Table 3.1).[56]

Additionally, because of its similarity to other hoards in this corpus, a single hoard from the Aegean (Eretria) has been included in this dataset. Recent scholarship has drawn attention to these similarities, interpreting the Eretria hoard with reference to the hoards from the southern Levant.[57] Including it here allows us to qualify these comparisons on a more detailed level; how that comparison should reflect on our understanding of money-use in the economy of Early Iron Age Greece is a different matter that will be addressed later.[58]

3.2.2 Methods and Issues: Context

We can approach the context of a hoard on various levels. In some cases, there is evidence for a container, such as a textile bag and/or a pot, testifying to the way the hoards were packed and stored. The direct archaeological context and possible associated finds can provide us with clues as to how and why hoards were deposited and in what sort of physical and social context or space they were kept and used. The wider setting in which its use should be placed (e.g., administrative, cultic or domestic) is also reflected by the location of a hoard within the larger site, most commonly a settlement. Finally, the wider geographic context can potentially provide an insight into the economic systems in which these hoards functioned.

Previous scholarship has dealt with these issues to varying degrees. As noted in Section 3.1.1, evidence for the use of textile bundles has been interpreted as an integral part of the practice surrounding money-use and storage, identifying it with the biblical *ṣrôr kesep̄*, or money-bag.[59] Other contextual information, such as the deposition, location within the site and the geographical distribution of the hoards, has drawn attention, but we should be cautious to draw conclusions.[60] As pointed out in the Section 3.1.2, we need to be aware of the restrictions of our dataset and the fact that our data are also a consequence of the research agenda. Excavations have focused in particular on large settlement-sites (tel-sites) and within those on public areas with administrative and cultic functions. In contrast to this, excavation efforts of Early Iron Age

56 Not all hoards are available in their entirety for study on the object level: often a selection of the material was left untreated for future reference and research (e.g., Arad, Megiddo D) or out of practical considerations (e.g., Dor, Eshtemoa). However, hoards were only included in the analyses when the available data was considered representative. See also Appendix.

57 Kopcke 1992, 12; Kroll 2001a, 77–78; 2003, 317; 2008a, 34; 2013a; Le Rider and Verdan 2002, 141–152; Thompson 2003, 91–92; 2007, 199. Cf. Hoffman 1998, 203.

58 See Section 5.4.

59 Stern 1998, 48; 2001, 22–23; Kletter 2003, 146, 149; Thompson 2003, 78–87.

60 Kletter 2003, 146–148; Thompson 2003; Eshel 2014, ch. 2.

Greece have been mostly directed towards cemeteries and sanctuaries, leading some to argue that this would explain the lack of similar finds.[61] Similarly, a close sequence of destruction strata, characteristic of the Iron Age archaeology in the southern Levant, might very well have affected the preservation of hoards (and possibly the lack thereof in Greece). Hoards from Ein Ḥofez, a small extra-urban settlement, and especially Wadi el-Makkuk, a desert cave, and Timna, an extra-urban sanctuary (and possibly also Eshtemoa and Tawilan, both lacking (settlement) contexts), pose exceptions to the main picture. To what extent these are representative is difficult to assess, and we need to keep in mind that hoards remain chance finds.

3.2.3 Methods and Issues: Metrology

The study of metrology focuses on how something is measured. In subjecting the hoards to metrological study, the basic assumption is that the precious metal was measured by its weight and quantified by means of standard weight systems. Evidence for the use of such weight systems in the Ancient Near East as well as the eastern Mediterranean throughout the Bronze and Iron Ages is abundant,[62] and for our current purpose, it is sufficient to point out that weighing systems were known in the southern Levant and are commonly assumed to have been used to measure out the precious metal in the hoards. When dealing with weights or coinage – objects of a certain denomination within a weight system – basic metrological analysis has been rather straightforward. It has focused on the individual objects in order to examine to what extent these reflect or conform to a (known) weight standard, and if so, what weight standard. The silver hoards, as we will see, demand a different approach in this respect, because their contents are not the result of a standardised production. In systematically documenting the weight information of all individual objects in the hoards, the question should therefore be asked how we can read the data and what exactly we are looking for.

Interestingly, however, with regard to precious metal hoards, there has been no discussion so far of the basic premises underlying the study of metrology. Scholarship has drawn attention to the weight of individual units – objects, bundles and complete hoards – with the sole purpose of associating (or dissociating) these individual weights with standard weight systems.[63] Where weights have been found conforming to whatever known or unknown system of

61 Kroll 2001a, 78; 2008a, 34–35.
62 E.g., Alberti, Ascalone and Peyronel 2006; Rahmstorf 2010; 2016a.
63 Balmuth 1971; 5–7; Bivar 1971, 105–106; 1982, 56–60; Kroll 2001a, 78; Stern 2001, 24; Thompson 2003, 81–87; Kletter and De Groot 2007, 369–374; Painter and Hunter 2013, 232. Cf. Gitin and Golani 2001, 39; Kletter 2003, 146–148; Eshel 2014; Eshel et al. 2018, 211–213.

fractions, this has been taken as further ground for assigning significance, thereby disregarding those weights not reflecting a possible standard as 'random'.[64] The premise underlying this approach is that a 'monetary' use of the metal can only be confirmed when the objects of value individually adhere to a weight standard, as in the case of coinage. These objects would then have to be produced or partitioned (broken or cut up) with the intention to match a standard weight denomination, thereby reflecting a reliance on weight systems. It is unlikely that this approach leads to a fruitful understanding of the hoard material presented here.

Criteria used to suggest such correspondence to a weight standard have been rather loose and undefined,[65] especially when considering the fact that early coins, even in the smallest fractions, display a remarkably high level of precision. If anything, the accurate weights of early coins suggest that high-precision weight systems were already used prior to the minting of coins.[66] Moreover, as the analysis in this chapter will show, there seems to be no empirical basis to suggest that individual objects from our hoards were produced to adhere to a weight standard. Also when focusing the analysis on a particular type of object suited for standardised production, tokens (see Section 3.2.4 for typology), no pertinent clustering of weights can be observed (see Section 3.3.2). Although it cannot be ruled out that finished objects were in some cases made to correspond to a weight standard,[67] the objects in the hoards generally do not fit any. Additionally, while it is possible that in other *hacksilber* corpora, such as Mesopotamian Bronze Age hoards, larger objects were fragmented in order to roughly fall into standard weight ranges,[68] this does not yet indicate a systematic and precise adherence of individual objects within a hoard to a weight standard.

This should not be surprising. Most hoards under discussion here consist predominantly of cut or broken objects, and it is difficult to imagine how these would neatly fit a precise weight in the way coins do. More importantly, since scales and weights were used, there was no absolute need to produce objects in set weights,[69] although fragmenting objects in order to approximate certain weights might have been convenient, particularly in the case of larger objects, as is suggested by some Mesopotamian Bronze Age hoards.[70] In any case,

64 Gitin and Golani 2001, 39; Kletter 2003, 148; Thompson 2003, 87; Eshel et al. 2018, 213. Cf. Wiseman 2018.

65 Cf. Bivar 1971, 105–106.

66 Kim 2001, 18; Kim and Kroll 2008, 64–67.

67 E.g., Powell 1978; Peyronel 2010, 933–934.

68 Cf. Bachhuber 2018, 272; Ialongo, Vacca and Peyronel 2018; Ialongo, Vacca and Vanzetti 2018.

69 Wallace 1987, 388, n. 23.

70 Ialongo, Vacca and Peyronel 2018.

precious metal was measured and quantified with the use of weight systems, and in order to meet a specific weight, one could simply add fragments of metal to the scale. The objects were therefore not cut up *at random*, but rather in order to balance the specific weight in the scale. Moreover, the use of precise weighing equipment was not made redundant by the introduction of coinage. The reliance on weights for measurement arguably continued in order to facilitate the use of coins of different weight standards, as is reflected by several mixed archaic coin hoards.[71]

So, contrary to what has been assumed in previous scholarship, it would be incorrect to qualify the weights of the individual objects as random, in the sense that they have no significance.[72] They rather result from a specific need to add up to a certain weight required in transaction, and a closer study of these weights could help us understand how this was done in practice.

In order to make sense of these weights, and thereby attempt to gain insight into this use of the metal, we should direct our attention to the assemblage of weights as a whole, instead of the individual data.[73] A dynamic system in which the metal is fragmented at will in order to facilitate transactions in certain weights would likely result in a gradual distribution of the objects' weights, with a high prevalence of weights within a certain range implying a high demand for such size objects in conducting transactions.[74] Moreover, this potentially reflects on the level of precision exhibited in the weighing. A closer study of the weight distributions should therefore contribute to our understanding of the hoards, their use and the extent to which they were part of the same practice.

3.2.4 Methods and Issues: Typology

Before laying out a typological framework for the current analysis of the hoards, I should address some issues related to how the hoard material has so far been described. As noted, previous scholarship on the hoards has proposed different typological subdivisions of the objects present in the hoards.[75] This has been mostly aimed at describing the material at hand, rather than serving as a basis for further analysis.[76] In order to more properly understand the

[71] Wallace 1987, 388, 394; Osborne [1996] 2009, 251–255; Kim 2001, 18; Borek 2020. Cf. Goodenough 2011, 131.

[72] Cf. Gitin and Golani 2001, 39; Kletter 2003, 148; Thompson 2003, 87. Cf. Wiseman 2018.

[73] Cf. Schon 2015; Ialongo, Vacca and Peyronel 2018.

[74] Cf. Kim 2001, 12–13, 18.

[75] Yeivin 1990; Gitin and Golani 2001; Thompson 2003; 2009; Eshel 2014; Eshel et al. 2018, 199, 202.

[76] Cf. Gitin and Golani 2001, 36; Shalev, Shechtman and Shilstein 2013, 222–223; Eshel 2014, ch. 3.

composition of the hoards and allow for comparison between them, it is necessary to critically assess the types or categories of objects that have been defined. In laying out a new typological framework, it is important to point out some general difficulties in assigning and identifying types and to reassess some specific types that have been identified.

It seems evident that in order to make a clear and straightforward subdivision of the material, a strict and exclusive use of terms is needed. However, the inherently fragmented state of the hoard material has proven a complication to this. Types have been identified on varying bases, such as the process of production, their supposed function or the way the object was later manipulated (i.e., cut, broken, etc.), resulting in an altogether confusing overlap of qualifications and categories. Ingots, *hacksilber* and jewellery (in complete or fragmented state) are often listed as separate types, while the term *hacksilber* in fact denotes any silver object that has been cut up, implying that the original object could have been an ingot as well as a piece of jewellery.[77] Moreover, if, for example, an ingot – an object serving as a source or storage of processed silver (whether as a form of economic value or as raw material) – would be cut in half, would those halves no longer be ingots themselves? And how are we to consider the difference between complete jewellery and fragmented jewellery? It can be safely assumed that once an earring is cut in two, it would no longer function as an earring; it cannot however be assumed that a complete earring, kept in a hoard, is necessarily and only used and valued as a piece of jewellery. And how does a category of 'silver fragments'[78] relate to other categories of fragmentary objects? To avoid confusion, and in order not to make assumptions regarding the function of individual objects, it would be helpful to separate the 'original type of object' from the extent of its completeness. Moreover, by attempting to identify the original state of the object prior to (and disregarding) its manipulation/fragmentation, we can get an impression of the types of objects that were appropriated for the use and circulation as represented by the hoards. Terms such as *hacksilber* or scrap rather emphasise the general fragmented state of the material and are thus more suitable as a general term for the material in these hoards.

In addition to this, two specific object types mentioned in the literature warrant discussion. The so-called chocolate-bar or pre-portioned ingot is described by Thompson as the most common type in the *hacksilber* hoards (Figure 3.2), stating that these are 'not simply pieces carelessly hacked off any sort of silver object', but that they had rather 'been deliberately portioned in much the same way that chocolate bars are today'.[79] Although the objects

77 Cf. Gitin and Golani 2001, 37; Thompson 2003; Eshel 2014.
78 Cf. Gitin and Golani 2001, 37.
79 Thompson 1999, 48; 2003, 71; Vargyas 2007, 300; Meadows 2008, 770.

3.2 So-called chocolate bar ingots (1.1/87, courtesy of the Israel Antiquities Authority [photo by author]; 1.2/9, 289, courtesy of the Oriental Institute of the University of Chicago [photos by author]; 4/59, courtesy of the Swiss School of Archaeology in Greece [photo by Pascal Simon]; 9.2/100, courtesy of the Penn Museum [photo by author]; 10.1/31, courtesy of the Israel Antiquities Authority [photo by author])

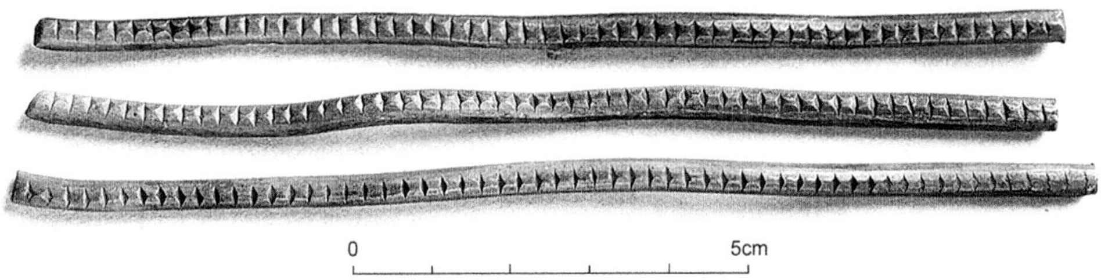

3.3 Three electrum rods from Troy (nos. 128–130, courtesy of Pushkin State Museum of Fine Arts, Moscow)

described by Thompson have indeed been cut, there is little reason to assume that they were (evenly) portioned in advance, let alone that they were 'cast in a preportioned form'.[80] The parallel referred to by Thompson, a series of sixteen electrum rods from EBA Troy with indentations (Figure 3.3),[81] is hardly comparable to the cut pieces in the hoards. They were presumably from stratum IIg and date around a millennium or more before our hoards. Moreover, while it has been suggested that the notched portions were standardised in weight,[82] though likely a result of the fact that they were regularly spaced, they are generally regarded as having been used primarily for the production of jewellery.[83] In contrast, most of the cut pieces from our hoards are rather irregular in shape; relatively few pieces actually have incomplete cuts across the surface (cf. Figure 3.2, object 5 and also Figure 3.11, object 1), and even fewer have more than one, but none appear regularly spaced (like the Troy rods).[84] If they had indeed been produced in a pre-portioned form, we

[80] Meadows 2008, 770.
[81] Schliemann 1881, 553; Antonova, Tolstikow and Treister 1996, nos. 128–132.
[82] Bobokhyan 2006, 87–90; Rahmstorf 2016a, 27; Bachhuber 2018, 272.
[83] Treister 1996a, 215, 225–229.
[84] Of over two thousand objects from 12 hoards, of which I have systematically recorded the manipulations, only 114 objects have (signs of) incomplete cuts; of these, only 21 have more than one cut.

would expect more pieces preserved in attachment to one another. However, none of this material brings to mind a 'chocolate bar', or in any case the idea that the metal would be pre-portioned in order to be broken off at will.[85]

If these incomplete cuts were not necessarily the result of the supposed portioning of a larger ingot, what could they have been? Although it is clear that objects were often partitioned (either broken or re-cut) – if only for practical reasons – along incomplete cuts (cf. also Figures 3.14 and 3.26), this might not have been the only reason they were made. Interestingly, these cuts do not disappear with the introduction of coinage but are rather well known from early coins, in particular those found outside or on the margins of the Greek world, where they were not necessarily accepted at face value.[86] Referred to as chisel cuts, it is generally understood that these were made in order to test the purity of the metal, whereby a deep impression into the metal would expose the core in much the same way as the incuse punch marks on the reverse of early coins.[87] A silver ingot with a copper core, discovered by Thompson in the Beth Shean D hoard, provides a tangible pretext for this practice.[88] In general, the colour of the core of silver (or gold) objects formed a way to check their purity, as is also implied by the passage from the *Heimskringla* discussed in Chapter 2 ('silver pennies . . . white in the fracture'), Herodotus' mention of the 'gilded lead coins' given by Polykrates to the Spartans[89] and the so-called Law of Nikophon of 375/4 BCE from Athens. This law was preserved on an inscription, found built into a wall of the Great Drain on the Athenian Agora. Lines 8–11 of the inscription read: 'If anyone brings forward [foreign silver currency] which has the same device as the Attic, [if it is good,] let the Tester give it back to the one who brought it forward; but if it is [bronze at the core,] or lead at the core, or debased, let him cut it across.'[90]

Additionally, the composition of the metal not only affects its colour but also its hardness. To judge from Pliny's suggestion that past a certain silver ratio electrum would offer no 'resistance on the anvil',[91] it seems that there was some kind of ancient understanding of this. Although this could hardly have been a reliable method and is, moreover, not mentioned in the existing

85 Cf. Kletter 2004, 207; Eshel 2014, ch. 3, but see Kletter and De Groot 2007, 369.

86 E.g., Kraay and Moorey 1968; 1981; Reade 1986.

87 Cf. Gitler and Tal 2019.

88 Thompson 2003, 74; 2009, 605–606. Cf. Pulak 2008, 357; Gestoso-Singer 2013, 250. The same interpretation has been suggested for three ingots from the Beth Shean A hoard (Vargyas 2007), but these are in fact folded packages of gold foil (see Appendix).

89 Hdt. 3.56.2

90 *SEG* 26.72; Stroud 1974; Rhodes and Osborne 2003, 113–115; Engen 2005; Psoma 2011. Cf. Kroll 2000, 89, n. 1.

91 Pliny *HN* 33.27.

3.4 An example of a 'caked' ingot from the Ein Gedi hoard (7/25, courtesy of the Israel Museum, Jerusalem [photo by author])

literature on ancient assaying,[92] it cannot altogether be ruled out that this formed an incentive for people to test the hardness of the metal by means of (incomplete) cuts.

The other object type singled out for further discussion is the so-called cake ingot. Although known before as a literal translation of the German *Silberkuchen* or *Gußkuchen*,[93] Thompson seems to re-coin the term as a type of ingot produced 'by melting together (by baking) numerous pieces of chocolate bar ingots' or *hacksilber*.[94] As the silver would not reach a completely liquid state, the objects would be 'caked' onto each other, with the outline of individual objects partially remaining visible. Thompson alleges that most objects in the Ein Gedi hoard are of this type,[95] but, after detailed restudy of the hoard, I have not been able to confirm this claim. Although there are examples of such 'caked' ingots, these are in fact very rare (notably Figure 3.4). Objects might appear scrappy and not solid due to the presence of cavities of varying sizes, visible in the cut or break. These cavities, though, are likely examples of gas porosity, resulting from the higher solubility of gases in liquid metal (molten silver can absorb over twenty times its volume in oxygen), whereby gas is expelled during the cooling and trapped in the solidifying metal. Larger cavities or cracks could also be the result of solidification shrinkage, caused by the uneven shrinking of the metal during cooling (Figure 3.5). However, as implied, these are typical casting defects, and cannot be related to the supposed 'caking'.

Thompson, however, relates this 'caking' to the Akkadian *aklu/akalu*, a term generally used to describe baked (flour) goods, in particular, a loaf of bread. Based on two documents referring to a certain quantity of silver 'of the excellent alloy of Ištar of Arbela' in the form of an *aklu*, Lipiński identified

92 E.g., Oddy 1983; Craddock 2000b.
93 Bivar 1971, 98, 100–101.
94 Thompson 1999, 50; 2007 48, 156–157.
95 Thompson 1999, 50; 2003, 71, 98; 2007, 48.

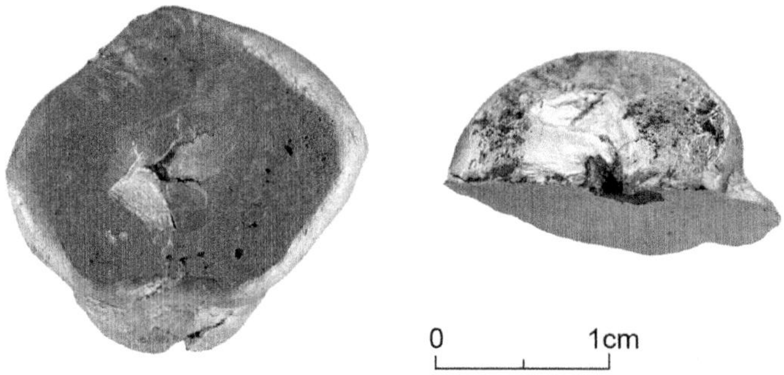

3.5 Examples of solidification shrinkage from the Eretria hoard (4/2–3, courtesy of the Swiss School of Archaeology in Greece [photo by Pascal Simon])

this term with the 'cake ingots' from Zincirli (Figure 4.6);[96] Thompson then draws on this in connecting the term to the supposed 'baked' cake ingots.[97] This reading has little basis, though, and rather than referring to the process of production of the silver ingots, the term is more likely to refer to their shape.[98] As already hinted at by Lipiński, it can in that regard be compared to the Hebrew *kikar*, which also appears in relation to bread and silver,[99] and of course to the English 'bun ingot', both designating the rounded shape of the object. Similarly, the Greek φθοῖς – cake – is used in the Athenian treasury inscription of 345/4 BCE to denote the unminted silver ingots stored in the Parthenon.[100]

Many of the round silver ingots, identified as *Gußkuchen* (cast-cakes), and known, for example, from Tall Munbaqa/Ekalte,[101] Zincirli,[102] Babylon[103] and possibly Ugarit[104] and Egypt[105] appear to have been cast in the bottom of a ceramic pot or on a rough surface, sometimes with small stones imprinted in or still adhering to the bottom surface (Figure 3.6); in some cases they appear to have also been hammered after the casting (Figure 3.7). Kletter and De Groot suggested that most of the Ein Gedi ingots were cast 'onto a rough surface,

96 Lipiński 1979, 574–576; Powell 1996, 236–237. One is a Neo-Assyrian contract from Nineveh; the other a contract from Tell Halaf.

97 Thompson 1999, 49–50; 2007, 157–158.

98 Singer 2006, 253, n. 44.

99 Lipiński 1979, 574. In relation to bread (*kikar leḥem*; Jer 37:21; Prov 6:26) it is translated as 'loaf', while in relation to silver (*kikar kesep*) it is commonly translated as talent, based on the use of the Greek τάλαντον in the LXX translation. Additionally, the term occurs as a geographical designation, in the meaning of a plain or valley (kikar hayarden; e.g., 1 Kgs 7:46), also relating to the shape of the landscape.

100 *IG* II^2, 1443 lines 12–88; Harris 1995, 123–127; Kroll 2001b, 9, n. 11.

101 Czichon and Werner 1998, 179, 210, no. 2368.

102 Von Luschan and Andrae 1943, 119–121, pl. 58t–v; Balmuth 1971, 5–7, pl. 2–3. Cf. Thompson 1999, 50. See also Section 4.3, Figure 4.6.

103 Reade 1986, 82. Cf. Thompson 1999, 50.

104 Schaeffer 1937, 153, fig. 18.

105 Kroll 2001b, 2, 7–10, pl. 1.

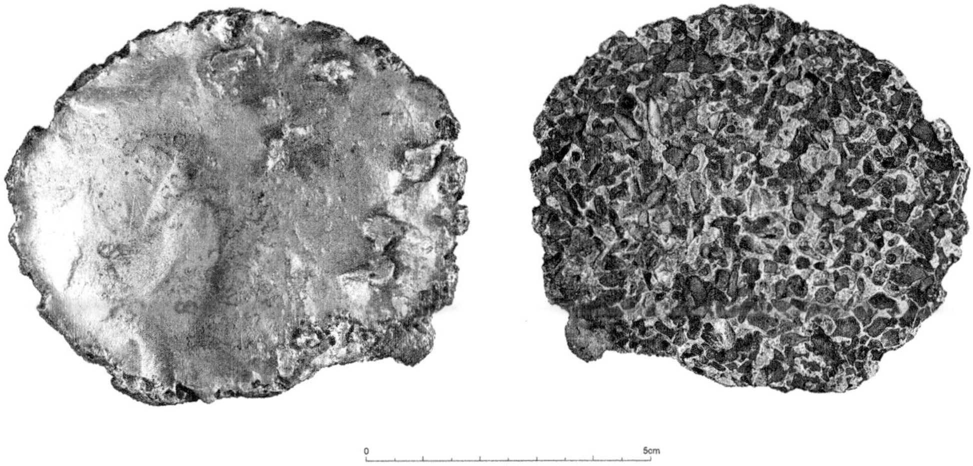

3.6 Cast ingot from Babylon (BM 1882,1220.38) (© The Trustees of the British Museum)

3.7 An example of a hammered ingot from the Beth Shean B hoard (9.1/1, courtesy of the Israel Antiquities Authority [photo by author])

perhaps even a layer of sand'.[106] There is, however, also another possible interpretation.

Many of the Ein Gedi ingots are complete or large cut fragments of irregular rounded flat ingots.[107] Generally, the convex underside has a wrinkled or mottled/grainy appearance, while the concave upper surface can be very irregular and rough, with protuberances and bubbles in the surface (Figure 3.8). In some cases, the ingots thicken towards the edges, which are more or less rounded in section, and projected diameters range between ca. 2.5 and ca. 10 cm. Moreover, the relative lack of wear on the ingots is notable. Although there are visible differences between the different objects (and it

[106] Kletter and De Groot 2007, 369.
[107] E.g., 7/1–23. See Appendix.

3.8 Examples of ingots from the Ein Gedi hoard (7/1, 19, 22, courtesy of the Israel Museum, Jerusalem [photo by author])

cannot be ruled out that they were produced in different ways), their general appearance allows us to suggest that they are possibly the primary product of cupellation.[108]

Cupellation is the process by which silver is extracted from argentiferous lead and was arguably practised from the early phases of silver production in the fourth millennium BCE.[109] During the process, the silver is purified from the lead, which oxidises into litharge (PbO) under a continuous flow of oxygen, leaving a 'button' of silver floating on top of the litharge 'like oil on water', as described by Pliny.[110] Direct archaeological evidence of this process is mostly known in the form of litharge-impregnated hearth lining and solid litharge cakes. Large preserved fragments of the latter, such as those from the refinery area at Sardis (Figure 3.9), show a large central impression from which the silver was removed after the process.[111] These impressions appear consistent

[108] This possibility was first suggested to me by Samuel Verdan, whom I thank for his input.

[109] Nriagu 1985, 668; Pernicka, Rehren and Schmitt-Strecker 1998, 123–124.

[110] *NH* 33.34.

[111] E.g., Rehren and Klappauf 1995, 22–26; Pernicka, Rehren and Schmitt-Strecker 1998, 124–128; Craddock 2000a, 208–209; Ramage 2000, 81–83, 90, fig. 4.35–36. This has also been confirmed by means of experiment, see Söderberg 2004, 117–121.

3.9 Lead litharge from a cupel found at Sardis (© Archaeological Exploration of Sardis/ President and Fellows of Harvard College)

with the morphological characteristics of the Ein Gedi ingots (shape, the wrinkled bottom surface and approximate size range); the irregular and bubbly upper surface could be explained as the result of oxygen violently breaking through the solidifying surface, a phenomenon known as 'spitting', or possibly by impurities or waste (e.g., stones and charcoal) removed after cooling. It should be noted that spitting can occur whenever silver is molten, so it does not directly indicate cupellation. However, in absence of evidence that the silver was cast in a mould, it is perhaps more likely that this is related to cupellation.

Although this interpretation of the Ein Gedi ingots is attractive, even more so because I am not aware of any other clear example of a primary silver ingot from cupellation described in the literature,[112] it cannot be proven and remains therefore a mere suggestion. If, however, this interpretation is correct, it could imply that this material (and possibly also very similar examples from the Tel

[112] A silver ingot from the archaic Asyut hoard is also a possible product of cupellation; it was noted as affected by 'spitting' (Price and Waggoner 1975; Gale, Gentner and Wagner 1980, 18–21). I thank prof. Ernst Pernicka for bringing this object to my attention and for his additional comments. Cf. also Wertime 1973, 883.

Miqne/Ekron C hoard) concerns not necessarily recycled silver but possibly *newly mined silver* being refined and imported to the region.

Coming back to the issue of the typological framework to be employed here, it can be concluded that if this typology should have any analytical value, more than being just descriptive, there should be a strict use of terms without commonsensical assumptions as to what these might imply. The assemblages in the hoards are the result of a dynamic use of different types of objects, made initially for different purposes and often manipulated in different instances over longer periods of time. As described, the way to appreciate this is by differentiating between the 'original object' and its subsequent manipulation. This focus on what object an individual item had once been part of allows us to map what types of objects entered the sphere of the hoard material.

To this end, all objects have been entered into a database where a basic division is made between ingots and ornamental objects,[113] both with subdivisions. The term ingot is used here as a wider label for all artefacts that are regarded primarily as a source of value and raw material, without functional or ornamental properties.[114] A subdivision is made between rough ingots (Figure 3.10), globules (unworked prills, Figure 3.11), tokens (flattened/hammered discs, Figure 3.12), rods (coiled/bent bars, Figure 3.13), and finished ingots (Figure 3.14). In contrast to ingots, the label 'ornamental object' is used for objects that are primarily understood either for their functional or ornamental properties or as semi-finished product used in the production of functional or ornamental objects. This includes rings (ear- or finger rings), bracelets, sheet metal, wires, refuse/parts from jewellery production and miscellaneous objects such as beads.[115] Additionally, the extent to which an object is complete, and the visible manipulations it underwent, have been recorded separately.

3.3 ANALYSIS

3.3.1 Context

As noted in Section 3.2.2, different aspects of the hoards' context have been the focus of previous scholarship. Of these, the use of textile and/or pottery as a primary container, and the historical evidence for the use of bundles, has been explored in detail;[116] beyond what has been commented upon already in

113 Cf. Kershaw 2017, 177–178.
114 Kruse 1988, 288.
115 These types are not illustrated separately but can be clearly identified in Figure 2.1 and Figures 4.5, 5.4, A.4, A.7 and A.9.
116 Kletter 2003, 146, 149; Thompson 2003, 78–87; Silver 2006. Cf. Eshel 2014, ch. 2; Eshel et al. 2018, 211–212.

3.10 Rough ingots (1.2/496, courtesy of the Oriental Institute of the University of Chicago [photo by author]; 4/31, courtesy of the Swiss School of Archaeology in Greece [photo by Pascal Simon]; 6/31, courtesy of the Megiddo Expedition, Tel Aviv University [photo by author]; 9.1/2, courtesy of the Israel Antiquities Authority [photo by author])

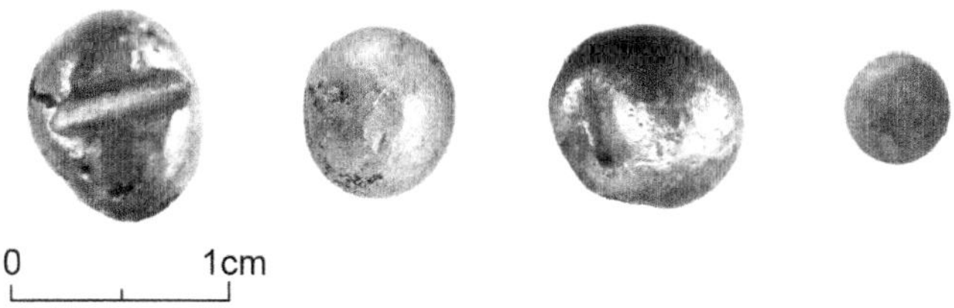

3.11 Globule ingots (1.1/78, courtesy of the Israel Antiquities Authority [photo by author]; 4/254, courtesy of the Swiss School of Archaeology in Greece [photo by Pascal Simon]; 6/15, courtesy of the Megiddo Expedition, Tel Aviv University [photo by author]; 9.2/66, courtesy of the Penn Museum [photos by author])

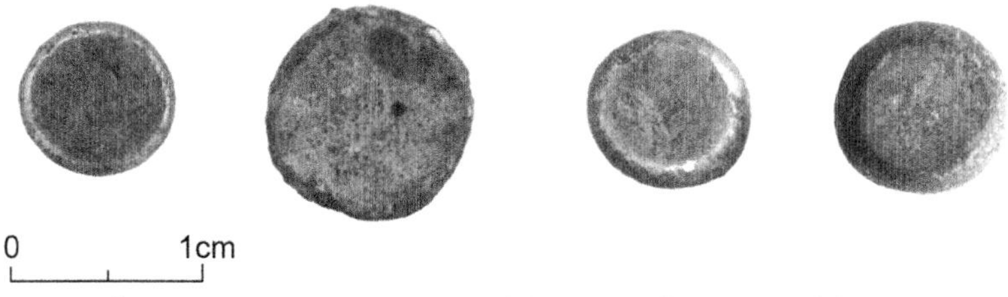

3.12 Token ingots (1.2/274, courtesy of the Oriental Institute of the University of Chicago [photo by author]; 9.2/70–71, courtesy of the Penn Museum [photos by author]; 10.1/8, courtesy of the Israel Antiquities Authority [photo by author])

3.13 Rod ingots (1.2/300–301, courtesy of the Oriental Institute of the University of Chicago [photos by author]; 4/361, courtesy of the Swiss School of Archaeology in Greece [photo by Pascal Simon]; 6/25–27, courtesy of the Megiddo Expedition, Tel Aviv University [photos by author])

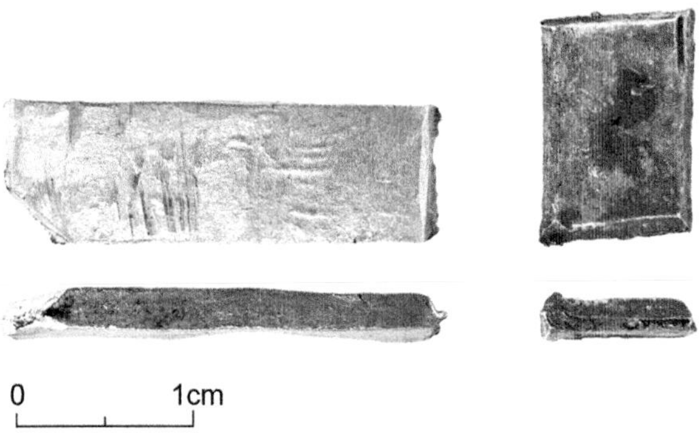

3.14 Finished ingots (4/359, courtesy of the Swiss School of Archaeology in Greece [photo by Pascal Simon]; 1.2/522, courtesy of the Oriental Institute of the University of Chicago [photo by author])

this chapter, there is no need here to add to that. With regard to other contextual elements, such as the hoards' location within sites and their geographical and chronological distribution, it has already been noted that caution is required due to the restrictions of the dataset.

In particular, the chance aspect of the hoard finds and the small number of hoards in general form a serious complication to any effort to draw straightforward conclusions concerning their development through space and time.[117] For example, neither the presence of six hoards in late seventh-century Tel Miqne/Ekron, nor the sheer size of the Eshtemoa hoard, provides a secure basis to identify an increase of actual hoard silver, compared to the Iron I period. However, two tentative observations regarding the diachronic geographic distribution of the hoards can be made (see Map 3.1).

[117] Kletter 2003, 147–148.

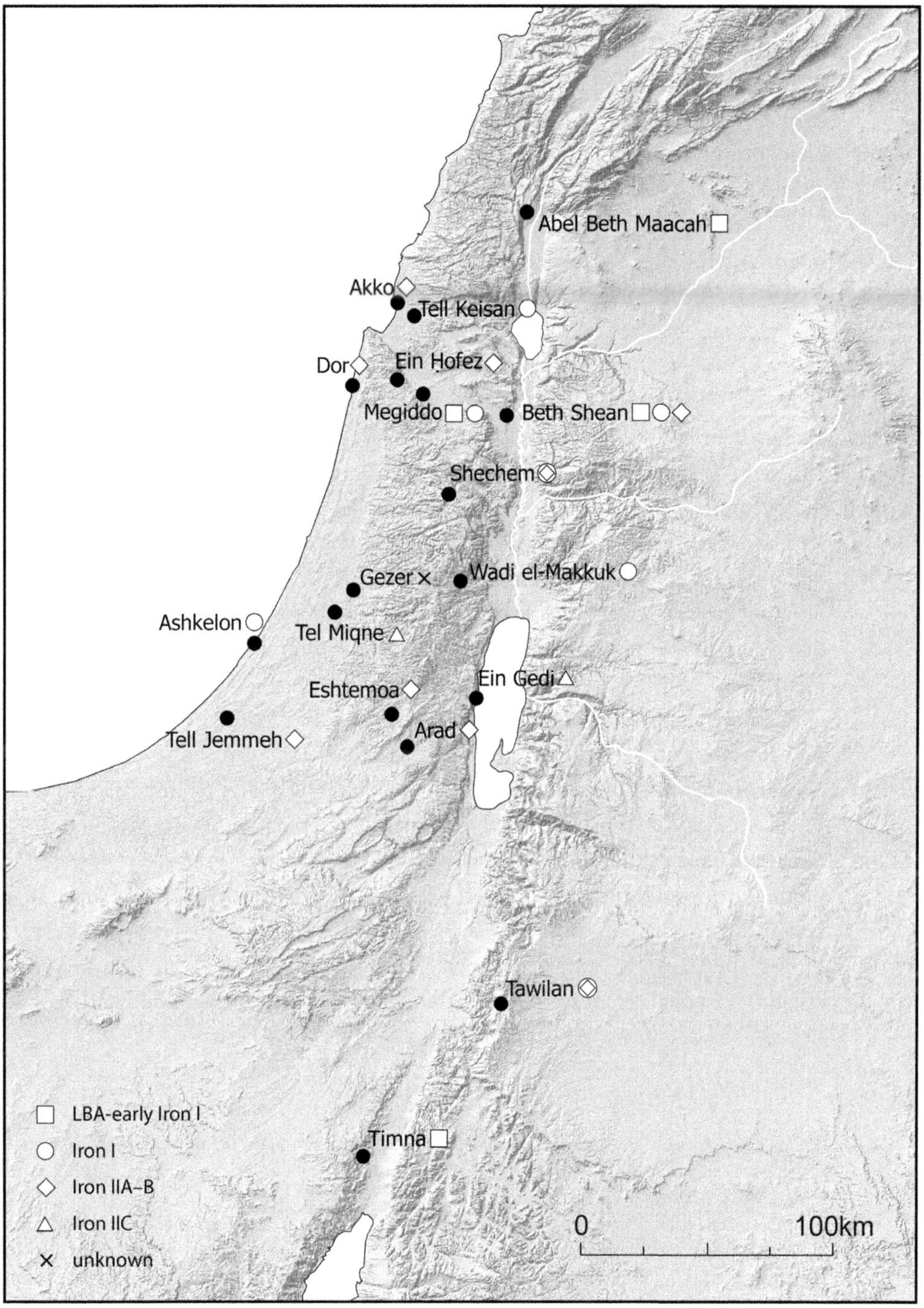

MAP 3.1 Precious metal hoards from the Iron Age southern Levant

Firstly, hoards dating to the end of the Late Bronze Age or the transition to the Iron Age (Beth Shean D, Megiddo D and Abel Beth Maacah), as well as hoards from the Iron I proper (Beth Shean C, Megiddo A–C, Tell Keisan, Ashkelon and possibly Shechem B), are from sites that are associated with the Late Bronze political geography.[118] These concern important settlement sites, characterised by a relative continuity of traditions between the end of the LBA and Iron I, of which Ashkelon, Beth Shean and Megiddo had been important Egyptian strongholds down to the end of Egyptian presence in the region. In the Iron I, these lowland sites continue or pick up after a possible occupational gap following the destruction of the LBA city,[119] as centres of (a revival of) Canaanite material culture, a phenomenon described as 'New Canaan'.[120] This association with LBA and New Canaan settlement sites is further emphasised by the fact that, with the possible exception of the Shechem B hoard, no single hoard datable to the end of the LBA or Iron I was found in the central highlands, despite a sharp increase in the number of settlements – especially newly established settlements – and built-up area documented in this region for the Iron I.[121] Whether this is the result of different preservation dynamics and/or research focus or indicates an actual difference in the use of hoard-silver between different regions and/or settlement types, will be addressed in Section 4.1.3.

Secondly, although equally few, hoards datable from the Iron IIB period onwards are restricted to the southern highlands and surrounding areas. These concern Arad and presumably Eshtemoa from the Iron IIB and Tel Miqne/Ekron A–F and Ein Gedi from the Iron IIC.[122] This pattern appears consistent with the collapse of the northern kingdom of Israel and the decrease of population following the conquest of Samaria by Sargon II in 720 (Iron IIB) and the growth and prosperity noted in the south, in Judah and Philistia, during the Iron IIB and C periods.[123] Population increase in these regions could have (partially) resulted from refugee immigration from the north[124] but

118 Cf. Kletter 2003, 148.

119 Cf. Mazar 2010, 260.

120 Finkelstein 2003. Research at Abel Beth Maacah has only taken off in recent years, and our knowledge of its LBA–IA history remains limited for now (Panitz-Cohen, Mullins and Bonfil 2013; 2015). Cf. n. 48.

121 Finkelstein 1988; Zertal 2007, 81–85; Zertal and Mirkam 2016, 38–41. Two hoards from the central highlands have been found at Shechem, one of which appears to be earlier of date (MB IIb–LB I). While the other one cannot be dated securely, a date in the Iron I–IIB and specifically the Iron I is most likely (see Appendix). However, Shechem also fits the LBA political geography. Also worth noting is the hoard discovered in a northern Judean desert cave at Wadi el-Makkuk, dating to the Iron I.

122 See Appendix.

123 Broshi and Finkelstein 1992, 50–53; Ofer 1994; Zertal 2007, 85–90; Finkelstein 2013, 154–155; Zertal and Mirkam 2016, 41–42.

124 Broshi 1974; Finkelstein 2008; 2015, with references; *pace* Na'aman 2007; 2014.

was likely buttressed by natural growth occurring simultaneously in other regions of the Mediterranean.[125]

With regard to the location of the hoards within a site, little can be said with certainty. Eshel has categorised the known contexts as either of a domestic or public nature, suggesting that the larger hoards are usually found in public areas, while the smaller hoards are more common in domestic spaces.[126] While this does not appear counter-intuitive, close scrutiny of the at times inadequate context information reveals that such identifications are not always straightforward. The Megiddo D hoard, for example, was identified as domestic, although found in a paved courtyard adjacent to the stratum VII A palace.[127] The Arad hoard, qualified as public,[128] was found in a Judahite border fortress, but this does not necessarily negate the possibility that its direct context was domestic, as is assumed in the case of the Beth Shean D hoard, found in the Egyptian garrison dwelling quarter.[129] It appears in general that the data are limited and often ambiguous, complicating any attempt to better understand where specifically and by whom these hoards were kept and used.

Alternatively, an assessment of the type of deposition appears more straightforward, although context information is lacking in several cases. With the notable exception of the hoards from the end of the LBA (Beth Shean D, Megiddo D, Abel Beth Maacah), which were located on the floor, most of the hoards have been discovered placed or buried under floor levels (Akko, Arad, Beth Shean A–B, Dor, Ein Gedi, Ein Ḥofez, Megiddo A, C, Tel Miqne A, C) and into or under walls (Beth Shean C, Tel Miqne E, Eretria, Tell Keisan).[130] Many were supposedly deposited in shallow pits, although these have not always been detected in excavation. For example, the Arad hoard was initially incorrectly assigned to stratum XI due to the fact that it 'was buried some 15 cm below the stratum X floor in a depression that apparently went unnoticed'.[131] In other cases, doubt has been expressed as to whether the hoard belongs to an earlier floor level or was deposited under a later floor (Akko, Ein Ḥofez), although the excavators have noted a

125 Cf. Morris 2007, 218–219, 236.

126 Eshel 2014, ch.2; Eshel et al. 2018, 200–201, 220. Cf. Golani 2013, 12.

127 Arie et al. 2019, 90.

128 Cf. Eshel et al. 2018, 201.

129 Thompson 2009.

130 Within the Iron Age proper exceptions to this are Tel Miqne B (on the floor) and Tel Miqne F (on a floor, covered by a bowl, possibly after having fallen down). While not buried under the floor, Tel Miqne D (perforated olive press weight) was clearly hidden as well. The Timna hoard (end of LBA or transition to Iron I) might have been a foundation or votive deposit in the temple. With regard to Beth Shean D, doubt has been expressed as to whether it was found on the floor or in an accumulation of striated floor layers, although 'there is no clear evidence that these groups of silver had been either hidden with the intent of later recovery, or buried as a deposit' (Thompson 2009, 597, 602, 609).

131 Singer-Avitz 2002, 161.

preference for the latter interpretation.[132] Additionally, an interpretation as foundation deposit has been raised with regard to some of the hoards (Beth Shean A–C, Dor, Tel Miqne E), and although the possibility cannot be rejected out of hand, there is no straightforward reason to suggest that these depositions are different from the other sub-surface depositions. Moreover, discussing the Beth Shean A and B hoard, this interpretation has been rejected with reference to the vast corpus of Ancient Near Eastern evidence.[133] Like most other hoards from the Iron I onwards, these hoards appear to have been discreetly deposited under the floor and out of sight, conforming to what appears to be a rather consistent pattern.[134]

The question is, however, what this typical deposition signifies. The preservation of these hoards in the archaeological record has generally been regarded as unintended and the result of some catastrophe, such as a violent destruction or earthquake.[135] Such references to impending danger have been made in order to provide a pretext (and explanation) for why these hoards would have been intentionally hidden in the first place: 'In a time of impending crises, if they could not be taken, such collections of wealth must have been hidden or secured with the intent of future retrieval'.[136] The same reasoning has also been invoked with regard to the deposition of some hoards in Ugarit, claiming that 'some city dwellers probably attempted to hide their valuables before fleeing',[137] 'in the vain hope of recovering them when the storm was over'.[138]

However, the urge to explain the type of deposition in the context of this projected *histoire événementielle* only keeps us from understanding how hoarded valuables were kept and dealt with under regular circumstances. In fact, whether a hoard was actively used and therefore easily accessible or temporarily stored in a secure location, there is good reason to suggest that hiding the hoard from sight, often by means of a discreet burial under the floor (or wall), was common practice under normal circumstances, rather than a last-minute effort in the face of disaster.[139] The safe storage of hoarded valuables must have been important and necessary in everyday life, also considering the fact that extended periods of stability and security must have been rather rare, and theft was never uncommon.

[132] Alexandre 2013, 20; Eshel 2014, ch.2; Eshel et al. 2018, 204–207.
[133] Vargyas 2007, 296–298; *pace* Golani 2013, 12. See Appendix.
[134] Bjorkman 1994, 7; Kletter 2003, 146; Peyronel 2010; 2014, 369. With regard to Mesopotamian hoards from ca. 3300–2000 BCE, Bjorkman notes that 'many, though by no means all, hoards were contained in sealed jars and buried under floors'.
[135] Kletter 2003, 144, 147.
[136] Golani and Sass 1998, 61. See also Matthews 1994, 299; Alexandre 2013, 20; Golani 2013, 12.
[137] Yon 1992, 117.
[138] Singer 1999, 731. See also Schaeffer 1963, 206.
[139] Kemp 2006, 315–317; Peyronel 2010, spec. 931; Bachhuber 2018, 274–276; Eshel et al. 2018, 215, 220.

There are, moreover, literary sources that refer to the hoarding of valuables under the ground. In the book of Joshua it is related how a man took for himself part of a booty intended for dedication, among which was two hundred shekel of silver, 'and buried/concealed it under the ground in [his] tent, with the silver at the bottom'.[140] A Late Bronze Age Egyptian letter gives instructions as to the burial place where a jar containing a hoard of gold and silver items was concealed.[141] And in a Mesopotamian poem, 'The debate between Silver and Copper', dating to the Middle Bronze Age, copper derides silver: 'Silver, you are forgotten in the soil inside the house .... You snake, get back in the darkest part of the house and lie down in your grave!'[142]

Euripides' lost tragedy *Palamedes* recounted a fifth century rendition of Odysseus' and Diomedes' conspiracy to bring down the title figure. Standing accused of treason on account of a forged letter from Priam promising a reward in gold, the gold was found buried under his tent – planted there on purpose – and Palamedes was stoned to death.[143] Xenophon also alludes to the burial of money in *Ways and Means*: 'No one ever yet possessed so much silver as to want no more; if a man finds himself with a huge amount of it, he takes as much pleasure in burying the surplus as in using it.'[144] Similarly, Pindar refers, albeit with disapproval, to keeping hidden wealth or treasure in the house (πλοῦτον κρυφαῖον).[145] Interestingly, in Classical Greece, the god of wealth, Ploutos, was imagined to live underground and complexly related to Hades, that is, as the Latin Pluto. Demetrius of Phaleron notes that the silver miners in Attica 'were digging so eagerly, as if they were expecting to drag up Ploutos himself from under the earth'.[146] Aristophanes also locates Ploutos in the underworld, joking that 'in weighing, the full pan goes down, while the empty one goes up to Zeus'.[147]

This aspect of buried and hidden wealth can be related to the conception of money or hoarded wealth as representing a hidden potential to act, explored

140 Josh. 7:21–2. Cf. 2 K 7:8.

141 Wente 1990, 146, no. 196.

142 Segment D, 38–46, translation from The Electronic Text Corpus of Sumerial Literature; http://etcsl.orinst.ox.ac.uk/section5/tr536.htm. Quoted in Peyronel 2014, 355. See also Stork 2015, 129; Bachhuber 2018, 275–276.

143 Hyg. *Fab.* 105; Schol. Eur. *Or.* 432. See Collard, Cropp and Gilbert 2004, 92–103; Collard and Cropp 2008, 46–59. Note that the account in the Scholia on Euripides, *Orestes* 432.6, 8, has the 'money ... [being] placed under Palamedes' bed'.

144 4.7 (transl. Loeb)

145 Pind. *Isthm.* 1.67; *Nem.* 1.31.

146 *FGrH* 228 F 35; Ath. *Deipnosophistaí* VI, 233e (transl. Loeb); Posidon. fr. F 239, 240a Kidd.

147 Ar. fr. 504. Moreover, Ploutos is represented as being blind (Ar. *Pl.*; cf. Hipponax fr. 36) Although in the context of Aristophanes' comedy, his blindness is explained as not being able to see who he endows with wealth, wealth's blindness could also be seen as an inversion of the intrinsic hiddenness of wealth.

by Graeber and discussed briefly in Chapter 2.[148] The buried hoard, as precious metal withdrawn from use and circulation and safeguarded for the future, is an expression of this conception of money. Interestingly, this understanding was foreshadowed by Marx, who described how money, in its abstract sense, is intricately related to the act of hoarding, referring *inter alia* to merchants in Delhi who bury their money under the ground.[149] The same practice is also hinted at by Peter Martyr d'Anghiera, the early historian of the New World, who praises the use of cocoa as a sort of money in Mexico, noting that 'it protects its innocent possessors from the infernal disease of avarice, since it cannot be long hoarded, nor hidden underground!'[150] A similar notion can also be recognised in the idea of *chullpa*, a word that relates to money as an underground buried treasure and a source of unpredictable wealth in the silver mining region of Potosí, Bolivia.[151]

It appears from this discussion that the deposition of precious metal hoards under the floor need not be seen only as a short-term reaction to impending danger, crisis or upheaval. There are good reasons to suppose that this particular type of deposition, dominant among Iron Age precious metal hoards, would have been prevalent under regular circumstances just the same. Even more so, the type of deposition is consistent with the content of the hoard and its significance. In hiding the hoarded valuables from sight, these depositions echo a conception of the hoards and their contents as a means to future action and should be seen as reflecting a characteristic of money itself.

3.3.2 Metrology

The weight of individual hoards, and their comparison to other hoards in the corpus, is a significant aspect of their materiality and their social, economic, political and historical meaning. For example, the Eshtemoa hoard with its ca. 26 kg (Figure 3.15) should be understood in a different context than most other hoards, generally weighing up to 500 grams. Its sheer size is surely indicative of an economic system able to accumulate and concentrate such wealth; however, as pointed out, it is very difficult to evaluate the extent to which this chance find is representative of a certain development. The same applies to the number of hoards from a specific period or site: despite attempts to overemphasise the historical importance of the six hoards from Tel Miqne,[152] previous discussions of the data have pointed out that no

148 Section 2.3; Graeber 1996; 2001, 91–115.
149 Marx 1970, 125–137, 149; 1976, 227–232; Graeber 2001, 100–101.
150 Quoted in Marx 1970, 154.
151 Harris 1989, 259–260.
152 Gitin and Golani 2001.

3.15 Eshtemoa hoard (Adapted from © User: Chamberi / Wikimedia Commons / CC-BY-SA-3.0)

straightforward historical pattern or development can be deduced from the number of hoards or their weight through time.[153]

As mentioned in Section 3.1.1, both Kletter and Thompson have been careful to document the evidence for the bundling of silver in textile bags and the presence of stamped seals.[154] The hypothesis, promoted by Thompson, that these bundles were of standard weight (and quality) guaranteed by a stamped bulla,[155] is, however, unwarranted. It was mostly based on the likeliness of the weight of one of the Dor bundles (490.5 g; the only bundle weighed at the time) to a 60-unit Babylonian mina, as well as the approximate coincidence of the weight of two bundles from Tell Keisan (24.5 g and 25 g, with the other two bundles weighing 100 g and 32 g). The weight of the other

153 Kletter 2003, 147–148; Eshel 2014, ch. 2.
154 Kletter 2003, 149; Thompson 2003, 84.
155 Thompson 2003, 78–87; Silver 2006; Richter 2017, 32–33. Cf. Noeske 1993, 204–205; *pace* Kletter 2003, 146.

Dor bundles was extrapolated based on a total weight of ca. 8.5 kg and the assumption of a total of seventeen bundles.[156] Most of the bundles were never separated, though, and one wonders how the number of seventeen bundles was reached in the first place. Moreover, an additional bundle, separated in recent years, was found to weigh ca. 420 g, refuting the idea that the Dor bundles were of a standard weight.[157] Furthermore, no support for this idea has been found in other hoards. The Beth Shean D hoard contained three supposed bundles of diverse weight (ca. 56, ca. 35 and ca. 66 g),[158] and also new data from the Megiddo A and B hoards show no sign of standardisation.[159] One of the Megiddo A bundles has a weight of ca. 88 g, while the two other bundles (regrettably mixed prior to weighing) have a combined weight of ca. 337 g, negating the likeliness of any direct correspondence. The single bundle from the contemporary Megiddo B hoard weighs ca. 38 g. Although evidence for bundles certainly has significance for our understanding of the use of silver, as it functionally allowed people to carry it around, no additional significance can currently be deduced from the weight of the bundles.

A focus on the weight of the individual objects and their distribution within the assemblages is more likely to offer a better view of the material characteristics, as laid out above. The purpose here is to evaluate the coherence of the corpus by comparing between the hoards and to assess their possible use. Due to reasons discussed in Section 3.2.1, not all known hoards were included in the current analyses (see Table 3.1). From each individual hoard that was included, data were selected with the aim of providing a thorough image of the hoard in question, based on criteria excluding non-(precious) metal and uncleaned conglomerates of objects.[160] Regretfully, none of the Tel Miqne hoards are included in these analyses, since the weights of individual objects in the hoards are currently not available.

There are different ways to visualise and gain insight into the characteristics of the weight distribution of a hoard and enable the comparison with other hoards. In order to illustrate this, we will first focus on the case of the Megiddo A hoard. This hoard is suited in particular for this purpose, because it is the largest dataset currently available of any single hoard, with data of 707 objects

[156] Cf. Stern 2001; Thompson 2003, 83.

[157] Eshel 2014, ch.2. Cf. Eshel et al. 2018, 204, 209, 211. I thank Eran Arie of the Israel Museum for his comments on the matter.

[158] Thompson 2009, 597, 601, 605.

[159] See Appendix.

[160] An exception to this is the Beth Shean B hoard (9.1, see Appendix), where several conglomerates were included. For the resulting distortion, see n. 177.

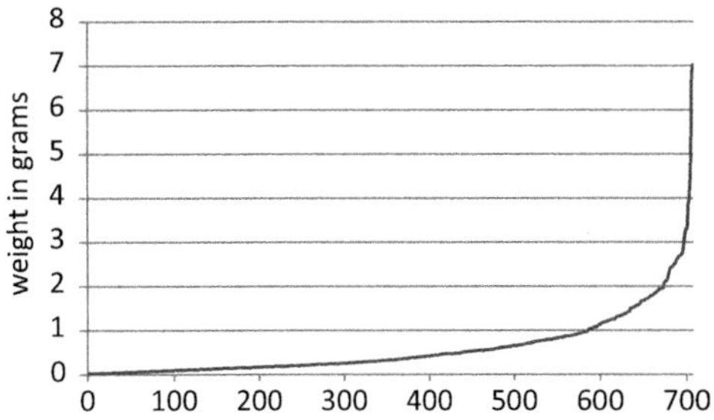

3.16 Weight distribution of the Megiddo A hoard

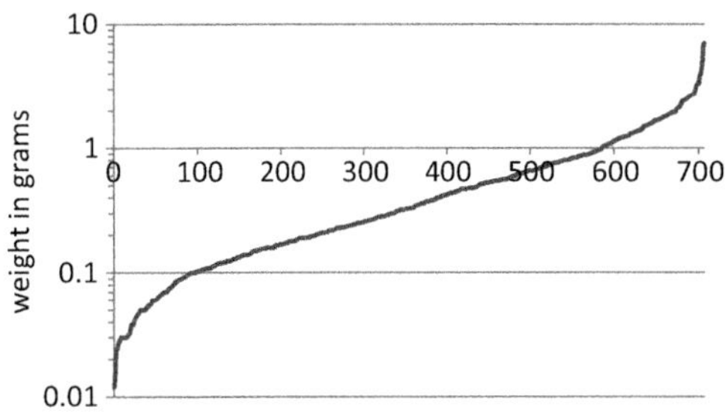

3.17 Weight distribution of the Megiddo A hoard (logarithmic scale)

(see Appendix and Figures A.9 and A.10).[161] There are of course larger hoards in terms of total weight and the number of objects, but in no other case has such a large number of objects been studied systematically.

One way to visualise the weight pattern is by plotting the weights of the individual objects arranged on an ascending scale (Figure 3.16). It becomes clear that a large portion of the objects (ca. 83 per cent) weigh up to one gram, with the increase in weight being exponential. Up to one or one-and-a-half grams, the increase in weights is slow and gradual, after which the curve steepens very quickly. With a concentration of weights in the range between zero and one gram, most of the objects are displayed in a relatively small part of the graph, at the bottom, potentially obscuring details in the weight distribution of the largest part of the hoard. This can be solved, however, by plotting the weights on a logarithmic scale (Figure 3.17).[162] The resulting graph is roughly symmetrical, with the curve sloping steeply at the start, bending towards a linear progression in the first decile and steepening again in the last decile. The most notable feature is this straight line between ca. 0.1 and 1 g., covering roughly 75 per cent of the sample and reflecting the underlying exponential curve. Two important characteristics can be deduced from this

[161] Although the Megiddo A hoard consisted of three bundles, the compositions of these bundles are similar, allowing us to treat the whole hoard as one assemblage (see Appendix).

[162] Cf. Wiseman 2018.

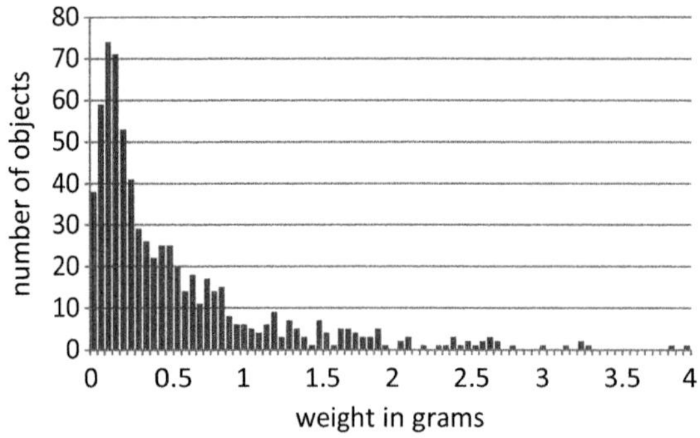

3.18 Weight distribution histogram of the Megiddo A hoard (binning of 1/20th gram)

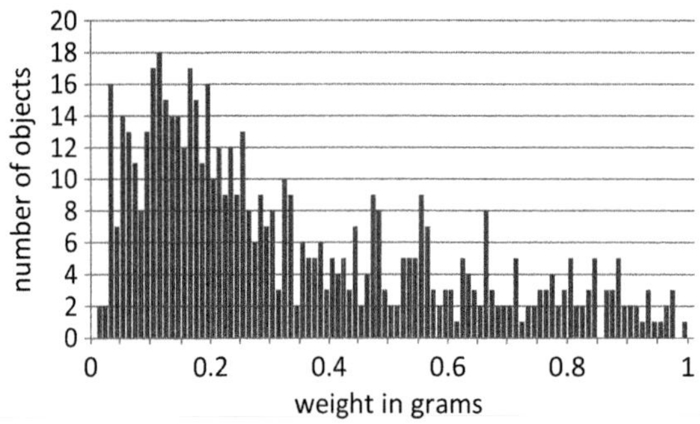

3.19 Weight distribution histogram of the Megiddo A hoard (binning of 1/100th gram)

aspect: there is a neat gradual increase in weight of the individual objects over most of the hoard and a high prevalence of objects with a low weight, mostly between ca. 0.1 and 0.2 g.

The same characteristics can also be visualised in a histogram, displaying the incidence of objects within set weight ranges. One needs to be aware though that this type of visualisation of the data leads to a loss of detail through the binning (combining data within a range); because the larger one defines the range, the less detailed information is displayed in the graph. Moreover, the graph is always a result of data manipulation, due to the fact that the information plotted is the outcome of a particular binning. A histogram with each bar/bin representing 1/20 gram (Figure 3.18) reveals a so-called right-skewed distribution with a clear peak (unimodal) between 0.1 and 0.2 g., after which there is a gradual decrease. Additionally, a small potential peak can be observed around 0.5 g., but it is uncertain whether this signifies anything. The same distribution can be observed in a histogram with a binning of 1/100 gram (Figure 3.19).

When comparing the weight distribution of the Megiddo A hoard on the basis of these visualisations to those of other hoards (Figures 3.20 and 3.21), it is generally notable that the smaller the sample, the more irregular the curve.

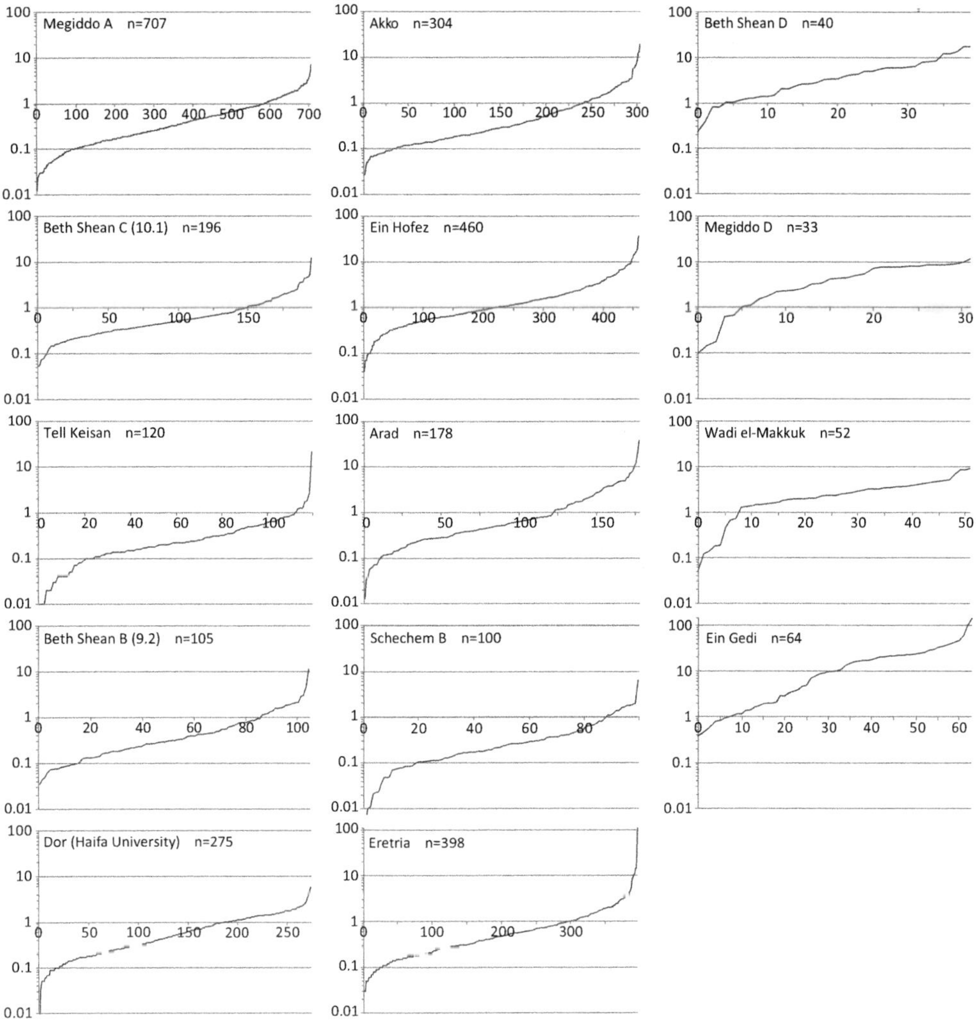

3.20 Weight distribution of hoards (logarithmic scale)

This is potentially due to the so-called law of small numbers, which basically says that the smaller the sample, the larger the potential bias. More importantly, it becomes clear that many of the hoards are similar in terms of their graph shape and their qualitative characteristics (Akko, Arad, Beth Shean B and C, Dor, Ein Ḥofez, Shechem B, Tell Keisan *and* Eretria). The range of the gradual increase in weight within these hoards, indicated by the linear progression of the curve, is approximately situated in the middle seven to eight deciles of the sample, reflecting values of approximately 0.1 to 1–2 grams. Accordingly, the mode of the distribution (the most observed value) varies between 0.1 and 0.3 g., and also the mean (average weight; ca. 0.5–1.6 g.) and median (middle weight of the sample; ca. 0.2–0.5 g.) are relatively similar (see Table 3.2). As can be observed in the graph, the Ein Ḥofez hoard is somewhat deviant with a mean of

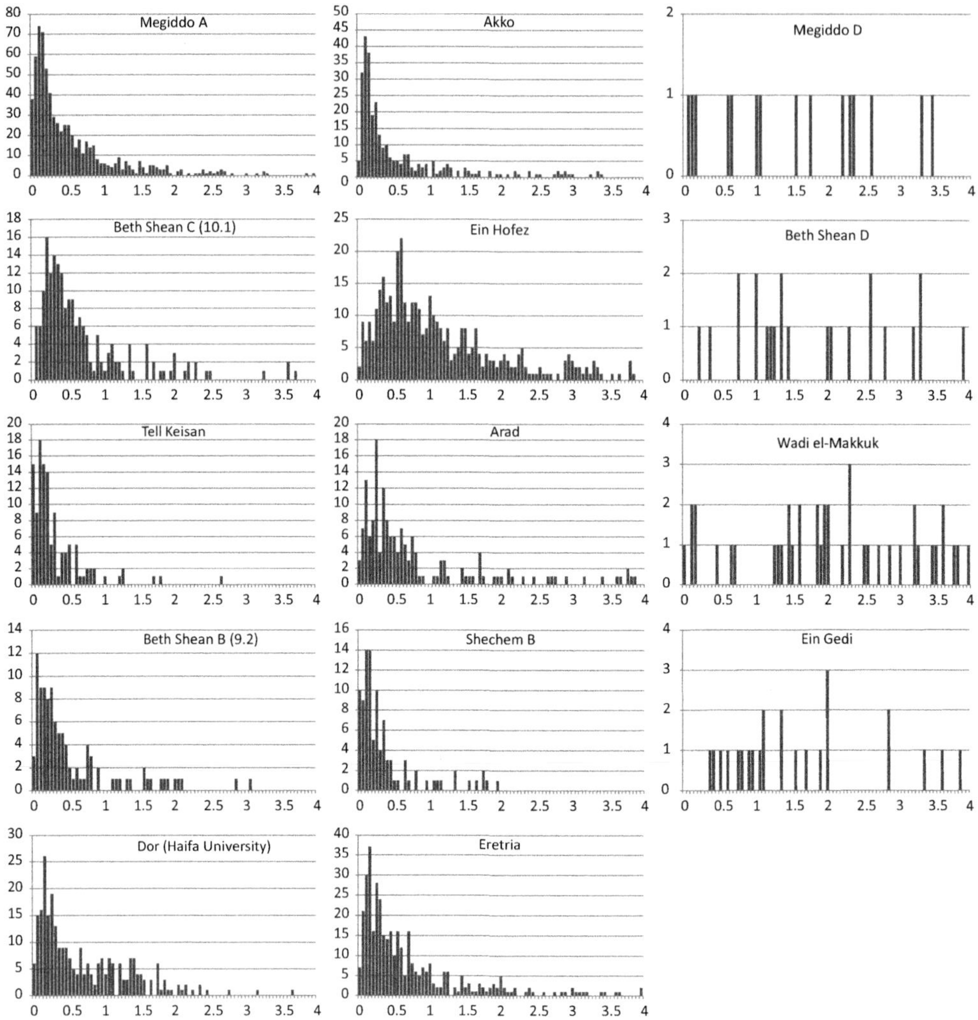

3.21 Weight distribution histograms of hoards (binning of 1/20th gram).

2.13 g. and a median of 1.05 g. This could however be the result of the mixing together of material from three distinct juglets (see Appendix).

The weight distributions of the Beth Shean D, Ein Gedi, Megiddo D and Wadi el-Makkuk hoards are clear exceptions to this pattern. Not only are these hoards significantly smaller in terms of the number of objects, the mean and median of these hoards are substantially higher, with the Ein Gedi hoard being notably deviant (see Table 3.2). In addition to the fact that they generally consist of larger objects, their weight-distribution curves do not show a straight line, but a more irregular pattern (Figure 3.20). In contrast to the other hoards, no gradual distribution can be demonstrated; with a binning of 1/10 gram there are no regular peaks visible in the distribution (Figure 3.22), and with a larger binning (½ and 1 gram), the distribution shows some multimodal but irregular clustering (Figure 3.23). In general, the collections of objects in these

TABLE 3.2 *The mode, mean and median of each hoard*

Hoard	Mode	Mean	Median
Akko	0.1	0.9	0.3
Arad	0.3	1.6	0.5
Beth Shean B (9.2)	0.1	0.5	0.3
Beth Shean C (10.1)	0.2	0.9	0.5
Beth Shean D	mm	4.8	3.3
Dor (Haifa University)	0.2	0.8	0.5
Ein Gedi	mm	17.2	10.0
Ein Ḥofez	0.6	2.1	1.0
Megiddo A	0.1	0.6	0.3
Megiddo D	mm	4.7	4.3
Shechem B	0.1	0.5	0.2
Tell Keisan	0.2	0.5	0.2
Wadi el-Makkuk	mm	2.8	2.4
Eretria	0.2	1.3	0.5

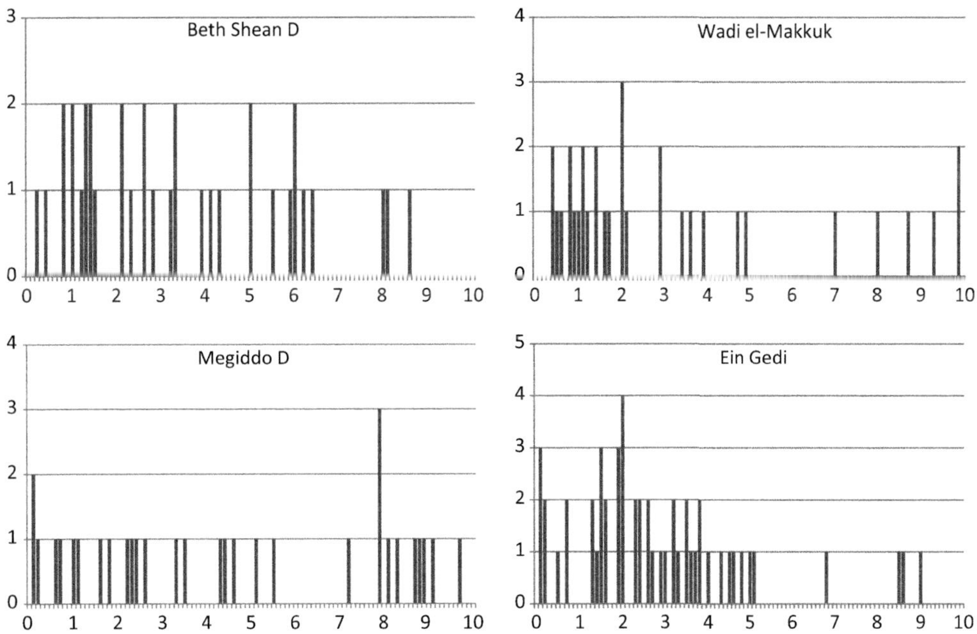

3.22 Histograms of the Beth Shean D, Megiddo D, Wadi el-Makkuk and Ein Gedi hoards (binning of 1/10th gram)

hoards appear random in terms of weight. Although this could result from the fact that the sample size is smaller, this is not very likely due to the relative consistency between hoards and the significantly higher weight of the objects. We can assume from the obvious differences that these hoards must have been used in a different way than the previous group (exemplified by Megiddo A). Interestingly, with the exception of the Wadi el-Makkuk hoard (see Section 3.3.3; Appendix), they also

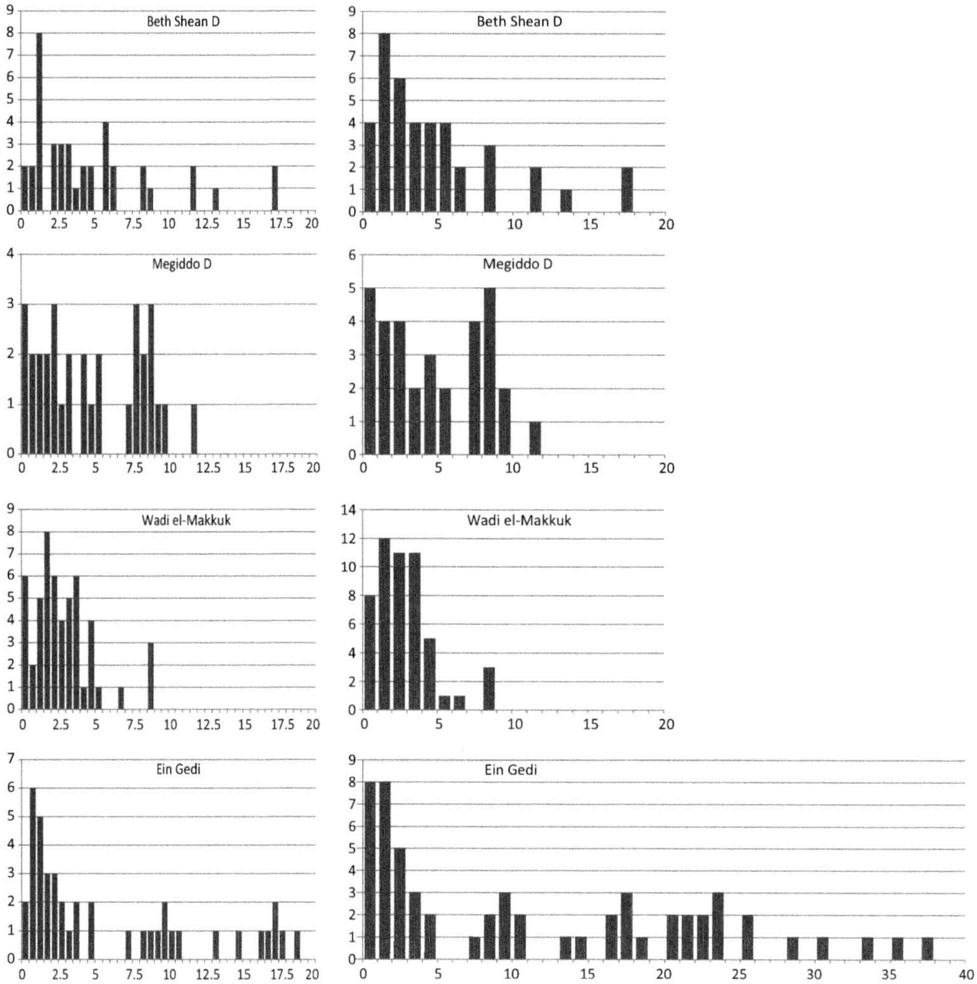

3.23 Histograms of the Beth Shean D, Megiddo D, Wadi el-Makkuk and Ein Gedi hoards (binning of ½ gram and 1 gram)

stand apart from the other group in terms of dating: while all of the hoards in the Megiddo A group are from the Iron I–IIB (including the LG II Eretria hoard), the Beth Shean D and Megiddo D hoards date to the end of the LBA–Iron I transition and the Ein Gedi hoard to the Iron IIC.

An additional way to evaluate the uniformity or coherence of the corpus, and visualise some of the above observations, is by plotting the average object weight for each hoard against the percentage of objects under 1 gram. The resulting scatter graph (Figure 3.24) reflects the difference between the two groups described above. The cluster visible on the upper left side represents the Megiddo A group, with the Ein Ḥofez hoard plotted below the cluster. The other hoards are visible at the bottom of the graph, with the Ein Gedi hoard far to the right due to its high average weight.

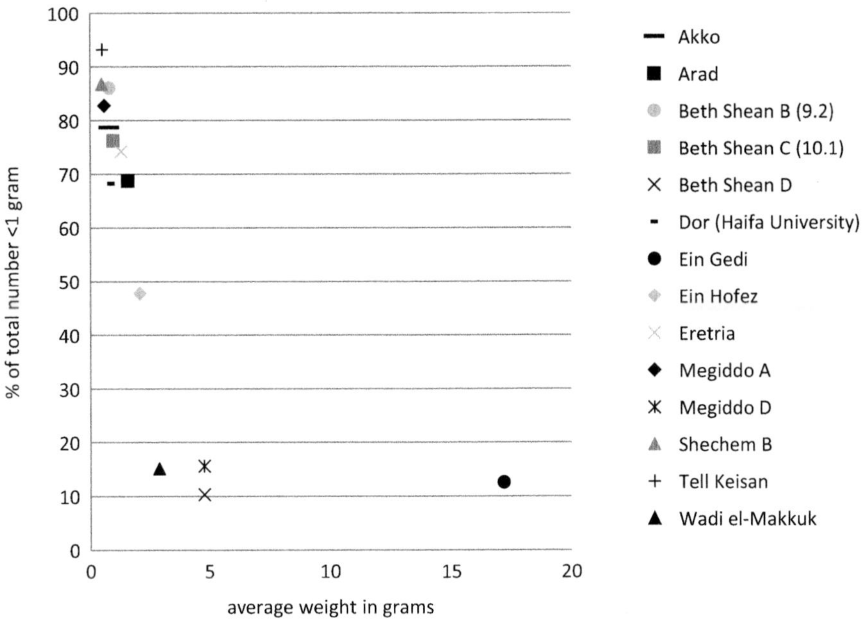

3.24 Weight scatter graph

When excluding the Ein Gedi hoard from the sample, a clear trend line can be observed (Figure 3.25), demonstrating an obvious negative correlation between the two factors: the higher the average weight, the smaller the percentage of objects under the 1 gram mark. This reflects a certain proportional consistency in the distribution of weights, offering a basic insight into the coherence of these assemblages, their use and the way in which they were shaped. Consequently, this trend line cautiously suggests an additional basis to evaluate the coherence of the corpus. All hoards adhere rather neatly to the trend, with exception of the Ein Gedi hoard. Within this trend, a clear divide can be noted between the Iron I–IIB hoards and the late LBA–Iron I transition (including Wadi el-Makkuk) in terms of their fragmentation, reflecting the observations made above on the basis of the weight-distribution graphs. This allows us to conclude the following: The fragmentation of Iron I–IIB hoards is rather consistent, with the object weights being gradually distributed and a high incidence of low-weight fragments. Alternatively, the object weights of the two late LBA–Iron I transition hoards are significantly higher and not gradually distributed.[163]

[163] Although specific data on the individual objects in the Abel Beth Maacah hoard (the third known precious metal hoard from the end of the LBA; cf. n. 48) are not available, the hoard appears on the whole relatively similar in terms of object weights. Taking into account that the sample error of this tiny hoard with only twelve objects must be considerable, with for example six complete earrings, the average object weight appears relatively high (see Appendix).

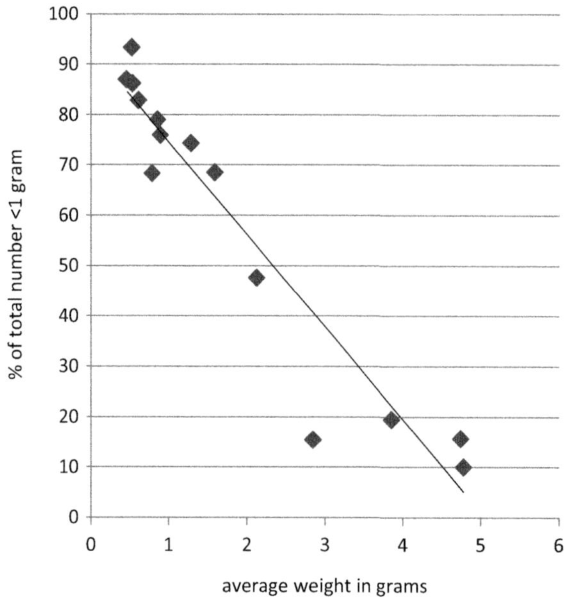

3.25 Weight scatter graph (with trend line), excluding the Ein Gedi hoard

We are left to consider what these observations imply in terms of the use of the silver in the hoards. Assuming that transactions were carried out by adding pieces of silver to the scale-pan and that, if needed, pieces were severed so as to match the required weight, it follows that the composition of the hoards was shaped through transactions and that it forms a reflection of what was used in these transactions. The high incidence of objects with a low weight, demonstrated by the Iron I–IIB hoards, suggests that these objects were most frequently used. This offers a sense of the scale of the transactions, as well as the level of precision applied in weighing. Similarly, hoards consisting largely of heavier objects were ill equipped for carrying out small-scale transactions of high precision, and it seems only obvious that they were shaped through and featured in a different type of behaviour.[164]

In the context of Viking Age silver hoards, Birgitta Hårdh has suggested that 'the degree of fragmentation shows the intensity in circulation and the degree to which silver was used in everyday transactions'.[165] We may add to and refine this by suggesting that the more gradual the distribution of weights (and thus the more uniform the graph), the more it is well adjusted through manipulation and exchange to a certain range of transactions. Pieces of silver were severed, sometimes on multiple occasions, and small pieces were kept in circulation (rather than being re-melted), in order to complement other pieces

164 An example is the Ein Gedi hoard, which has an average weight of 17.2 grams and only contains 2 objects out of 64 below 0.5 grams (0.38 and 0.44 g). Cf. n. 168.

165 Hårdh 1996, 84.

in high-precision weighing, resulting in a gradual weight distribution in the assemblage. As noted, the hoards from the Iron I–IIB demonstrate these characteristics to a high and comparable degree: they were apt for weighing out small denominations, with a high level of accuracy. The silver pieces most frequently used have a weight between ca. 0.1 and 0.3 grams, above which there is a gradual decrease in apparent use, suggesting that objects above approximately one gram were less often used and higher denominations less likely compiled. To put this into perspective: the smallest denominations of early coins, such as, for example, the 552 coins of 0.21 grams and the 353 coins of 0.43 grams from the archaic Kolophon hoard,[166] fall in a similar range as the amounts of silver that were most easily taken from the hoards. Also considering the fact that these pieces of silver get as small as can conveniently be handled or weighed,[167] it is likely that they functioned as small change used for compiling small denominations, with the hoards indicating an abundance of small-scale transactions, possibly in the context of retail trade.[168]

A high degree of circulation, implied by this use, is further indicated by the fact that only few objects were found to have belonged originally to the same artefact, with joins between objects being rare.[169] The Megiddo A hoard, for example, contains nine examples of a bracelet with herringbone incision, eight of which are small fragments, while one is complete.[170] Although very similar, minute differences in size and decoration indicate that none of the fragments had actually belonged to the same bracelet. Rather than being cut up or broken before entering the hoard, this implies that the fragmented objects themselves circulated over a longer period of time.[171]

This is further confirmed by the ample traces of wear notable on the objects. Examples of this can be seen where a decoration or the grainy structure of the

[166] Kim 2001; 2002; Kim and Kroll 2008. Cf. Velde 2020.

[167] Kim and Kroll 2008, 64–67; Velde 2020, 512.

[168] *Pace* Kletter and de Groot 2007, 372–373; Eshel et al. 2018, 204, 220. Kletter and the Groot (followed by Eshel et al.) argue against the use of hoard silver in small-scale transactions (instead suggesting that small pieces were only used to balance the scales) but base their claim on the Ein Gedi hoard. With an average weight of 17.2 grams and only 2 objects out of 64 weighing below 0.5 grams (0.38 and 0.44 g), this hoard notably does not fit the pattern of the Iron I–IIB hoards described here (cf. Eshel et al. 2018, 213–214). Additionally, Eshel et al. dismiss as unlikely the possibility that small quantities of silver were weighed out, because of the inaccuracy of the smallest weights. However, this does not negate the fact that these weights and small denominations existed and thus had a functional use. The Mesopotamian *girû* and Judahite *gerah* (derived from a carob seed; cf. carat) weighed 1/24th of a shekel (i.e., 0.35/0.47 g). The smallest Mesopotamian fractional unit was the barleycorn (1/180th shekel). See Powell 1992, 897–898; Kletter 1998, 80–84.

[169] Cf. Hårdh 2007, 98.

[170] These fragments are recorded as 1.2/351–356, 371, 485; the complete bracelet is recorded as 1.1/149, and visible in Figure A.10, bundle A.

[171] *Pace* Thompson 2007, 47–49.

3.26 Examples of wear: two objects from the Megiddo A hoard (1.2/484, 503, courtesy of the Oriental Institute of the University of Chicago [photos by author])

3.27 Examples of wear: two objects from the Eretria hoard (4/35, 59, courtesy of the Swiss School of Archaeology in Greece [photos by Pascal Simon])

metal in a break is obliterated by wear (Figure 3.26)[172] or where the straight edge of a cut or a surface appears worn down (Figure 3.27).[173] Although it has not been possible to systematically study and document all hoards in such detail, considerable wear appears to be a particular characteristic of hoards from the Iron I–IIB, while a lack of wear is notable in other (earlier and later) hoards such as that from Ein Gedi, which reflect a different type of use.

In contrast to the high level of circulation suggested for the Iron I–IIB hoards, the non-gradual distribution of weights (e.g., a multi-modal distribution) in the other hoards (end of LBA–Iron I transition and Iron IIC) may

[172] E.g., objects 1.2/484, 503, 2/120.
[173] E.g., objects 4/22, 35, 74, 59. See also Appendix.

indicate that these were less actively used and that their use was less apt to small-scale transactions. Their supposed use is not characterised by an emphasis on small change, and they do not fit the economic-behavioural context suggested for the Iron I–IIB hoards.

3.3.3 Typology

Following the typological framework laid out in Section 3.2.4, a division between ingots and ornamental objects was made for twenty hoards (Figure 3.28). A specification of these categories, based on the described subdivision, could be

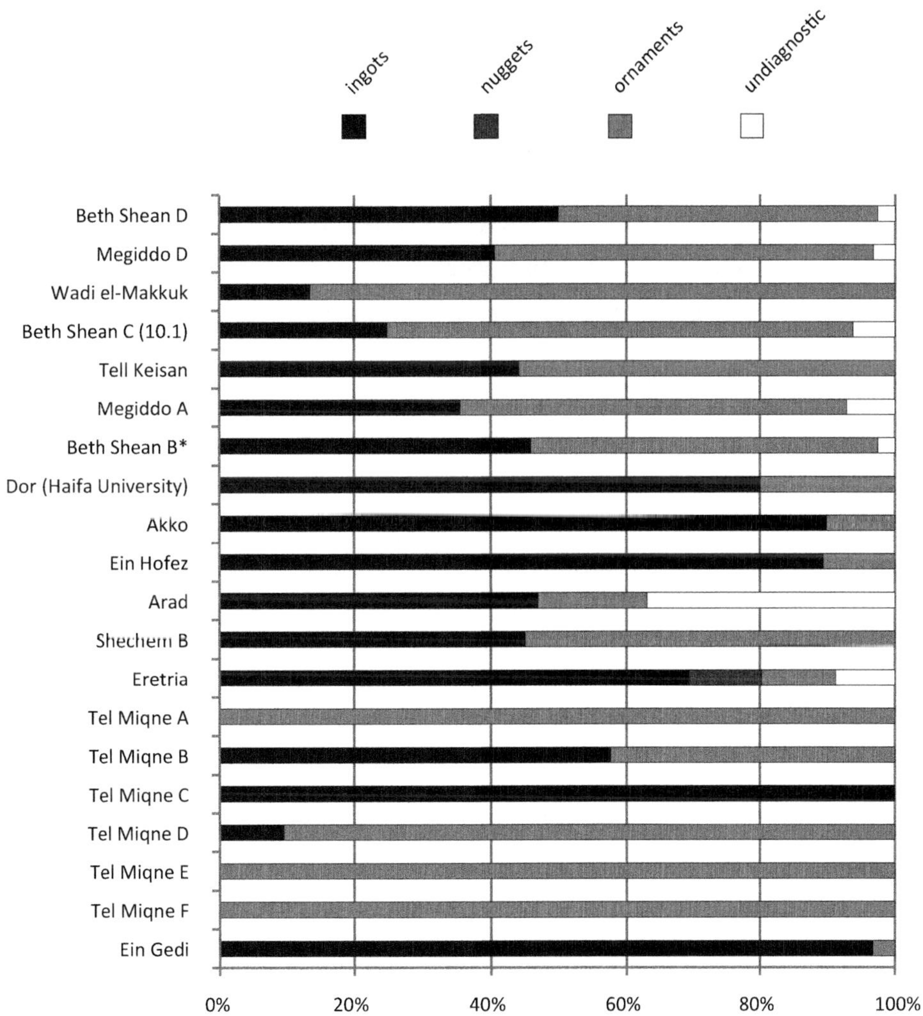

3.28 Typology: ingots and ornamental objects
The data for Beth Shean B contains uncleaned material (9.1): 31 objects counted here as ingots are conglomerates listed in the database as original object: not clear (inadequate obs.). See n. 177.

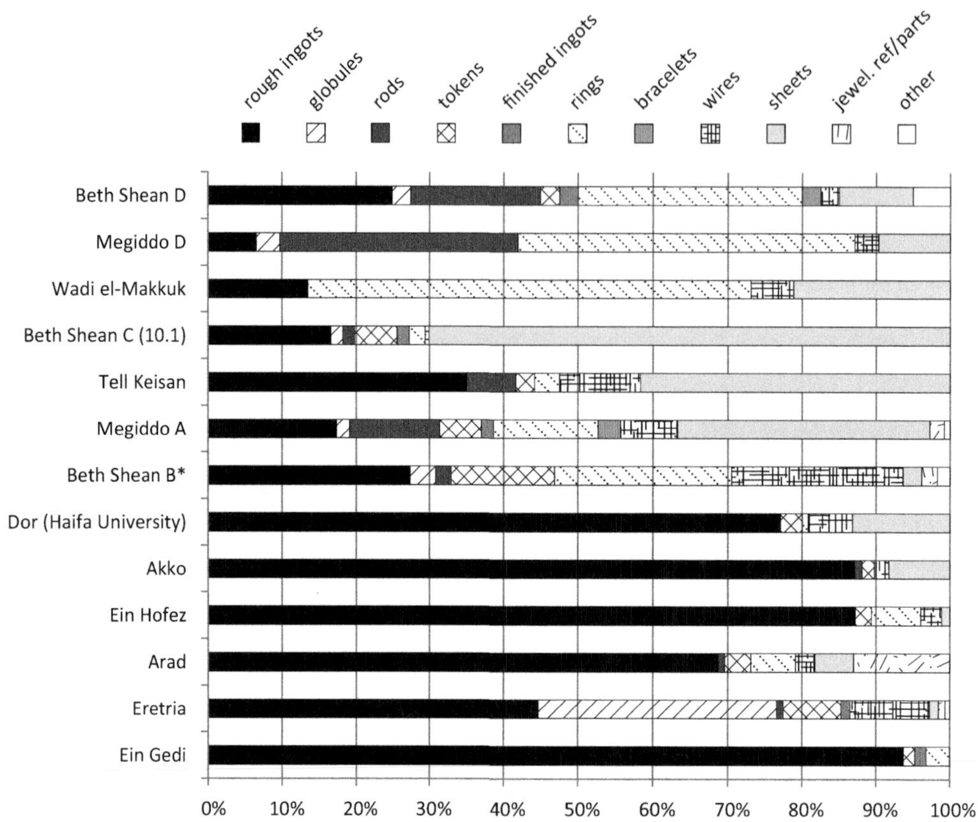

3.29 Typology: subdivisions
Nuggets are not accounted for in the data for Eretria (cf. Figure 3.28); for Beth Shean B, see n. 177.

made only for thirteen of these hoards (Figure 3.29).[174] These data, ordered in two bar diagrams with the hoards roughly in chronological order, allow for the following observations to be made.

Hoards from the end of the LBA and the Iron I contain a large proportion of ornamental objects as opposed to ingots (between 49 per cent and 74 per cent). A further differentiation of ornamental objects indicates that the hoards from the end of the LBA contain more jewellery (rings, jewellery refuse and miscellaneous objects such as beads),[175] while Iron I hoards feature a larger proportion of sheet fragments. Another exception in this regard, the hoard from Wadi el-Makkuk, dated to the Iron I,

[174] The seven remaining hoards (Shechem B and Tel Miqne A–F) were not available for study at first hand, and available or published data were not sufficiently detailed to allow for further subdivision. See Table 3.1.

[175] Although not included (see n. 48), this certainly appears to be the case with the Abel Beth Maacah hoard with its six earrings and two additional objects that are either ring or wire fragments.

contains a large quantity of rings, making it appear more similar to the LBA–Iron I transition hoards.

Moreover, considering the fact that the objects in the LBA–Iron I transition hoards are generally larger and more complete, it can be said that between the end of the LBA and the Iron I hoards, the objects were increasingly fragmented. As argued above on the basis of the low incidence of connections/joins and the traces of wear, these fragmented objects were likely circulating as such in the Iron I, as opposed to being severed upon entering the hoard and kept stationary. Furthermore, we should seriously consider the possibility that a significant part of the objects in Iron I hoards were originally Late Bronze products that remained in circulation.[176]

In contrast to the large proportion of ornamental objects noted for LBA and Iron I hoards, Iron IIA and B hoards are characterised by a predominance of ingots, mostly in fragmented state.[177] An additional difference can be noted in the strong decrease and almost complete disappearance of rod fragments, relatively common in LBA and Iron I hoards. The increase of ingots between the Iron I and Iron IIA–B points to a stronger emphasis on silver as a raw material processed primarily for the purpose of exchange or hoarding, away from its potential ornamental or functional qualities. Additionally, although difficult to prove on typological grounds, it could imply the melting down of hoarded silver and/or the influx of new silver – whether through import of ingots or the appropriation of objects previously not in circulation – primarily designated for use as a form of material wealth.

Despite the similarities, the Eretria hoard has particular typological characteristics that deviate from the Iron IIA–B hoards from the southern Levant.[178] Among other things, it contains gold nuggets (11 per cent), absent from other hoards, and as a specific type of ingot, a large amount of globules was identified (27 per cent), with relatively few or none in other hoards. Such differences might be regarded as resulting from the inherently different properties of the gold and electrum in the Eretria hoard versus the predominantly silver hoards from the southern Levant. However, the large presence of globules is also

[176] For this reason, Iron I hoards cannot be held as straightforward evidence for Iron I silver imports or alloying practices. Cf. Eshel et al. 2018, 220–221; 2019; Wood, Montero-Ruiz and Martinón-Torres 2019.

[177] The available data on the Beth Shean B hoard offer a distorted picture. The part of the hoard in Philadelphia is currently incomplete and might contain more ingots (see Appendix). The part in Jerusalem contains a large portion of untreated ingot fragments stuck onto one another. In a cleaned state of this part of the hoard, both the average weight and the proportion of ornamental objects would be adjusted down significantly, consistent with the Iron IIA–B trend. The Beth Shean A hoard, which could not be fully inventoried due to the sheer number of small ingots, also appears to confirm to these characteristics (see Appendix).

[178] *Pace* Thompson (2007, 199), who suggests that 'the ingot shapes all have remarkably precise silver parallels in the East'.

related to the specific way in which gold was processed, testified by ceramic melting plates identified at Sardis and more recently at Eretria and Methone.[179] These coarse ware sherds were used in the production of gold globules or pellets, as is evidenced by microscopic gold inclusions in the vitrified layer and the globule-sized impressions into the viscous surface (see also Figure 5.5).[180]

Departing from earlier patterns, the hoards preserved from the Iron IIC (Ein Gedi, Tel Miqne A–F) do not appear to conform to any particular set of characteristics. While the Ein Gedi and Tel Miqne C hoards consist almost completely of ingots (97 per cent and 100 per cent), many of them very large, Tel Miqne A, E and F contain only jewellery, predominantly in small fragments.[181] Alternatively, Tel Miqne B and D contain respectively 58 per cent and 10 per cent of ingots, with the objects generally relatively heavy and almost all jewellery in the D hoard being complete. This apparent divergence in the typological characteristics of the Iron IIC hoards stands in stark contrast with the relative consistency noted between hoards from earlier periods and confirms the observation made in Section 3.3.2, on the basis of the metrology, that the Ein Gedi hoard deviates from the trend indicated by the other hoards.

Notable, though, is the possible appearance of primary silver ingots, described above and tentatively identified in the Ein Gedi and Tel Miqne C hoards. Although it is equally possible that silver ingots were imported during the end of the LBA and Iron I, this is typologically not visible, suggesting that if so, they were appropriated directly for the production of finished objects or smaller (secondary) ingots.

The metrological and typological observations made so far can be summarised and further explored with the help of a single graph in which both aspects of the hoards' material characteristics are combined. The graph depicted in Figure 3.30 plots the average weight of the objects against the ratio between ingots and ornamental objects per hoard. A hoard plotted at the top contains only ingots and no ornamental objects, while one at the bottom is the opposite. The graph displays three discrete clusters, each representing a

179 Ramage and Craddock 2000, 90, 100, 102–117, 126–127, 132–134, 160–161, 207; Meeks and Craddock 2013, 271–273, pl. 127–129; Verdan 2013, 148–149, pl. 114; forthcoming; Verdan and Heymans 2021.

180 See also Section 5.4.1.

181 In their typological breakdown, Gitin and Golani list a category of 'silver fragments' that remains however undefined (2001). With regard to Tel Miqne A, this category is substantial in numbers (39 out of 74 silver objects), although less so in weight (3.5 g. out of 24.5 g.). 'Silver fragments' were also recorded for the C and E hoards, but relatively few (2 out of 87 and 9 out of 53) (Gitin and Golani 2001, 37). Because these objects could not be qualified as either ingot or ornamental object, they have been perforce left out of the analysis presented here, although it should be emphasised that only with regard to Tel Miqne A does this lead to a serious potential distortion.

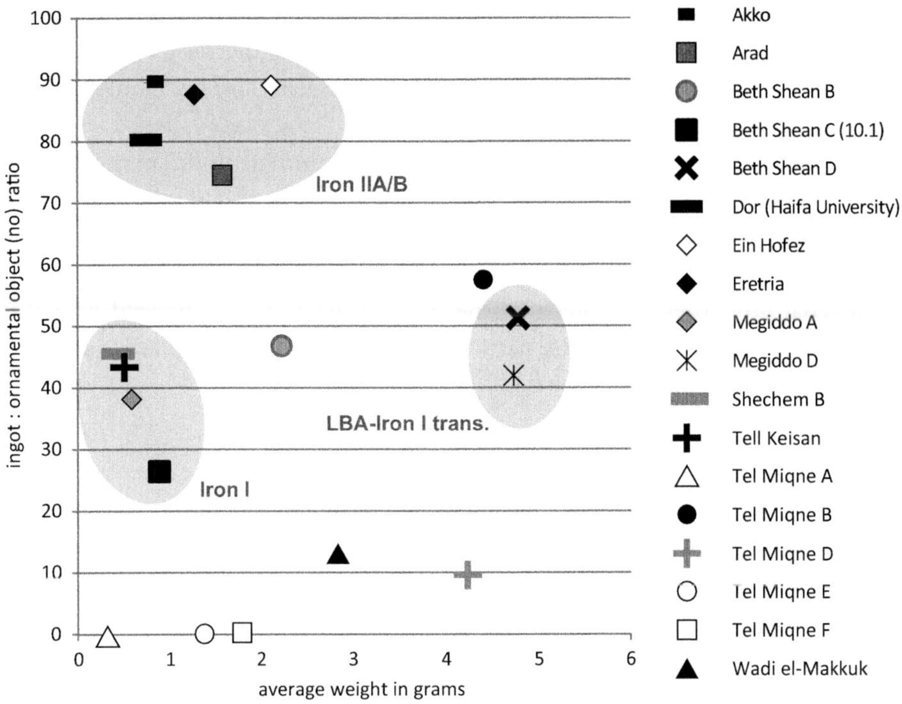

3.30 Weight-type graph

chronologically coherent group, for the end of the LBA–Iron I transition, the Iron I and the Iron IIA–B. As anticipated, the hoards from the Iron IIC are a visible exception to this. They show a dispersed pattern, being generally diverse both in term of average object weight and in terms of typological composition.[182]

In addition to these chronological groups, some comments on specific hoards should be added here. Appearing on the graph in isolation from the clusters, the Wadi el-Makkuk hoard was already identified as an exception (see Section 3.3.2). Although dated to the Iron I on the basis of specific objects in the hoard, this is ultimately based on the assumption that the assemblage is homogenous.[183] Also in terms of its context, located in a niche of a cave in the northern Judean desert, the hoard is a clear exception. With regard to the Shechem B hoard, found in a disturbed context, no specific dating has been proposed.[184] However, as indicated by the graph, its material characteristics

[182] The hoards from Tel Miqne (C) and Ein Gedi conform to this picture of diversity but have been excluded from the graph in Figure 3.30, due to the fact that their average weight is substantially higher than that of other hoards (10.9 g., resp. 17.2 g.), causing them to fall off the graph. Also, the fact that they almost exclusively contain ingots is notable (100 per cent, resp. 97 per cent).

[183] Hirschfeld and Riklin 2002, 7; Sass 2002a, 21. See Appendix.

[184] See Appendix.

suggest an association with hoards from the Iron I. Moreover, following the above remarks on the Beth Shean B hoard, adjusting the relative number of ingots upwards and the average weight down, as seems correct, would cause it to fall within the Iron IIA–B cluster.

In general, the graph demonstrates that down to the Iron IIC period hoards tend to conform to specific material characteristics. This implies that, as a material correlate, these hoards featured in a certain normative behavioural practice. The fact that these clusters shift over time, reflecting shifting trends in material properties, indicates that the implied practice also changed over the course of the time. How these particular shifts in practice can be explained in a diachronic framework, will be addressed in Section 3.4.

3.4 TOWARDS AN UNDERSTANDING OF THE HOARDS

In order to understand the historical significance of the hoards, it is necessary to carefully set out a historical framework that can help to account for the evidence brought forth by our analysis of the hoards. This preliminary historical framework will be subjected to further discussion in Chapter 4, with the purpose of exploring not only the practical historical development of money-use but to place this in the context of wider social, economic and political developments. It will therefore suffice for now to draw out a historical picture that deliberately stays close to the hoard evidence. These historical projections are tentative, due to the nature of our dataset, as previously discussed.

3.4.1 Silver and Money in the Iron Age

The historical setting for the first hoards in our corpus is provided by the final stages and direct aftermath of Egyptian rule over the region under the twentieth dynasty around the second half of the twelfth century.[185] The clear differences between the hoards found in strata associated with the retreat of the Egyptians and those from a later phase during the Iron I suggest the development of a silver cash economy involving small change. Presumably, these first hoards should not be seen as representing a pre-monetary economic stage during which silver did not circulate as a means of exchange; rather, they can be regarded as signalling a gradual transition towards the moneyed economy of the Iron I.

This moneyed economy, involving small-scale transactions and small change used in compiling small denominations, is indicated by the increase in fragmentation and the high level of circulation of objects during the Iron I.

[185] Singer 1988–1989; Ussishkin 1995.

A significant portion of the objects used in transactions were objects of an ornamental or functional nature, such as jewellery and sheet fragments, suggesting that the use of silver in exchange was strongly associated with objects whose value was at least in part based on their significance in social discourse. This value must have formed a partial basis for the acceptability of these objects in exchange.[186]

The dissolution of Late Bronze Age trade networks and the collapse of Egyptian centralised authority provide a context for the rise of a silver moneyed economy. Although the Egyptians were motivated by their own political and economic interests,[187] infrastructure for trade, such as harbours and trade routes (most prominently the Via Maris), was safeguarded and agreements enforced as a result of their presence, thereby contributing to the maintenance of a relatively stable trade environment. The weakening of Egyptian rule in the course of the twelfth century, also as a result of the Sea Peoples' incursion, culminated in a final retreat around 1130.[188] As a result of this gradual demise, local agents in the New Canaan centres[189] found themselves in need of new economic strategies in order to cope with changing economic realities and reverted to the use of precious metal, in part, objects with social value, for carrying out trade. Whether agents within the Late Bronze Age political hierarchy, or alternatively, entrepreneurial merchants and intermediaries taking advantage of the economic upheaval of the twelfth century, as posited *inter alia* by J. D. Muhly, E. S. Sherratt and M. Artzy,[190] had a role in initiating this process, is considered in Section 4.1. This will be followed by a discussion of the change in trade environment between the twelfth century (LBA III) and the subsequent Iron I, as dramatically reflected in the so-called Report of Wenamun.[191]

From the Iron IIA onwards, the silver moneyed economy consolidates its presence, with a stronger emphasis on ingots in hoards, likely reflecting the circulation of silver. Although there are no particular signs of a development towards standardisation in form or quality of the metal,[192] as in the case of coinage, the relative increase in the share of ingots suggests a stronger appreciation of silver as a material used for exchange and hoarding.

It is likely that arising central authorities related to state formation during the Iron IIA–B start to manifest themselves as important players in the circulation

186 See also Section 2.3.
187 Na'aman 1981; Redford 1992, 209–213.
188 Weinstein 1981, 17–23; 1992; Singer 1988–1989; 1994, 284–295; Ussishkin 1995; Knapp and Manning 2016, 135.
189 Finkelstein 2003.
190 Muhly 1992; Sherratt 1998; Artzy 1997; 1998.
191 See Section 4.1.4.
192 Cf. Shalev, Shechtman and Shilstein 2013; Eshel et al. 2018, 221.

of silver money. In the territory of Israel, this rise to statehood can be placed in the later tenth and early ninth century, while in Judah this might only occur around a century later. Although this historical development has been the subject of considerable interest,[193] little attention has gone out to exploring specific institutions of statehood. However, the rise of these territorial states can be associated with a more complex organisation of resources, and the use of silver money certainly offered opportunities to this end. State activity is therefore likely to offer at least a partial context in which the hoard evidence can be understood. It is also significant, in this regard, that hoards appear in the south particularly from the eighth century onwards.

Not knowing to what extent these hoards are representative, we cannot necessarily extrapolate a larger quantity of silver in circulation from the large size of the Dor and Eshtemoa hoards. As pointed out Section 3.3.2, their size is, however, significant. Testifying to what appears like an exceptional organisation and centralisation of resources, an accumulation of wealth the size of the Eshtemoa hoard is difficult to imagine as some private individual's hoard.[194] Such a financial tour de force is more plausibly connected with a centralised organisation, and in particular with a fiscal institution. A hoard of silver money this size should be regarded as a possible collection of tribute, booty or tax in the wider sense of the concept.[195] With this in mind, Section 4.2 will explore specific evidence for the existence of such institutions and forms of centralised management of financial resources.

The picture suggested by the hoard evidence changes fundamentally by the seventh century. The dissolution of a coherent pattern in the material characteristics of the hoards suggests the absence of a consistent behavioural practice in relation to hoarded silver, as would be expected in the case of money. This is clearly at odds with an interpretation of the Tel Miqne hoards as evidence for a monetary economy following the Neo-Assyrian conquest.[196] Gitin and

[193] Finkelstein 1999; 2001; 2013; 2019; Master 2001; Herzog and Singer-Avitz 2004; Na'aman 2013.

[194] Cf. Yeivin 1971a.

[195] Cf. Yeivin 1972; 1987; 1993; Kletter and Brand 1998; Kletter 2003, 144. Kletter and Brand reject the interpretation of the hoard as tax, writing *inter alia* on the basis of an observation by the excavator that 'all the pieces were cut with the same tool', which 'negates the notion that the small pieces of silver were collected as such from different individuals, a notion that was the basis for the interpretation of the hoard as collected taxes' (Kletter and Brand 1998, 152; Kletter 2003, 144). However, the original publication actually mentions that of twenty-one pieces selected specifically for study by the forensic department of the Israel Police (selected on the basis of typology, rather than to provide a representative cross-section) only five displayed possible traces of the same tool (Yeivin 1990, 50). Additional arguments, such as that the different jugs of the hoard would fail to reflect ancient weight units, or that taxes would supposedly have been paid in kind (however lacking reference), do not contradict an interpretation as a collection of taxes.

[196] Gitin 1995; 1997; Golani and Sass 1998, 62; Gitin and Golani 2001; 2004.

Golani claim that these seventh-century hoards are 'indicative of a new economic development in which silver was used . . . as a form of money';[197] but this claim appears to be mistaken on at least two counts: for one, the use of silver money was not a development new to the seventh century, and two, these particular hoards are not themselves a strong indication for the use of silver money. Although it is plausible that the silver in these hoards was hoarded as a means of value and might very well have been used in exchange as a relatively inarticulate form of money, the fact that the hoards deviate so clearly from earlier trends suggests that they do not reflect a silver-moneyed economy in the way the Iron I–IIB hoards do. Moreover, it should be pointed out that none of the Iron IIC hoards actually date to the period of Neo-Assyrian domination but rather to the subsequent phases of Egyptian and Babylonian influence over the region at the end of the seventh and early sixth century.[198]

This does not necessarily mean that there was no silver money in circulation or that a monetary economy would not have existed in any form. Perhaps we simply have not yet found the hoards suggesting this. However, the hoards that we do have provide no clear evidence for a consistent practice, not for the use of silver in transactions involving small denominations or for the use of small change; and they certainly do not provide evidence for a linear development towards monetisation and coinage.[199] Rather to the contrary, they appear more like a regression in this regard. In general, the use of money should be understood as part of a certain social reality, and it is very possible that the Iron IIC reality was one in which the circulation of silver cash – at least on a local level – had declined. The historical context for this decline will be discussed in detail in Section 4.3.

At the same time, the Iron IIC hoards provide evidence for the first time of newly imported silver entering the system. Ingots that can be tentatively identified as primary products of silver extraction from argentiferous lead through cupellation are found in at least two of the hoards and were presumably used directly in exchange without being processed into other objects first. This hypothesis of newly imported silver that had not yet, or hardly, circulated is supported by results from lead isotope analyses of silver pieces from Tel Miqne and Ein Gedi, indicating a strong presence of Aegean silver.[200] This is

197 Gitin and Golani 2004, 203.

198 Cf. Golani and Sass 1998, 74; Na'aman 2003, 86. In addition to the dating of the Tel Miqne stratum IB to 604 BC, Golani and Sass emphasise a dating for the jewellery in the last third of the seventh century, based on the Egyptianising influence of the objects, with only two pieces showing Neo-Assyrian elements (1998, 74).

199 Cf. Gitin and Golani 2001, 43; Thompson 2003. Cf. Kletter and de Groot 2007, 372–374.

200 Stos-Gale 2001, 61–62; Thompson 2007, 44; Thompson and Skaggs 2013; Wood, Montero-Ruiz and Martinón-Torres 2019; 11–15, 27.

significant in the light of the apparent suspension of trade relations between the southern Levant and the Aegean during the period of Neo-Assyrian dominance and the strong resumption of contact after the rise of the twenty-sixth dynasty in Egypt and its takeover of the southern Levant in the thirties or twenties of the seventh century.[201] Thus, if it had not already been imported in the eighth century or before, Aegean silver could only have arrived to the region in the last third of the seventh century, making it highly likely that the ingots represent fresh imports. These renewed contracts between the Aegean and Egypt, and through Egypt with the southern Levant, stimulated the production and trade of silver and provided impetus for considerable developments in the Aegean. This will be further explored in Section 5.4.

3.4.2 Social Aspects of Early Money-Use

A monetary economy can function in diverse ways that do not always or necessarily find expression in the physical use of money itself. The reliance on credit or the keeping of accounts are examples of monetary forms that can exist side by side or in alternation with actual money. However, when considering the active circulation of money within an economy, the existence of small change used to compile small denominations is a significant, if not fundamental, characteristic, indicating the appropriation of a material medium as money for small-scale transactions allowing precision. This characteristic has been shown to be typical for money-use in the Iron I–IIB periods, thereby demonstrating that, historically, small change or small fractions of weight standards are neither a later consequence of the introduction and use of coinage[202] nor did they arise out of particular financial needs associated with the development of the polis, such as pay for civic and military duties.[203] Although this had been theorised already,[204] it is now confirmed on an empirical basis.

There is, however, more to the hoard evidence presented here than identifying the functional utility of money and small change. In general, as explored in Chapter 2, money is a deeply social thing, intricately tied to social and cultural strategies and dynamics. Changes in use and the meanings attached to it offer a valuable view into that arena.

Specifically, how are we to understand the significance of ornamental objects within the hoards? As argued, the nature of the objects – their form and not only the material – is significant. The strong presence of ornamental

[201] Na'aman 1991, 33–41; Fantalkin 2006, 201–204; 2008a, 170–292; 2015, 238, n. 8.
[202] Kim 2001; 2002. Cf. Kraay 1964. Von Reden 1997, 156; but 2010, 22.
[203] Cf. Cook 1958; Pritchett 1971, 13–14; Rutter 1981, 5–6. See Section 6.2.2.
[204] Kim 2001; 2002.

objects in LBA–Iron I hoards, down to the level of small change, together with the continued presence of complete jewellery items, cannot be disregarded and is therefore irreconcilable with a singular interpretation of the silver as a mere commodity.[205] Rather, a certain token function is represented in the use and circulation of objects with a social significance, even if they had been appropriated for use within a new setting. Following our discussion on money and the state in Section 2.2.4, the emergence of this type of money might tentatively be associated with a weaker (non-autocratic) central authority.

Moreover, when concerned with the nature of the objects, rather than only the material from which they are made, what significance should be ascribed to the high influx of ornamental objects and the continued presence of complete jewellery in these hoards? Should these be partially regarded as prestige objects in a status economy or the remnants thereof? And if so, what is the significance of the fact that these objects were hoarded – taken out of circulation and concealed – as opposed to being used for bodily adornment? Does this presume a shift of emphasis from an enhancement of the social body to a potential economic tool?[206] Assuming that ornamental objects were in fact produced primarily to serve the purpose of the former, it can be argued that LBA–Iron I hoards in particular reflect a reality wherein prestige objects meant for purposeful display were appropriated for an alternative purpose, indicating a shift in social strategy.

This corresponds to what Appadurai refers to as the diversion of commodities from their path.[207] He uses these terms with reference to scholarship on *kula* exchange, where the concept of *keda* represents the path along which valuables circulate, implying not only the physical route that the valuables follow but also the social links between men of status among which the valuables were exchanged.[208] This is seen as crucial to the social life of things in general, where the movement along a path is driven by social and political dynamics and frequently subjected to social restrictions. Diversions from a path are made in order to wrest things from the confines of their social setting, for the purpose of gain, often moving them towards commoditisation. In turn, diversions can lead to the constitution of new paths in the flow of goods.

What factors could have led to this diversion of Late Bronze ornamental objects to a use in exchange and hoarding? Appadurai claims that the diversion of commodities from their path is 'always a sign of creativity or crisis, whether aesthetic or economic' and is potentially regarded as morally ambiguous. Additionally, he regards diversion generally as the act of the entrepreneurial

205 Cf. Sections 2.3 and 3.1.
206 Cf. Graeber 1996; 2001, 91–115. See Section 2.3.
207 Appadurai 1986a, 16–29.
208 Munn 1983. Cf. Leach 1983, 25.

individual in defiance of the politically and economically powerful.[209] This assumes a level of social stability, wherein strategies of diversion are necessarily interpreted in the framework of an endogenous struggle for power and challenge of those who have it. From our vantage point, however, it seems equally possible that in times of upheaval and insecurity, when the cultural basis for systems of valuation is being eroded, elites are forced to develop strategies of diversion in order to maintain their position.

These strategies of diversion can be seen at work in the appropriation of prestige objects meant for display for the purpose of calculated exchange and hoarding. This is particularly significant, because, as Appadurai concludes, 'change in the cultural construction of commodities is to be sought in the shifting relationship of paths to diversions in the lives of commodities'.[210] It is in the diversion of valuables from their path and the creation of a new path, reflected in the practice of monetary exchange and hoarding, that we can see how silver prestige items came to be valued as money.

Graeber has explored this transformation from bodily adornment to hidden economic tool, identifying the latter as money.[211] The transition from one to the other is not, however, one that can be ascribed to a single phase or moment in time. Money comes into being not as a result of a historical transition from one stage in the economy to the next. In reality, this process is rather more dynamic, characterised by what Graeber describes as 'the constant transformation of the visible into the invisible and back again'[212] and is tied in our case to the dynamic quality of precious metal to move back and forth between object and material or between being displayed and being hoarded. This understanding was developed in detail in Chapter 2, and although this transformation is particularly well reflected in the LBA–Iron I hoards, the continued presence of complete jewellery and jewellery fragments in hoards throughout the Iron Age indicates that it is an ongoing facet in the make-up of the hoards and the early use of money.[213]

Whether the strategies of diversion seen in the appropriation of prestige objects for use in exchange and hoarding and the resulting spread of money in society were negatively evaluated, as often suggested for money regardless of the historical context,[214] is hardly a straightforward matter. Changes in economic strategy are perhaps always met with a degree of what one could refer to

[209] Appadurai 1986a, 25–27.
[210] Appadurai 1986a, 29.
[211] Graeber 1996; 2001, 91–115. See Section 2.3.
[212] Graeber 2001, 104.
[213] N.b.: Only a single hoard from the Iron IIC (Tel Miqne C) contains no ornamental objects; even the similar Ein Gedi hoard, notable for its large silver ingots, actually contains two complete earrings.
[214] See Section 2.1.

as moral reluctance, whereby the contesting of pre-existing structures is negatively viewed by those feeling threatened and framed in that sense. This does not, however, mean that the spread of money has an intrinsically negative bearing on society.

3.5 CONCLUSION

The main objective of this chapter was to provide a thorough assessment of the evidence from the Iron Age silver hoards, dealing with previous scholarship on the topic, the archaeological and material characteristics of the hoards and the implications of the hoard evidence for our understanding of money-use in the Iron Age. Although recent research on these hoards has generally emphasised their economic function as a supposed precursor to coinage, approaches and interpretations diverge. In order to find a way forward and create a better and more detailed conception of the historical and social significance of the hoards, I have laid out a methodological approach that is geared towards understanding the behaviour behind the hoards and their historical and social context.

This approach emphasises the importance of material characteristics, taking all objects, rather than a particular selection, into consideration, as a way of understanding how the hoards – as assemblages – took shape and how they were used. The focus here is placed on the context and the metrology and typology of the objects in the hoards. Although such features by themselves do not determine the meaning attributed to the hoards, just as material features do not determine the meaning attributed to money,[215] material culture is always related to practice, thus allowing us to get a grasp of the behavioural practices of which they were part. It is argued that the degree to which the hoards adhere to a consistent pattern in terms of characteristics, corresponds to the degree of normative behaviour implied by the hoards.

A critical assessment of the methodology employed in previous research stands at the basis of the approach laid out here. This has led us to redefine the terms and categories employed in describing the material and reject the search for a correlation between known weight standards and individual objects or bundles. Drawing on new data, Thompson's claim of a standardisation of sealed bundles as a conceptual precursor to coinage is refuted.[216] Instead, a focus on the weight distribution within the hoard is argued for, with the aim of assessing the suitability of an assemblage of objects for performing certain transactions.

Thorough analysis of various aspects of the hoards has demonstrated that up to the Iron IIC period the hoards confirm to certain defined patterns,

[215] See Section 2.1.

[216] Thompson 2003. Cf. Eshel et al. 2018, 211–212, 221.

suggesting a consistent behavioural practice. These patterns are chronologically specific, with shifting trends in material characteristics being the basis for a historical reconstruction of money-use.

At the basis of this reconstruction stands the postulation of a moneyed economy. This economic practice started to take shape during the final phase of the Late Bronze Age, against the background of waning Egyptian dominance over the region but appears to gain momentum in former LB and New Canaan centres during the Iron I period. Characterised by small change and a high degree of circulation, hoards from this period reflect a degree of monetisation, whereby small-scale transactions were carried out with a level of accuracy comparable to that of early coinage. Rather than being hidden in anticipation of some catastrophe, these money hoards were likely kept underground under regular circumstances as a normal way to safely store valuables.

This practice of money-use continues under the rise of territorial states in the Iron IIA period, down to the Iron IIB. The accumulation and centralisation of resources reflected by some large hoards requires a certain political organisation and infrastructure, suggesting the involvement of institutions of central authority in the flow of money.

However, evidence for this moneyed economy seems to disappear after the Iron IIB period. The hoards from the Iron IIC, all post-dating the period of Neo-Assyrian dominance, do not form a coherent pattern, breaking with earlier trends, and it is argued that they did not (consistently) feature in a set behavioural practice as one would expect in a moneyed economy. Although this does not imply that money disappeared from the economy altogether, it is likely that the use and circulation of silver money as known from the preceding periods had declined.

The changes in practice and the apparent decline of small-change use in the seventh century argue against a linear or evolutionary model for the development of money from ingots (bullion) to coinage. Despite strong evidence for the use of silver in exchange during the Iron I and IIA–B periods, none of the evidence implies a clear development towards coinage, and there is no intrinsic reason why the use of money should have culminated in coinage. The fact is that the Iron IIC hoards all date after the introduction of coinage in western Anatolia and rather suggest a slowdown in the moneyed economy of the seventh and early sixth century. It follows that neither the development of money-use nor the monetisation of the economy is a path of no return.

Rather than reflecting a linear or evolutionary development of economy and society, it is argued that the introduction and use of money indicate changes in social-economic strategies, taking place under specific political circumstances. Where money comes into being, valuables are diverted from their path, and it is suggested with regard to this historical context that a substantial part of the objects were appropriated for monetary exchange by diverting them from use as prestige objects meant for display. The significant presence of such objects in the hoards, and the sophisticated practice in which they featured, imply that an understanding of the material as a mere commodity being valued in weight fails to appreciate the duality of the phenomenon at hand. In addition to being a commodity, appreciated for its material value, the social significance associated with these objects must have played a role in emphasising the token function of money and in consolidating the social practice of which they were part.

FOUR

MONEY IN THE IRON AGE SOUTHERN LEVANT

4.1 SILVER MONEY IN A CHANGING WORLD (THE END OF THE LATE BRONZE AGE)

4.1.1 Introduction

Chapter 3 has shown that the material study of silver hoards can provide essential evidence for money-use throughout much of the period under study. However, any attempt to grasp the use and significance of silver and money through time should include a consideration of the wider historical and social context in which this evidence can be placed. This chapter will therefore build on a variety of textual as well as archaeological sources pertinent to the conclusions drawn in Chapter 3 in order to provide the much-needed framework for the development of money-use in the Iron Age southern Levant.

Although the earliest known silver finds, made from native silver or electrum, might go back as far as the sixth or fifth millennium BCE, the first evidence for the systematic extraction of silver from argentiferous lead ores through cupellation is dated to the fourth millennium BCE.[1] Although much remains unknown as to the circumstances and reasons behind the start of silver production in relation to the production of lead,[2] silver finds and industrial evidence for its production appear at several sites across the Ancient Near East, from Iran to Anatolia. Towards the end of the fourth millennium, during the Early Bronze Age or Late Uruk Period in Mesopotamia (starting in the thirty-fourth century), an increase in the production of silver is noted,[3] likely corresponding to the appearance of litharge in the Aegean[4] and – interestingly – roughly contemporary with the emergence of cuneiform writing in Mesopotamia.

Although silver appears to have been used primarily for ornamental and prestige items, circulating as objects down to the third millennium, there are clear indications for a changing use and function in the centuries thereafter. These developments are likely to be understood in relation to wider changes in the perception of value of metal commodities.[5] Lorenz Rahmstorf has drawn attention to the use of scales and weights in the Aegean, possibly as early as the twenty-ninth/twenty-eighth centuries, but most clearly during the middle of the third millennium (EH II; until ca. 2300 BCE), as well as its relation to the increased production of silver.[6] More significantly, it is from this period (Early Dynastic III) onwards that *hacksilber* hoards are attested in Mesopotamia and the Levant, while the use of silver as a means of exchange and payment, and a unit of value in weight, is reflected by textual sources.[7] Although other commodities, such as barley and copper, were also used as currencies, it is clear that silver was considered the primary metal of value and was functioning as a form of money.

The basic principles underlying the use of silver as money – using standard weights and a balance – were to remain in place in the Ancient Near East until the spread of coinage in the Hellenistic period. At the same time, however, there is little reason to assume continuity in the practical use of silver cash and its circulation throughout this time frame. Economic, social and political

1 Nriagu 1985, 668; Pernicka, Rehren and Schmitt-Strecker 1998, 123–124; Nezafati and Pernicka 2012; Helwing 2014, 215.

2 Yahalom-Mack et al. 2015.

3 Helwing 2014, 414–416.

4 Rahmstorf 2015, 164; Bassiakos, Nerantzis and Papadopoulos 2019, 2751–2752. Silver objects are also known from fourth millennium Sardinia (Late Neolithic), increasing significantly in the third millennium, but no evidence for extraction from or mining of argentiferous lead ores is currently known (Melis 2014, spec. 487).

5 Bachhuber 2011; Wengrow 2011; Stork 2015; Rahmstorf 2016a.

6 Rahmstorf 2010; 2015, 163–166; 2016b.

7 Powell 1978; 1996; Peyronel 2010; 2014, 362–369; Helwing 2014, 416–418; Bachhuber 2018. Data on these hoards have been collected in Peyronel 2010, with discussion and references.

circumstances could differ significantly through time and across regions, and the supply of silver was not always constant. Moreover, as noted already in Chapter 2, with written accounts being kept, a form of monetary economy with reference to silver could exist also without the need for silver to change hands.

In fact, preceding the Iron Age hoards dealt with in Chapter 3, the first silver hoards in the southern Levant date from the Middle Bronze II to Late Bronze Age I.[8] Most of these concern *hacksilber* hoards, seemingly comparable to other Ancient Near Eastern hoards from the late third and second millennium, although there are some apparent exceptions.[9] Despite the fact that the number of hoards from this period seems small compared to the Iron Age, their appearance in the archaeological record is certainly significant, especially considering the fact that no similar hoards are known from the region after the Late Bronze Age I until the twelfth century. Whatever the specific historical and social context of these MB II–LB I hoards, they indicate the use and hoarding of silver as a form of value. Beyond this, a more proper understanding of their significance can only be obtained on the basis of a detailed and comparative study. Such a study lies, however, outside of our current scope.

Following the absence of silver hoards throughout much of the Late Bronze Age, the relative abundance of them in the southern Levant from the twelfth to the early sixth century is unparalleled in the world of the Ancient Near East and Mediterranean. In order to gain further insight into the use and significance of the first of these hoards – those dating to the end of the LBA and the transition to the Iron I – it is necessary to explore the ways and contexts in which silver was used and appreciated in the Levant in the period preceding the hoards. In other words, in order to understand what silver meant and how we can regard the suggested development in its use, we need to take a step back in time and start with the period prior to the crisis that hit the centres of the Late Bronze Age in the twelfth century. Following this, we will focus on the changing circumstances under which trade took place and what this meant for the role of silver towards the end of the Late Bronze Age and thereafter.

8 Hoards are known from Megiddo (str. XIIIa; Loud 1948, 183, fig. 397, pl. 228), Gezer (hoards A and B, see Appendix; for additional MB hoards, see Seger 1976; Eshel et al. 2018, 200), Nahariyah (Dothan 1981), Shiloh (Finkelstein and Brandl 1985, 17–26, 57–62; Brandl 1993, 238–245, spec. 244; Bunimovitz and Finkelstein 1993, 96; Finkelstein and Lederman 1993, 49–64), Tell el-Ajjul (Petrie 1934, 5–9/11; Negbi 1970) and presumably Shechem (A, see Appendix). The Gezer A and B and Shechem A hoards were listed previously among the Iron Age hoards (Kletter 2003; Thompson 2003) and have therefore been included in the catalogue in the Appendix. See also Table 3.1; Eshel et al. 2018, 200.

9 Cf. Peyronel 2010. The additional Gezer hoard (Seger 1976) and possibly also Gezer A are jewellery hoards. The silver objects from the Nahariyah temple can be connected to a smithy, as indicated by metallurgical refuse at the site (personal communication, Dr N. Yahalom-Mack).

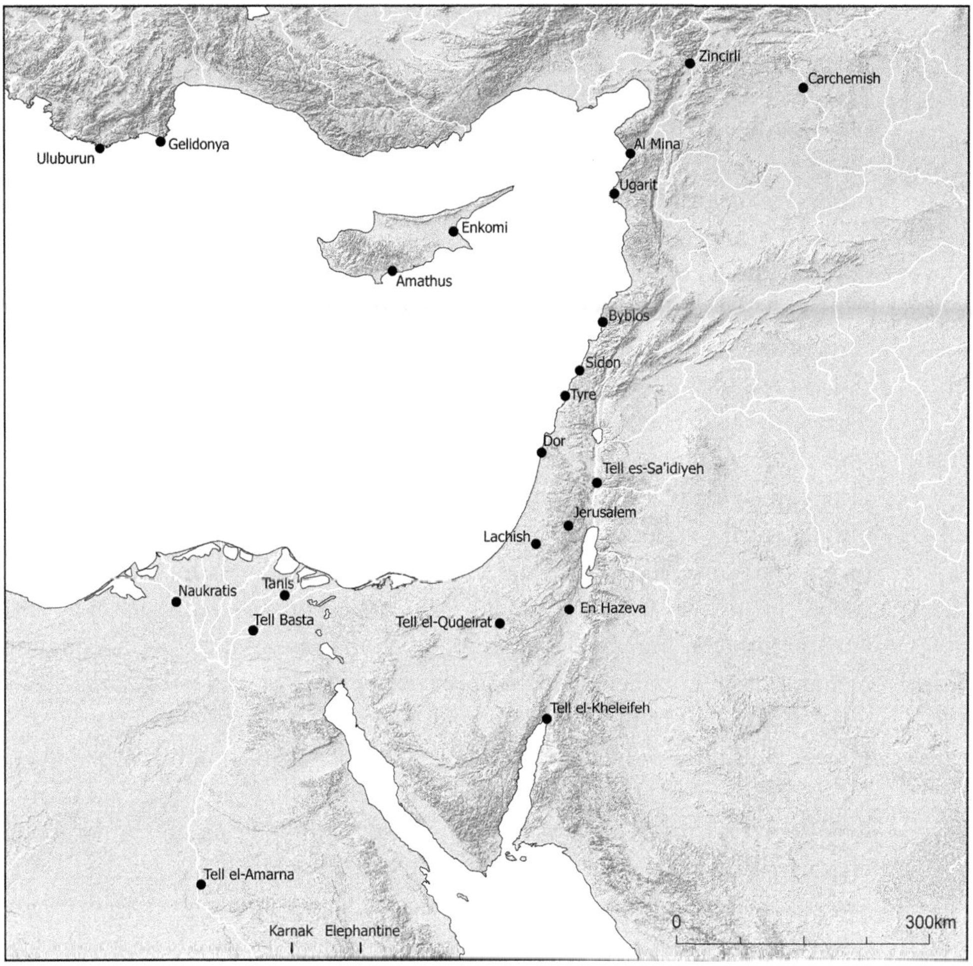

MAP 4.1 The Levant with sites mentioned in the text

4.1.2 Silver and Money in Late Bronze Age Ugarit

It is hard to think of any case that could serve as a better starting point in this than the northern Levantine port-city of Ras Shamra/Ugarit (see Map 4.1) with its rich archives that have preserved a vivid image of the city and its international contacts right up to its destruction in the early twelfth century. Fulfilling a central economic role in the international trade of the Late Bronze Age, Ugarit has been described as 'the hub of eastern Mediterranean trade'[10] and 'probably the first great international port',[11] prospering, in particular, under the so-called *Pax Hethitica*, following the Egyptian-Hittite peace treaty in 1259/1258 after the battle of Qadesh.

[10] Singer 1999, 647.
[11] Culican 1966, 46.

While appearing relatively absent from circulation and records in contemporary Kassite Babylonia and Middle Assyria, where gold and tin functioned as a standard,[12] references to silver in the archives of Ugarit are plentiful. In fact, value and exchange were much intertwined with the use and appreciation of silver in this city – tied to Mediterranean trade like no other – and this was inevitably coupled to the use of silver in Mediterranean trade. In what follows, the aim is not to give a systematic overview of the use of silver but rather to provide a selective discussion of the contexts in which silver was used and the significance it held.

Ample texts record the use of precious metal, most often silver, in trade. Particularly in international trade, silver was the primary commodity, weighed and its value assessed in standard weight-units (shekels, minas and talents). It was referred to as a unit of value and used as a means of exchange and, as such, can be seen as functioning on the basis of money-characteristics.[13] However, while silver certainly had a special and preferential status in trade transactions, it was not necessarily exclusive as a means of exchange in such contexts. We have transactions on record involving commodities in addition to silver, such as copper, oil, textiles and other goods in exchange for luxury items such as horses, but also for grain imports from Egypt.[14] Often, some of these goods complementing silver in transaction have been interpreted as *gifts* and regarded as a social supplement to the paid price, with silver qualified as a mere *commodity*.[15] However, as discussed in Section 2.2, such a strict distinction between certain goods identified as commodity and others identified as gift has an essentialist undertone – regarding silver in and of itself as a commodity and additional goods (e.g., textiles) as gift – that should not be taken for granted.[16]

In addition to the use of other goods in exchange alongside silver, sources also note prices and transactions wholly based on goods, such as grain, oil, textiles and copper/bronze.[17] Like silver, these were commonly used as a means of exchange and a unit of value in standard measures. Wool, for example, was measured on a special weight standard, apparently based on the theoretical weight of one sheep's shearing. Evidence for this sheep-fleece unit has been found across the eastern Mediterranean, and its standard likely functioned in relation to the weight systems that were employed across different regions, indicating that it was directly commensurable to other units of value.[18]

Copper was also used as a means of exchange, counted in shekels.[19] Its use in economic exchange had a long tradition in the Ancient Near East and is

[12] Oppenheim 1977, 86; Rosa 2011; Kleber 2016.
[13] Cf. McGeough 2007, 166–167, 199, 203–206.
[14] Cf. Singer 1999, 655–656, 671, 716.
[15] Peyronel 2014, 357–362, 370. Cf. Singer 1999, 716.
[16] Bachhuber 2018, 272–273.
[17] Cf. Heltzer 1999, 446–447; Singer 1999, 668; Fappas 2012.
[18] Zaccagnini 1999–2001, 48–54; Alberti and Parise 2005, 383–384; Breniquet and Michel 2014.
[19] Cf. Heltzer 1999, 451; Singer 1999, 668, 676; Jones 2007, 46.

particularly well attested in the Old Assyrian Period.[20] During the Late Bronze Age, it became an important if not a key commodity in international trade, circulating in the form of oxhide ingots as well as other objects, sometimes as a means of exchange in order to facilitate trade transactions.[21] Textual sources and archaeological data reflect both the use of copper in bulk transport and trade and in smaller quantities suitable for smaller-scale transactions.[22] The Uluburun and Cape Gelidonya shipwrecks (dated to the end of the fourteenth and thirteenth centuries BCE, respectively) carried large quantities of standardised copper ingots, while the latter in particular contained fragments of ingots and a particular type of slab ingot – possibly made in a standard weight of approximately 1 kg – found in the area of the 'captain's cabin' and thought to represent a form of currency.[23] Metallurgical research on ingots from the Uluburun ship, including the experimental production of ingots, suggests moreover that these were deliberately produced to have a high level of porosity, causing them to break easily into fragments for further use or processing.[24] In contrast to large ingots used in bulk trade, such fragments would have been more convenient for use in exchange, suggesting the possible use of copper in smaller transactions.

However, the suitability and use of copper in exchange does not necessarily contradict the singular importance attached to silver, as reflected in the textual record. Although copper was measured and recorded in the same units, silver was the more valuable metal, and the importance of both, but most significantly silver, is reflected by the widespread use of balance weights. By 1990, over 600 weights had been uncovered in excavations at Ugarit and of these the masses are known of 566. J.-C. Courtois has identified at least six different weight standards among these weights, befitting the international nature of the city's trade involvement. Of the known weights, more than half (314) correspond to the Ugaritic shekel of ca. 9.4 gram in denominations ranging from 1/8 to 3,000 shekels.[25] Although there are notably few textual references to the practical use of weights, it is likely that their use was so established and widely known, as to make further mention superfluous.[26] There are also various examples of ellipsis of the measure in texts, further testifying to the lack of need to specify the unit used.[27] Whoever conducted business in the city knew, or was sure to learn, how transactions were carried out.

20 Dercksen 1996.
21 Sherratt 2000; Jones 2007.
22 Singer 2006; Gestoso Singer 2013, 250–253.
23 Bass 1967, 82; 2010, 800; Singer 2006, 252–258; Gestoso Singer 2010; 2015, 102–111.
24 Hauptmann, Maddin and Prange 2002; Hauptmann, Laschimke and Burger 2016.
25 Courtois 1990; Pulak 1996, 25–48.
26 Monroe 2009, 55–56.
27 Heltzer 1999, 451; Singer 1999; 656, 668, 671–672, 716; and spec. Millard 2011, 41 with references.

The large numbers of balance weights found in both the Uluburun (149) and the Cape Gelidonya shipwrecks (67) confirm the interregional use-context of such weights.[28] These were used in carrying out different types of transactions across regions with precious metal at hand, as is also suggested by the presence of scrap gold and silver (coils, foils and small ingots) on the Uluburun ship.[29] Moreover, different regional weight systems of the Late Bronze Age, used from the Aegean to Mesopotamia, were integrated to the extent that valuables measured in different standards became commensurable, allowing the conversion of an amount from one system to the other. This integration demonstrates that weighing, most significantly of silver, was part and parcel of international trade in the Late Bronze Age.[30]

Aside from their use in trade, it is clear that precious metals had a special status in exchange. Although, as noted, silver in the Ancient Near East has been assigned 'to the sphere of subsistence/commodity', it has also been suggested that silver is featured in the context of gift exchange, albeit exclusively in the form of manufactured items.[31] There is indeed evidence for the circulation of silver and gold cups or vessels of standard weight and form as gifts, whereby the supposed singularity of the object, or its 'personality', rather than the material value of the silver is thought to have formed the basis of its value.[32] Without meaning to detract from the importance of international gift exchange in the Late Bronze Near East,[33] this distinction between silver as gift and silver as commodity carries the risk of circularity, whereby the exchange modality is identified on the basis of the type of goods involved in the exchange. We need to keep in mind, though, that silver 'objects' such as vessels could have functioned as well in economic or commercial exchanges.[34] Moreover, this distinction is at odds with the appreciation of silver, previously argued, for being both object and material at the same time.[35]

Moving beyond this dichotomy of silver as commodity or gift, its special significance is indicated by its prominent use in what are arguably blood compensations, or so-called *wergeld* payments. Such payments have been noted to be a profound characteristic of early forms of money,[36] and various examples can be identified in the texts from Ugarit. Several documents, for example,

[28] Pulak 1996; 2000; 2006; Alberti and Parise 2005, 387.
[29] Pulak 2008, 357–358; Gestoso Singer 2010, 265–272; 2015, 102–108.
[30] Pulak 1996; Alberti and Parise 2005; Alberti, Ascalone and Peyronel 2006.
[31] Peyronel 2014, 359.
[32] Zaccagnini 1991; Heltzer 1999, 445–447; Peyronel 2014, 357–360.
[33] See Zaccagnini 1973. Cf. Sherratt 2000, 83; Zangani 2016.
[34] Cf. Section 2.2; Bachhuber 2018, 272–273.
[35] See Sections 2.3 and 3.4.2.
[36] See Section 2.1; Grierson 1977.

testify to the existence as well as the enforcement of an accord between Ugarit and Carchemish that determines a price of three mina of silver to be paid as compensation for each merchant killed in the territory of the other.[37] As the perpetrators of the crime were often not known, responsibility lay with the ruler in whose territory the murder had taken place, and these cases were often settled under royal authority. In another lawsuit, the people of Apsuna, a northern town in the kingdom of Ugarit, are sentenced to a payment of one silver talent in recompense for killing the associates of the merchant Talimmu.[38]

Closely related to its use as compensation for a person's loss, silver was also used for buying, or redeeming people from captivity. One document notes that seven men from Ugarit, held by men from Beirut, were redeemed for the price of a hundred shekels silver;[39] another text records the payment of seventy shekels by the queen of Ugarit to a Hittite palace official for the redemption of 'her compatriot'.[40] Additional documents confirm the use of silver for the trade in slaves.[41] In general, it appears that silver was considered commensurable to, and an appropriate compensation for, a person's life.

Another interesting example of silver used as compensation is the case, documented in a series of texts, of the 'great sin' committed against the Storm-god of Sidon. Apparently, some citizens of Ugarit desecrated (part of) the temple of the god, causing a diplomatic riot. Itamar Singer's account of the affair suggests that while the Sidonians demand the stoning and impalement of the transgressors, the king of Sidon seems willing to settle the conflict by accepting as compensation for the offense a large monetary payment in addition to offerings for the gods to atone for the sins.[42] Offering an escape from what would have seemed like a certain and cruel death, the suggested payment would be a way to secure the lives of the offenders, while at the same time providing compensation for a moral transgression.

A rare instance where not silver but gold is documented to function as a blood price is provided by the affair of the so-called *bittu rabīti*, the estranged wife of the king of Ugarit, who was extradited at the cost of 1,400 golden shekels as part of what has been referred to as 'one of the most notorious scandals of antiquity'.[43] Ammiṯtamru II, king of Ugarit from 1260 to 1235, had married a princess from the neighbouring kingdom of Amurru, who is never called by her name but is variously denoted with reference to her royal

[37] Heltzer 1999, 440–441; Singer 1999, 651–652, 661.
[38] Singer 1999, 651–652; Monroe 2009, 173–176.
[39] Kienast 1979, 449–450; Singer 1999, 669, see also 652, 663–664.
[40] Singer 1999, 657.
[41] Heltzer 1999, 445; Singer 1999, 663–664, 673.
[42] Arnaud 1992, 189–191; Singer 1999, 670.
[43] Singer 1999, 680.

descent, such as the *bittu rabīti* ('daughter of the Great Lady'), referring to her mother who was a princess of Ḫatti. Although the circumstances are not specified, it is noted that she 'sought trouble for Ammiṯtamru', and the marriage did not hold, escalating into a diplomatic conflict of serious proportions. She was sent back to Amurru, but not long after, Ammiṯtamru came to demand her extradition, even threatening the use of force. Tensions were only dissolved with the intervention of the Hittite King Tudḫaliya IV, who was also her uncle, and a deal was struck to resolve the conflict. In the end, for his right to dispose of the *bittu rabīti* in any way he saw fit, Ammiṯtamru paid a blood price of 1,400 golden shekels to her brother Šaušgamuwa, the king of Amurru.[44] The use of gold as recompense, as well as the exceptional amount, should perhaps be understood as the superlative form of a blood price in silver, appropriate to the high profile of the individuals involved and the sensitive nature of the affair. In this extraordinary context, the use of gold, rather than silver, is the exception confirming the rule.

These examples of blood-money payments, and the near-exclusivity of silver as acceptable compensation for a person's life, provide insight into the value and significance of silver. In Ugarit, and specifically within the international relations it maintained, silver could be used as a form of *wergeld*. Moreover, its circulation in the form of gifts within the spheres of diplomacy and trade affirms its pertinence with regard to the multilateral relations that were maintained in the international world of the Late Bronze Age. Evidently, this provides insight into how silver was appreciated and the symbolic value with which it was associated. If silver could function as recompense for severe loss and moral transgression negatively affecting the relationship and trust between international players, then surely such compensation was perceived as a restoration and expression of that trust. From this perspective, it is particularly significant that the single most important peace agreement of the era, that between Ramesses II and Ḫattušili III following some sixteen years after the battle of Qadesh in 1259/1258, was originally inscribed on two silver tablets, one prepared in Hattusa and sent to the court of Ramesses II in Pi-Ramesse, in exchange for an Egyptian version moving in the opposite direction.[45] What could better represent the mutual restoration of trust between these two powers than the two-way exchange of silver tablets bearing the words of what is accordingly known as the Silver Treaty?

Silver was indeed a means of exchange suitable for trade but one that moreover had the significance and appropriate symbolic value to reinstate or affirm trust between those involved. Needless to say, such trust was essential in

[44] Singer 1999, 680–681, with references.
[45] Edel 1997; Van de Mieroop 2011, 222–223.

maintaining the multilateral relations that served as the basis for Ugarit's role and success in the international trade.

Towards the end of the Late Bronze Age and the fall of Ugarit in the early twelfth century, trust was indeed becoming a matter of increasing importance in maintaining stable trade relations. Prosperity under the *Pax Hethitica*, as is so evident from contemporary sources, also had adverse consequences in the form of robbery, theft and other security related issues.[46] The mobility of people and goods along trade routes in the eastern Mediterranean must have been under continuous strain from these perils, in particular, the murder and hijacking of merchants and travellers along these routes. The monetary compensations for the loss of life and property, and their common occurrence to judge by the regular textual references to the topic, imply that safety along trade routes was a serious matter that warranted diplomatic involvement. Apparently, murders and hijackings frequently took place, and for communities that were tied up with trade networks and whose livelihood was at least in part dependent on safe routes of transport, these were likely seen as a severe threat to the existing order. Agreements made between rulers with the purpose of preventing such mischief from destabilising trade and diplomatic relations, such as the treaty mentioned between Ugarit and Carchemish, indicate that this was a clear matter of concern to political elites. Legal cases were adjudicated and agreements ratified by the king or a representative, as is reflected by the case of the above-mentioned lawsuit of the merchant Talimmu that bears the seal of Ḫattušili III and Puduḫepa.[47]

Already in the Amarna letters, written around a century earlier, we can read that the murder of merchants was of special concern to rulers. Two letters, addressed by the king of Babylon to Akhenaten, bear witness to the robbery of caravans and the murder of merchants. In the latter, the king of Babylon calls upon Akhenaten to act against the murder of Babylonian merchants in Canaan, saying 'Canaan is your country and its kings are your servants .... Bring them to account and make compensation for the money they took away. Put to death the men who put my servants to death and so avenge their blood'.[48] However, compared to the more proactive involvement that developed under the *Pax Hethitica* and is exemplified by the noted agreement, the concern expressed in the Amarna letters appears to be of a more ad hoc character. In any case, the documents from Ugarit attest to a growing concern among rulers with stability and safety of movement along trade routes. As will be further discussed in Sections 4.1.3 and 4.1.4, this concern, and especially the

[46] Singer 1999, 651–652.
[47] Singer 1999, 651. See also Monroe 2009, 173–178.
[48] EA 7 and 8; Moran 1992, 16.

growing difficulties related to maintaining secure trade routes, formed a key factor in the increasing use of silver in transactions.

It should be pointed out that this concern for secure trade routes does not so much reflect a trade environment of independently operating entrepreneurial merchants but, as will be argued in Section 4.1.3, a system in which ruling houses had significant influence on the circumstances under which interregional trade was carried out. Although, in the end, their authority and power to enforce was relatively weak, they formed important power blocks and acted as patrons in the trade. As Routledge and McGeough explained, they did so by virtue of being 'the biggest household in a network of households',[49] but this was not the only reason. Ruling elites also wielded influence in accordance with their political status, but this political status was put under increasing pressure in the period to come.

4.1.3 *The End of the Late Bronze Age*

The increasing concern for safe trade routes and stable trade relations augurs the advent of an era in which such a trade environment was less and less taken for granted. With the destruction of the Late Bronze Age centres and the decline of the associated political order, long-distance trade networks came under severe pressure, resulting in their disintegration. It is significant in this regard that this period, starting towards the end of the thirteenth and especially during the twelfth century, witnessed a growing circulation of (precious) metal in the form of scrap (see below). Most likely, this suggests that metal, precious metal in particular, was increasingly employed as a form of money in the context of smaller-scale transactions.[50]

Who was responsible for initiating and/or picking up on this trend of increasing precious metal use in transactions is difficult to tell. As already mentioned in Section 3.4, Susan Sherratt has been one of several scholars to explain the collapse of the Late Bronze Age system as 'a replacement of the old centralized politico-economic orders by a decentralized economic system which steadily encroached from within or from the margins of the former', by the hands of initially marginal and therefore independent merchants or entrepreneurs who superseded the palace administration in its central economic function.[51] It is altogether possible that such entrepreneurial forces were, if not instrumental, at least involved in pushing the use of precious metal as money.[52]

[49] Routledge and McGeough 2009, 28–29.

[50] Sherratt 2000, 87–89; Singer 2006, 252–258; Gestoso-Singer 2010, 265–272; 2015; Moreno García 2016b, 15–20.

[51] Sherratt 1998, spec. 307. See also Muhly 1992; Artzy 1997; 1998; Liverani 2003, 128–137.

[52] Cf. Sherratt and Sherratt 1993, 361; Sherratt 2000, 87–88.

However, there are good reasons to reject a strict opposition between the palace and the merchant, between 'state' and 'private', and indeed the borders between different categories of actors and exchange modalities must have been rather fuzzy. Focusing on Late Bronze Age Ugarit, Bruce Routledge and Kevin McGeough have made a good case for the palace as the largest household, rather than the controlling institution and supreme authority, thereby rejecting an understanding of the twelfth century reality as one of two opposing classes.[53] Accepting this perspective, it becomes problematic to singularly identify the agents promoting the use of precious metal money with Sherratt's supposedly independent merchants as an outside force subversive to the system. Rather, it is possible that these forces not only came from within but would remain part of the decapitated and disabled old political order for the period to come. As will be noted further below, this explanation appears likely considering the presence of Iron I hoards in the New Canaan centres.[54]

However, regardless of the changing social organisation of the Late Bronze Age centres, and what role our reconstructions give to what group or social sector, it is clear that over the course of the twelfth century the larger-scale movement of people and destruction of urban centres damaged the already vulnerable control of the central authority.[55] Under the chaos and decline of authority, secure and stable trade relations, based in part on mutual trust and credit and formerly guaranteed and protected by the authority, were the first to suffer collapse. As mentioned, robberies already posed a continuous threat; it is likely that also piracy featured in this changing environment.[56]

This could have led to the increase in the physical use of metal in conducting trade and carrying out smaller transactions. In addition to its significance, the clear advantage of precious metal was that it was portable and could be hoarded, and as the reliance on precious metal for conducting transactions grew, hoarding became, within the new environment, an increasingly important strategy of insurance in the face of unstable trade relations.[57] The disruption of trade relations must have led to a fallback in premeditated trade ventures and a growing uncertainty concerning the supply in certain key trading commodities, such as copper and grain, that played an important part in bulk exchanges.[58] Letters from Ugarit, for example, already indicate increasing problems in the supply of grain by the late thirteenth century,[59] and these

[53] Routledge and McGeough 2009. See also Schloen 2001, spec. 252–254; Zangani 2016, 239–241. Cf. Monroe 2009, 151–205.
[54] See also Section 3.3.1.
[55] Joukowsky and Ward 1992; Cline 2014; Knapp and Manning 2016.
[56] Sherratt and Sherratt 1993, 366; Temin 2006, 149–151.
[57] Cf. Knapp, Muhly and Muhly 1988.
[58] Cf. Moreno García 2016b, 21–22.
[59] Singer 1999, 712, 715–719. Cf. Langgut, Finkelstein and Litt 2013, 165.

problems continued into the twelfth century, with soaring grain prices in Egypt during the latter half of the century.[60] Disruptions in the supply of such commodities would inevitably affect wider exchange mechanisms and communities' access to and ability to acquire a wider range of goods. At the same time, this must have put redistribution mechanisms within the patrimonial household, the dominant unit of social organisation,[61] under increasing pressure, threatening people's supply of a range of commodities, including basic subsistence needs. This collapse of trade relations and the related circumstances are likely to have stimulated a growing reliance on precious metal in conducting small-scale transactions. Because silver, also due to its status and significance, remained desirable, people could always resort to it in the context of exchange and in settling their debts.

Already around 1300 BCE, the presence of gold and silver jewellery, scrap, coils and ingots found together on the Uluburun shipwreck points to the need for an adjustable means of exchange in carrying out on-the-side trade transactions that were conducted by the ship's crew alongside the bulk trade represented by the ship's main cargo.[62] Around a century later, the above-mentioned interpretation of the smaller-type ingots and the many fragmented ingots on the Gelidonya wreck as a form of currency, as well as the presence of alloyed ingots, presumably produced themselves from scrap, reflect an increase in the use of scrap metal.[63]

Slightly later, dating to the time of the destruction of Ugarit, a series of precious metal hoards containing gold, silver and bronze excavated in the city suggest that by the early twelfth century, the cutting up of silver vessels, jewellery, coils and other ingots, to be used in transactions, as well as their hoarding, had become common practice.[64] None of these Ugarit hoards have been subject to detailed study, but of two of these, photos of a selection of the material were published at an early date, allowing for some tentative comparison to the hoards from the end of the LBA–Iron I transition, discussed in Chapter 3 (Beth Shean D, Megiddo D, Abel Beth Maacah). The first hoard, excavated in 1931 and found together with a limestone weight, consisted of

[60] Černý 1933; Janssen 1975, 551–552.

[61] Schloen 2001.

[62] Pulak 1988, 26; 2001, 24–25; 2008, 357–358; Sherratt 2000; Gestoso Singer 2010, 265–272; 2015, 102–108. A similar use can be suggested for the collection of gold jewellery, jewellery fragments and other scrap found together with a group of balance weights in the sea near the Yavne-Yam anchorage (Golani and Galili 2015).

[63] Bass 1967, 78, 81–82; 2008, 800; Sherratt 2000, 87–88; Singer 2006, 252–258; Gestoso Singer 2010; 2015, 102–111.

[64] Caubet and Yon 2001. Six of the hoards listed by Caubet and Yon contained scrap, jewellery and ingots; one excavated in 1931, two from 1934, one from 1937, one from 1960 (pt 2837) and one from 1962. Caubet and Yon note that the material from these hoards is divided between Paris, Aleppo and Damascus.

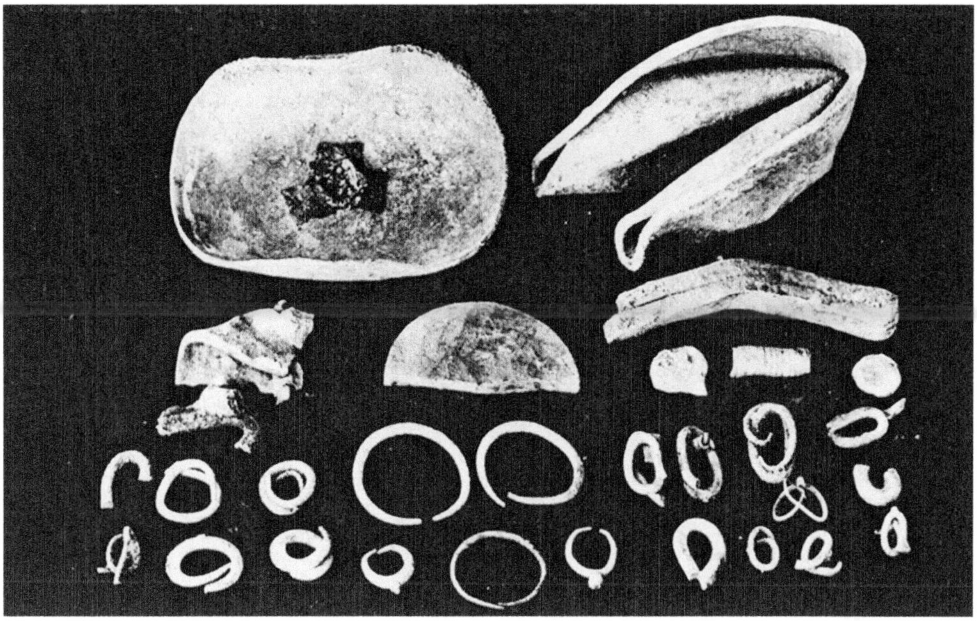

4.1 Silver objects from the 1931 hoard from Ugarit (After Schaeffer 1932, pl. 16.1, courtesy of Ifpo)

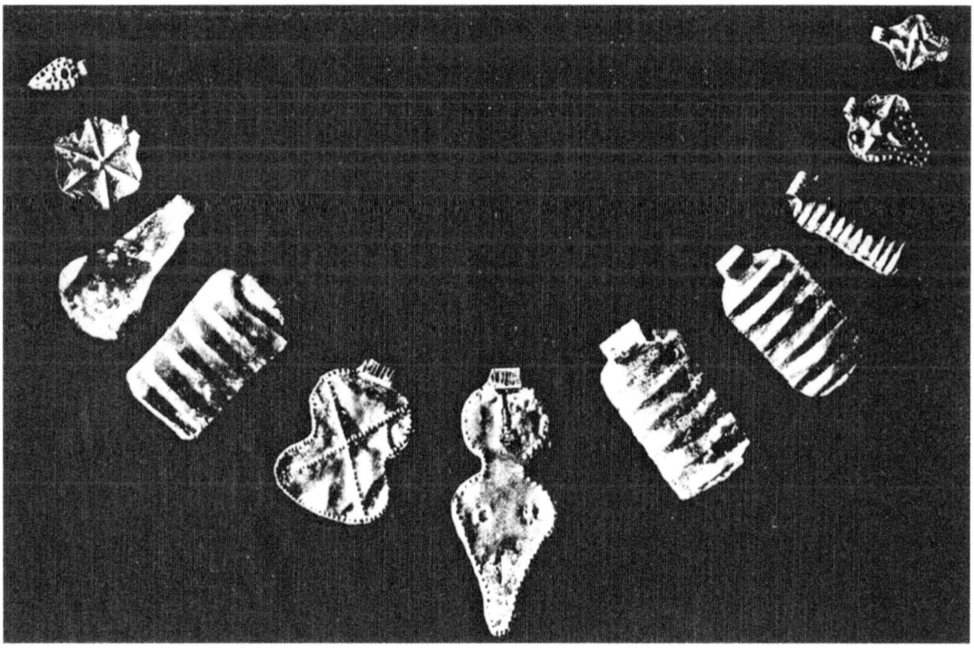

4.2 Gold pendants from the 1931 hoard from Ugarit (After Schaeffer 1932, pl. 16.2, courtesy of Ifpo)

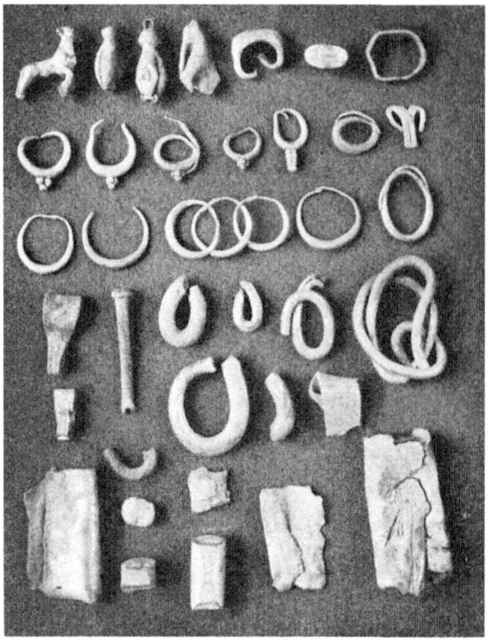

4.3 Objects from the 1934 hoard (RS 6.193) from Ugarit (After Schaeffer 1935, fig. 6, courtesy of Ifpo)

close to two kilos of silver and gold objects wrapped in textile and kept in a vase (Figures 4.1 and 4.2);[65] a hoard found in 1934 contained silver, gold and electrum objects of a total of 849 grams, kept in a jar (Figure 4.3).[66] Although the weight of both hoards is significantly higher than the somewhat later hoards from the southern Levant, when judging from the photos (Figures 4.1–4.3) the composition of the hoards in terms of the types of objects present appears very similar to the slightly later hoards from the southern Levant, containing a significant proportion of ornamental objects.[67] At the same time, however, it appears that the hoards from the southern Levant, dating to the latter half of the twelfth and perhaps the early eleventh century (Beth Shean D, Megiddo D), consist of relatively smaller, more fragmented objects, compared to the often large and less fragmented (if not complete) objects from the Ugarit hoards. Although we lack the data needed to calculate an average weight for these hoards, it would likely be higher than that of the hoards discussed in Chapter 3. This could suggest that the development postulated in Chapter 3, whereby precious metal objects were increasingly cut and broken into smaller pieces between the end of the LBA and the Iron I, can already be observed

[65] Schaeffer 1932, 22–23, pl. 16.1–2; Caubet and Yon 2001, 150–152.

[66] RS 6.193: Schaeffer 1935, 144–146, fig. 6; 1939, 42–44, fig. 31; Caubet and Yon 2001, 152–153.

[67] See Section 3.3.3; Appendix.

4.4 The Tell el-Amarna hoard as discovered in 1930 in a jar, covered by a bowl (Courtesy of the Egypt Exploration Society)

within the twelfth century. This appropriation of precious metal items and their fragmentation for the purpose of hoarding and exchange provides a clear confirmation for the suggested increase in the use of precious metal scrap.

This pattern is also reflected by contemporary evidence from Egypt. The circulation and even weighing of gold and silver ingots during the eighteenth dynasty is known from various sources, such as the annals of Thutmose III, a dedicatory relief in Karnak recording the booty from his campaigns in the Levant and the paintings in the tomb of Rekhmire.[68] Moreover, a large hoard from Tell el-Amarna, dating to the mid-fourteenth century and buried in a jar under a courtyard of a house in the Northern Suburb (Figures 4.4 and 4.5), provides direct evidence for this. Currently divided between Cairo and London, the hoard consisted of 23 gold and 2 silver bar ingots, a silver figurine and 93 pieces of coil, rings, ingots, sheet, and other scrap, adding up to a total of 3,375.36 grams of gold and 1,085.85 grams of silver.[69] Despite some small

[68] Sherratt and Sherratt 1991, 360–362; Gestoso Singer 2015, 89–90.

[69] Pendlebury 1931, 236, pl. 76; Frankfort and Pendlebury 1933, 59–61, pl. 43; Bell 1986; Kemp 2006, 315–317, fig. 110; 2012, 216–217, fig. 6; Vargyas 2010; Gestoso Singer 2013, 254–256. The number of objects is counted from the two photos in Frankfort and Pendlebury 1933, pl.

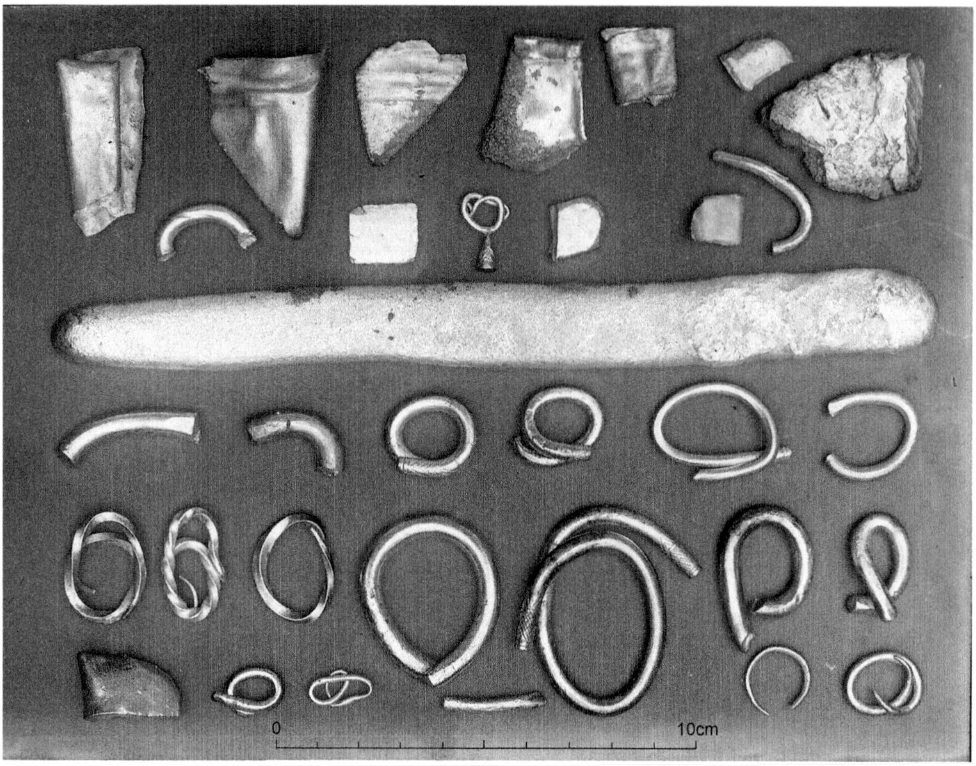

4.5 Selection of silver objects from the Tell el-Amarna hoard (Courtesy of the Egypt Exploration Society)

objects, the hoard mainly consists of sizable bar ingots and large pieces of coil, indicating a use of precious metal in substantial quantities.

In confirmation of what we have seen so far, the use of precious metal in large units changes markedly by the twelfth century, as is shown by the so-called Tell Basta treasure. It consisted of two hoards, discovered not far from one another in 1906.[70] The first hoard consisted of fine tableware, mostly exquisite vessels of silver, and some of gold, and contained a bowl with the cartouche of Twosret, the last pharaoh of the nineteenth dynasty (1191–1189 BCE). The second hoard was deposited in a heap, the lower part of which contained gold and silver vessels and exceptional pieces of golden jewellery. The top part consisted of silver jewellery, such as rings, bracelets, wires and pins, many bent or broken, pieces of (wrapped) sheet, ingots and other small scrap.[71] The cartouches of Merneptah (1213–1203 BCE) and Ramesses II (1279–1213 BCE) on torn and worn fragments of silver sheet provide a clear

43.4–5. Note, however, that Gestoso Singer (2013, 254) mentions 24 bars of gold and 95 other items.

70 Ogden 1990/1991; Lilyquist 2012; Jurman 2015, 57.

71 Lilyquist 2012, 14–20, 51–52, figs. 28–37, 63–65.

terminus post quem for the second hoard.[72] The jewellery and other silver items from this second hoard are not dissimilar from the two Ugarit hoards discussed above and the twentieth dynasty hoards from the southern Levant, considering the types of objects represented and the extent of their fragmentation, suggesting that these hoards are all related to a wider phenomenon in the eastern Mediterranean. While the possibility of a post-Ramesside date has been raised,[73] the *terminus post quem* after the nineteenth dynasty and the material resemblance to the other twelfth-century hoards suggest that a twentieth dynasty date is probable.

Whether dating to the twelfth century, or later still, the Tell Basta hoard provides clear evidence for the suggested trend of increasing use of precious metal (scrap) in transactions, and there is reason to assume that the circulation of silver further increases into the Third Intermediate Period (TIP; ca. 1069–664 BCE). An additional hoard from Tell Basta, discovered in 1992 and containing worn gold jewellery among other things, has been dated to the TIP on the basis of typology.[74] Moreover, the increased presence of silver in burials, such as known, for example, from the royal necropolis at Tanis and textual references to the use of silver in domestic exchange starting in that period, have provided basis for the assumption of a significant increase during TIP.[75] It is difficult, however, to deduce information regarding the circulation of silver from its use in funerary contexts and to generalise the available evidence for the whole period. We should therefore be cautious to conclude a net increase in silver during all of TIP.[76] At the same time, it should be emphasised that clear evidence for silver consumption in a period that is generally associated with economic decline is in itself indicative of the use and appreciation of silver.

Considering the evidence above, it is likely that the twelfth century proved a turning point in the Mediterranean Near East regarding the use of silver in exchange, and small-scale transactions in particular. I have argued that this change was related to changing power structures and the effects on trade relations and the way trade was conducted. Although the details of this development in the case of Egypt are uncertain and, moreover, not of primary concern here, the disintegrating power base of its rule provides a credible context for the increasing reliance on silver.

The effects of this political change on the southern Levant, where the rule of the twentieth dynasty gradually weakened in the course of the twelfth century

[72] Lilyquist 2012, 19, fig. 37.
[73] Jurman 2015, 57.
[74] Lilyquist 2012, 14; Jurman 2015, 57.
[75] Jurman 2015, 51–57, 61.
[76] Jurman 2015, 57.

until its retreat around 1130 BCE, can be observed in more detail.[77] It has long been recognised that LB IIB Canaan witnessed a concentration of wealth in important urban centres, mostly located in the lowlands, coupled with a general decline in the marginal areas.[78] Urban settlements that prospered during this period were located in lowland areas that stood under Egyptian colonial control and often featured within their colonial infrastructure, as they were located along important trade routes. This is reflected by the wide distribution and consumption of luxury goods and exotica in these centres. Although these were in part Egyptian imports, there were also local or Levantine products (or locally finished, using imported raw materials, such as glass) that referred to Egypt, indicating that these were status references.[79] However, the weakening of Egyptian rule and increasing disruption of trade routes, posed a threat to the supply of luxury goods and could have placed local elites under increasing pressure. This likely caused political fragmentation and led to a fall-out of second-tier settlements, as is illustrated by the case of Tell es-Saʿidiyeh, a trading outpost in the Jordan valley that suffered decline and isolation after the Egyptian retreat.[80]

Following the retreat of the Egyptians, several of the lowland centres show signs of relative continuity, in some cases being resettled after a short occupational gap. These New Canaan centres recovered from the political shock and destruction and prospered again in the Canaanite tradition as Iron I centres of the lowland and coastal areas.[81] As noted in Chapter 3, it is telling that the clear evidence posed by the Iron I hoards for the use and circulation of scrap silver as money, particularly for the purpose of carrying out small transactions, is found in these centres. Whether employed by remaining or returning elites, coping with the collapse of the social-political order, or perhaps competing elements, profiting from the same situation, the increasing use of silver money was certainly one of the more striking economic strategies associated with these centres.[82]

In contrast to the lowlands, Egyptian influence had been much weaker in the central highland and Transjordan.[83] This is reflected by the insecurity notably commented upon in the Amarna letters and blamed on the Apiru. As the economic context for those areas had been significantly different in the

77 Weinstein 1981, 17–23; 1992; Singer 1988–1989; 1994, 284–295; Ussishkin 1995; Knapp and Manning 2016, 135.

78 Bienkowski 1989. Cf. Knapp 1989; Bunimovitz 1994, 193–202.

79 Liebowitz 1987; Lilyquist 1996; Heymans and Van Wijngaarden 2011, 30–31.

80 Green 2009, 86–87, 90.

81 Finkelstein 2003. Cf. Fantalkin 2008b, 29; Gadot 2008; Bunimovitz and Lederman 2011, 45–47.

82 See Section 3.4.

83 Bienkowski 1989, 59.

LB IIB, we see neither the continuity known from the New Canaan centres, nor the associated use of silver in these regions.

Altogether, the rising use of precious metal, in particular, silver, as money in the southern Levant was an inheritance of the Mediterranean Near Eastern world of the Late Bronze Age, associated with the former LBA lowland centres, such as Megiddo and Beth Shean, which sat on important trade routes. Paradoxically, the collapse of this Late Bronze Age world and the associated trade networks propelled the use of silver money into practice, as it enabled people to maintain exchange relations and acquire needed goods. Consequently, silver became a profound characteristic of the Iron Age.

Much later, the biblical text would come to use the term 'Canaanite' in various instances to refer to a merchant. Hosea, for example, rejects 'a trader [*k^{e}na ʿan*] who holds false scales in his hand'.[84] Although such references might well reflect Phoenician trade activity, it is not impossible that this designation at the same time preserves a memory that associated trading activities and the use of cash with the former Canaanite centres.

4.1.4 *The Report of Wenamun*

The changes that took place in the economic reality of the southern Levant from the Late Bronze Age to the Iron Age, the effects this had on the way trade was conducted and the importance of precious metal money in this context, can be illustrated by looking at one of the rare written sources to shed light on interregional trade in the Levant during the Iron I: the Report of Wenamun. This Egyptian text, known from a single copy, is preserved on a damaged two-sheet papyrus found in an illicit excavation in El-Hiba in Middle Egypt in 1891–1892 together with two other papyri and is currently located in the Pushkin Museum in Moscow (Pap. Moscow 120). Written in hieratic, it describes the voyage of Wenamun, a priest of Amun at Karnak, to Byblos in order to acquire lumber for the barge of Amun. The opening line of the text dates the events to the twentieth to twenty-first dynasty transition – that is, the early eleventh century.[85] A short recap is relevant for further discussion.

At the beginning of the text, Wenamun is sent off by Smendes (the ruler of lower Egypt) on a ship of a Levantine captain, departing from Tanis in the Nile delta. His first stop is Dor – mentioned as a town of the Tjeker (i.e., the Sikel – one of the Sea Peoples) – where he is robbed by someone from his ship. The thief takes one golden and four silver vessels and a bag of silver of a total of 'five

[84] Hs. 12:8; Elat 1979, 529–530. See also Isa 23:8; Ezek 17:4; Zeph 1:11; Prov 31:24.
[85] Wente 2003, 116.

deben of gold and thirty-one *deben* of silver'.[86] Wenamun then complains to the ruler of Dor, asking him to use his authority and get him his money back. Beder, the prince of Dor, refuses to take responsibility though, saying that the thief did not belong to his land.

Next, passing Tyre (the text is damaged here), Wenamun reaches Byblos, where its ruler, Tjekerbaal, repeatedly tries to make him leave. Only after a month does he manage to gain an audience with Tjekerbaal, and a long scene between the two is played out. When they arrive to the purpose of his visit, Wenamun explains that he has come to fetch lumber for the barge of Amun. Invoking Byblos' tradition in supplying the Egyptians with wood, he says 'What your father did and what your father's father did, you will also do.'[87] However, Tjekerbaal refuses and replies, 'They did in fact supply it. You have but to pay me for supplying it, and I will supply it.'[88]

Wenamun is thus forced to write to Smendes, requesting that he sends a payment, and only when a shipment from Egypt arrives, does Tjekerbaal order men to fell the trees. Wenamun now attempts to depart for Egypt with the timber, but being pursued by the Tjeker, he is blown off course and arrives in Alashiya. There, he is almost killed by the townsmen, but the princess of the town takes him in. This is where the text is cut off.

The report of Wenamun has elicited an extensive bibliography, with a wide range of issues – the nature of the text, its dating, language, orthography, political context, historical value and ideological/theological message – evoking scholarly debate and suggestions on these matters varying significantly. Recent contributions have covered much of these debates,[89] and although there is no need to repeat any of this (nor would this necessarily be the place), it is worthwhile to make reference to the current standing of the debate on some of these issues.

Following the work of Černý, the text was generally assumed to be an administrative report, providing ground for its use as a primary historical source.[90] However, this consensus was challenged most influentially by Helck, who interpreted the text as a literary fiction dating to the twenty-second dynasty,[91] and the composition is now generally characterised 'as a work of literature cast in the form of a documentary text' or a 'simulated report'.[92] The text and composition (depending on whether it concerns a copy) have been dated from the early twenty-first to the twenty-second dynasty, but

86 1.12. All translations are taken from Wente 2003.

87 2.4–5.

88 2.5–6.

89 Sass 2002b; Schipper 2005; Winand 2011.

90 Černý 1952, 21–22.

91 Helck 1986.

92 Baines 1999; Egberts 2001. See Sass 2002b, 247–248; Schipper 2005, 23–40; Winand 2011, 451–453. Cf. Galán 2005, 134–173.

palaeographical[93] and linguistic evidence have been shown to point to a later *terminus post quem*, not prior to the mid-twenty-first dynasty.[94] The same has been argued on the basis of its ideological context.[95]

With regard to the ideological, political or religious message of the text, various ideas have been presented.[96] Most commentators however agree that the unfortunate situations with which Wenamun is confronted, his inability to command respect from his antagonists and his difficulties in achieving the purpose of his journey, reflect the dire standing of Egypt in the international world and the implications of this position on its trade interests. In fact, as Wenamun rightly points out, Byblos had long been an important partner to Egyptians' foreign interests, offering the Egyptians a secure supply of cedar wood. Focusing on the Late Bronze Age, evidence indicates that various Egyptian kings imported cedar from the Lebanon.[97] The political importance of these imports is reflected by a monumental relief of Seti I in Karnak, showing the felling of trees by Lebanon subjects under the supervision of an Egyptian official.[98] Clearly, Egypt's ability to procure timber from the Lebanon should be understood here – and elsewhere – as representing its power in the world. As late as Ramesses IX, in the late twelfth century, there is evidence for Egyptian use of Lebanon cedars.[99]

Whether these imports were the result of an Egyptian prerogative to Lebanon cedars or simply a trade deal, perhaps based on credit or in exchange for political or military backing, luxury goods or grain, this relation with the rulers of Byblos was apparently suspended in the eleventh century. With the collapse of the centralised authority in Egypt at the end of the twentieth dynasty, evidence for Egyptian influence and control in the southern Levant and Phoenician littoral declines significantly,[100] and it is only from the start of the twenty-second dynasty that Egypt reasserted its imperial ambitions abroad. Sheshonq I's campaign to Asia in the second half of the tenth century, presumably aiming – among other reasons – to secure its economic interests in the Faynan copper region,[101] might have been the first step in this new

[93] H. Goedicke, for example, noted that the palaeography points to the twenty-second dynasty, but considered the text to be a later copy of an original administrative document (1975, 7–9).

[94] Ben-Dor Evian 2011, 97; Winand 2011; 546–549. Cf. Ben-Dor Evian 2017, 37–38.

[95] Helck 1986; Sass 2002b, 250–251; Schipper 2005, 315, 317–318.

[96] See Sass 2002b, 249–250.

[97] Meiggs, 1982, 61–67; Tyldesley 1996, 144; Panagiotopoulos 2006, 380–387.

[98] Meiggs 1982, 324.

[99] Ben-Dor Evian 2011, 95.

[100] Ben-Dor Evian 2011; 2017, 31–35. Dor forms an exception to this decline, with ceramic evidence for Egyptian commercial contacts continuing between the end of the twentieth and the twenty-second dynasty (Waiman-Barak, Gilboa and Goren 2014; Gilboa 2015).

[101] Fantalkin and Finkelstein 2006. Cf. Münger and Levy 2014, 748–749, 758–759.

policy. The increase in Egyptian pottery observed in early Iron IIA strata beyond the coast provides an indication of its growing influence.[102] The presence of a stele bearing the name of Sheshonq I in Megiddo, and statues of him and his successors Osorkon I and II (ruling until the mid-ninth century) in Byblos, testify to the reinstatement of Egyptian influence and even authority.[103]

It has been convincingly argued that a date for the composition of the text in the early twenty-second dynasty would plausibly fit this negative image of the preceding era characterised by a lack of Egyptian authority. Benjamin Sass explains that 'when Wenamun sets sail he knows that he is thrown on his own resources; he cannot expect Egyptian backup, military or diplomatic, en route. Emphasizing this woeful situation makes ample sense if it has since been remedied, if it can be contrasted with the glorious present'.[104]

However, the report also offers a telling insight into the trade environment of the preceding period. The trade environment in which Wenamun operates was not merely a negative fantasy conjured up in the late tenth century for ideological reasons. Its message was likely rooted in historical memory[105] or at least provides us with a historically relevant commentary on the period. Wenamun's lack of success shows that without the political presence and power to enforce, Egyptian credit was not worth much in international trade. In a trade environment lacking centralised authority and plagued by insecurity, money – in the form of precious metal – was required in order to acquire goods; Wenamun's dependence on money, provoked from the onset by its theft, confirms its importance in carrying out transactions and its pertinence to the sphere of trade.[106] To judge from the way money was framed in the story, one could think that the author of the story had a negative view of its use, associated with an economic reality shaped by insecurity and Egypt's lack of power abroad.

Alternatively, emphasising the commercial aspect of trade, Glenn Markoe has suggested that 'the era of Wenamun is one in which international trade is conducted by joint enterprises between state-sponsored shipping firms'.[107] However, the interactions between Wenamun and the rulers of Dor and Byblos give no such impression. Wenamun is on his own, and his claim to represent the king of Egypt appears of little relevance to or added value in the purchase of timber. The only thing that seems to have mattered was whether he was able and willing to pay for his order in cash.

102 Ben-Dor Evian 2011.
103 Ben-Dor Evian 2011, 96–97, 112; 2017, 35–36.
104 Sass 2002b, 251.
105 Ben-Dor Evian 2017, 37–38.
106 Jurman 2015, 61.
107 Markoe 2000, 27–28.

It has also been argued that Wenamun represents a clash between two economic worlds – a commercial one and a diplomatic, or tribute-based world.[108] However, such an interpretation, emphasising the opposition between two systems, implies that these are mutually exclusive and ignores the importance of commercial aspects in Late Bronze Age trade.[109] Moreover, as argued here, the story reflects not so much the absence of a 'tribute system' but the idea that where authority as the basis for maintaining stable trade relations lacked, trade agents would resort to the use of cash in exchange as the basis for trust.

This perspective on the increasing use of money and cash also has bearing on an issue that was raised before, the supposed revolutionising effect of money on society.[110] While we have observed an increase in the use of precious metal in trade and transaction from the Late Bronze Age into the Iron Age (the late thirteenth to early eleventh century), there is no basis to suggest that the stronger presence of money during the Iron I period did in itself bring about a revolution in the economy or stimulated further monetisation. Rather, changes in the trade environment and the sphere of exchange were a result of the collapse of a stable and secure trading network, following the decline of central authority.

The context of money-use in the Report of Wenamun suggests that money was required for carrying out transactions within this changing trade environment because the decline in stable trade patterns raised the need for money. As illustrated by the case of Wenamun, money was used where trade had previously been based on credit relations between familiar and credible partners. In other situations, the breakdown in regular trade relations based on the exchange of goods caused people to resort to precious metal money as the new ad hoc mode of exchange that allowed them to acquire needed goods in absence of a regular and premeditated supply through an established network.

4.2 SILVER MONEY IN THE IRON IIA–B

4.2.1 Money in the Biblical Record

As silver came to be increasingly used as money, control over its circulation and extraction for the purpose of hoarding would become a focus of the emerging states in the southern Levant. This enabled the political elite to organise resources and centralise wealth under its control. Historical evidence

108 Monroe 2005, 155; Gestoso Singer 2013, 257–258.
109 Cf. Section 2.2.
110 See Section 2.1.

for this during the Iron IIA and B periods (ca. 950–650 BCE) is provided by various written sources, most prominently the Hebrew Bible. Before turning to the historical evidence for money-use in this period, we will first look at what the biblical record can tell us in general about the use of money and in what way, using what terms, it does so.

Previous scholarship has often uncritically referred to biblical terms as a confirmation of the Iron Age reality concerning money-use, and it is the purpose of this section to assess the extent to which the biblical record actually reflects Iron Age money. It is important to keep in mind in this regard that some of the relevant verses were likely composed at a late or post-exilic date (i.e., during the Persian and early Hellenistic periods), although this does not necessarily rule out a potential earlier (i.e., Iron Age) use of the language.

Denying of the existence of money as such in the Iron Age, Raz Kletter boldly claims that 'the Old Testament does not even have a term for money', but only for silver (*kęsęp̄*).[111] Following the same reasoning, the ancient Greeks did not have a term for money either, only for wealth (πλοῦτος), riches or treasure (κειμήλιον) and coinage (νόμισμα). The plural term generally used for money (χρήματα) also means goods or things (sg. χρῆμα), and the term for a piece of silver/money or cash (ἀργύριον) is directly related to the word for silver, yet it could hardly be suggested that because the Greeks did not have a singular and exclusive term for money, they experienced difficulties in referring to it.[112] With regard to the Hebrew Bible the matter is plain: there is a term for money, but it happens to be the same as the term for silver.

In few instances is the use of silver as *wergeld* recorded in the Bible. In one instance, a *kikar* (talent) of silver is mentioned as recompense for losing a prisoner.[113] Another passage in 2 Kings 12 refers to '*kęsęp̄ ašam wekęsęp̄ ḥaṭaôt*' (כֶּסֶף אָשָׁם וְכֶסֶף חַטָּאוֹת);[114] these terms have not been fully clarified, but they translate as guilt-money and sin-money and are likely related to offerings in the temple. Based on a comparison of the latter term with the description of sin-offerings in Leviticus 4, the suggestion has been made that the 2 Kings 12 verse could be a post-exilic insertion.[115] The possibility that it has a pre-exilic origin cannot, however, be discounted. Additionally, a *wergeld* function for silver is also attested in eighth-century Babylonia, where monetary transactions for the ransoming and selling of prisoners are attested in the Nippur archive.[116]

[111] Kletter 1998, 148. See Section 3.1.1.
[112] Von Reden 1995, 173–175; 2010, 6–8; Schaps 2004, 16–17; Seaford 2004, 16; Gangutia 2011.
[113] 1 Kgs 20:39.
[114] 2 Kgs 12:17.
[115] Gray 1970, 587–588.
[116] Jursa 2016, 65. Cf. Schmid 2014.

Contrary to the possible *wergeld* function, biblical references to the use of silver in exchange and as a unit of value are abundant, also in pre-exilic sources. Commonly, this appears as the formula (amount-) weight-silver, that is, *šęqęl kęsęp̄* (שֶׁקֶל) or *kikar kęsęp̄* (כִּכַּר) (cf. 2 Sam 24:24, where this is turned around), indicating that the shekel was the unit and that silver was measured by means of its weight. In some cases, however, only an amount of silver is noted, and the weight-unit is omitted.[117] Such an ellipsis of measure is common in the Ancient Near East and can be found in various documents. The shekel was well known as a weight unit across the Ancient Near East, and there was little reason to mention it every time.[118] Alternatively, there are few cases where only the measure, the weight, is mentioned and the silver omitted.[119] It is obvious, though, that silver is meant: in the case of 2 Kings 7, these verses refer back to the preceding chapter where the prices during the famine in Samaria are mentioned in silver.[120]

It is clear that in the context of exchange, silver was measured by weight.[121] This is indicated by the various references to the act of weighing out the silver.[122] When Jeremiah buys the field in Anatot from his cousin Ḥanamel, he weighs out seventeen shekels of silver for him.[123] Demonstrating the legitimacy of the transaction, he describes in detail how he carried out the transaction: he signed the contract and weighed the silver out on a scale in front of witnesses (*wā ʾęšqol hakęsęp̄ bᵉmoʾznāyim* – וָאֶשְׁקֹל הַכֶּסֶף בְּמֹאזְנָיִם).[124] The importance of weighing in measuring silver and determining value is moreover suggested by the moral rejection of the use of false scales that can be read in the work of eighth-century prophets, as well as in the law of Deuteronomy.[125]

Also pointing to the weighing of silver are the many interrelated fractions referred to throughout the biblical text, the smallest of which was the *gerah* and the largest the *kikar*.[126] While a *kikar* consisted of 3,000 shekels, a shekel consisted of 20 *gerah* or, as has been argued on the basis of evidence from a seventh-century Hebrew ostracon from Kadesh Barnea, 24 *gerah*, meaning that this fraction had a weight of around half a gram.[127]

117 Gen 20:14–16; 37:28; 45:22; 1 Sam 13:21; 18:11–12; 2 Kgs 6:25; Zech 11:12–13; Nam 2012, 167–168.
118 Millard 2011, 40–42; Kleber 2016, 50–51. Cf. Redford 1992, 305.
119 2 Kgs 7:1, 16.
120 2 Kgs 6:25.
121 See also further in this section.
122 E.g., Lev 19:35–36; 1 Kgs 20:39; Zech 11:12; Prov 11:1; 16:11; 20:23.
123 Jer 32:9.
124 Jer 32:10.
125 Hos 12:8; Amos 8:5; Micah 6:10–11; Deut 25:13–15.
126 See De Vaux 1961, 203–206; Powell 1992; Kletter 1998, 93–107.
127 Kletter 1998, 108–117. This division of the shekel is also recorded in the Talmud, where it is suggested that the weight of the shekel was increased by a sixth (see Tos. B. Batra 90a).

In addition to the known fractions, there are several other biblical terms that appear to be connected to money. The phrase *ʾăḡôraṯ kęsęp̄* (אֲגוֹרַת כֶּסֶף) is mentioned once,[128] the context of which seems to imply that it concerns a small quantity. Its relation to Semitic terms for wages, such as Akkadian *igru*, is known and points to a meaning as small payment.[129] The term has, however, been regarded by many as signifying a particular weight unit, presumably based on the Septuagint's (LXX – the Hellenistic translation of the Hebrew Bible) use of *obolos*, a small coin or unit, although no additional reasons are offered for this interpretation.[130]

Bęṣaʿ kęsęp̄ (בֶּצַע כֶּסֶף) has been claimed to be the biblical term for money itself.[131] The word *bęṣaʿ* means something that is cut or severed, and the phrase in Judges 5 appears to be a straightforward reference to the cut and broken silver that is attested archaeologically. Its common use in the Bible carries the meaning of gain or greed,[132] which might well have been derived from the use of cut and broken silver in the Iron Age. Nonetheless, the conjunction with silver appears only once in the biblical record, in the poetic context of the Song of Deborah ('the kings of Canaan fought ... but took no *gain/spoil of silver*'),[133] and this hardly seems like sufficient ground to conclude that it was the standard biblical term for money or even that it had any practical use.

Another term connected to exchange is the word *qᵉśîṭa* (קְשִׂיטָה),[134] which occurs in three locations. In both Genesis 33:19 and Joshua 24:32 we are told that Jacob bought a plot of land in Shechem from the sons of Hamor, the father of Shechem, for a hundred *qᵉśîṭa*. Joshua 24 adds that Joseph was buried on that plot of land.[135] Its use in buying a plot of land, together with the mention of a quantity, implies that it concerns a unit of exchange. The term is again used in the final chapter of Job where everyone gives Job one *qᵉśîṭa* and one golden *nezem*.[136] Although ancient translations generally use words for 'lamb' or 'sheep' – that is, ἀμνάς in the LXX, and *ḥôrp̄an* in the Targum Onqelos and Targum Yonatan (both dating to the Roman period) – it has

128 1 Sam 2:36.

129 Koehler et al. 1996, 10.

130 I.e., Kletter 1998, 97, with references.

131 Judg 5:19; Golani and Sass 1998, 60–61; Kletter 1998, 148; Gitin and Golani 2001, 36; Gitler and Tal 2020, 37.

132 I.e., Gen 37:26; Exod 18:21; 1 Sam 8:3; Isa 33:15 etc.

133 Judg 5:19.

134 I am greatly indebted to professor Ran Zadok for sharing his comments, ideas and expertise on the topic.

135 Although the late date of Joshua 24 is known, attaching a date to the use of the term remains problematic. Genesis 33:19 could have been earlier (perhaps part of the Jacob cycle, but see Finkelstein and Römer 2014, 327), in which case Joshua 24:32 could be a copy; it could also have been inserted later to provide a pretext for the use in the late Joshua 24.

136 Job 42:11.

been interpreted as an archaic weight unit used as money.[137] This assumption, however, lacks any further basis. Alternatively, it has been linked to the Hebrew words *qyšut* (קִשּׁוּט – ornament) and *takšyṭ* (תַּכְשִׁיט – jewel), thereby claiming that it denoted a jewellery currency.[138] Although this seems attractive as an explanation for the presence of jewellery in Iron Age silver hoards,[139] it is based on a casual but incorrect reading and transliteration of the Hebrew, as *qšyth* or *qeshitah* (with a *shin* instead of a *sin*), and cannot be accepted. Biblical Hebrew *sin*, while corresponding to *samech* in Mishnaic Hebrew, does not interchange with *shin*, and the link with words for ornament or jewel is therefore baseless.

Koehler et al. note that the etymology is uncertain but refer to the suggestion offered in Levy, relating it to the Arabic *qisṭ* (part, portion) from *qasaṭa* (to divide, measure).[140] This has been picked up by Thompson, who sees in 'portion' a welcome description of some of the supposedly pre-portioned[141] silver ingots in the hoards.[142] However, this interpretation has also been rejected on the basis of methodology, because the Hebrew *ś* (of *qᵉśiṭa*) should correspond phonetically to Akkadian and Arabic *š*, rather than *s*, as in *qisṭ*.[143] Suggesting a link with Akkadian *kašāṭu* (to take off, to cut off) and building on the Greek and Aramaic translations as sheep or lamb, Lipiński argues for an interpretation as 'shearling' or sheep kept for wool, with the semantic association based on the shearing (taking off) of the wool. In addition to the evidence for the existence of a wool or sheep-fleece unit in the Late Bronze Age, as well as the Neo-Babylonian period,[144] a relevant parallel for this unit could be found in the example of King Mesha of Moab, who paid an annual tribute to the king of Israel in lambs and wool.[145] If this reading is correct, *qᵉśiṭa* is likely to be understood as an archaizing term,[146] reflecting a deliberate attempt to legitimise the acquisition of the plot of land by Jacob by making it appear old and thus authentic.

Similarly archaizing is the term *nezem* (נֶזֶם), which can denote a nose-ring as well as an earring. Various late references indicate that it functioned as a common piece of jewellery that was suitable for giving, either as a gift or

137 De Vaux 1961, 204, 207; Koehler 1996, 1150; Kletter 1998, 97; Gitler and Tal 2020, 40, n. 15. Cf. Schaps 2004, 227.

138 Golani and Sass 1998, 60, 77; Kletter 1998, 97.

139 Golani and Sass 1998.

140 Levy 1924, 396; Koehler et al. 1996, 1150.

141 Cf. Section 3.2.4.

142 Thompson 2003, 74; 2009, 605. Cf. Williamson 1894, 14. Note again the incorrect transliteration as *kešitah* (Thompson 2003, 74; 2009, 605).

143 Lipiński 1988, 131–132; R. Zadok, personal correspondence.

144 See Section 4.1.2; Bongenaar 1999, 169–170.

145 2 Kgs 3:4.

146 Cf. De Vaux 1961, 204, with regard to Job 42:11.

token of exchange,[147] or as a contribution made individually by members of the community for a communal good – an archaising rendition of a tax.[148] Aaron, for example, casts the golden calf, after having commanded the people to take all the *nizmê hazāhāḇ* (the golden rings) from the ears of their wives, sons and daughters and bring them to him.[149] Similarly, Gideon asks the people to each give him a *nezem* from the spoils of the Midianites, and with the proceeds (a total of 1,700 shekels) he makes the *ephod*, a part of the priestly attire.[150]

Also in this case, there has been an attempt to identify objects from hoards with a term from the biblical record. Yeivin has identified a type of earring present in the Eshtemoa hoard as a *nezem*,[151] but why this particular type of earring rather than any other type of ring should qualify as the biblical *nezem* remains unclear. Evidence for the association between jewellery and the use of silver money in the Iron Age has been duly noted,[152] although, as we have seen, not always for the correct reasons. There are, moreover, many ethnographic and historical parallels, testifying to the use of rings as a token of exchange and payment and as a store of value.[153] Not incidentally, biblical references to such use can be linked specifically to stories that were meant to appear as if from a distant past and were likely used as part of a deliberate attempt by the biblical authors to fashion these pre-conquest traditions in a constructed ancient reality.

This survey shows that the use of money in the form of weighed silver is evidently present in the biblical record, in pre- as well as post-exilic sources. It also points out that the eager search in the biblical text for terms that could match the archaeological reality of the Iron Age has in several cases led to wishful, rather than attentive reading. Previous scholarship has sought to link terms such as *bęṣaʿ kęsęp̄*, *qᵉśîṭa* and *nezem* to the material culture of the silver hoards, but a critical reading of these terms has indicated that, as always, caution is required in associating material remains of the past with biblical sources.

147 Gen 24:22, 30; Job 42:11. Note that in Gen 24:22 the weight of the *nezem* is accounted for.

148 Exod 32:2–4; 35:20–22, 29; Judg 8:24–26.

149 Exod 32:2–4. There are good reasons to believe that this example, as well as the one in Exodus 35, describing the collection of contributions for the temple, is post-exilic in date (Watts 2011, 417–430. Cf. Propp 2006, 565–578). Moreover, it brings to mind a story recorded by the fourth century historian Ephorus about the Corinthian tyrant Periander, who dedicated a golden statue at Olympia after collecting jewellery from Corinthian women in order to obtain the required gold (Ephor. *FGrH* 70 F 178 = Diog. Laert. 1.96).

150 Judg 8:24–26.

151 Yeivin, 1990, 52, 56.

152 See also Chapters 2 and 3.

153 Cf. Graham-Campbell 1982, 33; Balmuth and Thompson 2000, 165.

4.2.2 *States and Tributes*

The biblical record, and in particular the book of Kings, is an important source, however, for the political history of the kingdoms of Israel and Judah and can shed additional light on the importance of money in the organisation and centralisation of resources in the Iron Age society of the southern Levant. As suggested in Section 3.4, it is likely that as part of a growing central authority in the form of emerging states, political elites (i.e., the royal court) managed to take advantage of the circulation of silver money in order to control the organisation of resources and meet their increasing needs. We will next turn to evidence for that.

Most direct evidence for the levy of monetary taxes in the biblical record is generally regarded as part of the Priestly code, and of a late, post-exilic date.[154] Interestingly, in these cases the tax is calculated in the 'holy shekel' (*šęqęl haqoḏęš* – שֶׁקֶל הַקֹּדֶשׁ). Usually understood as referring to a standard weight kept in the temple, this particular unit appears only in the Priestly code in the Pentateuch and in Ezekiel and is conspicuously absent from Deuteronomistic works.[155] It is therefore considered to be a later, post-exilic (i.e., Persian period), unit.[156] An earlier example of taxation relates how King Menahem of Israel gave a tribute of one thousand silver talents to Tiglath-Pileser III (mentioned as *p̄ûl*), which he raised by imposing on all the wealthy Israelites (*gibôrê haḥayil* [גִּבּוֹרֵי הַחַיִל] – those belonging to the wealthy class, or landowners) a tax of fifty shekels each.[157] This tribute is confirmed by two Neo-Assyrian inscriptions (see Table 4.1).[158] It has been pointed out that this would imply that there were 60,000 wealthy people (or households) that contributed, already a considerable part of the population, presuming a high degree of monetisation in eighth-century Israel.[159] Alternatively, Cogan and Tadmor suggest that part of 'the payment came from the royal treasury, with the remainder exacted from the men of means'.[160] Although the generic number of a thousand talents could well have been inflated, the fact that imposing a tax would have raised at least part of a considerable tribute indicates that there must have been a considerable amount of silver available or in circulation in order to realise such proceeds.

154 Exod 30:12–16; Num 7:13–86.
155 E.g., Lev 27:25; Num 3:47; 18:16; Ezek 45:12.
156 Kletter 1998, 101–103; Nam 2012, 177.
157 2 Kgs 15:19–20.
158 Both inscriptions mention a large group of kings (seventeen or eighteen), among which Menahem, and the tribute Tiglath-Pileser III received from them, consisting of various metals, hides, ivory, garments and animals (Younger 2000b, 286; 2000c, 287).
159 Holladay 2009; Nam 2012, 148–149; Master 2014, 89.
160 Cogan and Tadmor 1988, 172.

TABLE 4.1 *Interstate tributes/booty mentioned in 1 and 2 Kings (excl. Solomon)*

From – to	Date	Basic description of tribute/booty	Reference(s)
Rehoboam (Judah) – Shishak	926	Shishak took the treasures from the temple and the palace	1 Kings 14:26
Asa (Judah) – Ben Hadad	885	Asa sent all the silver and the gold remaining in the treasuries of the temple and the palace	1 Kings 15:18
Mesha – Ahab (Israel)	Before 852	A yearly tribute of 100,000 lambs and 100,000 unshaven rams was imposed on Mesha	2 Kings 3:4
Jehoash (Judah) – Hazael	ca. 813	Jehoash sent all the votives that he and his ancestors Josafat, Jehoram and Ahaziah had dedicated and all the gold in the treasuries of the temple and the palace	2 Kings 12:19
Amaziah (Judah) – Jehoash (Israel)	ca. 785	Jehoash took all the gold, silver and all the vessels from the temple and the treasuries of the palace	2 Kings 14:14
Menahem (Israel) – Tiglath-Pileser III	740–738[a]	Menahem gave Pul (Tiglath-Pileser III) 1,000 talents of silver to win his support; two inscriptions of Tiglath-Pileser record the tribute[b]	2 Kings 15:19–20; Younger 2000b, 285-6; 2000c, 287
Ahaz (Judah) – Tiglath-Pileser III	734/733	Ahaz sent the silver and the gold from the temple and the treasuries of the palace; an inscription of Tiglath-Pileser III records the tribute[c]	2 Kings 16:8; Younger 2000e, 289
Hoshea (Israel) – Shalmaneser V	731/730	Shalmaneser V imposed a tribute on Hoshea; an inscription of Tiglath-Pileser III records a tribute of 10 talents of gold and x talents of silver	2 Kings 17:3; Younger 2000d, 288[d]
Hezekiah (Judah) - Sennacherib	701	Sennacherib demanded 300 talents of silver and 30 talents of gold, and Hezekiah gave him all the silver from the temple and the treasuries of the palace and golden sheeting from the temple (see text)	2 Kings 18:14–15; Cogan 2000, 303; Grayson and Novotny 2012, 55–69
Jehoahaz/ Jehoiakim (Judah) – Necho	609	Necho imposed a tribute of 100 talents of silver and one (or 10; Gray [1964] 1970, 750) talent of gold	2 Kings 23:33
Jehoiachin (Judah) – Nebuchadnezzar	597	Nebuchadnezzar took all the treasures from the temple and the palace and all the golden vessels made by King Solomon	2 Kings 24:13

TABLE 4.1 *(continued)*

From – to	Date	Basic description of tribute/booty	Reference(s)
Zedekiah (Judah) – Nebuchadnezzar	586	Nebuchadnezzar's commander looted the temple and took all bronze elements and objects and everything that was gold or silver from the temple	2 Kings 25:13–17

[a] Cf. Shea 1978; Na'aman 1986, 81.
[b] Both inscriptions mention a large group of kings (17 or 18), amongst them Menahem, and the tribute Tiglath-Pileser III received from them, containing a diversity of metals, hides, ivory, garments and animals (Younger 2000b, 286; 2000c, 287).
[c] The inscription mentions 23 kings, amongst them Jehoahaz, the Judahite, and the tribute Tiglath-Pileser III received from them, containing a diversity of metals, garments, luxury objects and animals (Younger 2000e, 289).
[d] For the Tiglath-Pileser III inscriptions, see also Tadmor 1994; Na'aman 1995.

The suggestion that silver was taken from the treasury is, however, reasonable, considering what we know of the treasuries in the palace and the temple. It is related in several instances that the temple, in particular, like other temples in the Ancient Near East, was a place where wealth was stored. Solomon, for example, is noted to have 'brought the dedications of his father David and the silver and the gold and the paraphernalia to the treasury of the temple'.[161] The same is said of Asa of Judah,[162] while Jehoash of Judah 'took all the dedications of his ancestors Jehoshafat, Jehoram, and Ahazyahu, and those of himself, and all the gold that was in the treasury of the temple and the palace and sent them to Hazael, king of Aram'.[163] Significantly, like with the case of Jehoash, these mentions of storing gold and silver in the treasury presage its depletion for the purpose of offering a tribute.[164] While the examples of Solomon and Asa should not be regarded as reliable historical testimony, these verses at the very least reflect what the authors knew to be real. Clearly, it was known in the seventh century that, presumably as far back as Jehoash (ca. 836–798 BCE), these treasuries held capital reserves that were used in times of need for paying tributes to foreign rulers.[165]

For the current purpose, we could expand the definition of a tribute: large payments to overlords were made in the form of taxation (whether regular or not), but also under the threat of siege (e.g., Sennacherib) or even as booty.[166] Whether a foreign ruler came down to collect his tribute by means of force or threats, or whether the payment was initiated by the vassal, is of little

161 1 Kgs 7:51.
162 1 Kgs 15:15.
163 2 Kgs 12:19.
164 1 Kgs 14:26; 15:18; see Table 4.1.
165 Cf. Richter 2017, 31.
166 Cf. Liverani 1992, 155–156; Holladay 2006, 314. Holladay opts for the term palace tribute/booty with the purpose of covering both forms.

pertinence to the economic question of how the funds for such a transfer were extracted and stored in the first place. With regard to the latter, the biblical account provided by the book of Kings consistently notes that the Judahite tributes were taken from the temple and treasury of the palace (with one exception: the tax imposed by Necho; see Table 4.1), suggesting that it was known that the state's financial capital was amassed at those locations. Although taking control over the temple's capital, including its religious dedications, might have been regarded as a religious transgression, examples from the Greek world relate that in case of war this happened anyway, making the temple's financial assets a regular and integral part of state finances.[167] The tributes recorded in the book of Kings (see Table 4.1) confirm this practice.

In several cases, contemporary extra-biblical sources corroborate the tributes mentioned in the book of Kings (see Table 4.1 for references); additionally, many other tribute-payments are known from the wider region through written sources. These can offer a complementary, often more detailed, image of tributes. A relatively early example of such a tribute was the booty taken by the Assyrian King Adad-Nerari III (810–783 BCE) from Mari, king of Damascus. This tribute is preserved in three different inscriptions, the most extensive of which lists '2,300 talents of silver, 20 talents of gold, 3,000 talents of bronze, 5,000 talents of iron, linen garments with multi-coloured trim, an ivory bed, a couch with inlaid ivory'.[168]

Another important case of such a tribute is the one paid by Hezekiah, king of Judah, to the Neo-Assyrian King Sennacherib upon his campaign against Judah in 701 BCE. Detailed information concerning this tribute is handed down to us through two sources, the biblical record and the so-called Annals of Sennacherib, which in itself has been preserved through different copies, each differing in the extent to which the tribute is described.[169] The biblical record describes how Sennacherib demanded 300 talents of silver and 30 talents of gold from Hezekiah, who subsequently 'gave all the silver that was found in the house of the Lord, and in the treasuries of the king's house. At that time Hezekiah stripped the gold from the doors of the temple of the Lord and from the doorposts which Hezekiah king of Judah had overlaid and gave it to the king of Assyria'.[170] The biblical record is largely corroborated by the inscription on the Rassam cylinder, containing one of the extant versions of the Annals of Sennacherib, compiled relatively shortly after the described events:

[167] Cf. Thuc. 2.13.5; Linders 1987, 115–116. For state-borrowing from temples, see Davies 2001; van Wees 2013, 40, nn. 4–5.
[168] Gray 1970; 624; Grayson 1996, 209–213.
[169] Luckenbill 1924; Grayson and Novotny 2012, 55–69.
[170] 2 Kgs 18:14–16

> (55–58) 'As for him, Hezekiah, fear of my lordly brilliance overwhelmed him and, after my [departure], he had the auxiliary forces [and] his elite troops whom he had brought inside to strengthen the city Jerusalem, his royal city, and who had provided support, [along with] 30 talents of gold, 800 talents of silver, choice antimony, large blocks of ... ivory beds, armchairs of ivory, elephant hide[s], elephant ivory, ebony, boxwood, garments with multi-colored trim, linen garments, blue-purple wool, red-purple wool, utensils of bronze, iron, copper, tin, [and] iron, chariots, shields, lances, armor, iron belt-daggers, bows and uṣṣu-arrows, equipment, [and] implements of war, [all of] which were without number, together with his daughters, his palace women, male singers, [and] female singers brought into Nineveh, my capital city, and he sent a mounted messenger of his to me to deliver [this] payment and to do obeisance.'[171]

This version of the tribute reveals that, in addition to large amounts of precious metals, the tribute contained an unspecified quantity but great variety of precious exotica, garments, weaponry, base metal vessels and slaves.

Comparing this version of the tribute to the much shorter biblical version, the differences are obvious. In general, the descriptions of tributes in the book of Kings (Table 4.1) are rather basic, often involving only a mention of silver and gold or simply 'treasures'. Aside from the Hezekiah tribute, only in two cases (the 1,000 talents of silver paid by Menahem and the 100 talents of silver and 1 talent of gold imposed on Jehoiakim) is the amount of precious metal actually recorded, although these numbers appear rather generic. It seems that the biblical author had little or no specific information regarding these tributes, and when compared to the Neo-Assyrian records, it is plausible that they often involved other commodities such as metals of lesser value, garments and exotica.

Exotica and luxury goods were presumably part of the tribute, as the state was able to collect them through its role in the Arabian trade. Especially during the late eighth century, as international trade intensified, did the kingdom of Judah manage to strengthen its hold on the caravan and trade routes that connected the Arabian Peninsula and Egypt with the Mediterranean and the northern Levant.[172] Royal control over these routes, through a series of fortresses, such as those at Tell el-Kheleifeh along the Gulf of Aqaba, En Hazeva in the Arabah valley and the sites in the Beer Sheba valley, and increased trade connections with the coastal region gave the Judahite administration access to the goods that accompanied that trade.[173] This was presumably also the reason that the otherwise economically small and insignificant

[171] Grayson and Novotny 2012, 65–66.

[172] I.e., Holladay 2006; 316–321; 2009; Finkelstein 2014a; van der Brugge 2017.

[173] Finkelstein and Silberman 2006, 167–171; Master 2010; 2014; Finkelstein 2014a.

kingdom of Judah was of interest to the Neo-Assyrian kings.[174] Vassals in the Assyrian Empire provided tribute in whatever they were good for.[175] Some provided wood, others grain (if close by enough to make the transport cost-efficient); Judah provided commodities from the Arabian trade as well as the money that was raised, possibly in part from transit duties through its function as a gateway economy.[176]

As noted already, it is interesting in this regard that the Neo-Assyrian records list a whole range of commodities, whereas the Bible only mentions gold and silver. One could imagine that the royal court's disposal over luxury goods was something the Deuteronomistic authors would rather not draw attention to and therefore deliberately chose to ignore. Nonetheless, it is evident that in general gold and silver featured prominently in the tributes. As Mario Liverani observes with regard to the tributes from the time of Ashurnasipal II (883–859 BCE), 'gold and silver are among the most usual component part of the tribute, almost always in association and quoted as first. They are in fact a form of concentrated wealth, easily transported and easily converted'.[177] Tributes of silver from the southern Levant became more common in the ninth and especially the eighth century, suggesting that the availability of silver money for circulation must have also increased.[178] As was suggested on the basis of the Iron IIA–B hoards in Chapter 3, new silver could have entered the system through trade at least from the end of the tenth century and particularly during the ninth and eighth centuries. Lead isotope analyses performed on silver from these hoards suggest that this was coming from various sources across the Mediterranean.[179] It moreover fits the picture of a cautious resumption of Mediterranean trade during that period, intensifying particularly during the late ninth and eighth century.[180]

This is not to say that the payment of tributes to overlords was the sole use of these metal reserves. It is altogether plausible that state institutions

174 Holladay 2006; 2009; Master 2014. Cf. Byrne 2003; van der Brugge 2017.

175 Postgate 1974; 1979; Elat 1982. Cf. Byrne 2003, 21–22; Holladay 2006, 310–312.

176 Holladay 2006. Cf. Byrne 2003; van der Brugge 2017, 327. For an alternative approach, emphasising the importance of agricultural taxes as the basis for Hezekiah's wealth, see Röthlin and Le Roux 2013. Cf. van der Brugge 2017.

177 Liverani 1992, 160.

178 N.b.: 'the tribute system was mostly about money and the things money could buy' (Holladay 2006, 312).

179 Thompson 2007, 44; Thompson and Skaggs 2013; Eshel et al. 2019; Wood, Montero-Ruiz and Martinón-Torres 2019. We should, however, remain aware of the possibility that (part of the) the silver sampled for LIA was residual – i.e., that it had arrived to the region earlier and had been in use or circulation (see also Section 3.3.3). This is potentially supported by the claim that some of the samples represent a mixture of silver from different sources (Eshel et al. 2019; Wood, Montero-Ruiz and Martinón-Torres 2019), although this offers no further indication as to the date of the mixing or the original import of the silver.

180 E.g., Fantalkin 2006; 2008a; Fletcher 2012; Gilboa, Sharon and Boaretto 2012.

developed active uses for the funds at hand.[181] However, the overview offered here shows that in the ninth and eighth centuries the demand for tribute payments was tied to a centralisation of resources, most prominently gold and silver money, likely sustained by an increase in import and circulation. An important focus of this centralisation effort was to stock up funds in the royal treasuries for when tribute was demanded.

4.2.3 A Fiscal Policy in the Temple

In addition to the storage of state finances in the temple, what do we know about the organisation and centralised management of financial resources? How did the state collect resources?[182] In dealing with this question, 2 Kings 12 is of great significance, as it provides a model for how a key institution in society, that is, the temple, accrued and processed financial contributions, thereby offering insight into what fiscal policy during the period might have looked like.

In the central part of 2 Kings 12,[183] it is related that during the reign of King Jehoash of Judah (836–798 BCE) a new system was devised in order to organise the maintenance of the temple. Supposedly, the old system, whereby the priests were responsible for repairing any damage, did not function properly, causing Jehoash to take this responsibility away from the priests.[184]

The biblical text describes the following reform. First, Jehoiada the priest took a chest or box (*arôn*), in which he made a hole, and placed it next to the altar. The *kęsęp̄* that was subsequently brought to the temple was collected in that box, and when it appeared that there was a lot of *kęsęp̄* in the box, the royal scribe and the high priest would together process and record the *kęsęp̄* and hand it over to those responsible for the maintenance of the temple.[185] The subsequent verses relate how the *kęsęp̄* is handed over to the craftsmen carrying out the actual work and that it should not be used to make (*ye ʿāśę̄*)[186] vessels and ritual paraphernalia but only on repairing the temple.[187] Also it is mentioned that no record is kept of their payment, because 'they do their work in good faith'.[188]

This whole passage, from verse 5 down to verse 17, has received extensive treatment in scholarly literature, with focus on various aspects of the passage.[189]

[181] See Sections 4.2.3 and 4.3.
[182] In general cf. Stevens 2006, 82–120.
[183] 2 Kgs 12:10–17.
[184] 2 Kgs 12:7–9; Montgomery 1951, 427–428; Wright 1989, 442–443.
[185] 2 Kgs 12:10–13.
[186] See Section 2.3.
[187] 2 Kgs 12:13–15.
[188] 2 Kgs 12:16.
[189] E.g., Eissfeldt 1937; Oppenheim 1947; Greenfield 1985; Wright 1989; Naʾaman 1998, 337–40; Lipschits 2006, 243–249, with references; Nam 2012, 141–143.

Much of this attention has focused on its relation to the passage in 2 Kings 22, with which it notably shares part of the language. Set during the reign of King Josiah, it describes to some extent the same steps regarding the temple repairs as those described in 2 Kings 12, but this time providing a direct pretext for finding the book of law that prompted Josiah's religious reforms (622 BCE). Whether or not the more extensive account in 2 Kings 12 was only written/recorded in reference to the events described in 2 Kings 22 or was copied as a framing device into the account of the discovery of the book of law, it records an extant practice whose instigation was apparently associated with Jehoash. The authenticity of both passages as testimony to this practice is generally accepted,[190] meaning that the passage can help us understand in what way the silver in the box was processed and what this implies in terms of the fiscal practice in the temple.

As mentioned above, verse 11 relates that when the box was filled, the royal scribe and the high priest would come to process (*wayāṣurû* – וַיָּצֻרוּ) and record (*wayīmᵉnû* – וַיִּמְנוּ) 'the *kęsęp̄* present in the temple'. The word *wayīmᵉnû* (וַיִּמְנוּ) means 'to count'; however, the question is, how was the *kęsęp̄* counted exactly? The word *wayāṣurû* (וַיָּצֻרוּ) has commonly been connected to the biblical word for bundle (*ṣrôr* – צְרוֹר),[191] and most translations describe accordingly how the silver, or money, was put in bags and was counted.[192] Naturally, if the 'money' was to be paid out directly to those responsible for maintaining the temple, the silver was to be bundled in convenient moneybags. This interpretation is also reflected in the Septuagint, where וַיָּצֻרוּ is translated with καὶ ἔσφιγξαν, and they bundled/bound together.

However, following a suggestion by C. Torrey, it was recognised by O. Eissfeldt that the verb should be read as *wayiṣᵉrû*, 'and they casted', consistent with other occurrences of the verb and supported by Ibn Ezra and Saadiah Gaon.[193] In Exodus 32:4, the golden calf is cast (*wayāṣar*) in a mould (*ḥęręṭ*),[194] and Zechariah 11:13 refers to the office of the temple founder (*yôṣer*), to whom he throws his 30 shekels pay.[195] Explaining the role of this official, Torrey writes that

[190] Lipschits 2006, 246–249, with references. Cf. Na'aman 1998, 337–340.

[191] Gen 42:35.

[192] E.g., Thompson 2003, 86; Silver 2006, 188; Richter 2017, 32–34.

[193] Torrey 1936; Eissfelt 1937.

[194] Torrey 1943, 300–301. Cf. Houtman 1996, 617–621; Propp (2006, 549) raises doubt but provides no further explanation. Compare also 2 Kings 5:23, where Na'aman thanked Elisha 'and tied up [*wayāṣar*] two talents of *kęsęp̄* in two bags [*ḥariṭîm*]'. Commentators refer to Isa 3.22 for the identification of the latter term as bags (Gray 1970, 509; Cogan and Tadmor 1988, 66). This is consistent with the LXX θυλάκοις, although the Greek translators might have been confused by *wayāṣar*, as appears from the recurrent use of the Greek ἔλαβεν (he took; also for *qaḥ*).

[195] Torrey 1936; 1943, 300–301.

> In the centuries before 300 B.C., while coined money was little known or scarce in Palestine, and also in decreasing extent in the later time, the precious metal which was brought to the temple, as regular revenue or votive offering, came in the form of lumps, fragments, utensils and trinkets of every description and shape. It was of course necessary to melt all this down, and to cast it in certain standard forms . . .. it was from the important product, the standard *form*, rather than from the smelting, that the craftsman of the temple foundry received his designation, יוֹצֵר.[196]

When verse 12 mentions *hakęsęp̄ ham^{e}ṯukān* (הַכֶּסֶף הַמְתֻכָּן), given to the officials responsible for maintaining the temple, it refers to the weighed-out silver (cf. τὸ ἀργύριον τὸ ἑτοιμασθὲν, the *prepared* silver), signifying that the silver had been refined in the foundry so that its value could be guaranteed.[197]

It has been pointed out, most conclusively by Leo Oppenheim, that this fiscal practice in the temple in Jerusalem was common throughout the Ancient Near East. A passage from Herodotus has served as an important model for this 'fiscal practice', providing a description of a similar practice in Persia under Darius I (522–486 BCE).[198] The passage is preceded by a lengthy catalogue of the empire's satrapies and tributes and concludes that Darius collected a yearly tribute (φόρος) of 14,560 talents.[199] Herodotus goes on to say that 'the king stores [θησαυρίζει, he stores it in the treasury] this tribute in the following way: having melted it down, he pours it into ceramic containers [πίθους κεραμίνους]; when the vessel is filled, he breaks away the clay. And whenever he is in need of money [χρημάτων], he cuts off each time as much as he needs.'

There are various indications that silver dedications, brought to the temple and deposited in a special cash-box (*quppu* or *arannu*) were smelted, refined and cast by an official founder, as to be uniform in shape, weight and quality.[200] Examples of such *thesauroi* are also known from the Greek world and Cyprus, albeit later – from the Classical period onwards.[201] Also, the presence of two officials for opening the cash-box, a royal scribe and a priest, has various parallels in the Near East,[202] as well as the Greek world;[203] and the refining of the incoming silver by a founder, as to guarantee a standard quality, is known through other examples.[204]

Clearly, the system attributed in the Bible to Jehoash was no unique or exceptional procedure, nor was it only restricted to temple institutions; rather,

196 Torrey 1936, 255–256.
197 Greenfield 1985, 83.
198 Hdt. 3.96; Torrey 1943, 289–299; Oppenheim 1947, 116.
199 Hdt. 3.89–95. Cf. Armayor 1978; cf. Diod. 17.66.1–2.
200 Torrey 1943; Oppenheim 1947; Bongenaar 1999, 168; Jursa 2013, 8–9.
201 Kaminski 1991.
202 Hurowitz 1986; Radner 1999, 135–136.
203 Kaminski 1991, 89; Dignas 2002, 21–23, with translations; *SEG* I, 344. Cf. *IG* I^3 52.
204 Oppenheim 1947; Jurman 2015, 61–62.

it was a common practice in fiscal administration in the ancient world, in particular in the Near East, presumably originating in Mesopotamia.[205] This lends further weight to its general pertinence.

With regard to the use of the processed silver, the description in 2 Kings 12 offers several possibilities. The text emphasises that the silver is meant to pay out the workers[206] and to purchase materials.[207] This emphasis is clearly related to the purpose of temple maintenance as a pretext for the events in 2 Kings 22. However, in explicitly stating that the silver is not to be used as prebend, a priestly allowance,[208] or to make ritual paraphernalia,[209] it reveals that these uses would otherwise have been considered normal. Moreover, as noted, the production of finished products from the silver did not necessarily detract from its use as a means of value. This is also demonstrated by the fact that some of the tributes were noted to have included such precious metal objects.[210] Whereas the description in Herodotus gives the impression that Darius I used the funds in the treasury at will, it rather seems that the Achaemenid fiscal administration re-circulated only a relatively small part of its wealth.[211] This would perhaps suggest that most of the fiscal income was hoarded.

Considering the evidence discussed in this section, it is likely that expanding state institutions were responding to the use and circulation of money in society by absorbing or redirecting part of that capital for its own arising needs. The evidence for tribute payments shows that these tributes were becoming a substantial part of state expenditure in the ninth and eighth centuries in the southern Levant. The increasing mobilisation of liquid wealth – money – as reflected by the hoard evidence from the period and the effort towards centralisation of this wealth, exemplified by the Eshtemoa hoard (whether or not this concerned a specific tax collection), should be seen as answering to the increasing demands of the international political economy of the Iron IIA–B period.

4.3 MONEY AND THE ECONOMY IN THE LATE IRON AGE

Obviously, the economic interests of the state were not restricted to fiscal policy. The political rise and territorial expansion of the kingdom of Israel during the ninth century and the kingdom of Judah in the eighth century was

205 Oppenheim 1947, 120.
206 2 Kgs 12:12, 15.
207 2 Kgs 12:13.
208 2 Kgs 12:8–9.
209 2 Kgs 12:14.
210 Cf. Radner 1999, 136–137 on the use of weighed metal for cult statues.
211 Asheri 2007, 495.

paralleled by a mounting political and economic centralisation that has been observed in the Iron IIA and B.[212] Especially starting in the early eighth century, and subsequently in the seventh century, there is a growing amount of evidence for the involvement of state institutions in the wider economy.

As mentioned in Section 4.2, the kingdoms of Israel and Judah moved to assert control over southern trade routes, perhaps with some level of cooperation.[213] A series of fortresses was erected, for example, at Tell el-Kheleifeh (Ezion-Geber) starting in the first half of the eighth century and at Tell el-Qudeirat (Kadesh Barnea) after the Assyrian expansion into the region, in order to control the Darb el-Ghazza; at the end of the eighth and early seventh century, a series of fortresses was constructed in order to secure the now preferred route along the Edomite plateau and Beer Sheba valley.[214]

The end of the eighth century also witnessed the introduction of a system of inscribed limestone weights in Judah.[215] This should be regarded as part of an effort by the central authority to organise the use and circulation of silver in exchange by standardising the weights used.[216] Along similar lines, the standardisation of storage jars in the northern kingdom of Israel already in the early ninth century[217] and the subsequent appearance of the *lmlk* ('belonging to the king') stamps on storage jars from the end of the eighth century reflect royal involvement.[218] In general, these efforts demonstrate a growing level of standardisation in the economy and supposedly encouraged trade by reducing transaction costs.[219]

In the northern Levant, a silver hoard from Zincirli, ancient Sam'al, reflects in a most tangible way its ruler's interest in the control over silver. Three large disc-shaped ingots[220] were inscribed in Aramaic with the text 'belonging to Barrekub, son of Panamuwa', demonstrating the appropriation of the silver in his own name (Figure 4.6).[221] Barrekub ruled Sam'al in the late eighth century as a vassal of the Neo-Assyrian kings, and although we do not really know how these inscribed ingots related to his policies, they are a physical reminder of the ruler's urge to assert control over objects of value.[222]

212 Holladay 1995.
213 Cf. Finkelstein 2014b, 99–102.
214 Finkelstein 2010; 2014a, with references.
215 Kletter 1998.
216 Cf. Kletter 1998, 128–131.
217 Kleiman 2017.
218 Lipschits, Sergi and Koch 2011; Sergi et al. 2012.
219 Temin 2006, 152.
220 Mentioned also in Section 3.2.4.
221 Von Luschan and Andrae 1943, 119–121, pl. 58t–v; Balmuth 1971, 5–7, pl. 2–3; Thompson 1999, 48–49.
222 Cf. Section 2.2.4.

4.6 Large disc-shaped cut silver ingot, presumably from Zinzirli, inscribed 'belonging to Barrekub, son of Panamuwa' (diam. 8.6 cm (BM 134918). © The Trustees of the British Museum)

From the final third of the eighth century, the southern Levant was firmly incorporated into the sphere of influence and control of the Neo-Assyrian Empire, which was to last until their retreat in the 630s, followed by periods of Egyptian and Babylonian ascendancy until the destruction of Jerusalem in 586 BCE.[223] It is obvious that these geopolitical developments would have had a profound effect on the way in which the state was involved in the economy and the effects of this involvement in the Iron IIC period (ca. 650–586 BCE). What these effects would have been, and, in particular, how these affected the use and circulation of money, is what will be discussed next.

4.3.1 Under Assyrian Rule

As discussed in Chapter 3, Gitin and Golani claim that the southern Levant underwent a process of monetisation in the seventh century, characterised by an 'increased use of silver as currency'.[224] They regard the Neo-Assyrian expansion as the driving force behind this assumed development, claiming that their imperial rule provides the historical context for the increased use of money. They point to the 'the increasing fiscal needs of the Neo-Assyrian Empire', and the 'unparalleled economic growth' stimulated by the Assyrian military campaigns, as the conditions under which silver developed 'into a form of money'.[225]

223 Na'aman 1991, 33–41; Fantalkin 2006, 201–204; 2008a, 170–292; 2015, 238, n. 8.
224 Gitin and Golani 2001, 40–41; 2004; Gitin 1995, 69; Golani and Sass 1998, 61–62.
225 Gitin and Golani 2001, 40; 2004, 203–204; Richter 2017, 35–37; Wood, Montero-Ruiz and Martinón-Torres 2019, 5.

However, it has been demonstrated in Chapter 3 that the silver hoards from the Iron IIC do not provide any substantiation for this theory. In order to provide an alternative explanation for these hoards, it is necessary to take a closer look at the basis of Gitin and Golani's claim and, specifically, the historical context they claim exists for the seventh century. What would the Neo-Assyrian involvement in the southern Levant have looked like, and how did it lead to monetisation and economic growth?

By referring to the 'fiscal needs' of the Assyrians in the context of economic growth, Gitin and Golani appear to suggest – although fail to actually state – that the administration was levying tax in money, in order to facilitate their own budgetary spending. The taxes would likely be raised by the vassal and paid in tribute to the overlord – the core. However, in order to enable economic growth, while at the same time allowing for continued taxation, this money would then have to be re-circulated by investing it in the subjected province – the periphery. This way, money would be kept in circulation, leading to an increase in the use of silver as money (granted there is additional silver entering the equation) and people's ability to continue to pay taxes, perpetuating the system. This role for the central authority was the premise underlying G. F. Knapp's claim that money was essentially a token that originated and functioned under the authority of the state.[226] It accompanied the effort of Western colonial governments to draw local populations into their economic orbit,[227] and it is to some extent still the core of modern-day fiscal administrations. It should be noted that this model is inspired by nineteenth-century Western colonialism and assumes a world-systems type of exploitation of the periphery by the core, whereby monetisation would have been stimulated in order to impose more taxes/tributes for the core. Needless to say, we should be wary of the influence of such colonialist projections and modernisms.

Notwithstanding the details of this imperial fiscal system, Gitin and Golani's perception of the Neo-Assyrian Empire in terms of the core–periphery model is informed by the work of Susan Frankenstein.[228] Her argument, which has set the debate on Phoenician expansion since its publication, identifies the Neo-Assyrian expansion as the driving force behind Phoenicians maritime expansion westward, with the Phoenicians acting as the middle men for the Assyrians in their desire for new silver sources. Gitin and Golani assumed that if indeed Assyrian pressure had provoked Phoenician colonisation and the import of silver to the core, it might also have stimulated trade and prosperity in the southern Levant, causing a critical increase in silver circulation in the

226 See Section 2.2.4; Knapp [1905] 1924.
227 Bohannan 1955; Bloch and Parry 1989, 12–16; Graeber 2011, 127–164.
228 Frankenstein 1979.

southern Levant.[229] However, the chronological basis for Frankenstein's reconstruction has recently been questioned by Fletcher, who has pointed out that the Phoenician exploration commenced in the late ninth and early eighth century, at a time when Assyria suffered political decay and was not involved in the Mediterranean littoral.[230] Increasing Assyrian demand, especially towards the end of the eighth century, likely stimulated the increase in commercial interactions, movements and colonisation in the Mediterranean. However, this should not be seen as the singular result of the expanding power base of the Assyrians but rather as 'intensifications of movements and structures that already existed'.[231] This chronological objection applies to the supposed Assyrian influence on money-use as well: silver circulated already prior to the Assyrian involvement in the region, and to assign its inception to the context of Neo-Assyrian expansion into the southern Levant would be simply incorrect.

Moreover, from all we know, Assyrian state finance and taxation did not function as the assumed model would require: their fiscal needs did not necessarily lead to an increase in foreign imports of silver to subjected areas, nor did it lead to a higher circulation of silver money outside of Assyria proper. First of all, as previously noted, each region under imperial rule or influence was exploited differently, based on what they had to offer. For example, the incorporation of the Taurus region within the empire gave the Assyrians access to lumber and metals, including silver, as implied by an inscription of Sargon II.[232] Alternatively, control of the Levantine coastal region allowed them to profit from passing maritime trade, which involved access to luxury goods and the potential of harbour taxes.[233]

The main element of this exploitation policy was the extraction of tribute, *maddattu*.[234] An example is the tribute, recorded on a clay sealing from Nineveh, of one light talent of silver paid by Padi, king of Ekron, to the Assyrians in 699 BCE.[235] Gitin and Golani assume that such tributes led local rulers to step up taxation, but one is left to wonder how this could have fostered monetisation. Rather than having stimulated the regions under its control, most scholars believe that the Assyrian policy was simply one of 'maximal profit with minimal investment'.[236] Altogether, as noted by David

229 Cf. Gitin 1995, 61; 1997, 77–78.

230 Fletcher 2012. Cf. Fantalkin 2006, 200–201; Faust 2011; Thareani 2016, 94.

231 Fletcher 2012, 216.

232 Lie 1929, vv.222–233; Postgate 1974; 1979, 199–200; Elat 1982.

233 Postgate 1974; 1979, 197–199; Elat 1982; Faust and Weiss 2005; Fantalkin 2006, 201–202; Fantalkin and Tal 2009, 200; Faust 2011, 72; Walton 2015, 408–409; Thareani 2016, 95.

234 See Section 4.2.2.

235 Postgate 1974, 21; Gitin and Golani 2001, 37; 2004, 204.

236 Berlejung 2012, 48. See also Grayson 1991; Faust 2011; Faust and Weiss 2011; Bagg 2013; Thareani 2016. Cf. Younger 2015.

Schloen, there is 'no evidence that Assyrians understood or were concerned with the economic development of the territory they ruled, except in the most rudimentary sense of making it easy for themselves to tax or confiscate its wealth'.[237]

In the southern Levant, the Assyrians used the fact that silver was already circulating on a considerable level to their own benefit by simply absorbing it. In the seventh century, silver had become of central importance to the economy of the Assyrian core area, being used for various payments such as the *iškāru* (contributions through conscripted labour), thus requiring a steady supply of silver.[238] But there had been no such need before the mid-eighth century.

In fact, silver is only attested in Neo-Assyrian records as currency after the reign of Adad-Nerari III (783 BCE) and became more common towards the seventh century. Nicholas Postgate observed that in sale texts in the governor's palace archive in Nimrud dating as late as 727 BCE, bronze and copper were still much more common than silver, concluding that 'consequently, we are justified in stating that in most of the eighth century copper was the standard medium of currency'.[239] The shift from copper to silver as the preferred currency is presumed to have occurred only after and as a consequence of the incorporation of western Semitic states, most prominently Carchemish and later the southern Levant, during the campaigns of Sargon II (ca. 721–705 BCE). The capture of significant silver reserves and the potential access to silver from the Taurus[240] caused its use to become much more frequent.[241] Although copper is still attested in the seventh century, silver clearly had become the dominant currency by that time.[242]

Once Assyria was expanding in western directions and – towards the end of the eighth century – incorporated regions where silver had been circulating as the dominant form of money, it adopted the medium of currency and the weight standard used in the west.[243] Having adapted to the possibilities offered by these economies and the capital they had available, it implemented an aggressive policy of exploitation that Holladay has referred to as *bullionism*,[244] a term that is generally used to describe the monetary policy of states in late medieval and early modern Europe aiming to increase the supply of precious metal by maintaining a trade surplus. Part of Assyria's success should no doubt be sought in its adaptability and consequent ability to profit from the existing

237 Schloen 2001, 146.
238 Postgate 1974, 212, 218; Radner 1999.
239 Postgate 1973, 25; Radner 1999, 129.
240 Lie 1929, vv.222–233; Postgate 1974; 1979, 199–200; Elat 1982.
241 Postgate 1979, 199–200, 218; Müller 1997, 20; Radner 1999, 129, 139–149.
242 Postgate 1973, 25; Radner 1999, 129.
243 Zaccagnini 1999–2001.
244 Holladay 2006, 312–314.

structures. It is, however, unlikely that its policy would have led to an increase in the use and circulation of silver money.

Assyrian involvement has also been identified as the decisive influence in the development of the *lmlk*-stamp impressions. This system for marking storage jars has been understood as a way to organise and collect taxes.[245] Although it is unclear how exactly it would have functioned as a system of taxation, Lipschits, Sergi and Koch are clear on why it was initiated: 'It is our opinion that the lmlk stamp impressions represent another feature of the administrative and economic system established in Judah when it became an Assyrian vassal kingdom ... encouraged by the imperial rule'.[246]

The suggestion that the system was put in use under Assyrian support, considering that it would benefit from it, is at odds with the fact that Lachish III, where by far most handles were found, was destroyed by the Assyrians. If the system served to organise revenues for the Assyrians, why would they have destroyed the main agricultural centre in western Judah and the pillar of this system? And, if the system had been established under Assyrian influence, why would other regions under Assyrian control not have developed similar systems?

Moreover, there is little reason to assume that the local economy in much of the southern Levant was oriented towards Assyria. Evidence rather suggests that Judah and the coastal region maintained a focus towards Egypt, as the region had done throughout history. The system of Judahite inscribed limestone weights (JIL's) was marked with hieratic numerals, and the metrology of the system followed Egyptian equivalents. Clearly, this system had been adjusted to the Egyptian *dbn*/*qdt* system in order to facilitate direct trade between Egypt and Judah.[247] International trade would likely have involved larger quantities of precious metal, and indeed only the heavier units were adjusted to the Egyptian system.[248]

The so-called torpedo jars, eighth century transport jars that featured prominently in the maritime trade, also point in the direction of Egypt as the dominant trade partner. Two Phoenician shipwrecks loaded with these jars were found off the coast of Ashkelon and are thought to have sailed for Egypt.[249] Also, analysis of their measurements and its relation to their volume suggests that Egyptian units had been used in order to cater to an Egyptian market.[250]

245 Lipschits, Sergi and Koch 2010, 7; 2011, 6, 15; Garfinkel and Mendel-Gabrovitz 2016, 9.

246 Lipschits, Sergi and Koch 2010, 7; *pace* Kleiman (2017, spec. 369–370), who argues against an Assyrian role in the development of the *lmlk*-system, pointing instead to influence from the northern kingdom of Israel.

247 Scott 1965; Aharoni 1966; Kletter 1998, 27–28, 118–122.

248 Kletter 1998, 121–122.

249 Stager 2003; Temin 2006.

250 Finkelstein et al. 2011; Zapassky et al. 2012.

While the southern Levant was under de facto control of the Neo-Assyrian Empire for the major share of the seventh century, in terms of trade relations, the region was still very much focused towards Egypt. The point argued here is that, contrary to the claim that Assyrian rule had led to monetisation, there is no evidence to suggest that the Assyrians actually stimulated the local economy through trade or investment. Rather, the purpose of their imperial rule was the extraction of available resources for the benefit of its core.

4.3.2 Resetting Silver Money at the End of the Iron IIC

Having argued that there is little ground for the claim that Assyrian expansion into the southern Levant prompted the local use of silver money, it remains to be asked what *can* be said with regard to the use of silver in the Iron IIC. In attempting to offer insight into this question, focus will be placed on how this can be related to the evidence we have from the hoards. As discussed in Chapter 3, the hoards from the Iron IIC date specifically to the end of the seventh and early sixth century, to the period after the Assyrian retreat in the 630s, when the region was dominated first by the Egyptians of the Saite dynasty and from 604 BCE by the Babylonians. It is therefore particularly relevant to ask how these political changes might have affected the economy and specifically the use of silver money.

The economy of the region in the increasingly complex society of the Iron IIC has received wide interest in recent decades, with attention for a range of related issues such as demographics, production, (international) trade, weights and administrative systems (e.g., JIL's and *lmlk*-stamp impressions).[251] It is not the intention here to delve deep into the debates surrounding these topics, nor would this be the appropriate place; however, some remarks on particular issues are relevant to our discussion.

As claimed by Gitin and Golani, there are indeed indications that the regions of Judah and the coastal plain witnessed some economic growth in the Iron IIC.[252] Gitin specifically referred to the massive amount of olive oil installations excavated at Tel Miqne/Ekron as evidence for this growth. Reasoning that oil production on this scale could only have been developed under Assyrian tutelage, being an efficient way of the core to exploit the periphery, he dated the peak of oil production to the first half of the seventh century.[253] Although the so-called *pax Assyriaca* and the decline of the Judahite Shephelah after the Sennacherib campaign of 701 BCE are circumstances from which

[251] E.g., Finkelstein 1994; Gitin 1995; Stager 1996; Kletter 1998; Faust and Weiss 2005; Lipschits, Sergi and Koch 2011; Master 2014.

[252] Gitin 1995; 1997; Gitin and Golani 2001, 40; 2004, 203–204.

[253] Gitin 1989, 30–39; 1995, 63–69; 1997, 87–91.

Ekron likely profited,[254] Gitin's dating of the period of oil production to the early seventh century has been called into question. It is not at all certain that all installations belong to stratum IC (first half of the seventh century),[255] considering the fact that almost all presses were discovered in stratum IB, the phase dating to the Egyptian domination and destroyed in 604 BCE by the Babylonians.[256] Although many scenarios have been discussed, it remains possible that the production of olive oil continued under Egyptian hegemony or prospered in particular during that phase in the late seventh century.

In Judah itself, there are some signs of a cautious economic recovery after Hezekiah's revolt, but this hardly detracts from the general tenor that the region had been hit hard.[257] Further signs of recovery and prosperity, such as the tentative suggestion that Judah supplied grain to the Mediterranean port of Ashkelon destined for trade,[258] are best understood in the context of the second half of the century, when Judah returned to the Shephelah (with the rebuilding of Lachish II), which had also previously functioned as breadbasket for Judah.[259]

At the same time, the presence of JIL-weights might indicate continuity in the weighing of silver for transactions throughout the Iron IIC. Giving secure dates to the development of this system is, however, difficult. Although the presence of the earliest weight stones in Iron IIB strata establishes the introduction of the system by the late eighth century, the major part of the known weights from securely datable contexts are from the Iron IIC, mostly from contexts dating to the late seventh or early sixth century, such as Arad VII and VI, Ein Gedi V, Lachish II and Ramat Rahel V.[260] It is therefore not unlikely that the system was most intensively used during the late seventh and early sixth centuries.[261] However, it cannot be asserted whether the presence of weights in late contexts is simply the result of depositional factors (being in use throughout most of the century), or whether it in fact indicates that the need for and use of weights increased by the end of the seventh century.

254 Finkelstein and Na'aman 2004.

255 Cf. Na'aman 2003, who dates the start of this stratum in the late eighth century

256 Stager 1996, 70*–71*; Na'aman 2003, 86, 88; Fantalkin 2004, 254–258. Cf. James 2005; 2006, who dates IC to the late sixth and IB to the early fifth century; *pace* Gitin 2003.

257 Finkelstein 1994.

258 Weiss and Kislev 2004; Faust and Weiss 2005. Cf. Fantalkin 2011, 98–99.

259 Lipschits, Sergi and Koch 2011, 27–28.

260 Of a total of 434 JIL's listed by Kletter, 211 are from a documented context, 3 per cent (6) of which date pre-701, 40 per cent (85) date 701–586, and 56 per cent (118) are listed as 'other date', indicating that their dating is uncertain (Kletter 1998, 42–48). The uninscribed weights might have started earlier but are likely to have been used alongside the JIL's, see Kletter 1998, 132–137.

261 Lipschits, Sergi and Koch 2011, 28.

Generally, some areas and settlements certainly would have benefitted in a relative sense from the conditions set by the Assyrian exploitation of the region, or, as Na'aman described, 'the prosperity of certain western vassals arose from the stability produced by the pax Assyriaca and from the new economic opportunities created by the empire – rather than the result of a deliberate imperial policy of economic development of these states'.[262] Ekron might have profited from these conditions, as would those areas that were of strategic importance to the Assyrians in securing their supply in trade goods and proceeds, notably the Beer Sheba valley and the Mediterranean coastal region. However, across the board, the image of economic activity and growth in the Iron IIC should rather be associated with the second half of the seventh century, in particular, the period after the Assyrian retreat from the region. It is important though to emphasise the obvious, that economic development was influenced by a myriad of factors, of which the geopolitical situation was only one.

Most relevant in the framework of our interest is the question how this image of the late Iron IIC can be related to the hoard evidence. In Section 3.4, the possibility was raised that 'the Iron IIC reality was one in which the circulation of silver cash – at least on a local level – had declined'. Considering the fact that the Assyrians had attempted to effectively drain the local economy of its available silver, it is likely that silver became less readily available for local exchange. It is plausible that international trade would still have relied on silver money to some extent, but because it was in the self-interest of the Assyrians to maintain and control this sphere of circulation, it is less likely that the participating networks and ports would have been negatively affected by the overall drainage.

Moreover, Mediterranean trade access, connecting the southern Levant with the Aegean, Sardinia and Spain, had been essential to the supply of silver.[263] With the tight control of commercial trade routes and seaports by the Assyrians, there was little chance for fresh silver imports to enter local circulation. Alexander Fantalkin has keenly observed that after the Euboian imports of the end of the eighth century, Greek pottery becomes conspicuously absent in the Levant (with the notable exception of Al Mina), indicating that Greek commercial ties with the region had been cut off under Assyrian surveillance. The sudden and noteworthy appearance of substantial quantities of East Greek wares in the coastal plain in the last quarter of the century marks the reappearance of Mediterranean contacts through Egypt, associated with

262 Na'aman 2003, 87.

263 Thompson and Skaggs 2013; Eshel et al. 2019; Wood, Montero-Ruiz and Martinón-Torres 2019.

4.7 Elephantine hoard (© DAI Cairo)

the Saite takeover of the region in the 630s.[264] Under these circumstances, Greek pottery found its way back to the southern Levantine coast, presumably accompanied by Greek mercenaries in the service of the Egyptians, although disappearing again when the region came under Neo-Babylonian dominance.[265]

It is equally noteworthy that after the absence of silver hoards during most of the seventh century, silver hoards appear again under the period of Egyptian rule at Tel Miqne/Ekron, in the 604 BCE destruction of stratum IB.[266] It is particularly significant in this context that the jewellery in these hoards demonstrate a strong Egyptian influence, with only two pieces pointing to Assyrian connections.[267] Moreover, as noted in Section 3.4, lead isotope analyses on the Tel Miqne silver provide additional testimony to the importance of the reinstated trade connections, pointing to the Aegean as the main source of the silver.[268] The supply of fresh silver to the region is also confirmed by the claimed presence of primary ingots that could not have circulated for an extended period of time, and presumably arrived through the reinstated trade connections, via Egypt.[269] A seventh century silver hoard, found in Elephantine in southern Egypt (Figure 4.7), provides an additional indication of the importance of Aegean silver in the Egyptian trade of the period. The

264 Fantalkin 2006; 2008a; 2015, 238, n. 8.
265 Fantalkin 2001; 2006; 2008a.
266 Cf. James 2006.
267 Golani and Sass 1998, 74; Na'aman 2003, 85–86.
268 Stos-Gale 2001, 61–62; Thompson 2007, 44; Thompson and Skaggs 2013; Wood, Montero-Ruiz and Martinón-Torres 2019, 11–15.
269 See also Sections 3.4 and 5.4.3.

hoard consisted of a jar, containing three bundles of *hacksilber* with a total of 118 pieces weighing 39.45 grams[270] and appears comparable to the Iron IIA–B hoards from the Levant, tentatively reflecting the use of silver as a form of money. Preliminary results of metallurgical research point to Siphnos as the origin of the metal,[271] giving further credence to the suggestion that Egypt was importing Aegean silver in the seventh century.[272]

The image suggested by the available Iron IIC hoards is one in which the use and circulation of silver money was picking up again in the late seventh and early sixth century, following the re-establishment of Mediterranean trade access under Egyptian rule. The new supply of Mediterranean silver was particularly significant in this regard, after a period of decline had left the local economy largely drained from silver. This decline had no doubt left people scrambling for silver and had inevitably also transformed the role of silver money in exchange and trade. It could well be that the role of silver did not immediately revert to what it had been during the Iron IIA–B once new sources of silver became cautiously available again. These circumstances might also explain the lack of consistent characteristics of the Iron IIC hoards, observed in Chapter 3.

What this reduced availability of silver during part of the seventh century would have meant for the value of silver and for its use as a unit of account is uncertain. It is certainly not the case that this would have automatically led to a fall in prices or a reversion to barter, as formalist analysis might perhaps assume. We know from various examples through time that reference to a silver unit of account could also be maintained without an at-hand availability of silver.[273] A pertinent example of this is the lack of physical silver available in Post-Kassite Babylonia while a silver standard was in use.[274] At the same time, alternative strategies of exchange had surely remained in use alongside silver money in the late Iron Age. The allotment of food rations on a fragment of a Neo-Assyrian cuneiform tablet found in Tell Keisan could represent one of the many non-monetary forms of (re)distribution that were likely to have persisted throughout the centuries.[275]

4.4 CONCLUSION

The purpose of this chapter was to explore the historical settings in which the evidence from the silver hoards could be properly understood. In

270 Noeske 1991; 1993, 203–205, pl. 38.a; Jurman 2015, 61–62.
271 Noeske 1993, 205.
272 See more in detail Section 5.4.3.
273 See Section 2.3. Cf. Bloch 1967.
274 Kleber 2016.
275 Sigrist 1982; Na'aman 1991, 35, n. 36.

reconstructing the use of precious metal, silver in particular, as money, the hoard evidence provides one perspective, albeit an essential one. An understanding of the historical context for the silver hoards is, however, critical for attaining a serious appreciation of the social and historical significance of its development.

As part of a long tradition as an important medium of value stretching back to the fourth millennium BCE, silver functioned in the Late Bronze Age Levant as an important means of exchange in the sphere of international trade. The textual records at Ugarit provide ample testimony to the importance of silver in trade but also suggest that it did not function as the exclusive medium of exchange in this context. Additionally, it featured in *wergeld* payments, implying a certain significance as an adequate compensation of damage and loss (in particular, of human life) and in reinstating trust between international parties. This was critical to maintaining secure trade relations.

With the gradual weakening of the Late Bronze Age central authorities, and when the secure trade routes and relations that were so important to the system came under increasing pressure and consequently disintegrated, people gradually became more reliant on metal – especially silver – in carrying out transactions. Also due to its significance as a material of value and trust, and the fact that it remained desirable, the role of silver in exchange expanded, as can be observed from the growing evidence for the use and circulation of silver scrap. Following the retreat of the Egyptians from the southern Levant and heading into the Iron I, it is telling that evidence of hoards is strongly associated with former lowland centres of the LBA southern Levant that occupied strategic points along the trade routes, showing signs of continuity into the Iron Age.

The need for money that had arisen in the absence of stable credit relations managed through international diplomacy (and, no doubt, force), is painfully exposed in the Report of Wenamun. This literary text offers a critical reflection on the lack of Egyptian control abroad at the start of the Third Intermediate Period, with the composition dating to the time of the twenty-second dynasty, when its authority in the Levant had already been reasserted. Clearly, Wenamun's Mediterranean was one in which the purchasing power of silver, rather than political credit, was the basis for conducting trade.

The rise of territorial states in the southern Levant during the Iron IIA and B provided new impulses to the use and significance of silver money in society. An important source for the Iron II society, offering detailed information at times, is the biblical record. Biblical language and descriptions provide significant evidence for the use of silver money in carrying out transactions and is arguably consistent with the archaeological reality of silver money as reflected by the hoard material. At the same time, a critical attitude towards the text shows that there are good reasons to apply caution in attempting to identify hoard material with specific terms in the biblical record.

Still, confirmed by extra-biblical sources, the biblical record offers a reasonable insight into the growing importance of fiscal institutions in order to meet the increasing costs of political organisation. One form of expenditure that appears to be particularly well documented concerns the tributes extracted by overlords. These tributes were one reason that no doubt forced local rulers to organise and manage their income through forms of taxation. Textual evidence, notably 2 Kings 12, demonstrates that the temple in Jerusalem functioned as such a fiscal institution, collecting and storing state capital.

The tributes extracted consisted of precious metals but also of goods and proceeds obtained through the control over various trade routes, notably the Arabian and Mediterranean trade that must have been significant sources of income for the local rulers. With the incorporation of the southern Levant into the expanding Neo-Assyrian Empire at the end of the eighth century, the Assyrians kept on vassal rulers in the south of the region in order to maintain the supply of such goods. The control over commercial activity enabled them to profit through taxation. The other goal of the Assyrians was no doubt to absorb the silver that circulated in the local economy through tributes.

However, contrary to what has been claimed, there is little reason to assume that this policy of exploitation would have caused or even stimulated monetisation in the southern Levant. Rather, with exception of a few areas that were exploited by the Assyrians to their own benefit, a general decline of most of the region in the Iron IIC under Assyrian rule and the extraction of as much silver as available adequately explains the absence of silver hoards during most of the seventh century.

Following the retreat of the Assyrians, the reopening of trade connections into the Mediterranean under a short period of Egyptian dominance provides a fitting context for a renewed availability of silver in the late seventh century. Although the physical use of silver in exchange presumably did not reach its previous level of intensity with regard to the types and scale of transactions served, silver once again entered into circulation, as reflected by the hoards of the late seventh and early sixth century.

FIVE

MONEY IN THE IRON AGE AEGEAN

5.1 INTRODUCTION

The development of money-use in the Iron Age southern Levant was never a purely local phenomenon. As we have seen, the changing patterns in consumption, circulation and hoarding of precious metal, indicating its use as a form of money, took shape under the influence of the movement of people and goods, changing trade patterns and political circumstances in the wider world of the Mediterranean Near East. These developments also affected the role and significance of forms of money in the early Greek world, where, although later and under very different circumstances, the use of precious metal in particular took on an increasingly important role. This was influenced by the Levantine practice of weighing silver in trade but also stimulated by wider Aegean and Mediterranean movements and trade interests, as well as social and political changes within the emerging Greek states.

In order to better understand how interregional dynamics in the eastern Mediterranean affected the development of money-use, the current chapter deals with the role and significance of forms of money preceding coinage in the Aegean, also touching upon examples from Cyprus. Specific focus will be placed on the increasing importance of precious metal, in local use and in the framework of the eastern Mediterranean.

Much of the scholarship on the early development and history of money in the Greek world appears to reflect a degree of binary thinking with regard to money. As discussed in Chapter 2, a professed strict distinction between primitive and modern money, with coinage identified as the latter and anything that preceded it as the former, has served as the basis to regard the invention of coinage essentially as a 'big bang':[1] the birth of money and the emergence of a monetary economy out of its primitive, social forerunners.[2] Additionally, the significance attributed to coinage as indicating the start of the monetary economy in the Aegean has stimulated an unbalanced focus on early coins as the embodiment and indicator of the exploitation of silver mines and the high-value trade in silver.[3] As a result, Aegean production and trade in precious metal prior to the introduction of coinage has received little attention.[4]

Scholars showing interest in the significance of money preceding coinage have often conceptualised these forerunners of coinage with reference to modern money, asking to what extent such potential forms of money performed the same functions as later coinage.[5] This approach has placed emphasis on the functional differences between these forerunners and coinage, either because they did not fulfil money's four basic functions at the same time,[6] or because they were restricted in use, that is, special-purpose money.[7] However, it should be objected, as previously discussed, that in any real society (as opposed to a formalist model) the use of money is inherently restricted; moreover, rejecting a strictly functionalist understanding of money, its significance cannot be derived from the extent to which it is practically suitable for performing certain functions.[8]

Examples of such potential forms of money are cauldrons (*lebetes*), and iron spits (*obeloi*), as well as the oxen standard referred to in the Homeric epics. Their supposed function as a measure of value has been emphasised over other functions, with several scholars assuming that the cauldrons and spits could not have practically circulated as means of exchange.[9] Recently, Hans van Wees

1 Bresson 2009, 75.
2 Balmuth 1975; Price 1983; Howgego 1995, 12–14; Weatherford 1997; Kurke 1999, 11; Schaps 2004; 2008; Seaford 2004. Cf. Descat 2001, 69–71; von Reden 1997, 156; 2010, 22–25.
3 Hopper 1979, 38; Gale, Gentner and Wagner 1980; Figueira 1981, 144–149; Treister 1996b, 132–133, 151–152; Boardman 1999, 130; Bissa 2009, 29–102.
4 Cf. von Reden 2010, 28–30.
5 Kroll 2001a; 2008a; 2012; 2013a; Schaps 2001; 2004; 2008; Seaford 2004; van Wees 2013.
6 See Section 2.1.
7 von Reden 2010, 22. Cf. Schaps 2004, 219–220.
8 See Section 2.1.
9 Kroll 2001a, 87–88; Peacock 2011a, 54; van Wees 2013, 112–115. Cf. Descat 2001; Schaps 2004, 69–71, 82–88.

has gone as far as claiming that these functioned as the *universal* measure of value in different regions – the ox in Ionia, the cauldron in Crete and the spit in the Peloponnese. While metal was not yet functioning as a measure of value, according to van Wees, 'value was expressed instead in terms of oxen, bowls or spits – not defined by weight or volume – by which one could measure everything from food and drink via slaves to gold and silver'.[10] In other words, although these media were restricted in terms of the functions they performed, there were no restrictions concerning what could be expressed on a common standard of value.

Although one could doubt whether a measure of value can actually be universal, the underlying assumption behind this reconstruction is that while everything had a price (i.e., commoditisation is optimal), the functional shortcomings of these forms of money – likely technological in nature (cauldrons do not transport or divide very well) – stood in the way of monetisation.[11] As discussed in Chapter 2, one should wonder whether this focus on the functional properties of money is conducive to a proper understanding of its significance in society. Though the evidence for such potential forms of money will be addressed in more detail below (Sections 5.2 and 5.3), the point to be made here is that in order to better understand the development of money-use, the question that should be asked is not what medium performed what monetary function, and whether this could be qualified as (modern) money or not, but rather *in what context* these monetary characteristics were displayed.

This focus on the context of money-use emanates from the understanding, explored in Chapter 2, that money's significance ultimately results from the 'cultural matrix in which it is incorporated'.[12] Money-stuff – material or objects that are potentially used or contextualised as money – and written references to forms of money are culturally constructed and their significance is tied to the context of use. By drawing attention to the different contexts in which we encounter such references and forms of money we can gain insight into what money meant to people in the early Greek world.

As our focus lies with the development of money preceding coinage in the Aegean, the topic of early coinage itself – its invention, production and spread – will remain outside our scope. While other studies have contextualised the rise of coinage within the development of early forms of money and fiscal institutions with merit,[13] coinage is considered here as representing a

[10] van Wees 2013, 112–115.
[11] Cf. Kopytoff 1986. See Section 2.2.
[12] Bloch and Parry 1989, 1; Parry and Bloch 1989; Robbins and Akin 1999, 2–3.
[13] Kim 2001; Le Rider 2001; Papadopoulos 2002; 2012; Schaps 2004; Seaford 2004; Kim and Kroll 2008; Kroll 2008a; van Wees 2013.

different development. As a form of money, coinage was strictly not a conceptual innovation;[14] rather, its rise was particular to the context of state formation and the emergence of independent political communities in the fragmented political landscape of the archaic Greek world.[15] Coinage represents the appropriation of money through the attempted control over its production and circulation by the expanding civic and state institutions (or powerful actors) that became an important and visible factor in the historical record of the late seventh and sixth century and should be understood in that specific historical and political context.[16] Although historically important, this full involvement of state institutions, by issuing coinage itself and by putting in place laws and regulations concerning the circulation of coinage, reflects a distinct development and a phase in the history of Mediterranean money that is altogether different from the one that is focused on here. By drawing a line on typological and historical grounds and excluding coined money from our considerations, we provide a clear framework for the material discussed but also for the political and historical circumstances that provide a context for the developments described.

This does not mean that numismatic evidence will be ignored altogether; numismatic data, for example, concerning weight standards, can provide important indications of earlier realities.[17] However, the circumstances under which the first electrum coinages of Lydia and the Greek cities of Asia Minor were invented, as well as the introduction of a bi-metallic system and the development of the silver coinages from the mainland will not be included in the discussion here.[18]

In dealing with money-use preceding coinage, I will focus in this chapter on the different contexts in which past behaviour can be observed with reference to concepts of money, the different contexts in which money is put to use and the different forms of money involved. In particular, the role of precious metals and its significance in the development of money-use will be of concern in this regard. The discussion will further address the case of the Eretria hoard, presented already in Chapter 3, as well as other hoard data in relation to the changing role of silver in the Aegean and the eastern Mediterranean.

[14] See Section 2.3.

[15] Osborne [1996] 2009, 250–259. Cf. Schaps 2007.

[16] This need not presume a monopoly of 'the state', i.e., a single central authority, but can include initiatives of elite actors, as argued by both Kroll (2020b) and van Alfen (2020).

[17] Kim 2001, 17–19.

[18] See, e.g., Wallace 1987; 2016; Kroll and Waggoner 1984; Le Rider 2001; Papadopoulos 2002; 2012; Schaps 2004; Seaford 2004; Alfen et al. 2020.

5.2 DEPOSITION AND DEDICATION

5.2.1 *Money As Prestige Item*

The weighing of precious metal was a known practice in the Mycenaean world of the Late Bronze Age Aegean. Although the palatial records offer only hints of information on how local transactions or payments were carried out,[19] it is clear precious metal played an important role within the international trade network through which the palatial elite were supplied with luxury items.[20] The three golden scales from shaft grave III of grave circle A at Mycenae (see Map 5.1), suggest that already at the start of the Late Helladic period (the sixteenth century) weighing with precision scales was considered a high-profile activity. As part of the rich and exotic grave assemblages in the shaft graves, these model scales emphasise the importance of long-distance trade as a source of prestige and wealth.[21]

Aegean merchants used their own system of scale weights,[22] and, as noted in Section 4.1.2, the integration of different regional weight systems from the Aegean to Mesopotamia testifies to the international context of their use.[23] The Uluburun shipwreck, possibly manned by Mycenaean merchants, provides an interesting context for such use.[24] The use of silver in carrying out the associated transactions was a long-standing practice that became increasingly important towards the end of the Late Bronze Age, and lead isotope analysis has demonstrated that Aegean silver from Laurion was well represented in one of the hoards from the southern Levant dating to the end of the LBA.[25]

The silver in this hoard had likely arrived from the Aegean prior to the collapse of the Mycenaean palatial administration around 1190 BCE and the disintegration of the associated trade networks. Although contacts did not completely disappear, state-sponsored directional trade of the sort indicated by the Uluburun and Gelidonya shipwrecks came to an end, and the unravelling of palatial networks appears to have led to a partial reorganisation in the LH IIIC period of activity into smaller-scale or local networks, as demonstrated for the Euboian gulf.[26] However, the local 'sailor-warriors' that moved along these networks did not engage in large-scale directional trade, nor did

[19] Schaps 2004, 57–62; Zurbach 2017; 2018, 5–8.
[20] Cf. Section 4.2.
[21] Karo 1930a, 53–57, nos. 70, 81–82, 91, pl. 34.
[22] Michailidou 2010. See Alberti, Ascalone and Peyronel 2006.
[23] Pulak 1996; Alberti and Parise 2005; Alberti, Ascalone and Peyronel 2006.
[24] Zangani 2016.
[25] Beth Shean D; Thompson 2009, 606. The isotopic fingerprint of the silver ingots from Pyla-Kokkinokremos on Cyprus, interpreted as belonging to a silversmith hoard, and dating to the end of the thirteenth century (Karageorghis and Demas 1984, 64–65), was also consistent with the Laurion mines (Gale and Stos-Gale 1984, 97; Stos-Gale and Gale 2010, 396).
[26] Kramer-Hajos 2016, 149–179. Cf. Tartaron 2013.

MAP 5.1 The Aegean with sites mentioned in the text

they maintain access to exotic raw materials,[27] and we may assume that the weighing of precious metal as a means of exchange, associated with palatial trade activity, became relatively obsolete. Continued activity at Laurion in the Postpalatial Period is reflected by unstratified pottery and several silver grave goods at the cemetery at Perati in eastern Attica, but no evidence for exploitation of the mines outlasts the LH IIIC period.[28]

Also postpalatial in date, the so-called Tiryns treasure contains rare examples of raw gold and *hackgold*, in the form of spools of folded wire, (cut) coils (Figures 5.1 and 5.2) and a few small pieces of scrap.[29] These objects were part of a larger, heterogeneous assemblage, with some objects dated prior to 1200

[27] Kramer-Hajos 2016, 176–178. See also Dickinson 2006, 202–205.

[28] Stos-Gale and Macdonald 1991, 271; Dickinson 2006, 83; Laffineur 2010, 719.

[29] Karo 1930b, 128–129, no. 6218, 6220, 6221, pl. 31–32; Maran 2006, 137–138.

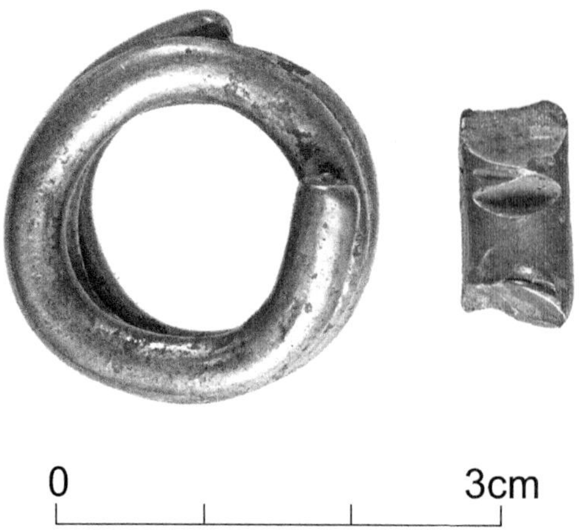

5.1 Gold coil and a cut fragment of gold coil from the Tiryns treasure (D-DAI-ATH-NM-3498. Photographer: H. Wagner)

BCE, and some after; the treasure mostly consisted of jewellery, among which were a famous Mycenaean golden signet ring, and bronze ceremonial feasting equipment, such as cauldrons, a Cypriot tripod stand and firedogs. Several of these objects had been intentionally damaged, raising the possibility of some ritual deposition of the treasure.[30] Whereas some of the metalwork reflects a strong Cypriot connection, other objects, such as two ‘sunwheels’ of gold wire with bronze spokes and large amber beads and the spools of gold wire (Figure 5.2) have parallels in the Urnfield culture of central Europe.[31] With exotic objects representing different contact zones, and palatial insignia suggesting an appropriation of traditional power symbols, the owners of the treasure were using former and novel forms of material culture to shape their social position.[32] But what does this tell us about the unfinished gold items?

Although very different in the type of deposition and assemblage, several items of gold found in a Cypriot tomb are worth taking a closer look at in order to better understand the scrap gold in the Tiryns treasure. These items, consisting of three rough ingots, two globules, six fragments of (cut) scrap sheet, two joining fragments of a hammered square-sectioned rod, two fragments of a twisted wire/ring and two large fragments of a drinking cup were found in tomb 93 in Enkomi (Figure 5.3; Map 4.1).[33] Known as the wealthiest tomb in the city, it contained a wide variety of local and imported pottery and

[30] Maran 2012, 124.

[31] Marinatos 1960; Maran 2012, 124–125.

[32] Maran 2006; 2012, with bibliography.

[33] Objects depicted in Figure 5.3: BM 1897,0401.529; 1897,0401.532; 1897,0401.533; 1897,0401.533.+; 1897,0401.639–643; 1900,0615.1. Additional objects: BM 1897,0401.534 (piece of cut sheet); 1897,0401.637–638 (two fragments of a wire or hair ring); 1897,0401.530–531 (two fragments of a cup); G.2130 (rough ingot, electrum); 1900,0615.21 (rough ingot, cut).

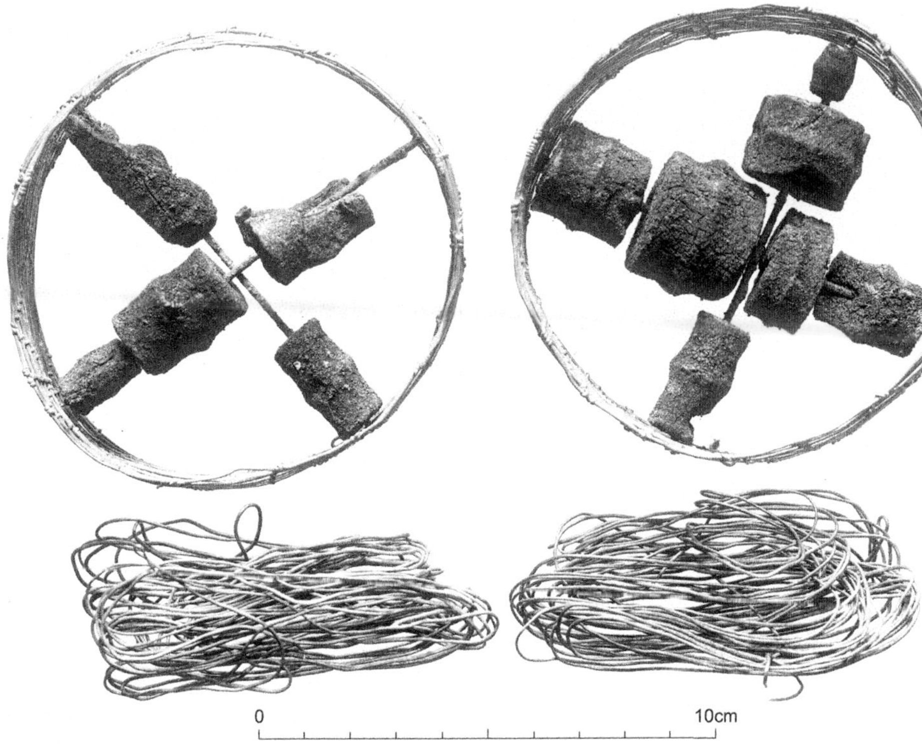

5.2 Spools of folded gold wire from the Tiryns treasure (D-DAI-ATH-Tiryns-0670. Photographer: unknown)

5.3 Selection of gold items from Enkomi tomb 93 (© The Trustees of the British Museum)

exotics, such as hematite cylinder seals and a scarab, as well as an impressive amount of golden jewellery.[34] The tomb has a wide chronological span, starting in the sixteenth century and continuing into the twelfth and possibly the early eleventh century (LC I–LC III), but most of the objects appear to date to the period before 1200 BCE and possibly the phase thereafter. Only Enkomi tomb 1, contemporary to tomb 93, also contained a few items of gold scrap (six cut fragments of jewellery, and a sheet fragment).[35] Considering the increase in scrap in the late thirteenth and twelfth century,[36] and the odd place of the unfinished golden objects within the grave assemblage, their deposition within tomb 93 could well be contemporary to the Tiryns treasure.

The presence of precious metal ingots and scrap in these explicit elite contexts of the LH IIIC and LC III period is interesting also in light of the contemporary increase in the circulation and hoarding of precious metal in the context of interregional trade. While many of these hoards had a utilitarian character and were meant to be retrieved,[37] the gold in the Tiryns treasure and Enkomi tomb 93 were not. Rather than representing objects hoarded in order to be later used in exchange, both contexts suggest that the gold items were deposited as luxury goods. When the infrastructure that had provided elites with access to exotics and luxury items for self-definition was collapsing, the availability of raw material, such as gold, as well as the specialised craftsmen needed to process the material into finished goods decreased. As a consequence, raw gold and available scrap became prestige items in themselves by symbolising or boasting continued access, thereby reflecting the changing role of precious metal in elite strategies.[38]

Another example of a burial with *hackgold* and *hacksilber* is t.198 in Amathus, Cyprus (see Map 4.1). This tomb contained twenty-nine cut ingots of gold, a few items of gold scrap, and thirty-three broken and cut ingots of silver. An additional group of sixty smaller pieces of broken silver ingots was recorded separately by the excavators as corroded bronze scrap, which could suggest that it was deposited separately.[39] The tomb furthermore contained six Egyptian or Egyptianising scarabs and various pieces of pottery, including twelve large amphoras, several so-called bird vases and a fragment of a Euboian pendent semicircle skyphos. The pottery assemblage can be dated between the Cypro-Geometric I and the Cypro-Archaic I, suggesting the tomb was in use from the tenth to the early seventh century.[40]

[34] Murray, Smith and Walters 1900, 36–37, 41–43, 54, pl. 5–7; Crewe 2008.
[35] Crewe 2008.
[36] See Section 4.1.3; Karageorghis and Demas 1984, 60–65.
[37] Knapp, Muhly and Muhly 1988. See Section 4.1.3.
[38] Cf. van Wijngaarden 2017.
[39] Heymans 2019, 48–49, 59–60.
[40] Murray, Smith and Walters 1900, 102, 123; Forgeau 1986, 147–149; Laffineur 1986, 56–57, 111–118, 127; Heymans 2019, 52–56.

Typologically similar to some of the cut gold ingots in the Eretria hoard and the silver ingots known from the southern Levant, the 'Amathus hoard' was long interpreted as belonging to a gold smith – in keeping with the interpretation of precious metal hoards from the Levant and Greece.[41] The observation that the ingots could be paired according to their weight gave rise to the suggestion that the pieces concerned raw material selected to be used for the production of pairs of earrings.[42] However, following the reinterpretation of the Iron Age hoards from the southern Levant and Eretria in an economic framework, as representing the use of precious metal as a form of money, the Amathus metal has been claimed to indicate similar money-use in Iron Age Cyprus.[43]

However, considering the fact that the material has a funerary context, we should be cautious to regard it as utilitarian or to draw a straightforward comparison with utilitarian hoards reflecting active use.[44] Moreover, the metrology of the Amathus material is fundamentally different from the other hoards in question. Whereas the Iron Age hoards from the southern Levant and Eretria are characterised by a gradual distribution in the weight of the objects with a low average weight, resulting from use over time,[45] the Amathus collection concerns a deliberate selection of objects, possibly made for the occasion of the deposition.[46] The typological similarity to the hoard material suggests that the ingots had at some point been used as a means of exchange, and the deliberate selection can be understood, not as reflecting active use in exchange, but as a reference to the monetary use of precious metal in interregional and Levantine trade. Well-connected Cypriots, engaged in maritime trade, were no doubt familiar with this practice, and the ingots were appropriated from this context in order to be used as an expression of identity within the cosmopolitan communities of Iron Age Cyprus.[47] Rather than exemplifying the use of precious metal money in Cyprus, the objects were given new significance through their deposition as a symbolic reference to the use of money.[48]

Referred to in recent years as a parallel for the Amathus ingots and the Eretria hoard, the famous Tekke tomb 2 near Knossos is another burial context that contains what look like golden ingots. The tholos was adopted as a family tomb from ca. 800 BCE, and two vessels were deposited on either side of the door inside the dromos, both containing a set of gold and silver jewellery, including

41 See Section 3.1.

42 Marshall 1911, 63–64. Cf. Laffineur 1986, 111–118.

43 Le Rider and Verdan 2002, 150–151; Thompson 2003, 71–73, 85, 92; Kassianidou 2012, 243.

44 Cf. Le Rider and Verdan 2002, 151; Kassianidou 2012, 243.

45 See Section 3.3.2.

46 Heymans 2019, 58–60.

47 Cf. Janes 2010; Heymans and van Wijngaarden 2011.

48 Heymans 2019.

an exquisite pendant with amber and rock crystal inlays. These vessels also contained several pieces of gold, silver and electrum, in the form of (bar)ingots, tokens and a piece of foil. Based on the Near Eastern influence of the jewellery, attributed to the 'Tekke Workshop', John Boardman argued that the tomb had belonged to a gold smith who had arrived from Syria.[49] In a recent study, Antonis Kotsonas demonstrated that the impressive assemblage in the tombs stands in contrast with a relatively limited distribution of such objects among other eighth-century tombs at Knossos. He concluded that 'the occupants of the Tekke tomb were an élite who enjoyed privileged access to foreign, precious materials and used them for the manufacture of skilfully crafted artefacts'.[50]

Aside from the identity of the people buried in the tomb, recent interest has focused on the ingots deposited in the dromos. Boardman initially identified the ingots as the stock-in-trade of the jeweller, remarking that 'a currency of gold, silver, and electrum dumps and bars in Crete about 800 B.C. – or for long afterwards – is unthinkable'.[51] Recent scholarship has referred to the precious metal ingots in comparison with other precious metal hoards, suggesting the use of the metal as means of exchange.[52]

This comparison should however be rejected. Although I have not been able to study the hoard first hand, it appears that the impressive yet small collection of ingots almost exclusively contains complete finished ingots, lacking visible manipulation. Although some objects, notably the tokens or globules[53] are common ingot forms known also from the Eretria hoard, it is likely that the ingots were selected for deposition, before even being used either as currency or as jeweller's stock. They were prepared and finished for the purpose of representing an aestheticised and symbolic version of the raw material, the supply of which (and its control) was arguably such an important part of the owners' social identity.

The use of money-related objects in the grave as an expression of social identity can also be observed in the case of T.79 in the Toumba cemetery in Lefkandi. Dated to the first half of the ninth century (SPG II) on the basis of two Attic EG II oinochoai, this grave contained an exceptional assemblage of grave goods, among which were a group of sixteen hematite balance weights and remains of a bronze scale.[54] Based on the weights and the presence of a 'killed' iron sword, typical of the so-called warrior grave in Iron Age

49 Boardman 1967; 2005. Cf. Hoffman 1997, 191–245.

50 Kotsonas 2006, 159.

51 Boardman 1967, 62.

52 Furtwängler 1986, 156; Kopcke 1992, 112; Hoffman 1997, 197–207; Le Rider and Verdan 2002, 150–151; Kroll 2003, 317; 2012; 2013a; Thompson 2003, 90–91. Cf. Kotsonas 2006, 154.

53 Boardman 1967, pl. 7.11–13, 8.27–28.

54 Kroll 2008b.

Greece,[55] the grave was identified as belonging to a 'Euboian warrior trader'.[56] The cremation remains had been placed in a bronze cauldron, closed off with a bronze lid with a handle of a type presumably produced on Cyprus and found from the Near East to Sardinia, with concentrations on Cyprus and Crete.[57] Other notable grave goods were two Phoenician bichrome jugs, an MBA North-Syrian cylinder seal and a group of thirty-four iron arrowheads.[58]

Belonging to a wealthy trader with foreign connections, the burial shows that the community of Lefkandi was involved in trade and was familiar with weight systems and their use. In a study of the weights, John Kroll has demonstrated that these do not represent a functional set. Of the eight sphendonoid weights corresponding to the 8.4 gram Mesopotamian standard, two had suspension holes drilled in them, while the other eight corresponded to diverse standards and did not make up a set, leading him to conclude that these were 'miscellaneous weights that were brought together specifically for funerary use, odds and ends from several old, broken sets that were contributed to the funeral pyre and burial as *symbolic* possessions or tokens of the deceased's way of life'.[59] Also here, the objects were severed from their original context of use and employed as a symbolic referent for the knowledge of and familiarity with precious metal money.

Another aspect of interest, echoing the above conclusions, concerns the thirty-four iron arrowheads in the grave.[60] Arrowheads in Iron Age Greece are notably rare: in 1964 Anthony Snodgrass remarked that there was little evidence for the use of metal arrowheads during this period, and little has changed since then.[61] Although arrowheads appear to be more common on the northern mainland,[62] few are known from the southern Aegean.[63]

[55] Cf. Whitley 2002.

[56] Popham and Lemos 1995.

[57] Matthäus 2001, 169–174.

[58] Popham and Lemos 1995.

[59] Kroll 2008b, 38–43.

[60] Bräuning and Kilian-Dirlmeier (2013, 35) identify the arrowheads as bronze and raise the possibility that they are Mycenaean antiques. However, awaiting the final publication of the Lefkandi III text, we refer to the data as presented by Popham and Lemos (1995; 1996). Cf. Nijboer (2008, 367), who compares the grave, including the arrowheads, to tomb N.1 at Achziv on the southern Phoenician coast (Mazar 2004). For the iron arrowheads, see Mazar 2004, 117–125.

[61] Snodgrass 1964, 144–156; Popham, Sackett and Themelis 1980, 256–257; Lemos 2002, 122–123; Dickinson 2006, 158.

[62] For Thessaly, see Georganas 2005, 68; Asderaki-Tzoumerkioti et al. in preparation; Lemos (2002, 123) mentions arrowheads from Pherai; there are also arrowheads from the Protogeometric tholos excavated near Aerino in the Volos museum. For Macedonia, see Andronikos 1969; Bräuning and Kilian-Dirlmeier 2013, spec. 34–36 with references.

[63] South of Thessaly, Lemos (2002, 123) lists an iron arrowhead from Athens (Popham, Sackett and Themelis 1980, 257, mentions two), and ten from the LPG grave T.26 at Toumba; n.b.: Popham and Lemos (1996) mention fourteen iron arrowheads in T.26. Coldstream ([1977]

Following Popham, Sackett and Themelis, Lemos has suggested their use on the basis of a vase painting on an MPG hydria, explaining their absence from the archaeological record as a coincidence.[64] Although the use of wooden arrowheads cannot be excluded as a possible explanation, the vase painting likely concerns a heroic depiction and need not reflect the Iron Age reality.

In light of the relative absence of iron arrowheads, it is remarkable that a single context would yield such a quantity.[65] Although a single iron arrowhead would have been rare and valuable as such, it appears that within the specific context of T.79 the basis of their significance was not their singularity but rather their quantity. Chris Gosden refers to objects in such a setting as 'quantifiable objects', objects that are disembedded from their social relations and that can be subject to the logic of calculation, since their value is conceptually constructed. On the opposite side of the spectrum he situates 'things of quality', objects that are singular, attract histories, relations and value, emanating from their definite qualities.[66] To Gosden, the key example of a type of quantifiable object is money, and we are to wonder whether this collection of otherwise rare arrowheads represented a store or hoard of valuables that could have functioned as an inarticulate form of money.

As noted, arrowheads were considerably more common in northern Greece, and more significantly, evidence for the use of arrowheads (or objects representing arrowheads) as a currency has been observed in the Black Sea region. An inscription from the sixth or fifth century on a skyphos from Olbia records a fine of eleven arrowheads, and large numbers of arrowheads, albeit bronze, are known from Greek colonies in the region, such as Apollonia Pontica, Olbia, Histria and Berezan, as well as their hinterland. Not being suitable as a weapon, their deposition in graves from the sixth century on has suggested their use as a form of money.[67] Like the dolphin-shaped coins from the region, coinage was presumably adopted in a form that was familiar as a means of value and therefore deemed locally acceptable.[68]

Considering the unconventional form of archaic arrow coins, it is not implausible that arrowheads had long functioned as a valuable that featured in local exchange practices. As Euboian exploring merchants expanded their influence in the northern Aegean as early as the Protogeometric period,[69] it is

2003, 38, 46) mentions an example from Corinth (Snodgrass 1964, mentions two) and one from Ialysos.

64 Popham, Sackett and Themelis 1980, 256–257; Lemos 2002, 123.

65 Grave T.26 contains an additional ten or fourteen arrowheads, albeit of a different type, see Lemos and Popham 1995, 157.

66 Gosden 2004, 36–39.

67 Graham [1994] 2001, 145–146; von Reden 1997, 158–159; Mitchiner 2004, 363–365; Schaps 2008, 41.

68 Cf. Descat 2001; Papadopoulos 2002; 2012.

69 Lemos 2002.

possible that eastern Macedonia or Thrace had functioned as a contact zone past which valuables from further regions were exchanged. These hoarded valuables were deposited in the context of the Lefkandi grave, severed from their original context of use – whatever exactly it had been – as a reference to a regime of value that was part of the long-distance trade contacts of Euboians to the northern Aegean and beyond.

At the same time, the importance of objects of quantifiable value in grave dedications is reflected by the dedication of bronze objects in Iron Age graves, especially in northern Greece. A typical presence in graves from the ninth to the seventh century, specifically in Macedonia and Chalkidike, are so-called arm spirals, or spiral bracelets, hair spirals and double-spiral or spectacle fibulae, object types that fit into a longer tradition of European bronze working.[70] These objects were dedicated as forms of jewellery or bodily adornment, but being in fact bronze coils adapted into an object, these could well be regarded as ornamentalised forms of raw metal coils. With bronze functioning as the dominant metal of value, coils were a convenient form, being both measurable and divisible, while at the same time suitable for further processing. By visibly preserving the form of raw metal coils within their design, these grave goods refer if not directly, then at least symbolically, to the quantifiable value of the raw material. The appropriation of such quantifiable wealth for the adornment of the body brings to mind David Graeber's identification of currencies with the adornment of the human body, as an attestation of past achievements.[71] While functioning as an adornment for the human body, pieces of bronze could be easily severed from the object for any arising need.

5.2.2 *Money As Sacred Payment*

In the southern mainland, vast numbers of metal objects, mostly bronze, were dedicated in sanctuaries in the eighth and seventh century. These offerings concern jewellery and ornamental implements such as fibulae, dress pins and rings, but also figurines and feasting equipment, such as tripods and cauldrons. One type of dedication has attracted considerable interest with regard to the early development of money in the Greek world. These are the iron sacrificial spits, *obeloi*, dedicated in graves during the eighth century, and appearing as dedications in sanctuaries in the seventh. The etymological connection between these spits, attested in some cases in sets of six – a *drachma* or 'handful' – and obols, sixth fractions of a drachma, has led to the suggestion in ancient and modern scholarship alike that spits had functioned as

[70] E.g., Misailidou-Despotidou 2011, 106–125, 169, 240; Bräuning and Kilian-Dirlmeier 2013, 48–52.

[71] Graeber 1996; 2001, 91–115; see Sections 2.3 and 3.4.

predecessor to coinage.[72] Although attractive due to the etymology, this interpretation of archaeological finds from the eighth and seventh century BCE, based on evidence from late antique written sources – being some thousand years younger – deserves scrutiny. The dissertation by Peter Haarer offers a systematic discussion of the available finds, as well as all relevant written sources, and it is therefore sufficient in this context to offer a short recap.[73]

The ancient tradition, preserved in the fifth century CE *Etymologicum* of Orion of Thebes, credits Pheidon of Argos with minting the first Aeginetan coins, at which occasion he had called in the preceding money, iron spits, and dedicated them in the Argive Heraion.[74] A large bundle of spits, discovered in 1894 during excavations at the Heraion, has been thought to confirm this tradition,[75] serving as the basis for the interpretation of spits in other sanctuaries as well, generally dating to the seventh or sixth century.[76]

Another story taken by modern scholars as evidence for the monetary value of spits is Herodotus' account of the courtesan Rhodopis, who dedicated a tithe of her income in spits at Delphi, which Herodotus notes were still visible behind the altar of the Chians.[77] Herodotus, however, does not suggest that her income was in spits; rather, she had spits made (ποιησαμένη) as dedication, referring to them as βουπόρος, ox-piercing. Clearly, to Herodotus, these spits were used to roast meat.[78]

Also, the account of Pheidon has been rejected as evidence for the theory that spits had preceded coinage as money. Not only is Pheidon generally dated too early to have been able to mint the first coins of Aegina,[79] the suggestion that the *obeloi* dedicated in the Heraion had represented the value of the later obols is hardly credible. As Haarer carefully demonstrated, the spits were not standardised, and the value of iron in the Early Archaic period was still much too high for a large spit to be equivalent in value to an obol,[80] although it might have been equivalent to approximately 1 gram of gold.[81] Herodotus, who credits Pheidon with the introduction of measures and weights,[82] does not refer to the story or to coinage or spits at the Argive Heraion, making

[72] Courbin 1983; Kroll and Waggoner 1984, 336; Strøm 1992; Treister 1996b, 96–97; Kroll 2001a; 2012, 34–36; Schaps 2004, 83–88, 101–103; Seaford 2004, 102–113; Peacock 2011a, 62–63; van Wees 2013, 113–115. Cf. von Reden 1997, 159–160; Haarer 2000, with bibliography.

[73] Haarer 2000.

[74] See Haarer 2000, 171–176.

[75] Waldstein 1902, 61–62, 77.

[76] E.g., Strøm 1992.

[77] Hdt. 2.134–135; Kraay 1976, 314; Courbin 1983, 151, n. 7; Strøm 1992, 45, 49.

[78] Haarer 2000, 97–104; Schaps 2004, 85–87.

[79] Figueira 1981, 65–76; Haarer 2000, 82–83.

[80] Haarer 2000, 82–92, 117–118; 2001, 262–264.

[81] Kroll 2012, 35–36.

[82] Hdt. 6.127.

Schaps' suggestion that the story was aetiological unlikely.[83] In fact, the Pheidon tradition cannot be traced earlier than the fourth century BCE, with the historian Ephorus being the earliest reference.[84] According to Figueira 'the story indicates the extent to which fourth century Greeks found it inconceivable for society to operate without a system of money'.[85]

The spits in the Heraion and in many other sanctuaries in the seventh and sixth century are rather to be seen apart from the tradition linking spits with coins. On the basis of a thorough survey of the known spits in different contexts, Haarer concludes that the presence of spits in the sanctuary should be related to their use as an implement for roasting sacrificial meat and that they were dedicated as votives, considering their associated value as prestige objects.[86] The presence of spits in graves is also interpreted with reference to their function in feasting, as testified by the presence of firedogs in some of the grave contexts.[87] Haarer concludes that there is no evidence for their use as money, citing the observed lack of uniformity in size or weight, while the appearance in multiples of six in grave contexts in Argos is no proof that they were used in a system of denominations but simply reflects a duodecimal count of the objects, hardly significant in itself.[88]

Although *obeloi* themselves were not ornaments, they were attributes in elite activity or at least symbolised elite activity. Being an attribute, or material extension of actors in an elite discourse, that is, the ceremonial consumption of meat, *obeloi* did function as an attribute of the social body, forming the basis for its prestige value. Despite the fact that the evidence does not substantiate its use as a direct predecessor to coins, Haarer notes that 'we need not exclude the possibility that spits functioned as money in its broadest sense in certain social contexts, such as the exchange of gifts in the form of a wide range of prestige goods'.[89] True, as David Schaps rightly points out, the use of utensils in exchange is known in many societies,[90] and spits were potentially exchanged as objects of value within an elite discourse. However, if they did, their use was likely restricted to such a setting. The suggestion that, rather than being objects of (elite) exchange themselves, they would have functioned as a measure of value, not to mention a *universal* measure of value, cannot be substantiated. The claim that this measure was associated with the Peloponnese[91] is not

83 Schaps 2004, 103.
84 Ephor. *FGrH* 70 F 115, 176 = Strab. 8.3.33; 8.6.16. See Haarer 2000, 82–92, 119–121, 171–176; Schaps 2004, 102.
85 Figueira 1981, 65–76, spec. 72–73.
86 Jeffery [1961] 1990, 122–124; Haarer 2000, 119–121.
87 Tandy 1997, 159–160; Haarer 2000, 52–56.
88 von Reden 1997, 159–160; Haarer 2000. Cf. Schaps 2004, 84–85.
89 Haarer 2000, 178–179.
90 Schaps 2004, 87–88.
91 van Wees 2013, 113–115.

confirmed by the wide distribution of *obeloi* in graves and sanctuaries.[92] This leads us to conclude that although *obeloi* might have functioned as objects of prestige exchange, this had nothing to do with the later coins. Haarer offers the idea that, given the division of half-staters in sixths, like the 'handful' of spits, their etymological connection could have resulted from the visual analogy between the spits and the spit-like tool used to strike the incuse mark into the coin.[93] While the origins of the term remain uncertain, it is clear that the monetary interpretation of the spits was later invented on the basis of the etymological connection, rather than vice versa.

Like *obeloi*, other types of votive offerings dedicated in sanctuaries during the Geometric and Archaic period reflect a level of standardisation. Although the votive assemblages found in different sanctuaries can be diverse, resulting from circumstances specific to the sanctuary, trends in the occurrence of certain types can be observed.[94] Previously, the deliberate disposal of wealth in the form of metal votive offerings was understood in the framework of gift exchange. Assuming the dominance of gift exchange in early Greece,[95] it was argued that objects that had previously functioned as a gift between men were now redirected as gifts to the gods.[96] Alternatively, rather than seeing these offerings as gifts with divine favour expected in return,[97] dedications can also be regarded as a form of payment.

A type of votive offering that forms an interesting example are the Archaic *krikoi*, bronze cast rings presumably dating to the Late Geometric and Early Archaic period (late eighth to early sixth century). Vast quantities have been excavated in the sanctuaries of Kalapodi, Olympia, the Argive Heraion and Pherai, while examples are also known from graves.[98] Possibly replacing coiled fingerrings during the Late Geometric period in southern Greece, these are simple round rings, sometimes with three or four knobs on the outer surface but mostly smooth, displaying a remarkable level of standardisation. Some could have been worn as fingerrings, as is known from burials in Anavra,[99] but many were too large (up to ca. 5 cm in diameter), and although it is assumed that they were worn as a form of adornment, scholars have raised the idea that

[92] Haarer 2000, 11–121.
[93] Haarer 2000, 181–186.
[94] E.g., Kilian-Dirlmeier 1985.
[95] Finley 1954. Section 5.3.1.
[96] Morris 1986a; Langdon 1987. Cf. Morgan 1990, 201–202.
[97] Cf. Parker 1998, 118–120.
[98] Kalapodi: Felsch 2007, 173–177, nos. 848–1362; Olympia: Felsch (2007, 177) mentions that they numbered in the thousands; Furtwängler 1890, 63–65; cf. Philipp 1981, 139–140; the Argive Heraion: Waldstein 1905, 251–261, nos. 975–1464; Pherai: Kilian 1975, 196–201; for references to grave depositions, see Dakoronia 1989.
[99] Dakoronia 1989, 115.

these rings, so simple and basic, were dedicated for their worth in metal.[100] Phanouria Dakoronia has even suggested that they represent a form of money.[101]

As long as there is no evidence that *krikoi* had a function outside of the dedicatory practices characterising burials and sanctuary life in early Greece, we should be reluctant to attribute some form of widespread universal use to these rings. However, the level of standardisation as a metal object reflects its significance as a conventional form of payment in the specific context of the sanctuary.

Whether these dedications are regarded as a tip of the iceberg, with increasing quantities of metal being in circulation, or the dedication of available resources into the emerging sanctuary, the general phenomenon of bronze votive offerings represents an impressive investment of wealth in early Greece.[102] The whole concept whereby (private) investment in the sanctuary as a focus of communal rituals and collective identity at least partly took the form of the dedication of objects of value – in this case bronze objects with a level of standardisation that in various cases also circulated outside the sphere of the sanctuary – demonstrates the potential role of such objects as a sacred contribution or fee. This brings to mind the work of Bernhard Laum, who placed the origins of money in the Greek sanctuary, arguing that contributions were valued with reference to sacrificial animals that formed the basic Homeric standard for currency.[103]

We know very little though about temple fees and taxes and how these were collected in early Greek cult. At least from the Classical period, inscriptions indicate the use of coinage in the payment of cult fees, and the use of *thesauroi* or cash-boxes – attested archaeologically – in order to collect and organise the incoming funds.[104] These *thesauroi* and the procedures surrounding their use strongly bring to mind earlier practices of collecting temple contributions in uncoined silver in cash-boxes known from the Ancient Near East and discussed in Section 4.2.3 Yet, it has been cautiously suggested that in Greek sanctuaries the payment of cult fees in coin was preceded by payments in kind.[105] Although this might reasonably be accepted for most local sanctuaries, it is not unlikely that early (inter)regional sanctuaries in particular, with visitors coming from afar and often significant quantities of bronze votives, would have customarily accepted contributions in metal.

100 Felsch, Kienast and Schuler 1980, 81; Philipp 1981, 140; Felsch 2007, 177.

101 Dakoronia 1989.

102 Morris 1989; Morgan 1990, 194–203.

103 Laum 1924; Peacock 2011a. It is less likely that such contributions were circulating back and forth between the temple and its visitors, as Laum suggested (1924, 94–97).

104 Sokolowski 1954; Kaminski 1991; Pafford 2006; 2013; Goodenough 2011, 8, 274.

105 E.g., Sokolowski 1954, 156; Davies 2001, 119–120; Pafford 2006; 2013; Goodenough 2011, 59–60, cf. 12–13.

Our reluctance to see in these bronze dedications a sanctuary fee – a form of money used in the context of the sanctuary – is understandable. If these votives were not convertible payments themselves, it is not unthinkable that they were paired with a contribution in the form of a cult fee made in metal. The fact that these sanctuaries were centres of metalworking[106] also points to the persistent need for the sanctuary administration to process metal and to produce or recycle (part of the) metal votive offerings.[107] The evident significance of bronze to the organisation of the sanctuary, and the fact that this high value commodity lent itself well to valuation by weight, does not however mean that bronze *was* necessarily measured by weight, not to mention by means of a specific bronze standard.[108] To what extent the circulation of bronze within the economic sphere of the early sanctuary was subject to regulatory control and quantification is uncertain.

At the same time, however, the financial characteristics of expenditure in the sanctuary become increasingly evident in the Late Geometric and Early Archaic period. A bronze scale pan with hanging wires and a hook, found under the floor of the Early Archaic temple and associated with the Late Geometric temple in Kalapodi, was used for weighing precious metal or dedicated as a votive.[109] It is early yet explicit evidence of the sanctuary as a context for financial transactions and as a financial institution.[110] Evidence for the financial role of the sanctuary in later (Archaic and Classical) times has come under increasing attention in recent scholarship, and the sanctuary has been described as 'a nexus of trade and economic interactions'.[111]

More specifically, there is increasing evidence for the monetary characteristics and financial value of sanctuary votives. The dedication of silver bullion, in some cases associated with coins, and bronze *aes rude* is known in Archaic sanctuaries in Magna Graecia and central Italy.[112] Illustrative of the monetisation of votives is an inscription from Samos dating to ca. 580–570 BCE. The inscription records that '[...]niskos son of Xenodokos, Demis son of Pythokles, colonists from Perinthos dedicated to Hera a tenth, offering a golden gorgon, a silver siren, a silver phiale, a bronze lampstand, altogether worth 212 Samian staters, the stone [with the inscription] included'.[113] This inscription brings to mind Herodotus' story of the Samian merchant Kolaios,

106 Risberg 1992, 39; 1997; Morgan 1993, 23–24; Treister 1996b, 76–77.

107 Lindenlauf 2006.

108 Cf. Kroll 2013b.

109 Felsch 2007, 245, 386, no. 2293, pl. 12.

110 Cf. Felsch and Siewert 1987.

111 Goodenough 2011, 235. See also Alroth and Linders 1987; Davies 2001; Seaford 2004, 75–87; von Reden 2010; Domínguez Monedero 2013.

112 Kroll 2008b, 24–29; Murgan and Kemmers 2016.

113 *IG* XII 6 2.577; Samos 218; *SEG* 12.391; Klaffenbach 1953. The gorgon and siren referred to are presumably vessels.

who had sailed for Egypt around 638 BCE but was blown off course by a storm. Ending up at the strait of Gibraltar, he brought back an unprecedented profit. Of six talents, a tenth of his profit, he and his crew (or the polis itself) had a cauldron with griffin protomes made that was dedicated in the Heraion.[114] Apparently, the monetary value of a votive was considered relevant to the dedication, and it was not uncommon that these were recorded in some way. In the Classical period, precious metal vessels, such as those stored in the Opisthodomos of the Parthenon, were also recorded by their weight.[115]

As noted, sacred payments, whether in the form of votives or as a separate cult fee, had an explicit monetary character by the first half of the sixth century, and evidence suggests that cult fees were increasingly formalised during the course of the Archaic period. Starting in the sixth century, coinage and particularly small denominations were important for the payment of cult fees.[116] But the organisation of contributions or fees and the regulation of cult costs almost certainly predate coinage.

The Athenian lawgiver Solon is thought to have established a ritual calendar for the Athenians, presumably together with his other reforms in 594 BCE. The ritual calendar was reinscribed in the late fifth century and listed prices for sacrifices in drachmas.[117] Prices for the choice sacrificial animals (τῶν ἐκκρίτων ἱερείων) were recorded in the sixteenth axon, one of Solon's laws, and for the valuations of the sacrifices (τὰ τιμήματα τῶν θυσιῶν) a conversion rate was applied, whereby 'a sheep and a drachma are counted against a *medimnos*' (a dry measure).[118] As coinage was introduced only later in the century, these drachmas could perhaps represent silver weight units.[119] The mentioned conversion rate poses problems of interpretation and, lacking a proper context, is not well understood,[120] but one possible implication is that it valued silver highly, thus encouraging the payment of contributions and taxes in silver.[121]

Although it remains uncertain whether the tradition recorded by Plutarch is historically correct,[122] or whether Solon was responsible for introducing a system of fixed sacrificial costs, it is certainly to be expected that a state such as Athens 'was from an early stage keen to quantify and control its sacrificial costs'.[123] Regardless of the details, the introduction of a ritual calendar with

[114] Hdt. 4.152; Shipley 1987, 56–57.
[115] Harris 1995, 63; Davies 2001, 126; Goodenough 2011, 182–183, n. 526.
[116] Goodenough 2011, 234–236.
[117] Lambert 2002; Lys. 30.20.
[118] Plut. *Sol.* 23.3.
[119] See Section 5.3.3.
[120] See Schaps 2004, 236–240; Davis 2012, 147–148.
[121] van Wees 2013, 89–90.
[122] Cf. Section 5.3.3.
[123] Goodenough 2011, 47.

fixed prices reflects this concern with cultic finance and the regulation of public costs.[124]

The monetisation of cultic contributions and costs had been part of the developing sanctuary economy starting in the Late Geometric period, and by the late seventh and early sixth century this took an increasingly explicit form, being accounted for in known monetary units, and reflecting a convergence of sacred money with other conventional units or form of money.[125]

5.3 COMPENSATIONS AND FINES

5.3.1 *Exchange in the Homeric Economy*

Any attempt to further explore the role of early forms of money beyond the sphere of the sanctuary in early Greece is bound to rely on the works of Homer, and indeed scholars who have ventured into topics related to exchange and the economy in early Greece have turned to the epics as a source for information. However, in view of the important role of the sanctuary as a context for value politics, as discussed in Section 5.2.2, it is perhaps surprising to find that the Homeric record is conspicuously quiet on the world of the sanctuaries and votives.[126]

In his pioneering work *The World of Odysseus*, Moses Finley argued that the Homeric epics represented the reality not of the Aegean Bronze Age, nor the polis society of Archaic Greece, but of the Dark Age.[127] Stimulated by archaeological exploration of the period (more neutrally referred to as the Iron Age),[128] critical research later rejected Finley's notion of a historical Homeric society, suggesting instead that the epics are to be understood as a literary pastiche preserving elements from different periods.[129] Moreover, it argued that the world painted by Homer was an ideologically motivated representation of a heroic society, serving the purpose of elite self-definition.[130] With regard to the economic reality of early Greece, in addition to the use of exaggerations and archaisms set to create 'epic distance',[131] the epics offer a strongly selective representation of aspects of the economy that suit its agenda of heroic elite self-legitimisation, while ignoring or marginalising those aspects and groups that do not fit this agenda.

124 Goodenough 2011, 47; van Wees 2013, 76–78.
125 Cf. Descat 2001, 70–71.
126 Cf. *Od.* 3.273–275; 12.335–337; 16.184–185.
127 Finley 1954.
128 Hägg 1983b, 7.
129 Snodgrass 1974.
130 E.g., Morris 1986b; Sherratt 1990; Raaflaub 1998; 2008. Cf. Donlan 1982.
131 Raaflaub 1998.

Often noted in this regard is the negative attitude displayed in the epics towards trade – reflecting its existence in reality. While a guest at the Phaiakans, Odysseus is openly insulted by Euryalos, who makes him out for 'one of those grasping traders that go about in ships as captains or merchants, and who think of nothing but of their outward freights and homeward cargoes'.[132] Also, Phoenicians, consistently appearing as tradesmen, are mostly described as untrustworthy folk (τρώκτης, a greedy trickster),[133] who had kidnapped Odysseus' swineherd Eumaios as a child and sold him off as a slave.[134] Alternatively, in several instances trade is implied or hinted at without specific negative connotations, such as in the case of Mentes, king of 'the oar-loving Taphians', who sails with a load of iron to Temese to acquire copper,[135] or Nausikaa, who describes the Phaiakans as proud sailors of the sea.[136] Certainly, sailing the seas and exploring the margins of the world in search of knowledge, power and treasures – κειμήλια – or luxury goods[137] was not viewed negatively but regarded as a feature of heroic life.[138] Exchange in this context was also accepted, preferably in the honourable form of gift exchange, so evidently emphasised in the epics; yet commercial trade, trade for the purpose of making profit – κέρδος – was regarded with distaste.[139] This negative attitude towards commercial trade could explain the Homeric reluctance to refer to value in terms that must have been common among traders: precious metal in weight units.

Rather than expressing value in precious metal on a weight standard, the basic way in which value is assessed in the Homeric epics is with reference to an amount of cattle. A prize tripod in the funerary games for Patroklos is valued at twelve oxen (δυωδεκάβοιον),[140] and the second prize, a woman skilled in handwork, is valued at four oxen (τεσσαράβοιον).[141] It has been argued that this standard was the universal measure of value in early Greece,[142] but rather than seeing the use of an oxen-standard in the Homeric epics as necessarily representing a practice in reality, its use and prominence in the Homeric economy might have been ideologically motivated, emphasising

132 *Od.* 8.158–164 (trans. Butler).
133 *Od.* 14.289; 15.415–416.
134 *Od.* 15.380–484; Stanley 1986, 7; Winter 1995; Sherratt 2010. Cf. Peacock 2011b.
135 *Od.* 1.181–184.
136 *Od.* 6.268–272; cf. Peacock 2011b, n. 37; cf. *Od.* 19.282–290; Stanley 1986; Schaps 2004, 74–77; Seaford 2004, 26–28; 2011.
137 *Od.* 19.272.
138 Helms 1988; Heymans and van Wijngaarden 2011.
139 Mele 1979; Stanley 1986, 10–11; Schaps 2004, 74–77; Seaford 2004, 26–30; Sherratt 2010. Cf. *Od.* 19.283–286; Peacock 2011b, 18–21.
140 *Il.* 23.703.
141 *Il.* 23.705.
142 Kroll 2001; Tandy 2011; van Wees 2013, 112–115.

cattle as the primary form of value.[143] By expressing transferable value in terms of cattle, the idea is reinforced that, ultimately, heroic wealth is based not on the amount of κέρδος one makes, sailing on a ship, or how much treasure one owns, but on the amount of cattle he possesses.[144] Likewise, Nestor's forceful taking of the Epeians' livestock, specifically cattle, as a way to settle a debt confirms their significance as a primary form of value.[145] The offer of cattle by means of sacrifice was, not coincidentally, the ultimate payment to the gods, while being a stage for elite activity, such as communal dining, dating back to the Early Iron Age.[146]

Moreover, the evidence hardly suggests that it functioned as a universal measure. Rather, the use of the oxen-standard in the world of Homer is restricted: only people and prestige objects, such as tripods and heroic armour, are referred to in oxen-worth.[147] In a single case, a fine (τιμή) as a form of recompense is expressed in oxen-worth, when one of the suitors, Eurymachos, attempts to appease Odysseus by promising him that in addition to compensating what they have eaten from his palace, 'each one of us shall pay you a fine [τιμή] worth twenty oxen, and we will keep on giving you gold and bronze till your heart is softened'.[148] The offer is rejected by Odysseus as an unacceptable price for dishonouring him and his house, and instead, he has them pay with their lives.[149] Also, bride wealth is expressed with reference to oxen, although cattle is explicitly mentioned, and not necessarily as a measure.[150] The reference to cattle as a measure of value evidently relates to goods of a higher level of prestige,[151] and as Laum argues, the standard was likely derived from animal sacrifices, further adding to the moral or prestige context of its use. The world of Homer is not unique in referring to cattle in such a moral context of use: blood money in the early Medieval Welsh and Irish laws was expressed in cattle, and in the 1920s the Nuer, a pastoral people in southern Sudan, employed a price for blood money and for bride wealth in cattle.[152]

This implies that although it is certainly possible that such a standard functioned in early Greece, it was likely restricted to certain social contexts.

143 Gallant 1982, 118; Sherratt 2010, 135.
144 *Od.* 14.96–104.
145 *Il.* 11.670–762. Cf. *Od.* 21.16–23.
146 Cf. Morgan 1999, 374, with bibliography; McInerney 2010.
147 For people (i.e., slaves), see *Od.* 1.430–431; *Il.* 21.79; for heroic armour, see *Il.* 6.235–236.
148 *Od.* 22.57–59 (trans. Butler).
149 *Od.* 22.45–67. This rejection should not be regarded as a 'breakdown in reciprocity', as claimed by Seaford (2011), approaching the proposal in the framework of gift exchange, but rather as an example of *poine*, a compensation payment for suffered damages, in this case in the form of a *timē*, a fine (see Section 5.3.2; Wilson 2002).
150 *Il.* 11.242–243; 18.593; Hes. *CW* fr.7, l.9; Grierson 1977, 9–10.
151 Cf. the concept of spheres of exchange, see Section 2.2.1.
152 Evans-Pritchard 1940, 16–50; Grierson 1977, 12; Graeber 2011, 98, 134–135, 171.

Considering the high value of a single ox, we should wonder what role it could have had in the wider economy. Items of less prestige (i.e., subsistence goods) that did not belong to the heroic sphere could hardly have been valued with reference to oxen.[153] Despite the many assumptions that it did function outside of the heroic economy, Homer is in fact the only reliable source testifying to its use.[154] In a single case, the late second century CE scholar Pollux mentions that 'the laws of Draco list a payment of twenty oxen-worth',[155] leading van Wees to reach the rather far-fetched conclusion that the standard was still in use during the time of Draco (late seventh century BCE) and presumably continued down to Solon, who would have reformed this measure.[156] However, it is more likely that Pollux rhetorically projected the Homeric oxen-worth on the laws of Draco, assuming that it must have been in use. The notion that it indicates the universal use of an oxen-standard in Ionia throughout the Archaic period is altogether unconvincing.

On the whole, the oxen-standard should be understood as part of a heroic economy, represented in the epics; another aspect of this heroic economy is the institution of gift exchange. The gift functions in this context as means to secure the friendship bond, as can be seen when Telemachos offers a gift to Athena, disguised as Mentes:

> 'I will then give you a present, and you shall go on your way rejoicing; I will give you one of great beauty and value – a keepsake such as only dear friends give to one another.' Athena answered, 'Do not try to keep me, for I would be on my way at once. As for any present you may be disposed to make me, keep it till I come again, and I will take it home with me. You shall give me a very good one, and I will give you one of no less value in return.'[157]

This passage is characteristic for Finley's understanding of gift exchange: 'Telemachus had said nothing about a counter gift. Yet he and "Mentes" understood each other perfectly: the counter-gift was as expected as the original gift at parting'.[158]

[153] Schaps 2004, 70.
[154] Cf. Hes. *CW* fr.7.9.
[155] Pol. 9.60–61.
[156] van Wees 2013, 112–115, 121–123. Pollux, believing that the 'ox' had been an early Athenian coin stamped with the image of an ox, also mentions that an number of oxen are said to be referred to as prizes at the Delian festival, noting that for each 'ox' two Attic drachmas are then given (9.61). As Schaps notes, this could hardly refer to an actual ox, but whether it might have referred to early coin type is uncertain (2004, 240. Cf. Ridgeway 1892, 4–6; Davis 2012, 144).
[157] *Od.* 1.311–318 (trans. Butler).
[158] Finley 1954, 63.

Although its prominence should likely be seen as illustrating heroic elite interaction, it was emphasised by Finley as the dominant mode of exchange in early Greece,[159] and widely accepted, affecting ideas on exchange in the historical societies of the Geometric and Early Archaic periods.[160] Critical readings were few and of limited influence.[161] Also with concern to archaeological finds, gift exchange became a prominent model to explain the spread of specific valued objects in graves and sanctuaries in Geometric and Archaic Greece.[162]

Partly as a consequence of this, the existence of commodity trade in early Greece has been downplayed,[163] and money, a topic only marginally addressed, was assumed to have only existed as coin.[164] However, looking past the deliberate marginalisation of trade, the epics do in fact hint at its existence. For example, an awareness of alternative modes of exchange can be seen seeping through in one of the most prominent examples of gift exchange. When Diomedes and Glaukos exchange armour on the battlefield, Homer deliberately notes the inequality of their exchange: 'And then did Zeus, son of Kronos take away Glaukos' sense, for he exchanged armour with Diomedes, son of Tydeus, gold for bronze, worth a hundred oxen for worth nine oxen'.[165] The mention of the exchange value in the gift exchange (whether on a heroic standard or not), and Diomedes' abuse of the situation seems 'antithetical to the spirit of gift-exchange', and suggests that the audience was familiar with calculative aspects of regular exchange.[166]

More explicitly, in several instances gifts are used as a means of establishing a market for trade. When the Lemnians provide the Greeks with wine, they first bring a thousand measures to Agamemnon and Menelaos, who allow them to establish a temporary market where the Greeks can buy wine in exchange for other products.[167] In a similar case, the Phoenicians offer a silver bowl as a gift

[159] Finley 1954.

[160] E.g., Qviller 1981; Donlan 1982.

[161] Cf. Murray [1980] 1993; Stanley 1986; Hooker 1989. Despite a shift in focus in explaining economic interaction in early Greece in scholarship of the 1990s, and the rejection of most of the Finleyan orthodoxy (see, for example Morris 2003), the supposed dominance of gift exchange was never fundamentally questioned and continues to surface (wherever modes of exchange are addressed) in mild forms in general studies of the period (see Jones 1999 for a less mild form; Whitley 2001; Hall 2007, 261, 272; Ulf 2009, 87–88; van Wees 2009, 458–459; Seaford 2011). In recent years, a sense of discomfort towards such overtly primitivist models has become more apparent in general scholarship (see, for example, Dickinson 2006, 206, 214).

[162] Coldstream 1983; Morris 1986a; Langdon 1987.

[163] Finley [1973] 1985; Hopkins 1983. Cf. Morris 2003.

[164] Finley [1973] 1985, 166–169, 174.

[165] *Il.* 6.234–236.

[166] Hooker 1989, 80; Seaford 2004, 34; 2011. Cf. Finley 1954, 63; Calder 1984; Donlan 1989.

[167] *Il.* 7.467–475.

for their anchorage in the harbour of Lemnos, suggesting that their gift provided them with access to a market.[168]

To sum up, the heroic economy reflected in the Homeric epics offers an ideologically constructed representation of reality, emphasising certain aspects, such as an oxen standard of value and the prominence of gift exchange, while marginalising others, notably trade. At the same time, the epics offer a distant reflection of the non-heroic economic reality, in which markets and commodity exchange were present.

5.3.2 Wergeld *in Homer*

In addition to these forms of exchange in the epics, there are also payments that are symbolic compensation for the value of a human life. Such payments are found throughout the Iliad in particular in the context of ransom (*apoina*) or recompense (*poine*)[169] and can both be understood as forms of *wergeld*. Such *wergeld* payments, also discussed in previous chapters, can be regarded as a typical context for the use of early forms of money, being associated with the development of money as a standard of value, or money of account.[170]

The concept of *poinē* (ποινή) refers to a compensation or recompense for suffered damage, ultimately the loss of life.[171] Of the many cases of *poine* in the Iliad, only in few is an actual transferable payment (payment of goods) implied. Criticising Achilles' blind anger, Ajax says (citing a theoretical case) that even someone whose brother or son is killed accepts *poine* from the murderer.[172] In the *ekphrasis* of the shield of Achilles, where a city is depicted, two men quarrel in the agora over the *poine* of a man that had been killed, with one claiming he had paid all and the other objecting (indicating a transferable payment, or fine).[173] In the middle, two golden talents are offered as a reward for fair judgement.[174]

However, in most instances in the epics (with their hot-headed egos) revenge and retribution in the framework of blood feud takes precedence over the regulation of damages through such payments.[175] Odysseus recounts how he made the Cyclops repay the *poine* for eating his comrades,[176] and Akamas avenges his dead brother by murdering Promachos, so that his

168 *Il.* 23.741–745; Stanley 1986, 8–9; Tandy 1997, 73. For other examples of trade or the reference to markets, see Stanley 1986; Schaps 2004, 74–77; Seaford 2011.
169 Wilson 2002.
170 See Sections 2.1 and 4.1.2.
171 Wilson 2002.
172 *Il.* 9.633–636. Cf. 3.285–290.
173 *Il.* 18.498–500; Wilson 2002, 159–161.
174 *Il.* 18.507–508.
175 Cf. *Il.* 18.109.
176 *Od.* 23.312–313.

brother's *poine* would not remain unpaid.[177] In another situation, Achilles takes twelve young Trojans prisoner, 'as a *poine* for the death of Patroklos', to later sacrifice them in his thirst for revenge.[178]

Closely related to this is the concept of *apoina* (ἄποινα), which is a ransom for redeeming a human life, or in the ultimate situation, a dead body.[179] The opening verses of the Iliad have the Trojan priest Chryses come to the ships of the Achaians 'in order to set free [λυσόμενός] his daughter, carrying a ransom past counting' (φέρων τ' ἀπερείσι' ἄποινα),[180] and in the final book, Priam goes down to the tent of Achilles to redeem the body of Hektor with an *aponia*.[181] The Trojans would redeem their captured sons by offering gold as *apoina*;[182] and *apoina* is also used in the sale of slaves, as the Lemnian Euneos paid an *apoina* for Lykaon.[183]

Although in the literary context of the epics *poine* is rarely offered, but usually exacted through blood-revenge, both *poine* and *apoina* are essentially compensation payments for a human life, and as such the Homeric equivalent of *wergeld*.[184] Appearing throughout the Iliad, these *wergeld* payments are transferable (implied by the verb φέρω)[185] and associated with high-value commodities. At the core of the payment, we often find gold.[186] The most elaborate description of such a payment is situated at the centre of the dramatic climax of the Iliad, when Priam descends from the city to redeem his son's body.[187] Preparing the *apoina* to offer to Achilles, he took out several robes, 'and having weighed it [στήσας], he took in total ten talents of gold, and two gleaming tripods and four cauldrons'.[188] In other cases, only gold, or gold and other metals are mentioned, indicating that gold was the most prominent or central element of the *wergeld* payment. It was measured by its weight, as

177 *Il.* 14.483–484.

178 *Il.* 21.27–28. Cf. 18.336–337; 23.175–176, 181–182. See also Wilson 2002, 153–164.

179 *Il.* 22.338–342, 349–352; 24.

180 *Il.* 1.12–13.

181 *Il.* 24.502, 555–556, 579, 594.

182 *Il.* 2.229–230

183 *Il.* 23. 746–747; cf. 21.34–135. See also Wilson 2002, 147–153.

184 See also Sections 2.1 and 4.1.2; Grierson 1977, 18. Within the world of the epics, heroic norms prescribe solidarity between companions (*hetairoi*), allowing them to exact *poine*, which is what Odysseus does for his companions (*Od.* 23.312–313), and Achilles for Patroklos. However, in addition to historical and ethnographic parallels, two passages suggest that historically, *wergeld* rights were kinship based: Ajax's reference to a man accepting *poine* for his brother and son (see above), and Lykaon's denial of blood-liability for Hektor, 'for I am not from the same womb as Hektor' (ἐπεὶ οὐχ ὁμογάστριος Ἕκτορός εἰμι; *Il.* 21.95–96). His supplication of last resort indicates that, customarily, blood feud and *wergeld* liability were kinship-based (*pace* Wilson 2002, 171).

185 *Il.* 1.13, 24.502, 556.

186 *Il.* 2.229–230.

187 Wilson 2002, 126–133.

188 *Il.* 24.228–237, spec. 232–233. Cf. Richardson 1993, 297–298.

indicated by the association with the verb ἵστημι,[189] and the reference to talents, a (symbolic) weight unit.[190]

In addition to its use in *wergeld* payments, talents of gold appear as a prize in the funerary games for Patroklos, and, as mentioned previously, as a reward for good judgement. As a prestige item, associated with the gods, it endowed the receiver with honour;[191] it was equally able to compensate damage (i.e., the loss of honour) and make amends in the case of a severely disrupted relationship,[192] symbolising honour and divine justice. In addition to the gold, the significance of the *wergeld* payment is further emphasised by the presence of prestige items – the tripods and cauldrons – known for their symbolic value as objects of dedication, payment and exchange.[193]

Additional examples of *apoina* give further context to the role of precious metal within the Homeric economy. When Agamemnon captures the sons of Antimachos, they offer him a ransom, referring to the treasures (κειμήλια) stored at their father's house:

> Take us alive, son of Atreus, and accept a worthy ransom; many treasures lie stored in the house of Antimachos, bronze and gold and iron worked with much toil; and from these would our father grant you ransom past counting if he should hear that we are alive at the ships of the Achaeans.[194]

This is an almost exact repetition of words used by Adrastos to ransom himself from the hands of Menelaos,[195] and similar words are also used by Dolon against Odysseus and Diomedes.[196] Although none of these offers are accepted, they all indicate that an *apoina* payment consists of κειμήλια, treasures of metal that are stored or hoarded (κεῖται) in their fathers house.[197] Likewise, Priam goes down to a treasure-chamber (θάλαμος) in order to collect the *apoina* for his son.[198] In a similar description in the Odyssey, Penelope goes up to a room or treasury

[189] *Cf. Il.* 19.247; 22.350; 24.232.

[190] *Cf. Il.* 9.122; 18.507; 23.269, 751; *Od.* 4.525–526. It has been observed that the quantities of gold mentioned by Homer are remarkably large by later (ancient) standards (e.g., two talents of gold as a reward for good judgement). Following earlier suggestions, van Wees claims that this suggests an earlier weight system had been in place, in which the talent had been significantly smaller (Ridgeway 1892, 7; van Wees 2013, 111–112). There is no reason to assume the existence of such a system, and the mention of talents can very well be regarded as a symbolic exaggeration, set to enforce the image of a wealthy heroic age (cf. Brown 1998; Nicolet-Pierre 2006).

[191] Brown 1998; Seaford 2004, 30–33.

[192] Cf. *Il.* 9.120–123ff.

[193] Cf. *Il.* 9.122–123. See Section 5.3.3.

[194] *Il.* 11.131–135 (trans. Loeb).

[195] *Il.* 6.46–50.

[196] *Il.* 10.378–381.

[197] Cf. Finley 1954, 58.

[198] *Il.* 24.191.

(θάλαμος) where they had stored the κειμήλια of the king, 'bronze and gold and iron, wrought with toil'.[199] De Jong refers to this as 'the "storeroom" type scene', denoting a standard scene with a standard set of elements, variously elaborated in different parts of the epic.[200] Additionally, a fragment of the seventh century poet Mimnermos refers to the location of the Golden Fleece as 'Aietes' city, where swift Helios' rays are stored in a golden chamber/treasury by the edge of Okeanos',[201] again reflecting a habitual association between gold (χρυσός; here used as adjective for θάλαμος, but also invoking the golden rays of the sun and the Golden Fleece), the act of storing (κεῖμαι) and a room or treasury (θάλαμος) as the setting. The recurrence of this formulaic description reflects something that was well understood: any significant household had disposal over hoarded valuables, most prominently metals, stored in a treasury.

Although the wealth of the *oikos* in the world of Homer was supposedly measured in livestock,[202] *wergeld* payments were made with hoarded treasures, such as gold. These payments constitute a form of compensation that could function as an alternative to revenge and retribution, and the dramatic choice between these stands at the centre of the Iliad. Its prominence in the heroic epic, moreover, reveals that *wergeld* laws, well known from other early societies,[203] were also known in early Greek historical society. Considering the increasing significance of gold and bronze in Late Geometric and Early Archaic society,[204] it is likely that these metals, measured by weight, featured prominently in such *wergeld* payments.

5.3.3 *Money in Early Law*

Several of the earliest Greek laws preserved in stone testify to the payment of fines. Generally known as the earliest Greek law, the Dreros law is recorded on a limestone inscription consisting of five lines from the Cretan polis of Dreros and dates to the middle of the seventh century.[205] Invoking the mandate of the community ('Thus has the polis decided'), the law sets the term for the local

199 *Od.* 21.9–10. Cf. *Od.* 2.337–381; 15.99–110.

200 de Jong 2001, 505–506, 598.

201 'Ἠελίοιο ἀκτῖνες χρυσέωι κείαται ἐν θαλάμωι'. Fr 11a W; after West 2011, 114.

202 *Od.* 14.96–108.

203 Grierson 1977.

204 Cf. Sections 5.2 and 5.4.

205 Dr1; Gagarin and Perlman 2016, 200–207. For the laws discussed (and quoted) in this section, I refer to the recent volume by Gagarin and Perlman (2016), which presents new editions of Cretan laws including translations, commentaries, accessible discussions of various aspects, and additional references. Most of these inscriptions have been previously published in the various volumes of *IC* (Inscriptiones Creticae, Guarducci 1935–1950) and follow its numbering, but have the place code replaced by an abbreviation, so *IC* 4.72, the Great Code from Gortyn, is listed as G72 (see Gagarin and Perlman 2016, x).

magistrate, the *kosmos*, determining that if someone has held the office of *kosmos*, he cannot serve in that capacity again for ten years. 'But if he should serve as *kosmos*, whenever he should give judgement, he [i.e., the kosmos] is to owe double, and he is to be without rights for as long as he lives, and whatever he should do as *kosmos* is to be void.'[206]

Apparently, one of the tasks of the *kosmos* was to serve as judge, in which capacity he would impose fines. Having to owe double implies that he had to repay twice the amount of the fine imposed. This double amount indicates that, within early Greek law, fines of a punitive nature developed, with the state or a god as its beneficiary,[207] or perhaps the double amount entailed the return of a possible reward for the judgement as we have seen on the shield of Achilles.[208] It is not mentioned in what medium the payment was to be made.

Although still the subject of debate, (extant) early Greek law has been argued to be largely procedural, focusing on what procedure to follow, rather than substantive, that is, pointing out right from wrong.[209] In these procedural laws, many aspects remain unmentioned or unexplained. This implies that the first written laws functioned within a judicial context of traditional custom and unwritten laws, which formed the basis for dealing with aspects of jurisdiction that were left unmentioned by these written laws.[210] Such customary laws formed the basis for the judgement and fines referred to in the Dreros law, and it is likely that these fines concerned compensation payments for suffered damage.

Many of the earliest inscriptions from the city of Gortyn contain laws that refer to payments and/or fines. Dating from the end of the seventh century to ca. 525 BCE, these laws were inscribed on the walls and steps of the temple of Apollo Pythios. Although the laws are often difficult to read, due of their fragmentary nature, eight of the laws mention specific compensation payments or fines, all of which were listed in *lebetes* (cauldrons).[211] The fines are set in the amounts of five, ten, twenty, fifty and one hundred *lebetes*.[212] The conventional use of *lebetes* in recording fines suggests that a *lebes* represented a set amount of value.

Although the laws explicitly mention that '*lebetes* are to be paid',[213] it is not likely that the payments physically involved cauldrons themselves.[214] More

206 l.2–3.

207 Gagarin and Perlman 2016, 109–110, 205. Cf. Cohen 2005, 173–174.

208 *Il.* 18.507–508.

209 Gagarin 1986, 78, 95. Cf. Hölkeskamp 1990; Pelloso 2013.

210 Thomas 2005, 53–57.

211 Outside of Gortyn, a law from Lyktos dating to ca. 500 BCE also lists a payment of one hundred *lebetes* (Gagarin and Perlman 2016, Lyktos1A6, 486–492).

212 G1; G21 (five *lebetes*); G8 (ten *lebetes*); G10; G11 (twenty *lebetes*); G10; G14 (fifty *lebetes*); G1; G5; G7 (one hundred *lebetes*); Gagarin and Perlman 2016.

213 Cf. 'πέντε λέβητας καταστᾶσαι', G21, 7–8.

214 van Wees 2013, 113; Gagarin and Perlman 2016, 107. Cf. Guarducci 1944–45; von Reden 1997, 157–158; Kroll 2001a, 87–88; Schaps 2004, 82–83.

likely, these prestige objects were referred to as a measure of value, suggested also by a specific law that imposes the payment of 'one tripod sworn to be (worth?) ten cauldrons'.[215] The tripod in this provision likely refers to an actual object, rather than a measure of value, as it would have sufficed otherwise to note just the amount in *lebetes*.[216]

It is notable though that such prestige objects (tripods and cauldrons) would feature in early laws. Both were known as objects used in the Homeric epics in contexts of (gift) exchange and payments, such as in the *wergeld* payments offered by Agamemnon to appease Achilles[217] and by Priam to Achilles in order to redeem his son's body.[218] Also, when Odysseus leaves for Ithaka, the chief men of the Phaiakans give him each a tripod and a cauldron.[219] We can infer that these objects signified honour, making them symbolically suitable for compensation payments and fines.[220] As such, it cannot be ruled out that tripods and cauldrons, prestige objects that moreover functioned as votive offerings or payments to the gods, were used themselves in contexts of elite exchange and payment.[221]

However, other than those citing *lebetes*, many early laws do not mention a specific fine, or a medium in which these are paid, but simply note in some cases: 'he shall pay the simple/double value'.[222] It is plausible that such fines were known through custom or depended on ad hoc judgement. At the same time, we can reasonably expect that people were able to pay in different media, something that is also implied by the mention of both grain and staters on two inscriptions from Eleutherna[223] and the payment of a wage (μισθόν) of a certain amount of grape 'must, [–] worth twenty drachmas (?), or bronze' (of equivalent value) on a bronze plaque from Datala of ca. 500 BCE.[224] It is altogether plausible that multiple media functioned as forms of money in the Archaic period,[225] and substitutes for conventional money were likely to remain important.

In this sense, considering the fact that other media of payment were likely accepted, it is clear that *lebetes* functioned as a measure of value. This measure

215 G81, a–f.

216 Gagarin and Perlman 2016, 107, 272–273. Cf. von Reden 1997, 158.

217 *Il.* 9.120–123.

218 *Il.* 24.232–233.

219 *Od.* 13.13–14.

220 The appearance of a fine in *lebetes*, together with staters on what might be an early law from Knossos that was reinscribed in the third century, indicates that the symbolism of the *lebes* as object of payment, object of value, enabled a continued association with money (*IC* I.8.5B; von Reden 1997, 158; Gagarin and Perlman 2016, 107, n. 280).

221 Schaps 2004, 82–88, spec. 87–88.

222 E.g., G13i2; G41.1.6–7.

223 Ele9; Ele13.

224 Da1A13–14; Gagarin and Perlman 2016, 110, 181–193.

225 Descat 2001.

of value was clearly not universal, as historical evidence for its use is restricted to the payment of fines.[226] The significance of these fines is often not clear though. The payment of a tripod in G8 is described explicitly as a *poine*, suggesting that the law could deal with homicide,[227] and also the other fines could concern *wergeld* payments, but often the fragmentary nature of the laws does not allow us to understand what these fines were based on.

However, when looking at later laws from Gortyn, we can observe more clearly how these laws reflect a formal kinship with the concept of *wergeld*. This is shown by the Late Archaic 'Little Code', of which seven columns with seventeen lines each are preserved.[228] A large part of the extant law (the first three columns) deals with damages relating to animals, including matters concerning rights and liability, and brings to mind the *Lex Salica*, known for its *wergeld*-laws that offer detailed provisions on animals.[229] More elaborate still is the early classical 'Great Code' of Gortyn,[230] which was presumably meant to systematise if not replace earlier laws and redefine penalties, previously in *lebetes*, in coined staters and drachmas.[231] After the first column dealing with the ownership of persons, the second column offers a particularly interesting example for the judicial reasoning behind the fines. It deals with sexual offences:

> if someone rapes a free man or woman, he will pay a hundred staters .... If a slave (rapes) a free man or woman, he will pay double. If a free man (rapes) a male or female serf, (he will pay) five drachmas. And if a serf (rapes) a male or female serf, five staters. *vac.* If someone should subdue by force a household slave woman, he will pay two staters; but if she has already had intercourse (he will pay) one obol during the day, but if at night, two obols ....[232]

Clearly, the fines listed are compensations for suffered damage, and the higher the status of the victim, or the lower that of the offender, the larger the damage incurred by the offence, and thus the higher the compensation is set.[233]

The dominant concern with compensating damages in these laws (and who is liable for those damages) indicates that the evidence for payments and money as available from early law texts, is related, as Grierson already argued in a wider sense, to *wergeld* payments. As we have seen Section 5.3.2, the phenomenon of *wergeld* payments in Homer, perhaps incipient in its procedural form,

226 Cf. van Wees 2013, 113–115.
227 Gagarin and Perlman 2016, 273.
228 G41.
229 Grierson 1977, 12.
230 G72.
231 Davies 2005, 308–309. Cf. Hölkeskamp 1999, 126–128.
232 G72 2.2–15; Gagarin and Perlman 2016, 345–350.
233 Grierson 1977, 18; Cantarella 2005, 245.

shows a concern with regulating revenge and restricting blood feud. The Gortyn laws indicate that this concern was to develop and expand in early Greek law.

The concern with regulating private revenge is also evident in Draco's homicide law. Enacted around 620 BCE, and reinscribed in the late fifth century, the law established procedures for the prosecution of homicide, prohibiting private revenge (with the notable exception of a man who had caught another man next to his kin), and thereby reforming traditional custom.[234] As elsewhere, it reflects the emerging civic body's concern for setting procedures in order to deal with offences.

With the exception of the homicide laws, the laws of Draco were repealed by Solon, who was said to have replaced them with a new law code.[235] In addition to the ritual calendar, he was credited with significant reforms, enacted during his archonship in 594 BCE,[236] and entering tradition as establishing the basis of the later Athenian democracy.[237] His laws were inscribed on *axones*, inscribed wooden poles that revolved within a wooden frame.[238] Plutarch writes that remains of these were still preserved in the Prytaneion in Athens in his time.[239] Several of these axons held fines that were listed in drachmas, such as a fine of five drachma for slander,[240] or a hundred drachmas for rape against a free woman, and twenty if she was seduced.[241] With Athenian coinage only minted after the middle of the sixth century,[242] it was suggested by Peter Rhodes that these drachmas refer to the weight of uncoined silver.[243] The same has been suggested in relation to the mention of a stater in a law inscription from Chios dating to first half of the sixth century: with the first known Chian coins dating well after the inscription, it is likely that the staters in the law refer to uncoined metal.[244] This would imply that

[234] *IG* I³ 104; Cantarella 2005, 239; Thomas 2005, 56–57. Gagarin (1986, 89, n. 23) suggests that homicide laws were rare, as homicide was usually covered through traditional custom, dealt with between families.

[235] *Ath. Pol.* 7.1; Plut. *Sol.* 17.1–2.

[236] Rhodes 1981, 121–122; Wallace 1983.

[237] Thomas 2005, 41; Davis 2012, 153, n. 144. In what was long considered the standard work on the laws of Solon, Ruschenbusch (1966) identified ninety-three laws or fragments of laws that he argued to be authentic (cf. Ruschenbusch 2010). In a new edition, Leão and Rhodes (2015) have further expanded the corpus, including another thirty-seven fragments. For Solon in general, see Blok and Lardinois 2006.

[238] Stroud 1979.

[239] Plut. *Sol.* 25.

[240] Three for the injured party and two for the treasury; Plut. *Sol.* 21.1; F 32.

[241] Plut. *Sol.* 23.1; F 26; F 30.

[242] Kroll and Waggoner 1984, 326–333.

[243] Rhodes 1975; 1981, 152–153; Kroll 1998; 2001a, 77–84; 2008a; 2012.

[244] Jeffery 1956, 160; ML no. 8.

either silver was used to pay fines that existed in law by the early sixth century or that silver was referred to in these fines as a measure of value. John Kroll has argued that a law on usury, attributed to Solon and referred to by Lysias, contains an archaic term (στάσιμον), referring to the obsolete procedure of weighing out silver in a scale.[245]

The suggestion that silver in weighed form was used as a means of exchange and payment in Solon's Athens could certainly be correct. Although appearing only marginally in the Homeric epics (mostly in association with Phoenicians), by the early sixth century, silver was regarded as an important form of wealth. Solon himself describes a wealthy person as 'having great possessions, silver and gold' as well as land and livestock.[246]

The Aristotelian *Athenaion Politeia* mentions that the laws of Solon, 'which are no longer in use', refer to the institution of the *naukrariai* (captaincies or ship-boards), and their officials, the *naukraroi* (captains or ship-chiefs), who were charged with raising the *eisphora*-tax and spending from 'the *naukraric* silver'.[247] The assumed purpose of this institution was financing the Athenian navy.[248] Van Wees explores in detail their role as an archaic naval institution with wide-ranging power and responsibilities going back to the late seventh century[249] and argues that they indicate the organisation of fiscal institutions using silver, going back to at least the early sixth century.[250]

It is possible that part of the *eisphora*-taxes (presumably ad hoc levies for funding the military) were paid in kind, especially if these levies concerned a proportion of the agricultural produce.[251] Yet a possible conversion rate from *medimnoi* of grain to silver would have allowed these taxes to be accounted for in silver.[252] In any case, the reference to 'naukraric silver' implies that in order for this fiscal system to have functioned, silver must have been circulating in

245 Lys. 10.18; F 68; Kroll 1998, 228–229; 2001a, 78–81. Cf. Schaps 2001, 97–98; Davis 2012, 154–156.

246 Plut. *Sol.* 2.2; Solon fr. 24 West.

247 *Ath. Pol.* 8.3; F 79.

248 Rhodes 1981, 50–53; Kroll 1998, 227–228.

249 It is generally accepted that they were active as early as the so-called Kylonian affair (Hdt. 5.71.2; Davis 2012, 153; van Wees 2013, 49–53).

250 van Wees 2013, 39–61. Sceptics have noted that the only explicit evidence for the use of *naukraric* silver was to pay for the expenses of the *naukraroi* on sacred embassy to Delphi (Androtion *FGrH* 324 fr. 36; Schaps 2001, 97; Davis 2012, 154). Van Wees argues that the sources for our information (notably the *Ath. Pol.*) were mostly compiled when the institution was already defunct, and consequently little was remembered of its former power and functions (van Wees 2013, spec. 55–56).

251 van Wees 2013, 29, 85.

252 Plut. *Sol.* 23.3. See Section 5.2.2. Gagarin and Perlman (2016, 110) note two examples of written laws from Crete that list or imply conversion ratios from silver to grain (Ele9; Ele13). One of these, a sixth or fifth century law from Eleutherna (Ele13), mentions the payment of a *medimnos* as a penalty, but this law appears to concern offences in relation to agricultural produce (Gagarin and Perlman 2016, 235–236).

society. Additionally, the possibility that the state imposed the payment of fines in silver suggests that expanding state institutions required silver for its policies.

The authenticity of the laws mentioning silver and the use of drachmas have been challenged in recent years, most notably by Gil Davis, who has consequently rejected the use of uncoined silver in Athens preceding coinage.[253] Evidently, our record of these laws is fragmentary, lacking in proper context, and most sources postdate Solon by at least two centuries; and it cannot be ruled out that the laws of Solon represent a complex and elaborate historiographical construct that only took shape by the fourth century BCE. But even if laws of later generations came to be associated with Solon in the fifth or fourth century as a point of reference for early Athenian law, the appearance of (written) laws and the incorporation of fines does not necessarily appear out of context in southern Greece of the early sixth century.[254] As we have seen, written laws appear in Crete from the second half of the seventh century, albeit fragmentarily preserved, and these show a clear concern with setting procedures for compensation and fines, thereby formalising and/or replacing customary law.[255]

Still, one could argue that the references to silver and drachmas are later injections, and indeed, Davis has argued that instead of silver, the *medimnos* would have functioned as the 'official measure of value'.[256] The *medimnos* was no doubt very important in the archaic Athenian economy as a measure of value in subsistence goods and a possible medium of exchange and payment in fines and obligations such as the *eisphora*.[257] Additionally, it functioned as a measure of agricultural wealth, forming the basis for defining the Solonian property classes, on which the *eisphora* might have been based.[258] However, parallels from the Ancient Near East testify to the common existence of a dry measure for grain (such as the biblical *ephah*)[259] alongside a precious metal weight standard that functions as the main form of money. Moreover, examples of *wergeld* payments, such as compensation in the Homeric record, as well as Gortynian fines, testify to the centrality of prestige items, symbolising honour and justice, if only as a measure of value, in denoting fines for moral

[253] Davis 2011; 2012. Cf. Schaps 2001. The revision of weights and measures attributed to Solon in antiquity (*Ath. Pol.* 10.1–2; Plut. *Sol.* 15; Andoc. I. 83) has been recognised to be problematic (Rhodes 1981, 164–169; Kroll 1998, 226; Davis 2012, 152; van Wees 2013, 115–121; cf. Kroll 2001a, 81–84), but many have accepted the fines.

[254] Harris 2006, 303–308. Cf. Davis 2011, 21.

[255] Gagarin 1986, 78–80, 95–96.

[256] Davis 2012, 143, 148, 151–152.

[257] The use of the *medimnos* in such contexts is accounted for outside of Athens as well. For example, a seventh-century law inscription from Tiryns describes that magistrates called *Platiwoinarchoi* are to levy a fine of 30 *medimnoi* from the *Platiwoinoi*, imposing the double amount if they fail to do so. The law is likely related to ritual banqueting (see Koerner 1993, no. 31, spec. 88–91).

[258] E.g., Davis 2012, 150–151; van Wees 2013, 85–90.

[259] E.g., Amos 8:5.

offences. It is therefore unlikely that a measure for subsistence goods would have functioned as the sole measure of value in the context of early penal law and early money-use.

Assessing the role of precious metal as a form of money in archaic Greece, we must admit that the textual evidence for silver-weight money in the laws of Solon is in itself not conclusive. Yet, the claim that we lack contemporary written evidence for the use of silver money should not be held as proof for the suggestion that silver had a marginal role in Greek society until the introduction of coinage.[260] Although it has taken up a significant place in the general debate on pre-coinage silver money in Greece,[261] in the end, the complex historical record of Solon provides only a very limited insight into the significance of silver in archaic Greece, confined moreover to a single Greek city, Athens. In order to place the potential evidence in a wider historical context, we need to turn to the development of precious metal use in the Aegean.

5.4 PRECIOUS METAL IN THE AEGEAN

5.4.1 *Euboian Pioneers*

In the course of the Archaic period, silver was to become the precious metal of choice in the Aegean economy. By the late sixth century, it circulated in significant quantities within the Aegean and across the eastern Mediterranean, as the preferred commodity of value and in the form of money. It is notable in this regard that silver is close to absent from the world of Homer.[262] As mentioned, it appears only in few and specific contexts, and never in weight (cf. talents of gold) but only as objects, such as the Sidonian bowl that the Phoenicians offered to Thoas, ending up as a prize in the funeral games for Patroklos,[263] or the krater, given by Menelaos to Telemachos, which he had originally received from Phaidimos, king of Sidon.[264] Elsewhere, a collection of silver gifts to Menelaos and Helena is mentioned to have been offered by Polybos and his wife Alkandra from Egyptian Thebes,[265] and the palace of Phaiakan King Alkinoos – an even more distant and exotic place – is described with columns, a lintel and a pair of watchdogs, all in silver.[266] The inspiration for this description was argued to have come from the Neo-Assyrian world, in

260 Cf. Davis 2012.
261 Kroll 1998; 2001a; 2008a; Schaps 2001; Davis 2012; van Wees 2013, 115–123.
262 Gray 1954, 1; Muhly 2011.
263 *Il.* 23.741–745.
264 *Od.* 4.614–619; 15.113–119.
265 *Od.* 4.128–132.
266 *Od.* 7.89–93.

particular the palace of Sargon II in Dur-Sharrukin.[267] Although silver is clearly a material of value, whenever gold and bronze are mentioned as the *keimelia* stored by Greeks and Trojans silver is absent.[268] References to silver in the Homeric record are strongly connected to the Mediterranean Near East (Egypt, the Levant, Assyria), where silver was commonly used as money during the late eighth century, while in the Aegean itself it was apparently still exotic.

Interestingly, this absence of silver is also reflected in the archaeological record.[269] For the Protogeometric period on the mainland, a single silver ring from the female inhumation grave under the Heroon in Lefkandi is reported,[270] and also for the Geometric period, silver finds remain exceptionally rare. Known examples are the silver fibulae from the MG Isis grave in Eleusis, an LG grave at the Odos Peiraios in Athens, and the LG Hygeionomeion cemetery at Eretria, although there might be more.[271] Crete and the Dodecanese, both with stronger Phoenician influence, have slightly more silver, among which are several silver objects from the Tekke tomb and several silver pins and rings in LG/EO graves at the Knossos North Cemetery.[272]

At the same time, evidence from eastern Attica demonstrates that silver production from the Laurion mines was taking place during the Iron Age. While industrial remains can be difficult to discern and date,[273] excavations at Thorikos exposed a large space with rock-cut basins, containing litharge and dated on the basis of EG II and MG I pottery to the ninth century. During the second half of the century, the space was buried in a rock collapse from the Velatouri hill, thereby preserving the remains.[274] Although the use of these installations was cut short, it is unlikely that this stopped silver production at Laurion in general.[275] With later activity potentially obliterating evidence, it cannot be ruled out that during the Middle and Late Geometric periods silver production continued on a small scale at Laurion, using what is known as the 'first contact', that is, ores that were exposed on the surface. Considering the lack of contemporary silver objects and the increasing contacts with the eastern Mediterranean, it seems likely that the silver produced was traded directly eastwards.[276]

267 Cook 2004.
268 See Section 5.3.2.
269 Dickinson 2006, 119–120, 215.
270 Lemos 2002, 128. The original publication refers to the ring as electrum (Popham, Calligas and Sackett 1993, 20).
271 Coldstream [1977] 2003, 79, 126, 198; Blandin 2007, 68.
272 See Kotsonas 2006, 157, 165–166.
273 See Section 5.4.3.
274 Mussche et al. 1967, 31–42; Coldstream [1977] 2003, 70; 1995, 399–400.
275 Treister 1996b, 23–24; Dickinson 2006, 83, 120. Cf. Davis 2012, 129; 2014, 260. Traces of silver production of PG date have also been identified at Argos (Lemos 2002, 138, n. 22; Dickinson 2006, 120).
276 Sherratt and Sherratt 1993, 363–369; Coldstream 1995, 399–402; Dickinson 2006, 214–215, 253.

Those Greeks involved in long-distance trade were surely familiar with weighing precious metal and using it in standard weights in exchange and payment, presumably through the increasing contacts and trade activity within the eastern Mediterranean in the ninth and eighth centuries. Clear indication is provided by the balance weights in grave T.79 in the Toumba cemetery of Lefkandi.[277] The person buried here is likely to have been a wealthy trader with connections in the eastern Mediterranean.[278] John Kroll showed that the balance weights, although not a coherent set, reflect active Euboian involvement in the Cypro-Levantine trade by at least the ninth century and argued that this led them to adopt an eastern weight standard that would become the basis for what came to be known in Archaic and Classical Greece as the *Euboic* standard, by adjusting the ca. 8.4 gram norm of the Mesopotamian standard slightly upwards to 8.64 grams.[279] The role of Phoenician intermediaries in this transmission is implied by the use of a 50-stater (or Euboic half-stater) mina in the Euboic-Attic system, like the Levantine 50-shekel mina, but in contrast to the Babylonian 60-shekel mina. The early prominence of this weight standard in the Greek world is also reflected by a bronze and lead weight of 8.79 grams found in a likely late eight/early seventh-century context in the artisanal quarter in Pithekoussai,[280] the Euboian-Phoenician trade colony in the gulf of Naples, and by its influence on the weight standards adopted by other Greek cities, such as Athens, Corinth and Samos. Clearly, the adoption of this standard by such powerful maritime trading cities of the Archaic period, while retaining the label 'Euboic',[281] suggests that the standard had originally been introduced within the Aegean by the Euboians or at least came to be associated with them at a time when they maintained a dominant position in maritime trade and colonisation, prior to the so-called Lelantine war of ca. 700 BCE.[282]

Direct evidence of the Euboian adoption of precious metal as a form of money is provided by the gold/electrum hoard from Eretria (Figure 5.4), previously discussed in Chapter 3. Although initially interpreted as evidence for a goldsmith workshop,[283] most recent commentators have compared the electrum hoard to the *hacksilber* hoards from the southern Levant, arguing for a monetary use.[284] Though this interpretation is justified, a thorough

[277] See Section 5.2.1.

[278] Popham and Lemos 1995.

[279] Kroll 2008b.

[280] Buchner 1970–1971, 66; Buchner and Gialanella 1994, 59; Verdan and Heymans 2021. Considering the fact that lead gains weight through oxidation, the weight could originally have been either the Euboic standard of 8.64 grams or the Mesopotamian of ca. 8.4 grams.

[281] Cf. Hdt. 3.89.

[282] Kroll 2001a, 81–82; 2008b, 44–46. Cf. Hall 2007, 1–8.

[283] Themelis 1981; 1983; Morris 1992a, 141; Treister 1996b, 82, 98.

[284] Furtwängler 1986, 156; Kopcke 1992, 112; Kroll 2001a, 77–78; 2008a, 34; 2012, 38; Le Rider and Verdan 2002, 141–152; Thompson 2003, 91–92; 2007, 199. Cf. Hoffman 1997, 203.

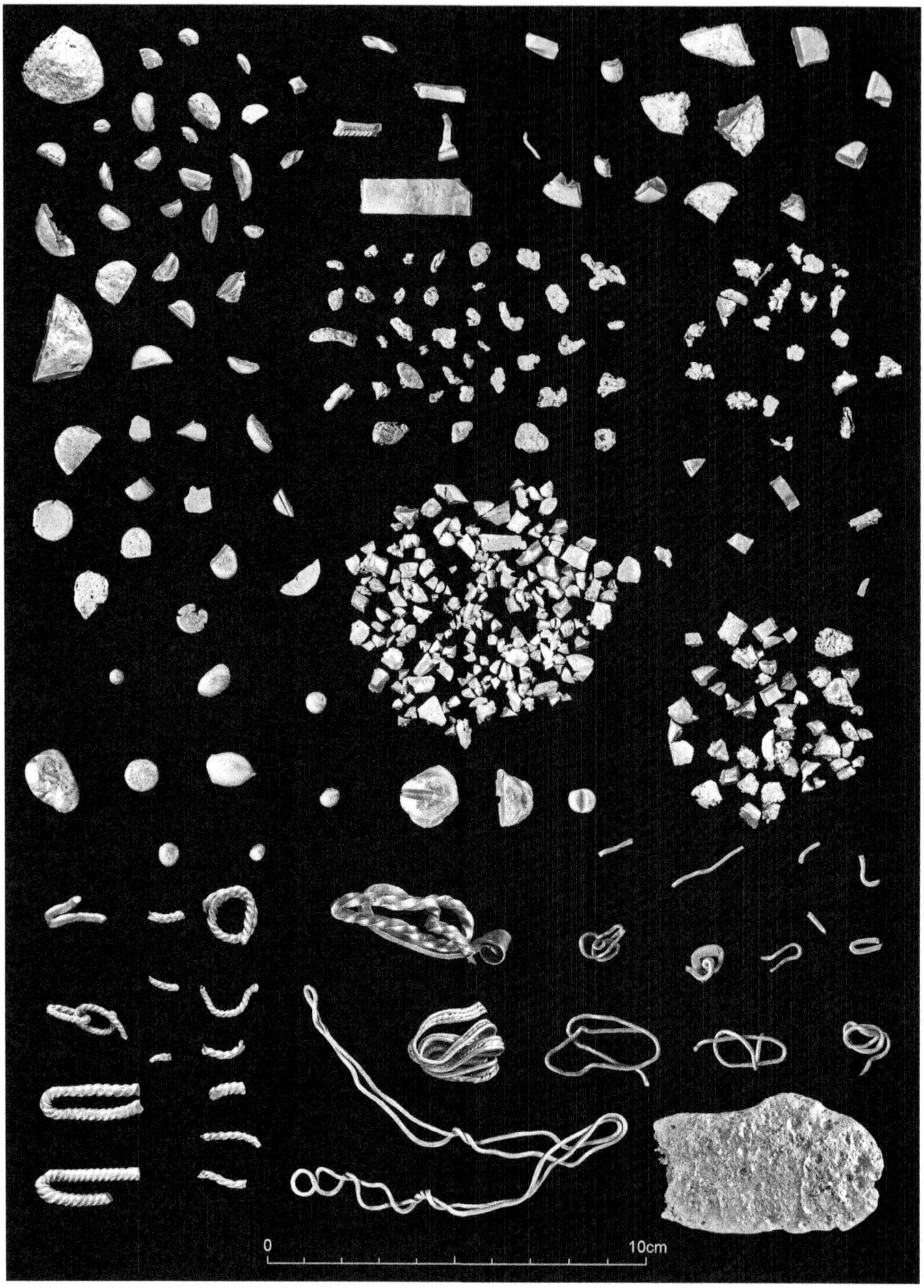

5.4 Eretria hoard (Courtesy of the Swiss School of Archaeology in Greece [photo by Andreas Skiadaressis])

comparison as a means of understanding its relation to the Levantine hoards can only be based on a detailed study of the hoard material, as presented in Chapter 3.

It was demonstrated there that the Eretria hoard shares clear metrological characteristics with contemporary hoards from the Levant, with a gradual weight distribution and a large proportion of small objects, indicating that the material was suitable for making small-scale and precise payments and featured in a dynamic exchange pattern involving the use of small change. A high level of circulation is furthermore confirmed by the many traces of wear on the objects. Also the hoard's typological characteristics are largely comparable to contemporary Levantine hoards, but – as noted – there are interesting differences here. The manipulation employed in order to fragment the objects was very similar, yet the original objects involved were somewhat different, with notable quantities of gold nuggets (11 per cent) and globules (27 per cent), contrasting with few or none of these objects in Levantine hoards. This reflects differences in the production process of the objects that initially entered into circulation, and the suggestion that the Eretria hoard would reflect 'a craftsman's dialogue between Phoenicians and Euboians'[285] fails to take into account these different production contexts.

While nuggets appear naturally in placer deposits (riverbeds) and are therefore specific to gold, globules can be connected to the specific production process of gold and electrum, testified by ceramic melting plates from Sardis, Eretria and Methone (Figure 5.5) that were used to process gold dust (placer gold) into a larger ingots, or globules, as a more convenient form for further use.[286] Although these differences hardly relate to the material's use in exchange, they are, as will be discussed below, significant for understanding how gold and electrum were produced and how they came to be appropriated for use as money. It is to this context that we now turn.

The prominence of Euboians in maritime trade and interaction during the ninth and eighth centuries was related to their increasing influence and presence in settlements abroad. Especially Euboian involvement in the northern Aegean, evident from the Protogeometric period onwards[287] and continuing into the Archaic period, is relevant to our effort to understand the role precious metal came to play in trade as a form of money. Although part of a wider phenomenon of Euboian exploration and expansion in the

[285] Thompson 2007, 199–200.

[286] Ramage and Craddock 2000, 90, 100, 102–117, 126–127, 132–134, 160–161, 207; Meeks and Craddock 2013, 271–273, pl. 127–129; Verdan 2013, 148–149, pl. 114; forthcoming; Verdan and Heymans 2021. For a detailed description of the production process, see Verdan forthcoming; Verdan and Heymans 2021.

[287] Lemos 2002, 212–217.

5.5 Ceramic melting plate from Methone (photo by Samuel Verdan)

Mediterranean,[288] a focus on the northern Aegean will prove helpful in exposing the context and circumstances in which this development took place.

Already during the Protogeometric period, Euboia and the northwest Aegean (Thessaly, the Sporades and parts of Macedonia) were linked in what Irene Lemos has described as a Euboian or Euboio-Thessalian *koine*.[289] In the course of the ninth and especially the eighth century, this involvement intensified across the area of the Thermaic gulf and the Chalkidike peninsula,[290] with evidence for direct links and substantial presence increasing, as suggested by Euboian ceramic imports as well as local production of Euboian-style ceramics.[291] Euboians were joining existing settlements, such as Sindos during phase 8 and 7,[292] and also establishing new colonies, such as Mende and Methone,[293] although it is likely that such foundations followed a local presence, as, for example, indicated by activity at the cultic site at cape Poseidi four kilometres west of Mende going back to the Late Mycenaean period.[294]

In the most extensive survey of Greek colonisation in the northern Aegean to date, Michalis Tiverios asserts that in the eighth and the early seventh century, newly established colonies were focused on agriculture.[295] It is,

288 E.g., Tandy 1997, 59–83; Lemos 2002, 212–217, 282–292; Luke 2003, 56–60. Cf. Papadopoulos 1997; 2011.

289 Lemos 1998; 2002, 212–217; Gimatzidis 2011a, 958–959.

290 Bats and Agostino 1998; Hammond 1998; Tiverios 2008, 1–51.

291 Papadopoulos 1996; Gimatzidis 2011a; Leone 2012.

292 Gimatzidis 2010; 2011b, 101.

293 Mende: Moschonissioti 1998; 2017; Methone: Bessios, Tzifopoulos and Kotsonas 2012.

294 Moschonissioti 1998, 260–267.

295 Tiverios 2008, 125. Tiverios refers to this as the first phase of the second colonisation, taking indications of earlier contact or influence (such as that at Poseidi near Mende) as evidence

however, becoming increasingly clear in recent years that other incentives for Euboian presence in the region were also at play.[296]

In contrast to local communities, Euboian colonies were predominantly situated on the coast, and settlements such as Mende, Sindos and Methone functioned as gateway communities, strategically located in order to allow access to local trade networks. Methone, founded according to literary tradition by Eretrians in 733/732 BCE, and Sindos, with substantial Euboian presence indicated from the first half of the eighth century, were both located on the edge of the Macedonian plain, along rivers that allowed access into the wealthy hinterland and into the Balkans: Methone on the edge of the Haliakmon estuary, some thirty kilometres downstream from Vergina, and Sindos, along the Gallikos river. Mende had access to arable land but was also the strategic stopover for ships sailing in eastern direction from the mainland coast. Evidently, these settlements were part of the growing maritime trade network in which Euboians played a key role.[297] Methone in particular has been identified in recent research as a major trade centre, with a large quantity of pottery from across the Aegean, most of which were transport amphorae, dating to the late eighth century.[298]

Significantly, the region also had abundant precious metal sources, likely attracting Euboian attention. Local gold sources, naturally appearing as electrum, were known already in the Late Bronze Age, but the scarce evidence for gold working, such as the two stone crucibles excavated in domestic contexts at Thessaloniki Toumba, suggest that there was very limited processing of gold and no indication of trade in gold as a high-value commodity.[299] The Iron Age offers indications that this could have changed: for example, it has been suggested that the substantial quantities of gold found in Lefkandi from the tenth and ninth centuries had a northern origin.[300] The Haliakmon, Axios and Gallikos rivers are known to contain placer gold, and in particular the Gallikos – known in antiquity as the *Echedoros* (gift-having)[301] – was likely exploited for its gold. Nea Philadelphia and Palatiano, two inland settlements along the Gallikos with Euboian pottery,[302] prospered between the ninth and

for a first colonisation of Ionian Greeks, following the Trojan war (Tiverios 2008, 1–17, 124–125). Rejecting such a phase as ahistorical, it seems rather likely that such evidence reflects long-term contacts and interaction within the Aegean (e.g., Papadopoulos 1996; Gimatzidis 2011a; Leone 2012).

296 Cf. Kotsonas 2012, 255–256; Leone 2012.

297 Cf. Papadopoulos 1997; 2011.

298 Bessios, Tzifopoulos and Kotsonas 2012; Clay, Malkin and Tzifopoulos 2017.

299 Vavelidis and Andreou 2008; Andreou and Vavelidis 2014. There are indications for Late Bronze silver exploitation at Chalkidike, see Wagner et al. 1986, 183–184.

300 Tiverios 1998, 249–250; Leone 2012, 232–233.

301 Hdt. 7.124, 127.

302 Tiverios 2008, 8.

seventh century, making it plausible that they benefitted from gold extraction; and with regard to Sindos, the seaport along the Gallikos, Tiverios concluded that 'there can be no doubt that the Euboians were attracted here chiefly by the gold in the Gallikos river'.[303] Although it need not necessarily have been what brought the Euboians to the Thermaic gulf and Chalkidike in the first place, or what kept them there, access to the region's precious metal resources, even if it concerned small quantities, was and would remain important to Euboian interests.

The gold in the Eretria hoard, the single largest find of gold during the Geometric period, was previously thought to have come from Egypt or Anatolia.[304] However, in the light of recent discoveries, the northern Aegean has become more likely as the source of the precious metal. The so-called Ypogeio at Methone, a subterranean structure that was filled up around 700 BCE, contained a huge quantity of material dating to ca. 730–690 BCE, among which were transport amphorae and decorated pottery from across the Aegean and a collection of sherds with alphabetic inscriptions.[305] It moreover contained several of the above-mentioned melting plates used for gold processing, with round impressions left by the globule-ingots into the molten vitrified layer (Figure 5.5). In addition to industrial waste, a single hammered globule, or token, cut in two, was found, with the halves weighing 3 and 7 grams respectively. Discussing this material in detail, Samuel Verdan convincingly argues that gold dust from the nearby placer deposits of the Haliakmon, Axios and Gallikos rivers was processed at Methone into ingots of the sort known from the Eretria hoard, a form that was suitable for further transport and trade. Considering the fact that Methone was an Eretrian foundation[306] and that both cities were strongly linked in the late eighth century, it is plausible that the gold in the Eretria hoard had been imported from its colony on the Thermaic gulf.[307] Only further analysis can provide a step forward in testing this specific hypothesis. In any case, the typological and the metallurgical links, in the form of the globule ingots and the melting plates found both at Methone and at Eretria, clearly indicate a pattern in Eretrian or Euboian activity with regard to the production of gold currency. Gold was the precious metal of choice in the Aegean, and it is presumably under these circumstances that the Euboic gold standard, mentioned by Herodotus, emerged.[308]

Methone provides an interesting context for the production and use of gold in weight units as money. As mentioned, Methone was a trading hub attracting

303 Tiverios 1998, 248–250; 2008, 21.

304 Le Rider and Verdan 2002, 147–148; Descœudres 2008, 306–307, n. 115.

305 Bessios, Tzifopoulos and Kotsonas 2012; Clay, Malkin and Tsifopoulos 2017.

306 Plut. *Quaest. Graec.* 11.

307 Verdan forthcoming; Verdan and Heymans 2021.

308 Hdt. 3.89.

activity and merchandise from across the Aegean and even beyond. Phoenicians were likely active in Methone as well, and two Phoenician torpedo jars were among the material in the Ypogeio.[309] Attracting considerable attention, the evidence for early writing at Methone is impressive, as at Eretria,[310] and being a meeting place for Greeks, Phoenicians, and others, the site has recently been suggested as a possible context for the transmission of the alphabet.[311] The use of a system of alphabetic writing no doubt proved helpful in marking pots and wares but also in matters of administration. Although the longest inscriptions from the Ypogeio were found on sympotic vessels and connected to drinking,[312] there was also a significant amount of simple potters' marks,[313] and it is not difficult to imagine that writing could have also served – as it did in the Levant – for keeping accounts and other forms of basic administration (presumably on non-ceramic media) including numerical notations that no doubt were pertinent to the trading activities at Methone.[314] Logically, such use of writing could have functioned as a positive condition for the development and versatility of precious metal use as money.[315]

Although Kroll has shown that Euboian traders were familiar with the weighing of precious metal in the context of long-distance trade as early as the ninth century, this does not yet indicate the appropriation of precious metal for local money-use. The surge in trading activity and the appearance of international trading hubs such as Methone likely provides a setting for this. The practices and know-how of weight systems and financial administration that eastern traders brought to Methone are likely to have stimulated this process. At the same time, the use of electrum was clearly a local Aegean practice. Levantine trade partners presumably accepted in exchange whatever commodity they deemed valuable, but the variable gold content of natural electrum, at a time they used silver of a high quality, suggests that the medium was not necessarily their preference. Electrum was naturally available in the northern Aegean as well as in western Anatolia,[316] and Greek traders from this part of the Aegean were well represented at Methone, to judge from the pottery in the Ypogeio. As long as it was accepted, there is little reason to believe that the variable gold content posed a problem for these people. Perhaps not coincidentally, it was in this region that electrum coinage was

309 Kasseri 2012; Papadopoulos 2016, 1244–1246.
310 Kenzelmann Pfyffer, Theurillat and Verdan 2005.
311 Papadopoulos 2016.
312 Bessios, Tzifopoulos and Kotsonas 2012, 337–343.
313 Papadopoulos 2017; Verdan 2017. Cf. Papadopoulos 1994, 473–478.
314 Verdan 2017.
315 Cf. Codere 1968; Section 2.2.3.
316 See, e.g., Vavelidis and Andreou 2008; Cahill et al. 2020, 317–319, with references.

introduced less than a century later.[317] The prominence of gold in the Aegean during this period, expressed also in the works of Homer, and the metrology of the Eretria hoard, indicating active use in precise transactions involving small change, suggest that precious metal money was most likely used for local and Aegean trade.

The value of electrum must have been significantly higher than that of silver, and, logically, *hackgold* was more valuable than *hacksilber*. On this basis, it could be thought that the Eretria gold was too valuable for use in retail trade or small-scale exchange, as suggested with regard to early electrum coins.[318] However, this should not have posed a problem. Gold was available, and the Eretria hoard clearly demonstrates – as do the smallest coin fractions – that it was used in as small a quantity as practically could be handled.[319] Its high value, as well as its variable gold content made electrum less than ideal when considered against the functionalist criteria for money as described by Mill and Jevons.[320] This does not, however, negate the fact that it could have functioned as money.

5.4.2 *Second Colonisation Wave in the Northern Aegean*

Precious metal resources in the northern Aegean would remain important after the eclipse of the Euboian dominance in Aegean and international trade following the so-called Lelantine war.[321] In addition to placer gold, there were various primary gold deposits and wealthy silver mines in the Chalkidike peninsula, in the area of mount Pangaion and on the island of Thasos.[322] These sources would continue to play an important role in the development of money-use in the Greek world.

Following the Euboian colonisation of the region of the Thermaic gulf and parts of Chalkidike, Greek settlements were founded in the northern Aegean during the middle and second half of the seventh century. Settlers from the Cycladic island of Andros established colonies on the east side of Chalkidike and to its east, while Paros colonised the island of Thasos and its opposite coast

[317] A hoard containing electrum ingots/*hackgold* of variable gold content and four electrum coins, which were identified as modern forgeries, appeared on the market in 2002 and was documented before being dispersed (*CH* X, 199; Kim 2004). Regretfully, its uncertain origin (possibly from Asia Minor or the Black Sea?) and the doubts concerning its authenticity disable us from using it as evidence for the use of electrum prior to and in connection to the development of coinage.

[318] Kraay 1964; van Wees 2013, 131.

[319] Howgego 1995, 7; Velde 2020, 512.

[320] See Section 2.1.

[321] Cf. Hall 2007, 1–8; Verdan and Heymans 2021.

[322] Wagner et al. 1986; Papadopoulos 1996, 171–174; 2011, 122–124; Descœudres 2008, 306–307; Bissa 2009, 33–38.

between the Strymon and Nestos rivers (with Stryme founded east of the Nestos). Additionally, although less relevant to our discussion, Abdera to the east of the Nestos was founded by Klazomenai and later refounded by Teos, while Samothrace was colonised by Samians. Tiverios maintained that settlements established during this second phase of colonisation were based on trade, in addition to agriculture.[323] However, also here access to precious metal resources appears to have played an important role, even if not necessarily from the onset.

The colonies of Akanthos, Sane and Stageira were founded by Andros on the east side of Chalkidike and Argilos on the other side of the Strymonian gulf, four kilometres west of the mouth of the Strymon, in the mid-seventh century or perhaps somewhat later.[324] It is thought that the Andrians were assisted in their colonisation efforts by Chalkidians, assuming that Andros would otherwise not have been capable of founding these colonies simultaneously.[325] At least in the case of Argilos, finds indicate that a local population had occupied the site before the arrival of the colonists.[326]

Around the same time, Parians colonised the island of Thasos, and soon after (already by the third quarter of the century) Thasos itself established colonies – presumably with the help of Paros – on the coast opposite the island, known as the *Thasian Peraia*: Galepsos, Apollonia, Oisyme and Neapolis (modern Kavala).[327] Also in the mid-seventh century, Thasos founded Stryme, east of Abdera. On Thasos itself, the colonists encountered a local population, and Phoenicians are also recorded to have been there before the Greeks in order to exploit the gold mines,[328] although evidence for a substantial Phoenician presence or dominance beyond mere activity has never been found.[329]

The locations of these colonies offer an insight into their economic focus. Many no doubt relied to some degree on agriculture; but being all port cities, commercial activities, based on the availability of timber and, of course, metals,

323 Tiverios 2008, 125.

324 Graham 1978, 95; Tiverios 2008, 52–66; 2012, 276; Perreault and Bonias 2012, 263–265. The traditional foundation date for Akanthos, Sane, and Stageira is 655 BCE; consequently, Graham assumed that Argilos would have been established around the same time (1978, 95). Although the earliest pottery (Thracian, regional, East Greek, and Cycladic) appears to date to the middle of the seventh century (Perreault and Bonias 2012, 264–265), it is debated whether Greeks arrived to the site prior to the last decades of the seventh century, with only few Late Protocorinthian sherds (Tiverios 2008, 53, 64; Neeft 2012, 192; 2020, 10–11; Perreault and Bonias 2012, 267).

325 Tiverios 2008, 53, 126.

326 Tiverios 2008, 63–64. Cf. Perreault and Bonias 2012, 264–265, 267; Neeft 2020, 13. Plutarch's account (*Quaest. Graec.* 30) implies that also Sane and Akanthos were native settlements before the arrival of the Andrians and Chalkidians.

327 Graham 1978, 61–86, 94–95; Tiverios 2008, 72–91.

328 Hdt. 2.44, 6.47.

329 Graham 1978; Morris 1992a, 144–145; Tiverios 2008, 74–76, 126.

must have been of central importance.[330] Akanthos, for example, had arable land at its disposal and produced famed wine for export, but the locations of both Stageira and Argilos offered limited possibilities for agriculture. Stageira was founded on a rocky promontory with natural harbours on both sides, directly south of the small alluvial plain of Olympiada with wealthy silver mines in its direct hinterland;[331] Argilos was strategically located as a gateway community with access to the Strymon valley and the Pangaion area with its precious metal sources to the east.[332] Also Thasos was famous for its wine, likely produced only after the seventh century,[333] but had gold and silver mines, and the cities of its *peraia* occupied the coast of the Pangaion region with its metal sources,[334] while Neapolis also secured access to the plain of Drama. In contrast to the Greek colonies in Magna Graecia with their large farmlands, these colonies appear to be more comparable to the Phoenician colonies on the Mediterranean coast of Spain: relatively small settlements with little accessible hinterland that functioned as way stations for the Phoenician trade.[335]

In addition to their strategic location, finds indicate how well some of these colonies were integrated within Aegean trade networks during the second half of the seventh century. The cemetery at Akanthos has yielded pottery from across the Aegean, and architectural fragments of an Archaic Ionic temple have been uncovered at the site.[336] The Parthenos sanctuary in Neapolis, excavated in the old town of Kavala, also had a splendid Ionic marble temple of a Late Archaic date, but the ceramic finds started already in the second half of the seventh century and included the finest decorated pottery from various places in the Aegean.[337] Also indicative of intensive trade is the Artemision on Thasos, where, in addition to gold jewellery, eastern ivories and terracotta votives, some 40,000 Corinthian sherds were excavated, several thousands of which are Late Protocorinthian, but the bulk being Early Corinthian in date.[338] Evidence of this scale can leave little doubt as to whether Thasos' metal resources had attracted the attention of Aegean traders by the late seventh century.[339]

Like the Euboian colonies before, these settlements functioned to some degree as gateway communities. This is evident especially in the case of the

[330] Tiverios 2008, 65, 73, 80; 2012, 278–279; Tsigarida 2011, 149–151.
[331] Wagner et al. 1986; Sismanidis 2003, 13; Bissa 2009, 34.
[332] Perreault and Bonias 2012, 266–270; Neeft 2020, 17.
[333] Graham 1978, 88.
[334] E.g., Hdt. 5.17, 23, 6.46–47, 7.112.
[335] Aubet 2006.
[336] Tiverios 2008, 56–60.
[337] Tiverios 2008, 82.
[338] Tiverios 2008, 77–78; Neeft 2012, 189–192.
[339] Cf. Kroll 2011, 35–36.

Pangaion region, where Thracians inhabited the interior, and Greeks settled the coasts and islands,[340] allowing for commercial exchange between these different spheres.[341] Considering the absence of colonies in the interior, mining was presumably carried out by and under authority of the local Thracian population, as indicated by Herodotus.[342] Also, the fact that Peisistratus continued to receive revenues from the Pangaion mines after his second return to Athens, has been interpreted as reflecting his role as middleman for the Thracian owners of the mines.[343] In this way, the Greeks were able to benefit from the trade in metal by providing a port and market for the interior. Interestingly, only when their supply of precious metal came under threat did the Thasians found the colony Krenides in the plain behind Neapolis in 360 BCE, but this strategy had only a short-term effect, because Krenides was taken over by Philip II four years later and refounded as Philippoi.[344]

5.4.3 A Mediterranean Market for Aegean Silver

Could the availability of gold and silver resources in the northern Aegean have played a part in its colonisation? The foundation of Andrian colonies on the east coast of Chalkidike and the establishment of Parian/Thasian dominance on Thasos and the opposite coast, the Thasian Peraia, in what appears to have been a remarkably short time span around the middle and the third quarter of the seventh century,[345] suggest some sort of coordinated effort by the colonial ventures. However, a complex historical process such as colonisation does not necessarily have a single specific cause. There might have been factors that drove people north, possibly as a consequence of the circumstances that caused the settlements of Zagora on Andros and Koukounaries on Paros to be abandoned around the same time.[346] It is equally possible that people on the move were attracted to settlements at different locations that offered diverse opportunities. These dynamics lie beyond our current scope.

Reflecting on the circumstances of this colonisation movement in the north, John Graham asserted that 'we need not doubt that one of the motives, if not the main motive, of this great colonial venture was the desire to obtain mineral resources, notably precious metals'.[347] If indeed the access to gold and

[340] Appian BC 4.13.102.
[341] Tiverios 2008, 127.
[342] 7.112.
[343] Hdt. 1.64; cf. *Ath. Pol.* 15.2; Isaac 1986, 14–15; Treister 1996b, 136–137; Lavelle 2005, 126–134.
[344] Cf. Tiverios 2008, 90.
[345] Graham 1978, 94–95; Tiverios 2008, 53, 74; Perreault and Bonias 2012, 263–265.
[346] E.g., Whitley 1991.
[347] Graham 1978, 95.

silver sources formed an important strategic asset to these settlements, what demand could have prompted the exploitation of these sources in the region?

Graham argued that Phoenicians had exploited the metal sources of Thasos, as recounted by Herodotus,[348] and that crisis in Phoenicia proper during the second quarter of the century left a power vacuum in the region of Thrace that was filled in by Greeks. The destruction of Sidon by Esarhaddon in 677, the suppressed revolt of Tyre and Egypt in 671 and the subsequent siege of Tyre by Assurbanipal in 668 BCE would have likely affected Phoenician activity in the northern Aegean,[349] and the *Elegy on the Fall of Sidon* in Isaiah 23 also reflects the dire implication the destruction of Sidon had on its maritime trade.[350] Although the case for Phoenician influence on Thasos is clear,[351] making it likely that they would have frequented the island in the eighth and early seventh century in order to procure its metal, more than a century of archaeological exploration has not yet uncovered evidence for a substantial Phoenician colonial presence on the island, or in any case a presence that would have kept the Greeks at bay.[352]

More significant in stimulating the exploitation of precious metal sources, if not from the initial settlement then at least in its growing success, was the opening up of contact routes with Egypt from the middle of the seventh century on. Psammetichos I, founder of the twenty-sixth or Saite dynasty, managed to unite Egypt in 656 BCE, according to Herodotus, with the help of Ionian and Carian mercenaries.[353] Contacts with Egypt were established in this period, and mercenaries, traders and craftsmen travelled to and settled in Egypt, resulting in a long-lasting influence on Greek culture.[354] An Egyptian statue found near Priene was dedicated by a certain Pedon and mentions Psammetichos, whom he apparently served as a mercenary, although it is uncertain whether this concerns Psammetichos I (664–610 BCE) or II (595–589 BCE).[355] From the middle of the seventh century, Egyptian prestige objects were arriving in the Aegean, such as the bronze statuettes found at the Samian Heraion in notable quantities.[356]

[348] 6.47.
[349] Graham suggested that this was due to a diversion of Phoenician activity towards the western Mediterranean (1978, 96–97).
[350] Lipiński 1978.
[351] Graham 1978, 72, 88–92.
[352] Tiverios 2008, 75–77, 126.
[353] Hdt. 1.152.
[354] Boardman 1999, 112–117, 280–281; Vittmann 2003, 197–235; Pfeiffer 2013, 4; Villing 2015. Cf. Kyrieleis 1996.
[355] Boardman 1999, 280–281; Vittmann 2003, 203–206; Barbaro 2018.
[356] Kilian-Dirlmeier 1985, 235–243, 252–253; Shipley 1987, 56; Boardman 1999, 112–115.

While people in the Aegean favoured gold and electrum as the metal of value and a form of money, silver offered lucrative possibilities for export. As the Neo-Assyrian overlords had attempted to extract as much silver as possible from its territories, including the southern Levant and Egypt,[357] there was a high demand for silver in Egypt.[358] Having now freed themselves from the Assyrian yoke, Egypt saw new possibilities to establish contacts with the Aegean in order to secure a supply of silver.[359]

As discussed in Section 4.3.2, evidence indicates that Aegean silver did in fact reach Egypt. Two independent analyses performed on the small seventh century *hacksilber* hoard from Elephantine (Figure 4.7), albeit preliminary, indicated Siphnos as the source of the metal.[360] At least three other hoards with raw silver/*hacksilber*, likely dated before the middle of the sixth century, based on the absence of coins, are known from lower Egypt, and testify to the increasing supply of silver, potentially from the Aegean.[361] After Egypt took control of the southern Levant, Aegean silver also found its way into the Levantine economy, presumably through Egypt. In addition to the Egyptianising character of the jewellery in the hoards from Tel Miqne,[362] the silver was demonstrated to come from Aegean sources: lead isotope analyses performed on seven objects point to Chalkidike (2), Siphnos (2), and Laurion (3),[363] and results from additional samples also clearly point to the Aegean.[364] The results from analyses on the Ein Gedi hoard further indicate the presence of Aegean silver.[365] Theoretically, it is possible that this Aegean silver would have arrived earlier, that is, in the eighth century or earlier, before the Neo-Assyrians had cut off contacts with the Aegean, but this

357 See Section 4.4.

358 Jurman 2015, 61–63.

359 Cf. Boardman 1999, 130, 230.

360 Noeske 1993, 205.

361 Dressel and Regling 1927, 6–7; Kroll 2001b, 4. Admittedly, these early hoards cannot be securely dated, but in light of the fact that a number of mixed bullion-coin hoards are known from Egypt (at least twelve are recorded: Kroll 2001b, 4–7; Bissa 2009, 92), the absence of coins places them squarely before the arrival of the first coins to Egypt around the end of the sixth century. Moreover, one of these hoards, found at Tell Athrib, consisted of two jars containing a total of 50 kg of corroded silver, among which a variety of amulets and jewellery that could be heterogeneous, and 'that seem to date between the 26th dynasty and Ptolemaic times', although an early date is likely (Engelbach 1924, 181; Dressel and Regling 1927, 6–7; Ogden 1990/1991, 13; 1995, 72).

362 Golani and Sass 1998, 74; Na'aman 2003, 85–86.

363 Stos-Gale 2001, 61–62.

364 Thompson 2007, 44; Thompson and Skaggs 2013. A total of fifty or fifty-seven samples have been taken and analysed. Some of the samples appear to be a mixture of predominantly Laurion silver with silver from a Spanish source (Wood, Montero-Ruiz and Martinón-Torres 2019, 4, 11–15).

365 Thompson (2007, 44) lists five samples: one from Siphnos, two from Laurion, one from Sardinia, and one from Spain (cf. Wood, Montero-Ruiz and Martinón-Torres 2019, 27).

is not plausible. Assyrian imperial tribute policy made silver increasingly rare in the provinces, and the specific presence of primary ingots with few traces of wear[366] suggest that a supply of fresh silver from the Aegean to Egypt had opened up before the end of the century.

It has been claimed that Greeks in return were only interested in grain,[367] but it is likely that bulk trade involving subsistence goods became interesting only in the sixth century, when trade had become more regular and the population in the Aegean expanded.[368] During the first decades of trade with Egypt, in the second half of the seventh century, luxury items were at least equally important. After the Assyrian retreat from the southern Levant in the 630s, Egypt had taken over its control of the Arabian trade routes,[369] thereby securing their supply of luxury goods. References to 'myrrh, cassia and frankincense' in the poetry of Sappho[370] indicate that from at least the last quarter of the seventh century aromatics and spices that came by way of the Arabian trade must have reached the Aegean.[371] Other high-valued commodities could have attracted Greek traders to Egypt as well.[372]

Much of the scholarly discussion on Greek presence in Egypt has focused on the trade colony of Naukratis.[373] Herodotus relates how Pharaoh Amasis, who became king in 570 BCE, offered up Naukratis to the Greeks that came to settle in Egypt and allowed them to establish their sanctuaries.[374] The largest of these, Herodotus explains, was the Hellenion, which was a joint foundation of the Ionian cities of Chios, Teos, Phokaia and Klazomenai; the Dorian cities of Rhodes, Knidos, Halikarnassos and Phaselis and the Aeolian city of Mytilene. Fantalkin observed that the privilege to build the Hellenion was offered specifically to these east Greek cities, not coincidentally the cities that found themselves by ca. the 560s BCE in the Lydian sphere of influence, and argued that Amasis' policy had been shaped through Lydian mediation.[375] However, Herodotus also mentions that the Aeginetans, the Samians and the Milesians had built sanctuaries of their own, implying that they had established ties already at an earlier stage.[376] In particular, Aegina's exceptional position, being the only Greek 'mainland' presence within an emporion dominated by east Greek traders, can be regarded as confirmation of the fact that it was given

366 As argued in Sections 3.2.4 and 3.3.3.
367 Figueira 1981, 258–259; Boardman 1999, 129; Merrillees 2003, 38. Cf. Bissa 2009, 73.
368 Osborne 1996; Scheidel 2007, 44–45.
369 See Sections 4.2 and 4.3.
370 Fr. 44.30. Cf. fr. 2.4.
371 Davies 2016, 306–307.
372 See van Alfen 2016.
373 Villing and Schlotzhauer 2006a.
374 Hdt. 2.178.
375 Fantalkin 2014, 42–44, with bibliography.
376 Lloyd 2007, 373. Cf. Figueira 1981, 251–264; Fantalkin 2014, 43–44.

formal access to Naukratis at an early stage. The fact that groups of traders, substantial enough to be identified by their city of origin, were granted the privilege to build a sanctuary, suggests that they had established a (semi) permanent presence at the site.

Indeed, archaeological excavations at Naukratis reflect an earlier foundation date than Amasis. Ceramic evidence – *inter alia* in the form of Wild Goat style and Early Corinthian sherds – indicates a presence of Greeks from ca. 615 BCE, at the same time that we see evidence for Greek mercenaries in the southern Levant.[377] The quantity and nature of the finds at Naukratis demonstrate the presence of groups of migrant Greeks, forming a Greek trade settlement within Egyptian territory,[378] and such a settlement could have only been established, as Herodotus implies, under a formal permission. Other examples of such settlements, potentially predating the Amasis charter, are the Nile islands named after Greek poleis or islands, mentioned by Hekataios: 'Ephesos, Chios, Lesbos, Cyprus, and Samos'.[379] Whatever the circumstances under which the Egyptians granted Greek traders the formal right to settle,[380] it must have been preceded by the establishment of informal trade relations. These early contacts, datable to the third quarter of the seventh century, had proven to the Egyptians that access to a Greek market, presumably for the supply of silver, was worth granting them a special status within Egypt. In addition to the few Egyptian imports,[381] a reflection of these early contacts is the voyage of the Samian merchant Kolaios, traditionally dated to ca. 638 BCE, who had sailed for Egypt before being blown off course.[382]

Aegina, and possibly also Miletus, both early participants in the emporion at Naukratis, no doubt had a pioneering role in the silver trade with Egypt. As a major force in the maritime trade of the Archaic period, Aegina was likely involved in Egypt in the second half of the seventh century.[383] While the late seventh-century presence of Milesians and other east Greeks at Naukratis is reflected by east Greek pottery, Boardman noted that Aegina did not produce painted pottery of her own but could have been responsible for carrying early Attic black-figured and Early Corinthian pottery.[384] Aegina was also an early

377 Boardman 1999, 121–125; Fantalkin 2006; 2014.

378 Boardman 1999, 118–133; Villing and Schlotzhauer 2006a.

379 *FGrH* I F 310; see Malkin 2011, 84.

380 E.g., Vittmann 2003, 197–199; Fantalkin 2014, 38–42; Villing 2015.

381 Boardman 1999, 112–115.

382 Hdt. 4.152; Shipley 1987, 55–56; Boardman 1999, 114.

383 Figueira 1981, 251–264.

384 Beazley and Payne 1929; Morris 1984, 99–100; Venit 1984; Boardman 1999, 125; Villing and Schlotzhauer 2006b, 6. Corinthian pottery was abundant in eastern Greece, but imports cease shortly before the end of Early Corinthian in ca. 600 BCE (Neeft 2012, 190–192). It is therefore equally possible that, for example, Milesians had brought the earliest Corinthian pottery to Naukratis.

centre in the Aegean slave trade,[385] and its role as a hub in the Aegean trade would be reflected later still by the dominance of its coins in the sixth and early fifth century international trade.[386]

Aegina had no silver sources of her own but tapped into other sources in the Aegean. The island of Siphnos was close by, and it is likely that Aegina had access to its rich silver mines. Aegina also enjoyed close contacts and trade relations with Athens in the seventh century, reflected by the presence of Protoattic pottery on the island,[387] and it is possible that it had secured mining concessions in the Laurion district enabling small-scale exploitation. Moreover, there are also indications that Aegina had access to silver from the northern Aegean. These three sources, Siphnos, Laurion and Chalkidike, are strongly represented among its early coinages.[388] While Aegina's interest in these sources and its role in carrying silver to Egypt has been acknowledged, they are predominantly associated with the period in which Aegina had adopted coinage.[389] However, Aeginetan involvement in Egypt during the late seventh century and the contemporary presence of Aegean silver in Egypt and the Levant clearly indicate that its role in the silver trade should predate coinage.

Demonstrating seventh-century exploitation of these Aegean silver sources is difficult, though.[390] It is important to keep in mind that industrial activity is often difficult to date, since little closely datable evidence has been left behind, and much has been obliterated by later activity at the site.[391] At the same time, not all known silver mines have yet been systematically studied.[392] Early historical activity at these mines is generally dated to the sixth century, although this is mostly based on the study of the silver sources of early coins.[393] Since silver coins were only produced starting in the sixth century, this confirms the contemporary exploitation of mines but does not rule out earlier activity. Large-scale exploitation of the so-called third contact at Laurion is argued to have started only in the late sixth century,[394] but, as previously noted, silver production on a smaller scale using first contact ores certainly

385 Figueira 1981, 238–240; Morris 1984, 94, 102–103.

386 Holloway 1971; Kraay 1976, 41–49; Figueira 1981, 148–149; Sheedy 2012, 106–109.

387 Cf. Morris 1984.

388 Gale, Gentner and Wagner 1980, 33–43; Wagner et al. 1986, 180–184.

389 E.g., Kraay 1976, 43–44; Gale, Gentner and Wagner 1980, 33–43; Figueira 1981, 258–259; Sheedy 2012, 106. Cf. Morris 1984, 96–101; Boardman 1999, 125, 130; Bissa 2009, 60–61, 90, 92, 99. Based on Aegina's coinage, John Kroll already assumed that Aegina's role in silver traffic should likely predate coinage (2011, 35).

390 Descœudres 2008, 306.

391 Kakavoyannis 2001, 366.

392 Sismanidis 2003, 13.

393 Gale, Genter and Wagner 1980; Gale and Stos-Gale 1981, 202; Wagner and Weisgerber 1985, e.g., 224; Wagner et al. 1986, 181; Andreou and Vavelidis 2014, 453. Cf. Pernicka and Wagner 1985, 205.

394 Davis 2014, with bibliography.

predates the sixth century. Such activity, it has been noted, would have left behind few traces.[395] Historical silver production at Thasos is also difficult to date but appears to go back to the pre-colonial phases of the island.[396] However, the emphasis in scholarship on coinage as the primary form in which silver historically circulated[397] has resulted in a lack of interest in the exploitation and trade in silver preceding coinage, further reinforcing the belief that mining was not a concern before the introduction of coinage.[398]

Numismatic data can, however, also reflect on trade prior to the introduction of coinage. As discussed, weight systems were in use during the eighth and seventh centuries,[399] and the weight standards of early coinages can reveal trade relations, potentially going back to earlier stages of archaic trade. Cycladic poleis, among which Paros, used the Aeginetan weight standard for their coinages, reflecting Aegina's dominance in archaic trade. Deconstructing what was long known as the 'Thraco-Macedonian standard', Selene Psoma argued that, in fact, Thasos and the cities of the Peraia minted coins on a reduced Aeginetan standard, thereby revealing early trade links between Aegina, Paros and its northern colonies.[400] At the same time, she pointed out, several cities in Chalkidike including Argilos directly to its east, minted their earliest coins on a reduced Milesian standard.[401] The colonies in the northern Aegean were minting coinage at a relatively early stage,[402] which is hardly surprising when we consider that silver was available in the region. But why would they have minted their coins on reduced Aeginetan and Milesian standards?

Presumably, these reduced standards were introduced when the first coins were minted in order to create a closed monetary zone and protect the local market.[403] In the Classical period, Xenophon would note that traders could make a profit exporting silver from Athens, suggesting that the price of silver outside Athens was higher than within its territory.[404] Considering the fact that the price of silver in these silver-producing colonies was lower than in the international trade, coinage on a reduced standard would render local coins more valuable (i.e., with a nominal value above that of the reduced metal

395 Kakavoyannis 2001, 366.
396 Wagner et al. 1981; Nerantzis and Papadopoulos 2013, 192–193.
397 Cf. Howgego 1995, 89–90; Bissa 2009, 60–61, 90, 92, 99; Kroll 2011, 35.
398 Hopper 1979, 38; Gale, Gentner and Wagner 1980; Figueira 1981, 144–149; Gale and Stos-Gale 1981, 202; Howgego 1995, 95–96; Treister 1996b, 132–133, 151–152; Boardman 1999, 130; Bissa 2009, 29–102; *pace* Kim 2001, 16.
399 Kim 2001, 17–19.
400 Psoma 2015, 175–179; 2016, 97.
401 Psoma 2015, 171–172; 2016, 91–92, 104.
402 Price and Waggoner 1975; Kraay 1976, 132–136, 148–149.
403 Psoma 2015, 179; 2016, 95. Cf. Stefanakis 1999, 260–262.
404 Xen. *Ways*. 3.2; Bissa 2009, 59–60; Kroll 2011, 28–29.

weight) and thus maintained a local circulation of coins, while protecting the silver export market.

The link with the Aeginetan and Milesian weight standards in these areas likely predates the first coins and reflects Aeginetan and Milesian trade interests in the region. Both Aegina and Miletus participated in early trade with Egypt, and both were possibly involved in the lucrative silver trade. For this trade, silver sources in the northern Aegean were an important supplier.

5.4.4 *Silver Money in Aegean Trade*

By the end of the seventh century, the economic importance of silver had been established within the Aegean through the growing interdependence of markets in the eastern Mediterranean.[405] Local production of silver, no doubt still on a modest scale, was now linked to the foreign demand of the Egyptian market through pioneering Aegean traders, thereby affecting the various spheres of the system, such as the colonial economy and potentially the slave trade. As a resulting back-ripple effect, the role of silver within Aegean trade was becoming increasingly important as well. This can be illustrated with reference to Corinth, an important trade power that also started to weigh in on the silver trade.

Already in 627 BCE, Corinth and Corcyra, itself a Corinthian colony, founded Epidamnus (Roman Dyrrhachium) and around the turn of the century Apollonia, both located along the Adriatic coast. These colonies increased Corinthian strategic control of trade into the Adriatic but, as suggested by Boardman, may also have served to gain access to the Illyrian silver mines in the region.[406] Around the same time (ca. 600 BCE) Corinth also established its presence in the northern Aegean, through its only colony in the wider region, Potidaia.[407] Strategically located on the isthmus of the Pallene peninsula, the western finger of Chalkidike, offering access to both the Thermaic and the Toronaic gulf, as well as the interior of Chalkidike, Potidaia was founded as a commercial settlement that served as an anchorage and basis for Corinthian activity in the region. Western Chalkidike had previously been colonised by Euboians, but Euboia was no longer a dominant force and the Corinthian trade might have offered advantages. The Corinthians were no doubt attracted by the timber resources in the north but certainly also by its precious metal. Soon enough, Corinth was expanding its active range and was conducting direct trade at Argilos by ca. 570 BCE,

[405] Cf. Osborne 1996.
[406] Boardman 1999, 226–227.
[407] Tiverios 2008, 41–43.

indicated by the sudden appearance of large quantities of Late Corinthian settlement pottery.[408]

Changing awareness of the importance of precious metal bullion in trade and its potential as a form of state revenue are reflected by developments at Corinth itself. The Diolkos, the trackway across the Isthmus, was constructed around 600 BCE under Periander and facilitated the movement of ships across the Isthmus to avoid the need of circumnavigating the Peloponnese. Corinth had harbours on both sides, Kenchreai on the Saronic and Lechaion on the Corinthian gulf, and the Diolkos therefore primarily served merchant vessels from other states, enabling Corinth to collect revenues in the form of a transit duty.[409] This strategic focus on transit trade as a source of revenue for the city is also indicated by the artificial construction of the Lechaion harbour by Periander.[410] Interestingly, Aristotle would later note that Periander was 'exacting no other tax and being satisfied with those from the agora and the harbours',[411] confirming indeed that trade was increasingly subject to fiscal regulation.

Naturally, the taxes raised on trade took the form of precious metal, the dominant form of money in interregional trade around 600 BCE. Direct evidence for this is provided by the Ephesos lead tablet, a folded and discarded tablet, found under the Archaic Artemis temple.[412] Based on the context, as well as the letter forms, the tablet can be dated to the late seventh or early sixth century and contains an inventory of various payments made to the sanctuary. These payments are listed in gold and silver in minas, and are noted as having been weighed out or paid (ἐστάθησαν); considering the fact that the tablet predates bimetallic coinage, this clearly concerns bullion.[413] One payment notes: '33 minas of silver were weighed out here, silver f[rom the] marit[ime] (revenue)'.[414] This concerned a form of harbour tax, with the Artemision located at the harbour, but other payments might also indicate taxes, such as those levied on the production of salt.[415] Although electrum coins were already used in Ephesos for local exchange, the tablet only mentions gold and silver, indicating the treasury preferred or relied on the use of precious metal bullion as money. The fact that specifically silver was recorded as the

408 Neeft 2012, 192–193; *pace* Neeft 2020, 19.

409 Snodgrass 1980, 147; Salmon 1984, 136–139; Bresson 2016, 93–94; *pace* Pettegrew 2011.

410 Salmon 1984, 134.

411 Arist. F 611.20 Rose; van Wees 2013, 29.

412 See Kroll 2008a, 18–21; 2020a, with bibliography.

413 Side B lists several payments with fractional weight units (i.e., staters, sixths, and twelfths), which also refer to bullion, rather than coin (Kroll 2008a, 19–20; 2020a; *pace* Davies 2001, 12).

414 A5; Kroll 2008a, 20; 2020a.

415 A7, B3; Davies 2001, 121; Kroll 2008a, 20–21.

harbour tax, or tax on maritime revenue, demonstrates that silver had become an important form of money in the Aegean trade.

Silver bullion remained important as a form of money in the Aegean, also after the introduction of silver coinage in the sixth century. The presence of *hacksilber* pieces in coin hoards from the late sixth century, notably the Kolophon hoard and a mixed hoard from Caria, currently in the Israel Museum, demonstrate the continued importance of weighed and uncoined silver.[416] In the case of the Kolophon hoard, the coins might have been used as a supplement to the bullion in large-scale transactions, for which the small-denomination coins alone were less suitable.[417] Moreover, an inscription from Eretria, dating to ca. 525 BCE, before the city had minted its own coinage, mentions a payment in 'χρέματα δόκιμα' – money that is current, or acceptable – and a fine of ten staters (Figure 5.6).[418] It is likely that the noted payment was made either in weighed silver bullion (of which the quality had to be acceptable) or potentially in foreign coins.[419] One wonders whether this distinction had any significance to the Eretrians at the time.

We can now offer some final remarks concerning the historical rise of silver money in the Aegean. The exploitation of precious metal sources and the related trade became significant in the Aegean during the second half of the seventh century BCE. With colonists tapping into local economies in the northern Aegean, but also with the exploitation of the silver in Laurion and Siphnos and contacts with Egypt taking shape, pioneering traders, presumably from Aegina and Miletus, succeeded in linking these disparate economic spheres through the trade in silver. The quantities in which silver was produced and traded might have been relatively modest during this stage, but its high value and the implications for the economic infrastructure of the eastern Mediterranean were disproportionate to the size of the trade.

The access to precious metal was not necessarily the primary focus of the colonisation of the northern Aegean from the start, and indeed, some have argued against the search for raw metals as a motivation for colonisation in general.[420] However, such generalisations are not helpful for better understanding the diverse incentives at play. The colonisation of the northern Aegean was historically complex, taking place under diverse conditions and with different incentives. If precious metal had not been the main objective from the start, the

416 Kim and Kroll 2008; Kroll 2008a, 23–24.

417 Kim and Kroll 2008, 63–68; Kroll 2008a, 22–23.

418 *IG* XII 9.1273–1274.

419 Cairns 1984; 1991; von Reden 1997, 158; Haarer 2000, 181; Goodenough 2011, 131–132; Leone 2017.

420 Treister 1996b, 176–179. Cf. Tsetskhladze 1994, 123–124; 1995, 307, 323–325; 1998, 64–65; Bissa 2009, 43; Fantalkin 2014, 35.

5.6 Inscription from Eretria (Courtesy of the Swiss School of Archaeology in Greece)

potential of its exploitation would have become apparent within a relatively short period, as local markets were being drawn into a wider economic system.

In due course, the increasing production of silver in the Aegean and the growing demand for silver from intermediaries for the purpose of trade had a back-ripple effect, which led to an increase in its significance and use within the Aegean by ca. 600 BCE and within local contexts as well. Rather than a supposed rejection of elitist gold motivated by a civic or middling ideology,[421] it was this growing use, for example, in the context of trade taxes and other payments to the state, that caused silver to become the preferred metal for money-use.

5.5 CONCLUSION

The significance of money within early Greek society is revealed in the contexts in which valuables take on a role as a form of money, being subject to a degree of relative standardisation and its use regulated by social convention. In this chapter, I have focused on such contexts in order to assess the

[421] Cf. Kurke 1999; Thompson 2007, 185. Cf. Morris 2000, 109–191.

growing importance of money-use and the convergence of different forms and uses of money in early Greek society.[422] Emphasis was placed on contextualising the changing role and significance of precious metals as a form of money. As illustrated by the current and previous chapters, this process cannot be properly understood if regarded as a geographically isolated phenomenon; it was strongly tied in with dynamics in the wider Mediterranean region. By offering the Aegean perspective, complementary to Chapter 4 that focused on the southern Levant, this chapter has aimed to place this complex development into a wider historical and geographic context.

During most of the Early Iron Age (ca. 1200–700 BCE) precious metals were rare, and there is little reason to assume that they were used as a form of money. The dedication of raw gold and silver in rich burials or other prestige contexts in the Aegean and Cyprus served as a reference, either to the availability of precious metal at times of restricted supply or to its use in exchange in the context of international trade, mostly associated with the Levant. But other objects and materials, most prominently bronze, also functioned increasingly as references to and expressions of quantifiable value and prestige.

This is particularly evident in sanctuaries during the Late Geometric and Early Archaic period (eighth and seventh centuries). The dedication of valuables, predominantly bronze votives, can be regarded as payments to the deity and shows that collective investment and expenditure at the sanctuary increasingly took the form of measurable value through standardisation and regulation. Through this form of expenditure, no doubt related to the organisation of cult finance, early sanctuaries formed an important context in which money-use was given shape, reflecting increasing convergence with other contexts of money-use.

Wergeld payments form another context for the development of money-use. The existence of such compensation payments, and the importance of gold and bronze as metals of value in these payments, is reflected already in the Homeric epics. Gold was evidently a material that symbolised prestige and honour, and as we have seen in Chapter 4 with regard to Late Bronze Age Ugarit, the significance attached to such metals made them particularly suitable for use in *wergeld* transactions.

Compensation payments were an important part of early Greek law, which regulated revenge and retribution by imposing fines against different offences. These fines stimulated the conceptualisation of money within a social and political framework, and although it is likely that different media were used across Greece (in payment and as a measure of value), such as the cauldrons

[422] Cf. Descat 2001, 70–71.

listed in laws from Gortyn, their character as prestige items made them appropriate for use in this context. By the late seventh or early sixth century, laws and regulations reflect the increasing use of money within early state finance, presumably in the form of weighed silver.

However, until the middle of the seventh century, silver had played no significant role as a means of value in the Greek world. Gold and electrum had been the precious metal of preference in the Aegean, and the use of *hackgold* in weight units as money in the context of exchange and trade during the late eighth century is testified by the hoard from Eretria. Euboians were a dominant player in Aegean trade during the Geometric period, and the materiality of the hoard suggests that they adopted the use of precious metal in exchange from Levantines, presumably Phoenicians, from whom they had also adapted their weight standard, using it for a similar range of transactions as reflected by the hoards from the southern Levant. One of the reasons that the Euboians had established a colonial presence in the northern Aegean was in order to secure a supply of native gold to be used as money in exchange. The Late Geometric international trade centre at Methone is likely to have served as the location for collecting and processing placer gold into ingots that were used in exchange and shipped to Eretria.

Around the middle of the seventh century, the colonisation of other parts of the northern Aegean made its precious metal sources available to a wider Aegean and Mediterranean market. Particularly silver from the region, but also from the mines at Laurion and Siphnos, formed the objective of a lucrative growing trade that had far-reaching effects. Saite Egypt, which opened up to Aegean trade from the middle of the century, had a high demand for silver, and pioneering traders, such as from Aegina and possibly Miletus, exploring the opportunities provided by expanding markets, stepped in to link the disparate economic spheres by bringing Aegean silver to the Egyptian market, thereby contributing to the establishment of Greek presence in Egypt.

By the end of the seventh century, silver had presumably become important within Aegean trade as well, and like the use of money in the context of fines, archaic states were now starting to levy trade and transit taxes in gold and/or silver. The integration of markets and the growing importance of money within the public sphere, such as in cult finance and fiscal policy, had fostered a high demand for silver within Greek society as well, and further stimulated the convergence of different forms and uses of money.

SIX

CONCLUSION

This book presents a reconstruction of the history of money-use prior to the introduction of coinage in the eastern Mediterranean Iron Age, with a specific focus on the southern Levant and the Aegean. At its core stands a detailed analysis of Iron Age precious metal hoards, predominantly from the southern Levant, reflecting the use of precious metal money in carrying out transactions. It argues how money developed historically, under what social, political and economic circumstances it did so and what significance it held in society.

Chapters 2–5 each offer a concluding section, summarising the main points raised in that chapter; together these offer a concise overview of the general argument laid out with regard to the specific historical development and social significance of precious metal money in the eastern Mediterranean Iron Age (ca. twelfth–sixth century BCE). Rather than rehearsing that argument here once more, I want to use this concluding chapter to revisit the wider issue raised in Chapter 1, of how money comes into being, and to draw attention to the perspective provided in this book to contribute to a general understanding of the circumstances under which this takes place. To do this, I will address a few of the overarching themes that have appeared throughout the book. This will also allow us to point out issues that require additional scholarly attention, as well as possibilities for future research.

6.1 HOW MONEY COMES INTO BEING

Upon revisiting the question of how money comes into being, it is important to emphasise again what was laid out in Chapter 1, that the 'genesis' of money and its development from a historical kernel to a full-fledged focus of economic and social life is not a single or unitary process. Money is heterogeneous, meaning that diverse social, political and economic circumstances can give way to its emergence in different historical contexts. But beyond the circumstances of its appearance, the nature of money in a set historical context and its development over time are also profoundly shaped by the cultural logic and framework in which it is embedded. One could say that the circumstances 'dress' money; they endow it with significance and provide a framework of use. The topics discussed here each reflect upon different circumstances that are pertinent to the rise of money in early historical societies.

6.1.1 *Value through Distance*

As described in Chapter 2, in considering where to search for the origins of the concept of money, several scholars have suggested that money existed as a standard of value before being used in exchange and that in early, premarket societies this standard enabled people to place a value on personal injury or damage, and the fines or compensation paid for it, known as *wergeld*.[1] We have seen that both in the Late Bronze Age Levant – specifically Ugarit – and in the early Greek world – in Homer and early law – *wergeld* provides a context for the use and significance of precious metal as standard of value and means of payment.[2] This evidence, some of which was already observed by Grierson, could be understood as support for his theory that the historical origins of money as a standard of value are to be sought in these compensation payments.

We should, however, be reluctant to assume, as Polanyi did, that money's functions in premodern society were necessarily institutionalised separately.[3] That precious metal was used as a standard of value in *wergeld* payments does not mean that its use in exchange was insignificant. Rather than isolating the *wergeld* context from the wider significance attached to precious metal, we should ask what made precious metal particularly appropriate for such use. As noted in Chapter 2, a standard of value or medium in *wergeld* payments is not just naturally endowed with the value and significance that warrant its acceptability as such. For that, its value has to be constructed through use.

[1] Polanyi 1968a, 157–158, 166–169; 1968b, 178–183, spec. 179; Grierson 1977, 10–19; Ingham 2004, 72–75, 89–93. Cf. Hudson 2004.

[2] For the Late Bronze Age Levant, see Section 4.1; for the early Greek world, see Section 5.3.

[3] Polanyi 1968b, 179.

Examples from the eastern Mediterranean suggest that the value and significance of precious metals could have partially been constructed through the cultural and physical distance that had to be overcome, as well as the effort, power and knowledge needed in order to procure the metals. Initially then, raw materials used for money-stuff are often not found or produced locally. Although appropriated for use as money within a local context, such materials are obtained from elsewhere. This was the case with silver in the Levant but also with the brass rods of the Tiv, which were acquired through interregional trade,[4] and the stone discs of the Yap, which were mined in Palau.[5] It is through distance that these are constructed as *tokens of value* – as a form of money.

An approach to this understanding of value was offered by Mary Helms, who argued that 'geographical distance from a given cultural heartland may correspond with supernatural distance from that center', thereby making exotic objects and materials but also foreign knowledge 'politically valuable "goods"'.[6] Associated with the owner's ability to overcome geographical distance, access to foreign knowledge and power, such materials were thus highly valued in local and regional exchange. The desire to obtain and pass on such exchange valuables likely made them the focus of social strategies, and this can be seen as an underlying principle of exchange systems such as the *kula*. The exchange of silver and gold in the early Mediterranean is no exception to this, and it has been aptly noted with regard to Viking exchange that 'silver and other valuables were not pursued by Viking-age Scandinavians as wealth in general, but because they had properties crucial for the maintenance of social networks'.[7]

Referring to Huizinga's description of *kula*-type exchange as a feature of *Homo Ludens*,[8] Grierson claimed that the exchange of such valuables had 'a political and not an economic basis', thereby rejecting them as a form of money.[9] This line of reasoning was in keeping with the distinction, held at the time, between primitive valuables and money, but it is at odds with the approach to money explored here.[10] If we steer clear from this binary opposition, it becomes possible to see how objects that were valued in exchange came to serve as a standard of value in expressing *wergeld*.

In the eastern Mediterranean throughout the Late Bronze and Iron Age, silver was traded as the dominant commodity of value, as was gold in the

4 Guyer 2004, 15, 28–31.
5 Furness 1910, 93–94; Fitzpatrick 2002; 2016.
6 Helms 1988, 4.
7 Sindbæk 2011, 41. See also Chapter 2.
8 Huizinga 1949, 62–63.
9 Grierson 1977, 7.
10 See specifically Chapter 2.

Aegean down to the seventh century. Being exchanged within interregional trade and obtained through the long-distance networks that were a source of prestige for their participants, it gained a local significance that it did not necessarily have on the other end of the exchange. This significance, which caused it to stand out from other, that is, local goods being exchanged, made it suitable for appropriation and use in certain contexts as a form of money.

6.1.2 From Object to (Hoarded) Material

Central to the conceptualisation of money-stuff in this book – in the nature of the material, as well as the historical context studied – is the idea that precious metal in the hoards was valued neither strictly as a token nor as a commodity, but both at the same time. As emphasised in Chapters 2 and 3, this duality was a characteristic of money already preceding coinage, with the material in the hoards being appreciated for the dynamic and transitory quality to move back and forth between object and matter, between substance and form. Rather than being distinct, these categories were argued to be interrelated, with the potential token quality being the basis for its value as a commodity and vice versa.

The increasing appropriation of precious metal objects (jewellery, vessels etc.) for transactions and the hoarding of wealth, observed in the Levant starting with the end of the Late Bronze Age, reflects a historic characteristic of Western money. Although this transformation of Late Bronze Age ornamental objects into Iron Age hoarded silver – *hacksilber* – is of historical significance to the question of how money came into being in the early eastern Mediterranean, it is not necessarily the case that precious metal can only be or become money through this transition. This would assume, as Marx postulated, that only when temporarily withdrawn from circulation and hoarded could something become money,[11] while the very use of ornamental objects in exchange should make us wonder if being hoarded should be seen as a prerequisite for being money.

Moreover, comparable processes of appropriation of precious metal objects can be observed in different times and places, suggesting the transformation or re-establishment of money in society under different circumstances. The silver hoards from the Viking Age, discussed in Chapter 2, represent one conspicuous example of this. However, the transformation supposedly reflected by these hoards – from prestige items to *hacksilber* – did not necessarily take place for the same reasons as the process in the eastern Mediterranean Iron Age.

[11] Marx 1970, 125–137; 1976, 227–232.

The development from objects to (hoarded) material or *hacksilber* is not a natural phenomenon but is brought about by human agents, who actively appropriate these objects for an alternative use. With reference to the approach to the circulation of objects in the *kula* developed by Munn and Appadurai,[12] I have described this appropriation as the *diversion of commodities from their customary path.* While far from certain, I have attempted to establish what actors (or groups) were involved in diverting precious metal objects, notably jewellery and vessels, or other forms of precious metal for use as money, and for what reason. This shows that only through detailed analysis of the historical context and its social, political and economic circumstances is it possible to develop a better understanding of why money came into being.

6.1.3 State Institutions

The basis for its significance as a form of money and its appropriation for such use is only part of what enables money to come into being. Another part is to be sought in the circumstances that cause it to emerge and become more pervasive in society. Although I have argued that the existence of a state that sanctions the use of money as legal tender under its umbrella is not a prerequisite for money to exist and circulate,[13] the existence of state authority or any form of centralised power and its institutions are an important part of the conditions under which money historically develops and functions in society. The character of such institutions and their effect on the political, social and economic environment in which money-use is embedded can be diverse, such as a military force that serves to secure trade routes, or a specialised fiscal administration that levies and spends silver money.

Rather than the intuitive assumption that the rise of money is positively correlated with the development of state institutions (i.e., more state means more money), it has become clear that this relation is by no means straightforward.[14] In fact, as posited in Section 3.4 and substantiated in Section 4.1, the increase in the observable use of silver money in exchange and as a store of wealth in the Levant from the end of the Late Bronze Age to the Iron I period was a result of the collapse of a central authority that had previously been instrumental in securing and maintaining an interregional and international trade system. As noted, the economic upheaval of the period led certain actors in the continuing urban centres to appropriate silver valuables for carrying out transactions – to divert them from their customary path. Rather than state institutions offering a context for money-use, it appears that the waning of

[12] Munn 1983; Appadurai 1986a, 16–29.

[13] See Section 2.2.4.

[14] Heymans and Termeer 2020a; Terrenato 2020.

state institutions cleared the way for the increasing use of silver money in certain transactions.

However, developing state institutions can also provide a context for money-use and its spread to different spheres of society. In the Aegean during the early Archaic period, various developing institutions, whether directly related to the state, such as laws recording fines, or less directly, such as religious fees and dedications, provide a context for an increasingly diversified role of money in society. At the same time, these different forms of money, appearing in different contexts, testify to a convergence of the concept of money and its use. Some of these contexts have received attention in our discussion in Chapters 4 and 5, but it is important to emphasise that the relation between developing state institutions and the development of money-use preceding coinage is hardly well understood. The construction of the Diolkos and the Lechaion harbour under Periander of Corinth were noted as pointing to a fiscalisation of trade because they enabled the levy of transit duties, but these concern only a small piece of a much larger puzzle, while future research can provide a more detailed image of the economic and fiscal significance of archaic state institutions. For example, the development of the agora as a setting for local exchange in various urban centres taking shape across the Greek world might well have formed a significant context for the spread of money into daily life,[15] but this topic has yet to contribute to a more complete understanding of pre-coinage money under the early Greek state.

6.2 CONNECTING MONEY TO CHANGE IN ARCHAIC SOCIETY

After reflecting along broader lines on the development of money and the processes that shape this development on a more abstract level, it is now worthwhile to draw attention to three specific historical phenomena that arose in the eastern Mediterranean and that could be pertinent to the rise and early history of money: writing, the military and coinage. The effect that these could have had on the development of money is not straightforward and moreover depends on the specific historical context. While suggestions can be made on the basis of theoretical considerations and a broad historical coincidence of these phenomena with the development of money in the ancient Mediterranean, only a detailed examination of the specific historical context and circumstances can clarify the implications for the development of money. In Sections 6.2.1–6.2.3, some preliminary remarks are offered, while emphasising the need for additional research.

[15] Schaps 1997.

6.2.1 *Money and Writing*

Broadly contemporary with the rise of precious metal money in the Iron Age southern Levant and the Late Geometric Aegean was the development and introduction of the alphabet in both regions.[16] The spread of alphabetic writing likely stimulated the use of writing for various purposes, among which were the keeping of accounts and fiscal administration. As suggested,[17] this potentially opened up new possibilities and contexts for the use for money with far-reaching implications. Think for example of the implications that financial record keeping could have had on the complexity of transactions taking place. Although the relation between early writing and money is relatively unclear beyond the fact that neither one is a prerequisite for the other, it is unlikely that such contemporary innovations would have occurred in relative isolation from one another, without affecting one another. In addition to the use of writing for administrative and financial record keeping, we know of one case – the Eshtemoa hoard (Figure 3.15) – in which writing appears to have been used to count or mark containers with hoarded silver.[18]

The development of the alphabet in the southern Levant is complex and chronologically spread out. Starting in the Late Bronze Age, inscriptions in the Proto-Canaanite script are found concentrated in the area of the Shephelah, a focus of Egyptian power, and associated with Egyptian activity.[19] This distribution of early inscriptions does not overlap with the distribution of silver hoards,[20] making a direct connection between both unlikely. Yet, it appears that in the development of both writing and silver money-use, proximity to Egypt could have been a distinctive factor.

The introduction of the alphabet in Geometric Greece can be more closely associated with the early use of precious metal money in the region, as discussed in Chapter 5. Presumably transmitted through contact with Phoenician trade partners, many early inscriptions were found in Eretria and its various colonies, notably Methone, while the Eretrians or Euboians were also early adopters of precious metal money and standard weights in the Aegean. As argued, the Eretrians used Methone, an international trading centre on the Thermaic gulf, in order to process placer gold from the region into ingots that were then used in exchange. It is attractive to consider how the use of writing there could have influenced the complexity of trade transactions carried out or the accounting of merchants. However, the potential use of early Greek alphabetic writing in financial administration and trade and its

16 Sass 2005 with bibliography; Finkelstein and Sass 2013.
17 Cf. Sections 2.2.3 and 5.4.1; Codere 1968.
18 See Appendix.
19 Finkelstein and Sass 2013, 183–184.
20 See Section 3.3.1.

influence on money-use deserves additional scrutiny. The relevance of non-alphabetic potters' marks and their significance in marking tradable commodities are also yet to be better understood.[21]

6.2.2 Money and the Military

The spread of money, specifically in the form of coinage, has been associated with the arising need to finance military activity, for example, by paying soldiers. Initially suggested with regard to early Greek coinage, assuming that the first coins were too high in value to have been used in retail trade,[22] military pay has been invoked in explaining the invention of coinage and monetisation in various parts of the ancient world.[23] Although this explanation might well fit the context of Latin colonies in southern and central Italy during the third century BCE, or the late Iron Age Celtic coinages in northern Gaul (ca. third century BCE–first century CE), this is not necessarily the case with regard to the rise of money in the southern Levant or the Aegean.

I have argued that precious metal money in the southern Levant from the Iron I to IIB period and in the Aegean from the Late Geometric period onwards was used for carrying out small-scale transactions characterised by a high level of precision, well before the use of small fractional coinage.[24] Moreover, the use of precious metal money has been placed in various contexts (trade, religious contributions etc.), and there are no clear lines connecting the east-Greek mercenaries in the late seventh century southern Levant to monetisation in either region. In any case, these processes had taken hold already before the appearance of these mercenaries.

At the same time, we should not ignore that the rise of money-use appears to take place in the southern Levant as well as Greece in parallel to the deployment of armies and the rise of military tensions between expanding territorial entities. This can be seen in the southern Levant from the Iron I down to the period of Assyrian rule, with the importance of silver testified to by its prominence in tributary payments and booty.[25] In early Archaic Greece, the emerging city-states and the military tensions between them, for example, the so-called Lelantine war,[26] could have given rise to the need to organise the polities' military force. It is not unlikely that the participation or contribution of citizens to the emerging hoplite force had a financial or fiscal side to it.

[21] Papadopoulos 2017; Verdan 2017.

[22] Cf. Kim 2002.

[23] E.g., Cook 1958, 261; Pritchett 1971, 13–14; Rutter 1981, 5–6; 1997, 71–72; Crawford 1985, 36–37; Wigg-Wolf 2011; Termeer 2016.

[24] Cf. Kim 2001; 2002. See Sections 3.3 and 3.4.

[25] See Section 4.2.2.

[26] Cf. Hall 2007, 1–8.

While initially this might not have provided a direct impetus for the rise of money, it is altogether not unlikely that in due time it affected its use and circulation. Also here, detailed analysis of specific historical and political contexts should provide a way forward in understanding the complex ways in which money came to be embedded in archaic society.

6.2.3 Money and Coinage

Most conspicuously connected to the rise of money in the scholarly as well as popular discourse is the introduction of coinage. While I have offered clear considerations at the start of Chapter 5 to exclude the introduction of coinage from our discussions, its supposed connection to the early history of money and its relevance as the historically subsequent chapter warrant some remarks and suggestions aimed at future research.

Around the time the east Greeks and Lydians started using electrum coinage (i.e., the last third of the seventh century), they also became increasingly involved in Egypt as merchants and mercenaries.[27] Could this have provided an impetus for the introduction of coinage in western Asia Minor? Several scholars, notably Thompson, have argued that coinage – as a stamped standard weight of precious metal – had evolved in a direct line from the Levantine silver hoards, which she (incorrectly) claimed were sealed in bundles of standard weight and quality.[28] However, various reasons have been offered to reject this evolutionary approach to the development of money on the basis of the theoretical approach to money,[29] the diachronic analysis of the hoards[30] and the historical context.[31]

Although the Lydian presence on the geo-political stage, its expansionist ambitions and its role in a wider economic system[32] provide a plausible context for financial innovation as a political tool, there is little reason to assume that the practice of precious metal use was adopted directly and singularly from either the Assyrians, the Phoenicians or the Egyptians. Neither is it likely that the idea of coinage, as suggested by Thompson, was transmitted through such a channel. East Greek and Lydian contact with eastern powers, such as Egyptians and Assyrians, was partially related to increasing economic activity, characterised by the integration of formerly disparate markets and economic

[27] See Section 5.4.3.

[28] Balmuth 1976; Thompson 2003; Gitler 2012, 7–8; Haselgrove and Krmnicek 2012, 239; *pace* Eshel et al. 2018, 203–204, 221. See also Chapter 3.

[29] See Chapter 2.

[30] See Chapter 3.

[31] See Chapters 4 and 5.

[32] Fantalkin 2014, 38–45.

spheres.[33] This economic integration, as well as the use of electrum in Aegean trade,[34] could have stimulated money-use and prompted the introduction of coinage, but it is unlikely that contacts with Egypt and the Levant provided the nexus for the transmission of the specific ideas or money forms reflected by coinage. Distinguishing the idea of money-use from the specific idea of coinage, it is clear that the concept of precious metal money in standard weights was already transmitted to the Aegean prior to the start of the seventh century, during the (Late) Geometric period.

Equally related to the increasing economic integration of markets is perhaps the introduction of bimetallism – the minting of silver and gold, rather than electrum coinage – in the mid-sixth century.[35] As suggested in Chapter 5, the high demand in foreign markets led to an increasing importance of silver in international trade, thereby stimulating its use within the Aegean, where silver was produced. In addition to the advantage of being lower in value than electrum (thus more suitable for lower-value transaction) and the availability in larger quantities, this provided a plausible context for the adoption of silver as the customary, agreed-upon (δόκιμον) form of local money. It is not improbable that the western Aegean preceded east Greece in adopting uncoined silver as the *dokimon* form of money, regardless of the question who minted the first silver coins.

As noted at the start of Chapter 5, the appropriation and development of money-use within archaic Greek cities was by and large a result of the specific social and political context of the later seventh and sixth centuries. However, the seed for this had been planted prior to this, with the development of money-use in interregional and local trade and the increasing presence of different forms of money in other contexts of society, such as in cult and fines. Descat argued that coinage posed not a radical break but an innovation of different pre-existing forms of money ('monnaie multiple'), by a decrease in the number of objects used as money and an increasing specialisation in their use.[36] Coinage is thus regarded as the convergence of different forms of money into a uniform phenomenon.

But was early coinage uniform? Coinage arguably reflects the appropriation of money by emerging central authorities, such as the state, not just for the purpose of making its use more efficient[37] but in order to pave the way for certain policies that expanded its control. In order to understand the nature of this innovation, we need to ask what reality coinage was a reaction to. Rather

33 See Sections 5.4.3 and 5.4.4.
34 See Section 5.4.1.
35 Cf. Wallace 2016.
36 Descat 2001, 71.
37 Cf. Wallace 1987; Bresson 2009.

than being uniform in this regard, the practices of money-use and its importance in different communities around the Greek world were diverse, depending on trade interests, (inter)regional contacts, natural resources, legal realities etc. Being a response to those realities, early coinage was more diverse and heterogeneous than generally assumed. Although this assertion lies beyond the scope of this study, the thorough investigation of the nature and significance of money-use prior to coinage presented here should offer a fruitful basis and new vantage point for the future exploration of early coinage and the development of money in general.

APPENDIX

A CATALOGUE OF IRON AGE PRECIOUS METAL HOARDS IN ISRAEL/PALESTINE

INTRODUCTION

As discussed in Chapter 3 (see also Table 3.1), this catalogue serves as a basic survey of the data set and can be regarded as updating, correcting, and expanding the earlier work of Kletter and Thompson.[1] It focuses on hoards datable to the end of the Late Bronze Age and the Iron Age from the southern Levant, including also one hoard from Eretria, Greece. Some of the hoards included by Kletter and Thompson can be re-dated to earlier periods; for the purpose of clarity, these have been included here as well. Most hoards contain (predominantly) silver, unless stated otherwise.

The object numbers referred to in the text and in several figure captions[2] consist of a number assigned to the hoard, combined with a number assigned to the object within the hoard (i.e., hoard/object). Under these numbers, hoards and the specific objects have been recorded in a MS Access database that served as the basis for the analyses. Separate bundles or parts of hoards that are kept in different collections have been recorded under a different decimal number. The following hoards (with hoard numbers) were included in detail in the database (see Section 3.2.1).

1. Megiddo A (1.1 Rockefeller Museum; 1.2 Oriental Institute Museum)
2. Arad
3. Wadi el-Makkuk
4. Eretria (Greece)
5. Beth Shean D (5.1–4)
6. Megiddo D
7. Ein Gedi
8. Beth Shean A (8.1 Rockefeller Museum; 8.2 Penn Museum)
9. Beth Shean B (9.1 Rockefeller Museum; 9.2 Penn Museum)
10. Beth Shean C (10.1 Rockefeller Museum; 10.2 Penn Museum)

[1] Kletter 2003; Thompson 2003. Cf. Eshel et al. 2018.

[2] See Chapter 3.

11. Megiddo E (MB/LB hoard; not included in this study)[3]
12. Megiddo B
13. Tell Keisan
14. Tel Dor (14.1 Haifa University; 14.2 IAA/Israel Museum)
15. Akko
16. Ein Ḥofez
17. Shechem B (17.1 Semitic Museum)
18. Amathus (not included in this study, see Section 5.2.1)[4]

1 ABEL BETH MAACAH

During the first excavation season at the site, in 2013, a small jug containing a silver hoard was found on a beaten-earth and lime floor abutting the north side of a large stone structure in area F, stratum F3. Fragments of a collared-rim jar were initially recorded to have been found on the same floor as the hoard, which in turn was dated to the end of the LB II, or to the final phase of the LBA,[5] contemporary to the Beth Shean D hoard.[6] A new report of the hoard now dates its context to the LB IIB,[7] thereby placing it outside of the chronological range of the corpus. It has been included here for the purpose of clarity.

The published report presents the hoard in detail, although lacking weights of the individual objects.[8] The hoard contains twelve silver objects, weighing a total of 59 g. There are five penannular earrings with cone-shaped pendants and one penannular twisted (square-sectioned) wire earring, suggesting a date for these objects between the MB IIb and the fourteenth century, with parallels for both types present in the Amarna hoard (Figure 4.5). In addition to these complete jewellery items, there are two pieces of bent wire/ring (one is broken/cut on one side), one rod fragment (bent and cut on both ends), one piece of folded sheet/plate, one rough ingot fragment (cut twice) and one large rough cast ingot of irregular shape (apparently complete).

Lead Isotope Analysis (LIA) suggests the Aegean and/or Anatolia as a likely source of the silver, although this could not be determined with certainty, possibly as a result of mixing.

Bibliography: Panitz-Cohen, Mullins and Bonfil 2013, 39–40; 2015, 46; Panitz-Cohen et al. 2016; Yahalom-Mack et al 2019.

[3] See Chapter 4, n. 8.
[4] Heymans 2019.
[5] LB III or 'early Iron Age I'. Cf. Chapter 3, n. 42.
[6] Personal communication, N. Panitz-Cohen; Panitz-Cohen, Mullins and Bonfil 2013, 39–40; 2015, 46.
[7] Yahalom-Mack et al. 2019, 132–135.
[8] Yahalom-Mack et al. 2019.

2 AKKO

During excavations on Tel Akko under M. Dothan in 1978, two juglets, one of which contained a silver hoard, were found in locus 762, area A, stratum 7 (previously listed as stratum 3). A preliminary discussion of the hoard and its context is offered by Eshel et al.[9] The unpublished excavation diary notes that the hoard was placed 'either on a lower floor or in a fill – set in and covered over, [the] latter is more likely'.[10] Although no final date for the stratum was provided by the excavators, it contained Phoenician and Cypriot pottery. Eshel et al. suggests an Iron II dating for the hoard.[11]

Kept at the Institute for Maritime Studies of the University of Haifa, the hoard has been studied in its totality by T. Eshel, offering weights, typology and XRF compositional analysis of part of the objects.[12] The recorded total weight of all the objects in the hoard is 259 g,[13] and it contained a variety of cut and broken objects (*hacksilber*) but lacked jewellery (fragments). Samples taken for LIA suggest origins in Sardinia and southeast Anatolia[14] and possibly Iberia.[15]

Bibliography: Dothan 1992, 52; Thompson 2003, 72, 97; 2007, 44; Thompson and Skaggs 2013; Eshel 2014; Eshel et al. 2018; 2019; Wood, Montero-Ruiz and Martinón-Torres 2019.

3 ARAD

Excavations in the Iron Age fortress of Tel Arad in the Judean desert in the late 1960s under Y. Aharoni discovered a silver hoard consisting of two corroded masses with textile remains inside a cooking pot (Figures 2.1 and A.1). The hoard was located in the southwest part of the fortress (locus 979) in a pit 15 cm under the floor of stratum X that went unnoticed at the time of excavation, leading the excavators to assign the hoard to stratum XI.[16] A restudy of the stratigraphy of the site, and the observation that the type of cooking pot was specific for stratum X, enabled Z. Herzog and L. Singer-Avitz to properly identify the context of the hoard in the preliminary excavation report.[17] Stratum X was identified as the first of three Iron IIB strata at the fortress, dated by Herzog to the middle of the eighth

[9] Eshel 2014; Eshel et al. 2018. 207.
[10] Thompson 2003, 97; Thompson and Skaggs 2013, table 3, Eshel 2014; Eshel et al. 2018, 207.
[11] Eshel et al. 2018, 201, 207. Cf. Eshel 2014, dating the hoard to the Iron IIA.
[12] Eshel 2014.
[13] 305 objects. Cf. Thompson 2003 lists a total weight of 257.6 g, followed by Eshel et al. 2018.
[14] Thompson 2007, 44; Thompson and Skaggs 2013; Eshel et al. 2019.
[15] Wood, Montero-Ruiz and Martinón-Torres 2019.
[16] Aharoni 1968, 392; Aharoni 1980.
[17] Herzog 2002, 33; Singer-Avitz 2002, 141, 161.

A.1 Cooking pot and bundles of the Arad hoard after discovery; close up of one of the bundles (Courtesy of the Tel Arad Publication Team, Institute of Archaeology, Tel Aviv University)

century. A hematite dome-shaped object – presumably a weight – of a shekel was found in the same locus as the hoard.[18]

A preliminary report of the hoard was published by M. Aharoni,[19] recording its weight as ca. 200 g. With the permission of Z. Herzog, the material was reinvestigated in the framework of the current study. While part of the hoard had been cleaned previously (61 objects), a large part of the hoard that had remained untreated since its discovery was subjected to conservation treatment (117 objects); a portion of the hoard remains in its untreated state (28 objects or conglomerates of objects). Textile fragments (linen), preserved on the corrosion, were documented and studied by Koen Berghuijs of the Textile Research Centre in Leiden.

The current weight of the hoard is ca. 328 g and consists of 206 objects (prior to the recent treatment of 117 objects, the total weight had been ca. 360 g). A total of 178 objects have been cleaned, representing a weight of 283.53 g and are included in the study. Why the hoard was previously recorded with a lower weight is unclear. The hoard consisted of a variety of cut and broken objects, including ingots and ornamental objects of different types (Figure 2.1). The objects show considerable traces of wear, and very few were complete (three) or almost complete (four). Compositional analyses of a selection of objects were published by Aharoni,[20] and samples for LIA were taken by T. Eshel but are not yet published.

Bibliography: Aharoni 1968, 392, pl. 40b; 1980, 39–40; Herzog 1997, 222–223; 2002, 33, 80; Singer-Avitz 2002, 141, 161, 169, 199; Heymans 2018a.

[18] Ca. 11.37 g. Herzog 2002, 33, 80; Singer-Avitz 2002, 161; personal communication, Z. Herzog.

[19] Aharoni 1980.

[20] Aharoni 1980, 40.

4 ASHKELON

In 1998, two corroded masses of silver (reg. nos. 50650 and 50651), were discovered together on a stone pavement in room 595, a side-room or alcove of room 530, in phase 18a of grid 38. Phase 18 is the second phase yielding bichrome ware and assigned by the excavators to period XV of the site ('late bichrome'/Iron I), which is dated before the end of the Iron I.[21] During phase 18a, room 530-595 of the Southern Building Complex was dominated by a hearth and the stone pavement on which the bundles were found.[22] Although the excavators do not give this option, the possibility remains that the hoard was in fact buried under a later floor.

The first bundle (50650) had a weight of 36.35 g (cf. 55 g before cleaning); the second bundle (50651) had a weight of 44.79 g (cf. 65 g before cleaning).[23] A photo of the cleaned material (Figure A.2) shows that it consists of a variety of cut and broken objects, including ingots and ornamental objects of different types.[24] Complete or almost complete objects are rare, if there are any at all.

A.2 Ashkelon hoard (Courtesy of the Leon Levy Expedition to Ashkelon)

[21] Stager et al. 2008, 217.

[22] Stager et al. 2008, 267–271; Aja 2009, 179–181, 194, fig. 3.6; Thompson 2020, 596–597.

[23] I thank prof. Daniel Master for providing this information. Cf. Thompson 2003, 97. Cf. Gitler and Tal 2020, 36, who record 36.64 g; 46.35 g.

[24] Stager et al. 2008, 270, fig. 15.42. For alternative images, see Gitler and Tal 2020, 36, fig. 1; Thompson 2020, fig. 22.2.

The bundles were wrapped in textile. Thompson took samples for LIA, but the preliminary results are still under debate.[25]

Bibliography: Balmuth 2001b, 15; Thompson 2003, 97; 2007, 44; 2020; Stager et al. 2008, 266–271, fig. 15.42; Aja 2009, 180–181, 194, fig. 3.6; Gitler and Tal 2020, 36, fig. 1.

5 BETH SHEAN A

In 1925, during the University Museum Expedition excavation of the so-called Southern Temple of Rameses III of Level V (room 1029), two hoards (A and B) were found placed against the east side of the middle column basis on both the north (hoard A) and south side (hoard B) of the central aisle. Both hoards were interpreted by the excavator as foundation deposits, presumably because they were found under the surface, although the exact circumstances of discovery have not been recorded.[26] However, as argued before,[27] hoards were habitually placed under the floor, against or under a wall, and both of these hoards were found placed against the column base rather than irretrievably under it, making it more likely that the hoards were left or stored at a later point in time during the use of the building.[28]

The dating of the Level V temples has been subject to several revisions. Initially dated to the time of Ramesses II,[29] Mazar has argued, following James,[30] for a building date of the Southern Temple during Iron I, after which it was reused as an administrative complex during the Iron IIA.[31] Considering that the hoard presumably dates to the end of the building's lifetime, we can put forward a date in the Iron IIA, while keeping in mind that the debate on the phasing and chronology of Level V remains unresolved. A full discussion of the hoard's context and contents was presented elsewhere as part of a preliminary report of the hoard.[32]

Deposited in a red-burnished jug, the hoard has a total weight of 2,436.18 g, of which are 479.81 g in gold and electrum. These weights were recorded in the framework of the current study but appear to match the original weights

[25] Thompson 2007, 44; 2020, 601–602. Cf. Eshel et al. 2018, 222; 2019; Wood, Montero-Ruiz and Martinón-Torres 2019.

[26] Rowe 1940, 26; James 1966, 38.

[27] Cf. Section 3.3.1.

[28] Cf. Vargyas 2007, 296–298.

[29] Rowe 1930.

[30] James 1966, 151–153.

[31] Mazar 1993, 221–223; 2006, 34–35; 2009, 10–11, 27–28; Mullins 2012, 145. Cf. Yannai 1996.

[32] Heymans 2018b, 277–286. The Beth Shean A, B and C hoards were studied in both Jerusalem and Philadelphia. Alegre Savariego of the IAA/Rockefeller Museum provided permission and support in studying the material in Jerusalem. Permission to study the objects in Philadelphia was granted by Katy Blanchard of the Penn Museum. Alessandro Pezatti and Eric Schnittke provided access to the Penn Museum Archive.

A.3 Gold foil ingot from the Beth Shean A hoard (8.2/4 courtesy of the Penn Museum, object no. 29-105-107D [photo author])

given by Rowe.[33] However, detailed investigation of the hoard, divided between the Penn Museum in Philadelphia and the Rockefeller Museum in Jerusalem, determined that not all objects are currently kept under their originally assigned number. Considering the fact that hoards A and B were found so close to one another in both space and time, it cannot be excluded that objects got displaced between them.[34] The hoard contains cut and broken ingots of various types, part of which is covered by heavy corrosion, and ornamental objects such as jewellery and fragments thereof, with most objects being small in size. Most notable are three large solid electrum ingots, hammered into flat blocks, and sixteen smaller ingots, made out of folded packs of gold foil (Figure A.3).[35] Of these 16 ingots, one, somewhat larger example, was hammered and clean, while the others have traces of corrosion on them. Assuming that the corrosion of a cheaper metal had burst out onto the surface, Vargyas suggested that these were in fact gold-plated ingots, meant as counterfeits and 'that somebody made the fake ingots in order to use them as money'.[36] However, close inspection indicated that this claim is unsubstantiated and that these are folded packs of gold foil; visible traces of iron corrosion are likely a result of contamination from other objects in the hoard.[37]

With the material of the hoard divided, and due to the sheer size of the hoard and the corroded state of part of the material, it was not possible to subject all objects to full study and inventory. Consequently, the hoard was excluded from the quantitative analyses in Section 3.3.

[33] Rowe 1940, 26. It is assumed here that the large weight of 5 pounds and 5 ½ ounces concerns the total weight, rather than only the silver as noted in Rowe 1940, 26. This weight is listed in Rowe's excavation diary of 1925 (p. 57) for 'electrum objects & ingots'.

[34] Heymans 2018b, 278–279.

[35] One of these was reportedly stolen while on loan at the Land of Israel Museum in Tel Aviv, and another is a wrapped-up spindle of gold strips.

[36] Vargyas 2007, 299–300.

[37] Visual inspection was supplemented by XRF analysis of the ingots in the Rockefeller Museum, carried out by prof. Yuval Goren, whom I thank for his help.

Bibliography: Rowe 1940, 26, 72, pl. 10, 29:32–44, pl. 66a:1–2; James 1966, 38; Vargyas 2007; Heymans 2018b, 277–286.

6 BETH SHEAN B

Hoard B was discovered ten days before hoard A in the same room of the Southern Temple of Level V (1029) and had been deposited under similar conditions.[38] It was deposited in a cooking pot, the rim of which had likely been broken off in antiquity[39] and was wrapped in textile.[40] A full discussion of the hoard's context and contents was presented elsewhere as part of a preliminary report of the hoard.[41]

As noted with regard to hoard A, detailed investigation of the hoard material, divided between the Penn Museum in Philadelphia (Figure A.4) and the Rockefeller Museum in Jerusalem, determined that some objects are no longer kept under their original inventory number. In the case of hoard B, a total weight of 438.35 g, recorded in the framework of the current study, compared to the nearly 2.5 kg recorded by Rowe, suggests that substantial quantities of material are currently missing.[42]

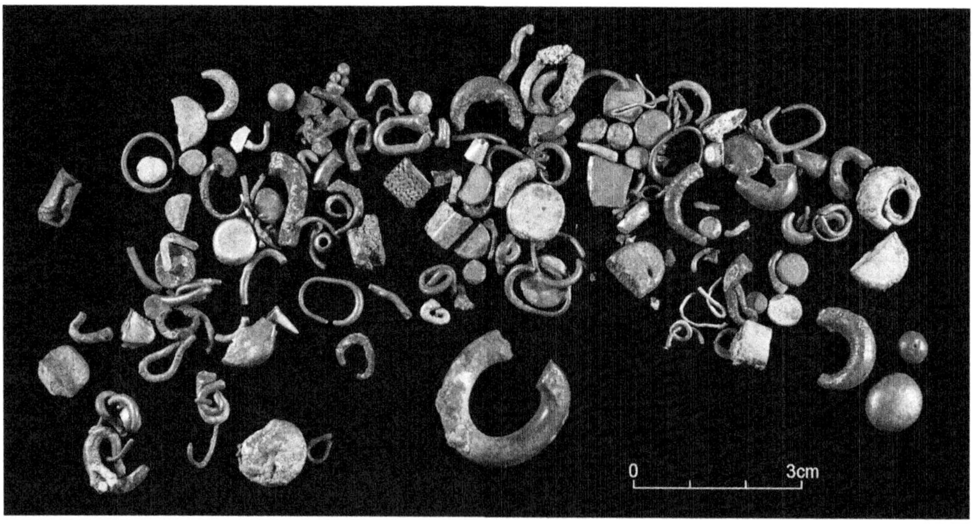

A.4 Selection of objects from the Beth Shean B hoard in the Penn Museum (Courtesy of the Penn Museum, object no. 29-105-159)

[38] Rowe 1940, 26; James 1966, 38.
[39] James 1966, 38.
[40] Rowe 1940, 19.
[41] Heymans 2018b, 277–286. See n. 32.
[42] Rowe 1940, 26; Heymans 2018b, 278, 285.

Although a significant part of the material at the Rockefeller Museum (9.1) remains uncleaned, with objects sticking together into conglomerates bound by corrosion, the metrology and typology of both the total hoard (9.1 and 9.2) and the Penn Museum part (9.2, specifically for the metrology) have been analysed and are included in Section 3.3. While only a fraction of the hoard at large, the weight distribution patterns appear consistent with other hoards dating to Iron I and Iron IIA–B, and show that ca. 80 per cent of the objects at the Penn Museum (9.2) weigh below 1 g. The graph in Figure 3.30, showing data for the combined hoard (9.1 and 9.2), suggests a higher average weight for the objects with slightly more than half of the objects weighing below 1 g, but we need to take into account here that the presence of conglomerates distorts the overall weight distribution, suggesting a lower number of objects for the same weight of the hoard.[43] The Beth Shean A hoard, with its large amount of small objects, seems to be similar in this respect.

Around half the objects can be categorised as ingots of various types and half as ornamental objects, including (broken) jewellery. However, with most (if not all) of the objects in the conglomerates appearing like ingots, this ratio would clearly shift in favour of the ingots. Moreover, descriptions of objects in the field register suggest that the missing part(s) of the hoard would predominantly consist of ingots.

Bibliography: Rowe 1940, 19, 26, 72, pl. 10, 29:12–31, pl. 66a:3; James 1966, 38; Vargyas 2007; Heymans 2018b, 277–286.

7 BETH SHEAN C

During excavations of the University Museum Expedition in 1926 at the central part of the tel, a hoard wrapped in linen was discovered under the south wall of room 1095 (part of structure 1093-99), directly north of the temple of Seti I. This structure was assigned by James to the Late Level VI, dating to the Iron I (eleventh/early tenth century).[44] Mazar has attempted to reassign this structure to the last phase of Egyptian presence in Beth Shean by identifying it as part of Building SL of stratum S-3 of the Hebrew University Excavations,[45] but there are several reasons to reject this reconstruction. Among others, none of the walls of the structure actually match the walls of Building SL, and, as Mazar and Panitz-Cohen acknowledge, the level of room 1095 is much higher than the floor level of Building SL in stratum S-2.

[43] See also Chapter 3, n. 177.

[44] James 1966, 21, 27, fig. 76.2, 77.

[45] Mazar 1993, 208, fig. 4; 2009, 7, fig. 1.5; Panitz-Cohen and Mazar 2009, 152.

A.5 Selection of objects from the Beth Shean C hoard in the Penn Museum (Courtesy of the Penn Museum, object no. 29-105-162)

Although the stratigraphic evidence remains inconclusive, there is no solid basis to down-date building 1096-93 (with room 1095) to Lower Level VI, that is, the end of the Late Bronze Age. An Iron I date for the hoard is moreover consistent with several characteristics of the hoard. A full discussion of the hoard's context and contents was presented elsewhere as part of a preliminary report of the hoard.[46]

Currently divided between the Penn Museum in Philadelphia (Figure A.5) and the Rockefeller Museum in Jerusalem, the hoard has a total weight of 1,350.3 g in metal objects, recorded in the framework of the current study. It appears to be complete, with the exception of a gold or electrum bracelet[47] and a strip of gold foil, which could not be located in the Penn Museum.

[46] Heymans 2018b, 277–286. See n. 32.

[47] Rowe 1940, pl. 34.17.

Contents consisted of cut and broken ingots and ornamental objects, a large proportion of which were sheet fragments. Much of the hoard bears traces of corrosion. Preliminary results of XRF analysis, carried out by Yuval Goren, indicate that several objects had a high copper content, appearing comparable to the composition of the silver in the Tel Keisan hoard.[48] Additionally, the hoard contained a slightly chipped grey sandstone sphendonoid weight of 43.256 g, likely related to the 'Carchemish' shekel of ca. 7.8 g (six) or the 'Hittite' shekel of ca. 11.4 g (four).

With the material of the hoard divided, and due to the sheer size of the hoard, it was not possible to subject all objects to full study and inventory. The quantitative analyses of the hoard presented in Section 3.3 were therefore based on the Rockefeller part of the hoard (10.1), assuming that it is representative for the complete assemblage.

Bibliography: Rowe 1940, 19, pl. 34:10, 11, 17, 21 and pl. 67a: 1–3; James 1966, 21, 27, fig. 76.2, 77; Mazar 1993, 208, fig. 4; 2009, 7, fig. 1.5; 2010, 259–60; Thompson 2003, 98; Panitz-Cohen and Mazar 2009, 152; Golani 2013, 12, n. 23; Heymans 2018b, 277–286.

8 BETH SHEAN D

Three corroded masses of silver objects and several associated objects were found in locus 88866 in room 10704 in building SD of stratum S-4 during the 1991 excavation campaign of the Hebrew University at Tel Beth Shean (Figure A.6). The area was identified as the Egyptian garrison quarter, and stratum S-4 was the penultimate phase of Egyptian presence at the site, presumably dating to the middle of the twelfth century. The hoard and its context are published in detail in the final report of the excavations.[49]

The three bundles had a respective weight of 56.18, 34.83 and 66.33 g. Only bundle three was wrapped in textile. Based on the proximity and the nature of the objects, several of the associated objects could have belonged to the hoard, in particular, two earrings, a signet ring and three silver fragments that were retrieved from sifting.[50] Regretfully, these three fragments were otherwise not published and no weight was recorded. Adding the weight of the former three items, the hoard has a total metal weight of 191.15 g. Most objects were cut or broken and concern ingots and ornamental objects alike. Of a total of forty objects, four appear complete and seven almost complete. Five samples were

[48] Eshel 2014; Eshel et al. 2018, 214.
[49] Thompson 2009; Panitz-Cohen and Mazar 2009, 122–124, 129.
[50] Thompson 2009, 602.

A.6 Beth Shean D hoard (Courtesy of the Tel Beth Shean expedition, The Hebrew University of Jerusalem [photo by Gabi Laron])

taken for LIA, identifying ores from the Taurus region (2) and from Laurion (3).[51] One of the ingots was identified as having a hidden copper-core.[52]

Bibliography: Thompson 2003, 74; 2009, 597–611; Panitz-Cohen and Mazar 2009, 122–124, 129.

9 TEL DOR

In 1995, a large jug was discovered *in situ* in locus 17321 in area D2, on the southern side of the tel, next to the harbour, and only lifted the next season. The jug had presumably been placed in a pit or fill under a courtyard, next to a public building.[53] Although the context information is not conclusive, the hoard has been assigned to phase 8c, which is dated by the excavators to their Iron I/II horizon (late tenth century). A discussion of the archaeological context and contents of the hoard is given by Eshel et al.[54]

The hoard (Figure 3.1) consisted of several linen bundles that appear to have been sealed and stamped with a Middle Bronze Age scarab with a pattern of interlocking spirals,[55] although it is unclear how many bundles there are and whether all bundles were sealed in a similar fashion. The hoard has a total weight of 8.5 kg. The bundle(s) that has/have been separated and cleaned consisted mostly of small cut or broken silver ingots and ornamental objects of various types. Various samples have been taken for LIA, pointing to the Taurus, Sardinia and possibly Iberia as possible sources of the silver.[56]

Bibliography: Stern 2001; 2008, 1698–1699; Thompson 2003, 79, 81–83, 98; 2007, 44, 245; Gilboa and Sharon 2008, 162; Gilboa, Sharon, and Boaretto 2008, 156; Eshel 2014; Eshel et al. 2018; 2019; Wood, Montero-Ruiz and Martinón-Torres 2019

10 EIN GEDI

In a pit under the floor of room 208 of building 207 in area D on the north slope of Tel Goren, Ein Gedi, a hoard was discovered in a cooking pot (Figure A.7), covered by a lamp. The room belongs to stratum V, which was presumably destroyed in the 580s BCE. Assuming that the hoard belongs to the end of the stratum, it can be securely dated to the early sixth century. The floor under

[51] Thompson 2009, 606. Cf. Eshel et al. 2018, 222; 2019; Wood, Montero-Ruiz and Martinón-Torres 2019.

[52] Thompson 2003, 74; 2009, 605–606.

[53] N.B., its neck was sticking out into L17309, see Stern 2001, 21, pl.1.1; Eshel 2014, chapter 2.

[54] Eshel 2014; Eshel et al. 2018, 204.

[55] Stern 2001, 22–24.

[56] Thompson 2007, 44; Thompson and Skaggs 2013; Eshel et al. 2019; Wood, Montero-Ruiz and Martinón-Torres 2019.

A.7 Ein Gedi hoard (Courtesy of the Israel Museum, Jerusalem [photo author])

which the hoard was found yielded bronze scale pans and Judahite stone weights of 1, 2 and 8 shekels.[57] A final publication of the excavations, including a study of the hoard, appeared in 2007,[58] but, regretfully, the object list is incomplete and the objects do not correspond with the weights recorded.

In the framework of the current study, the hoard was subject to a new investigation. Kletter and de Groot mention that the hoard consisted of sixty-seven objects but that five of these were lost before the hoard entered the Israel Museum in Jerusalem. Additionally, two earrings, visible on two photos (one of which taken at the time of the excavation),[59] but apparently lost and not mentioned by other studies,[60] were found misplaced among jewellery from

[57] Kletter and de Groot 2007, 368; Stern 2007, 174–175.
[58] Stern 2007; Kletter and de Groot 2007.
[59] Stern 2007, pl. 5.
[60] Kletter 2003, 143; Thompson 2003, 98; Kletter and de Groot 2007.

the Eshtemoa hoard.[61] The five small objects mentioned by Kletter and de Groot and shown by them on a photo with numbering are still missing.[62]

The hoard currently consists of sixty-four objects, with a total weight of 1,102.18 g (Figures 3.4, 3.8 and A.7). With the exception of the two earrings, all the objects are ingots, many of which have cut traces. Most large ingots have relatively few traces of wear. The common ingot-type in this hoard was discussed in Section 3.2.4 in detail, and it was suggested that these could be the primary product of cupellation, explaining their peculiar surface characteristics and shape. Thompson took LIA samples, with preliminary results indicating sources in the Aegean, Sardinia and Spain.[63]

Bibliography: Mazar 1963, 104; Gitin and Golani 2001, 38, 44; Thompson 2003, 71, 98; 2007, 44; Kletter and De Groot 2007, 367–375, pl. 5; Stern 2007, 77–85, 174–175; Wood, Montero-Ruiz and Martinón-Torres 2019.

11 EIN ḤOFEZ

During salvage excavations for the construction of a neighbourhood southwest of Yoqne'am near the Ein Ḥofez spring, about two kilometres east of the Elyaqim interchange and a kilometre south of the 70 highway, remains of two houses belonging to an Iron Age settlement were uncovered. In a backroom of one of the houses, three small dipper juglets filled with silver objects (Figure A.8) were found between two floors (L269, and 15 cm below it L277), the latest of which is dated to the late Iron IIA. The excavator assumes that the hoard belonged to the upper layer, having been placed or hidden under the floor, but the stratigraphy is not conclusive.[64] The necks of the juglets had been carefully broken, presumably to widen the opening. A discussion of the archaeological context and contents of the hoard is offered by Eshel et al.[65]

Regretfully, the contents of the three juglets were mixed together, possibly during conservation or study, and it is no longer possible to compare the contents of the different juglets. Eshel compiled an inventory of 462 objects, two of which were stone, and the rest silver.[66] It was noted earlier that the hoard contains gold as well,[67] but this is incorrect; several objects (jewellery)

[61] I am grateful to Dr Eran Arie of the Israel Museum for his help and for allowing me to study the material.

[62] Kletter and de Groot 2007, 371, photo 4.

[63] Thompson 2007, 44; Wood, Montero-Ruiz and Martinón-Torres 2019. Cf. Eshel et al. 2018, 222; 2019.

[64] Alexandre 2013; Eshel 2014, ch. 2; Eshel et al. 2018, 204, 207.

[65] Eshel 2014; Eshel et al. 2018, 204, 207.

[66] Eshel 2014.

[67] Alexandre 1997; Golani and Sass 1998, 77, n. 7.

A.8 Ein Ḥofez hoard (Courtesy of Warhaftig Venezian/Israel Antiquities Authority)

did, however, have a notable gold content (ca. 10–30 per cent).[68] The total silver weight of the hoard is 977.86 g, while it was previously noted to be over 1,200 g. Presumably, this concerns the weight recorded prior to conservation treatment. The hoard consisted of various large (cut or broken) ingots and ornamental objects, among which are many earrings and smaller cut or broken ingots. Thompson took samples for LIA and pointed to Sardinia as the source of the silver, but, more recently, Iberia and possibly the Taurus have been proposed instead.[69]

Bibliography: Alexandre 1997, 53–54; 2008, 1728–1729; 2013; Golani and Sass 1998, 77; Thompson 2003, 77, 98–99; 2007, 44; Thompson and Skaggs 2013; Eshel 2014; Eshel et al. 2018; 2019; Wood, Montero-Ruiz and Martinón-Torres 2019.

12 ESHTEMOA

In a natural cavity in the rock bottom, 60 cm under the floor of a room adjoining the ancient synagogue of Eshtemoa, five Iron Age jugs were found together, filled with silver objects (Figure 3.15). Two of the jugs had dipinti with the word *hamesh* (חמש – five), while a third bore traces of paint that appear

[68] Eshel 2014, ch.4; Eshel et al. 2018, 215. Cf. Thompson 2003, 99; Alexandre 2013, 20*.
[69] Thompson 2007; 44; Thompson and Skaggs 2013; Eshel et al. 2019; Wood, Montero-Ruiz and Martinón-Torres 2019.

to have been of a similar dipinto.[70] The jugs had different weights, but the total weight of the silver has been estimated around 26 kg, making it the single largest silver hoard that has been uncovered in the southern Levant. Discussing only a selection of the silver objects, the hoard and its context were published by Z. Yeivin.[71]

Since the archaeological context offers no further clues, the date of the hoard has been the subject of extensive discussion, with reference to diverse aspects, such as the historical context, the pottery, the letterforms of the dipinti and the jewellery in the hoard. In recent decades, consensus appears to have been reached to date the hoard either to the ninth or the eighth century.[72] Sass has assigned the jewellery, with its use of granulation and herringbone wire decoration, to the Iron IIA, based *inter alia* on the comparison with the Arad hoard.[73] As discussed, this hoard was later reassigned to stratum X, the earliest of the Iron IIB strata (see catalogue no. 3), although the wear on the granule-decorated earring from the Arad, used as comparandum (2/120), suggests that the piece was older at the time of deposition (i.e., late Iron IIA). Meanwhile, discussing the palaeography on the jars, Finkelstein and Sass have extended the date span slightly to include the early Iron IIB,[74] although Na'aman earlier drew the comparison with script of Arad IX–VIII, the later strata of the Iron IIB (pre-Sennacherib).[75] An eighth century date for the hoard would also be consistent with the typology of the jugs,[76] and the suggested eight century (pre-Sennacherib) existence of the town and a critical reading of 1 Samuel 30:26–31.[77] Thompson's suggestion of a pre-eighth century date (eleventh–ninth century), based on the comparison with the single other massive hoard (Dor),[78] not only ignores the evidence from the hoard itself but fails to appreciate the difference between the north and Judah in terms of their respective development as a credible social and political context for such an accumulation of wealth.

Only a fraction of the silver from the hoard (from one jug) has been cleaned, consisting of cut and broken ingots and ornamental objects, among which are a variety of jewellery types. All object categories known from other hoards and discussed in Chapter 3 (except for nuggets) appear to be represented, but regretfully, no quantitative data are available so far. Results from LIA are

[70] Yeivin 1987; 1990, 46–48.
[71] Yeivin 1987; 1990; Kletter and Brand 1998.
[72] Kletter and Brand 1998; Kletter 2003, 143–144.
[73] Sass 1997, 243; 2002a, 32.
[74] Finkelstein and Sass 2013, 170.
[75] Na'aman 1994, 220, n. 6.
[76] Kletter and Brand 1998.
[77] Na'aman 2010.
[78] Thompson 2003, 93, 99.

under debate: Thompson identified Taurus and Sardinia, but others are now pointing also to Iberia as (one of) the source(s) of the silver.[79]

Bibliography: Yeivin 1971a; 1971b; 1972; 1987; 1990; 1993, 426; Balmuth 1976; Eran 1990; Kletter and Brand 1998; Kletter 2003, 143–144; Sass 1997, 243; 2002a, 32, n. 11; Thompson 2003, 93, 99; 2007, 44; Na'aman 2010; Thompson and Skaggs 2013; Eshel et al. 2019; Wood, Montero-Ruiz and Martinón-Torres 2019.

13 GEZER A

Thompson lists a hoard from the early excavations at Tel Gezer, found in trench 17 and dated by Macalister to the 'fourth semitic period', although noting that 'the stratification was here rather disturbed'.[80]

The hoard is described as consisting of eighteen silver bracelets and fragments of bracelets and a small toggle pin. However, with a diameter of ca. 4 cm (ca. 1.5 inch using the scale bar in the photo),[81] the rings are perhaps too small to qualify as bracelets. They are presumably penannular earrings, a type that is dated to the MB or LB I.[82] Although difficult to see, the toggle pin also appears to fit this date. In absence of objects indicative of a later date, such as lunate earrings, an Iron Age date for this hoard cannot be supported.

Bibliography: Macalister 1912, 98–100, fig. 285; Thompson 2003, 99.

14 GEZER B

A second hoard listed by Thompson from the early excavations at Gezer from trench 'IV 10', consisted of (broken) silver jewellery, several other pieces of broken or cut silver scraps and two steatite scarabs, mounted in rings, all placed at the bottom of a broken jar.[83] Macalister actually dates the hoard to 'the time of the XIIth Dynasty or of the Hyksos', on the basis of the scarabs, while also referring to a scarab of Sheshi, a ruler of the Second Intermediate Period (seventeenth century), found at the same level nearby.[84]

Thompson, however, invokes the MB bullae in the Dor hoard in order to claim that early scarabs do not necessarily indicate an early date for the hoard,[85] but her suggestion that the hoard could date to the Iron Age should be

79 Thompson 2007; 44; Thompson and Skaggs 2013; Eshel et al. 2019; Wood, Montero-Ruiz and Martinón-Torres 2019.
80 Macalister 1912, 99.
81 Macalister 1912, 98, fig. 285.
82 Cf. Maxwell-Hyslop 1971, 112–116, 149–151; Sass 1997, 241.
83 Macalister 1912, 102–103.
84 Macalister 1912, 102.
85 Thompson 2003, 99.

rejected. None of the other objects in the hoard warrant a date after LB I. The penannular earrings, the toggle pins, and the open crescent pendant are all consistent with a MB date for this hoard.[86]

Bibliography: Macalister 1912, 102–103, fig. 288; Thompson 2003, 99.

15 GEZER C

Macalister recorded another hoard consisting of 'shapeless fragments of silver' that 'were found with a number of others in a jar. They evidently are waste scraps collected for re-melting by a silversmith'.[87] A drawing of the objects (possibly a selection) shows several pieces of cut and/or broken silver ingots and ornamental objects, such as folded sheet and wire, some visibly stuck onto one another.[88] Although no specific date can be given for the hoard, its composition certainly allows for an Iron Age date.

Kletter notes that a few weights were found in the hoard, referring to Macalister's mention elsewhere of weights found in 'a hoard in IV 21',[89] but the basis for this connection is not clear.

Bibliography: Macalister 1912, 262–263, fig. 408; Gitin and Golani 2001, 39; Kletter 2003, 144; Thompson 2003, 99.

16 TELL JEMMEH

A group of ten gold and silver earrings was found by Petrie in 1927 in room GA at a level of 185 ft., and interpreted as a jeweller's hoard.[90] The room belonged to level G–H, identified as the 'town of the XXth Dynasty'[91] Petrie's strata have been noted to be problematic, and the contexts unreliable, and their dating has been subject to general revision, with level G–H tentatively dated to the Iron IIA.[92]

Like the Tawilan hoard, the Jemmeh hoard appears to be a jewellery hoard. There were two damaged silver earrings, one with a knob on the underside and the other with a herringbone wire decoration around the edge, six golden earrings with herringbone wire decoration and a loop on the side for a pendant

[86] Cf. Maxwell-Hyslop 1971, 112–116, 149–151; Sass 1997, 241.
[87] Macalister 1912, 263.
[88] Macalister 1912, 262, fig. 408.
[89] Kletter 2003, 144. Cf. Macalister 1912, 283.
[90] Petrie 1928, 10, pl. 1.
[91] Petrie 1928, 6, pl. 7.
[92] Amiran and Van Beek 1976, 546–547; Van Beek 1993; Ben-Shlomo and Van Beek 2014, 4, 15, n. 3.

(?) and a pair of golden earrings with granules along the edge.[93] Photos of a pair of the golden earrings with herringbone decoration, published by Sass, offer a better impression of these fine earrings from different angles.[94] The Eshtemoa hoard contained silver examples of this type, as well as of the earring with the granules along the edge,[95] and the Tawilan hoard also contained two earrings of the latter type.[96] The homogeneity of the Jemmeh hoard and the presence of several pairs of earrings is not suggestive of heirlooms or long usage before deposition. A date in the (late) Iron IIA, consistent with the revised date of level G–H, is therefore plausible.

Bibliography: Petrie 1928, 10, pl. 1, 7, 69; Sass 1997, 243.

17 TELL KEISAN

Excavations at Tell Keisan discovered a silver hoard of six or seven textile bundles in a bichrome flask in stratum 9a, dated to the end of the Iron I. The hoard was found in locus 635 in the rubble of a burnt wall (between silo 6115 and locus 610, a small storage room with jars), and Nodet infers that the hoard had been hidden in a niche in the wall.[97] Four of the bundles were sealed with bullae.[98] Two of these and additional material from another possible bundle were cleaned in recent years in the framework of the study by Eshel,[99] who provides a preliminary discussion of the archaeological context and contents of the hoard.

The total weight of the untreated hoard was 354 g, and Nodet also records the weight of the untreated four large bundles (24.5, 100, 32, and 25 g). Additionally, he notes that the remaining material had a weight of 172.5 g of which 27 g was silver, but it not clear what is meant here. It is possible that due to the effects of corrosion, some of the objects were identified as other metals (i.e., copper) rather than silver. Eshel had two of the four bundles (those of 32 and 25 g), as well as additional material cleaned. The cleaned objects add up to a weight of 36.67, 16.43 and 8.49 g for the different bundles/groups, which could suggest that the objects might have got mixed up in the process of conservation or study.

93 Petrie 1928, 10, pl. 1.
94 Sass 1997, 243, fig. 4.
95 Yeivin 1990, 54, fig. 16.11–13, 20.
96 Ogden 1995, 72–73, nos. 10–11.
97 Briend 1980, 198–201, pl. 62.4; Nodet 1980, 325.
98 Keel 1980, 282, nos. 28–31; pl. 90.
99 Eshel 2014; Eshel et al. 2018, 204.

The material recorded by Eshel consists of 120 objects with a total weight of 62.13 g.[100] These are mostly small cut or broken ingots and ornamental objects, such as jewellery and sheet silver, and a single large bent rod of 20.89 g. Eshel carried out XRF analyses and noted a high ratio of copper in part of the objects,[101] comparable to the high presence of copper recorded in the contemporary Beth Shean C hoard.[102] Thompson took eight samples for LIA, with preliminary results pointing to southeast Anatolia (3), the northern Aegean (1), and Sardinia (4) as the sources of the silver, although Eshel et al. have countered that their isotopic fingerprint is distorted by the addition of lead-containing copper.[103]

Bibliography: Briend 1980, 198–201, fig. 51–52; Keel 1980, 282, pl. 90, 136; Nodet 1980, 325–326, pl. 132; Kletter 2003, 145; Thompson 2003, 82, 100; 2007, 44; Thompson and Skaggs 2013; Eshel 2014; Eshel et al. 2018; 2019; Wood, Montero-Ruiz and Martinón-Torres 2019.

18 MEGIDDO A

During excavations by the Oriental Institute of the University of Chicago in November 1935, a hoard was discovered in locus 2012 on the edge of the tel, near the palace in area AA (square K8). Loud noted in his excavation diary that the hoard was found under the stratum VI floor level, regarding it as 'the means whereby some VI woman concealed her jewelry by burying it under the floor of the house'.[104] Being part of the destruction of Chicago stratum VI A, the hoard can be dated to the latter part of the Iron I (early tenth century). A detailed investigation of the hoard was undertaken in the framework of this study, and a discussion of its context and contents was presented elsewhere as part of a preliminary report of the hoard.[105]

The hoard consisted of three corroded lumps with remains of textile (Figure A.9). The contents of one of the bundles are currently kept at the Rockefeller Museum in Jerusalem (Figure A.9A and A.10A). The contents of the other two bundles are at the Oriental Institute Museum in Chicago

[100] Eshel 2014.
[101] Eshel 2014, chapter 4; Eshel et al. 2018, 214.
[102] See catalogue no. 7.
[103] Thompson 2007, 44; Thompson and Skaggs 2013; Eshel et al. 2018, 222; 2019. Cf. Wood, Montero-Ruiz and Martinón-Torres 2019.
[104] Loud 1935-1936 excavation diary, 19.
[105] Heymans 2018b, 289–294. I am grateful to Alegre Savariego of the IAA and Fawzi Ibrahim of the Rockefeller Museum for allowing me to study the material in Jerusalem and to Jack Green and Helen McDonald of the OIM for allowing me to study the material and archives in Chicago and for their support during my visit.

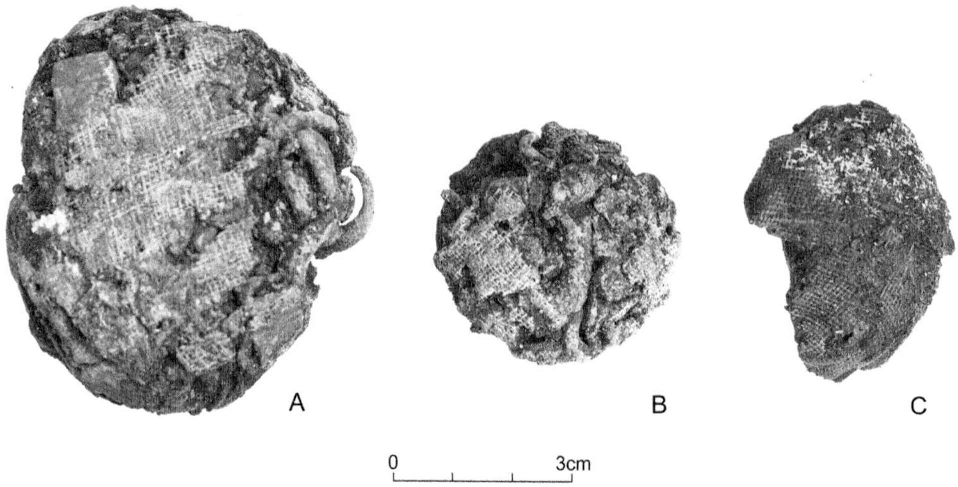

A.9 Megiddo A hoard bundles before treatment (Courtesy of the Oriental Institute of the University of Chicago)

(Figure A.9B–C and A.10B–C)[106] and were presumably already mixed together upon arrival to Chicago, making it currently impossible to reconstruct the weights of the individual bundles.

The hoard consists of 708 objects with a total weight of 425.15 g. The bundle in Jerusalem consists of 150 objects (87.99 g), from which a bronze arrowhead could not be traced, and also from the other two bundles in Chicago (558 objects; 337.16 g) a few objects appear to be missing.[107] As noted in Section 3.3.2, the weights indicate that the bundles were not of equal or standard weight. The contents of both parts of the hoard are very similar and contain mostly small cut or broken ingots and ornamental objects, among which are predominantly sheet fragments. Only twenty objects (17.76 g) of the total hoard were complete, among which are a single electrum lunate earring and a bracelet (both in Jerusalem).

The claim that the material circulated intensively is substantiated by the fragmented nature of the material, but moreover by the considerable traces of

[106] The field numbers assigned originally to the separate bundles and recorded in the original field negatives (as in Figures A.9 and A.10 here) were changed after the material was photographed. Presumably thinking that the largest bundle (A) must have contained the large group of silver (C), the letters identifying the silver groups on the field catalogue cards were amended: A–B, B–C and C–A. Consequently, bundles A and C were listed in the accession file for the transport of the objects to Chicago (dated 18 June 1936), where the objects still are recorded under field nos. a133 a & c. This identification of the bundle A (Figure A.9) with cleaned silver group C (Figure A.10) is as also reflected by Loud 1948, pl. 229, 7–9. This is likely incorrect. Both the bronze arrowhead and the large bracelet (Figure A.10A) are too large to have fit the smaller bundles B and C, and the earring sticking out on the right side of bundle A can be identified with the earing visible inside the bracelet.

[107] Heymans 2018b, 291.

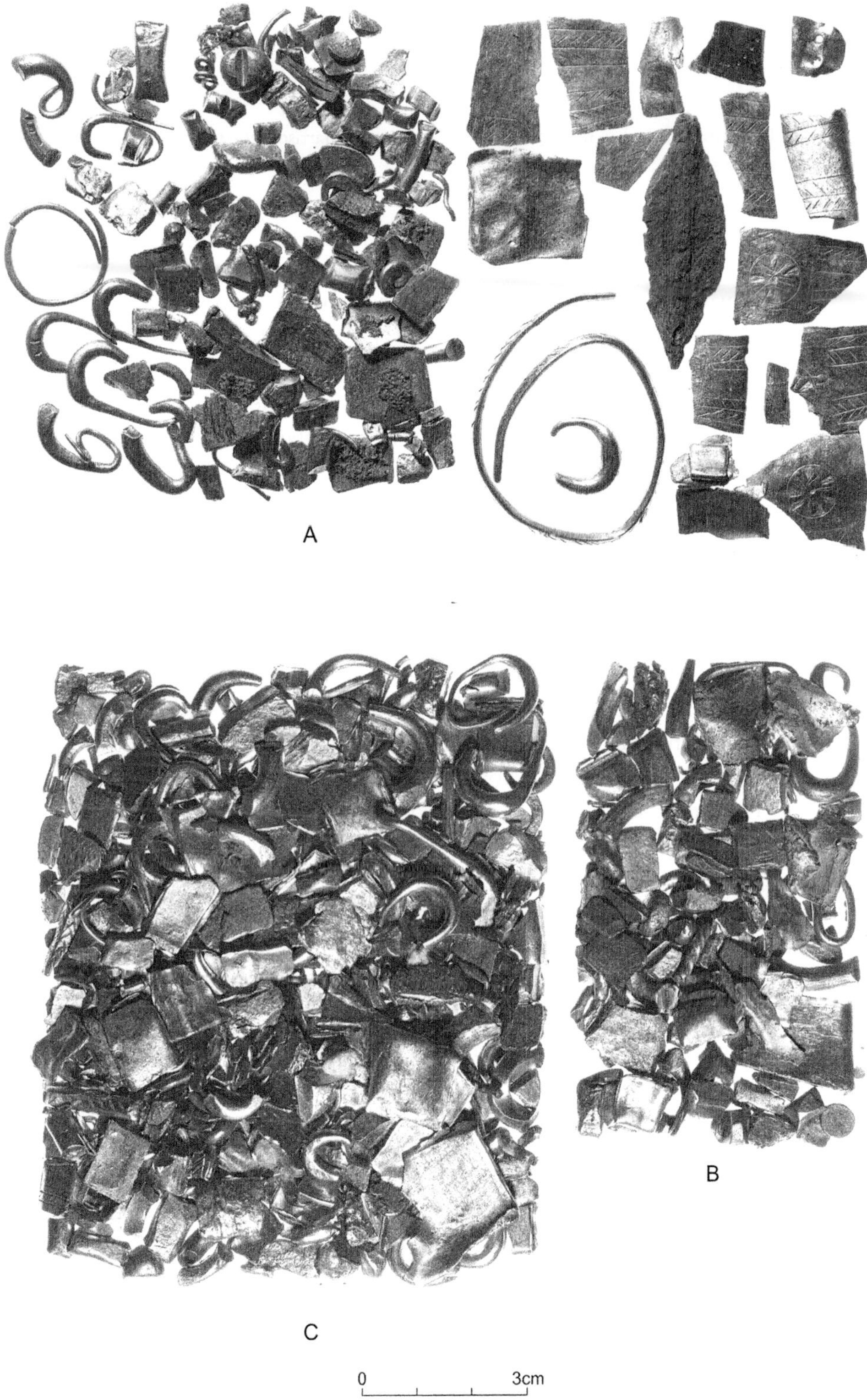

A.10 Megiddo A hoard bundles after treatment (Courtesy of the Oriental Institute of the University of Chicago)

wear and the fact that few objects were identified to have originally been part of the same object.[108] Only eighteen objects (15.69 g) had direct joins with other objects.

Bibliography: Loud 1948, 157, fig. 386, pl. 229.7–9; Harrison 2004, 17, 78, 181, pl. 29.9–11; Heymans 2018a, 89–96; 2018b, 289–294.

19 MEGIDDO B

In January 1939, a hoard, consisting of a corroded lump with textile remains and additional objects, was found near a stone wall in locus 5213 (area DD, square L11). It was attributed to stratum VI A and dates to the end of the Iron I. Presumably because the hoard was found near the end of the expedition's active work in the field, its discovery and details of its context were not recorded in the excavation diary. This might also explain why it did not receive the same conservation treatment as the Megiddo A hoard, and most of the hoard was shipped to Chicago uncleaned in the spring of 1939.[109] Although, following the division, a small part of the hoard is currently in the Rockefeller Museum in Jerusalem, the *hacksilber* objects are all in Chicago and are covered with heavy corrosion. Due to this, it was impossible to subject the hoard to a full investigation, but inspection of the material was nonetheless undertaken in conjunction with the study of the Megiddo A hoard. A discussion of its context and contents was presented elsewhere, alongside with and as comparison to hoard A.[110]

The hoard consists of a small corroded lump with textile remains and additional objects that also remain untreated, but have no traces of wrapping (Figure A.11).[111] A collection of beads (164 stone, mostly carnelian and one sard, 3 bronze spacer, and 4 gold) and a carnelian eye of horus amulet, found in the same locus (Figure A.12)[112] can be identified as belonging to the hoard itself. Wire fragments have been preserved in several of these beads, and similar bronze spacer beads (also with wire, so supposedly belonging to the same necklace) as well as golden beads are stuck onto some of the corroded silver pieces in the hoard. Part of this necklace is located in the Rockefeller Museum.

The metal objects in the hoard have a total weight of 92.57 g (total weight of the objects in Chicago is 119.14 g), with the single bundle weighing 38.05 g. The composition of the hoard, and specifically that of the bundle, appears to be comparable to that of the Megiddo A hoard, with fragmented ingots and

108 See Section 3.3.2.
109 Heymans 2018b, 290–291.
110 Heymans 2018b, 289–294. See n. 105.
111 Loud 1948, pl 228.4–6.
112 Loud 1948, 187, pl. 206.45, 216.122–123.

A.11 Untreated bundle and metal objects from the Megiddo B hoard (Courtesy of the Oriental Institute of the University of Chicago)

ornamental object of various types. Notable, however, is the presence (outside of the bundle) of several flat hammered ingots, of which one complete example (diam. 2.1–2.6 cm) has a golden lunate earring stuck onto its surface.

Bibliography: Loud 1948, 187, fig. 413, pl. 216.122–123, 228.4–6; Harrison 2004, 21, 70, 72–74, 184, pl. 26.21, 25–26, 27.5; Heymans 2018b, 289–294.

20 MEGIDDO C

A hoard wrapped in textile was found during excavations under Y. Yadin next to a doorstep in the north wing of palace 6000 (locus 6206, directly south of wall 155), in a pit under the floor, under an ash layer. The hoard was assigned to stratum VI A, like the Megiddo A and B hoards, and dates to the end of the Iron I. The context was published by Zarzecki-Peleg.[113]

The hoard consisted of nine ivory or ebony whorls, beads of different materials (bronze?), a scarab, several iron objects (*inter alia* rings) with cloth remains on them, weight stones, two bronze pomegranate pendants and two

[113] Zarzecki-Peleg 2005, 13–14, map 4.

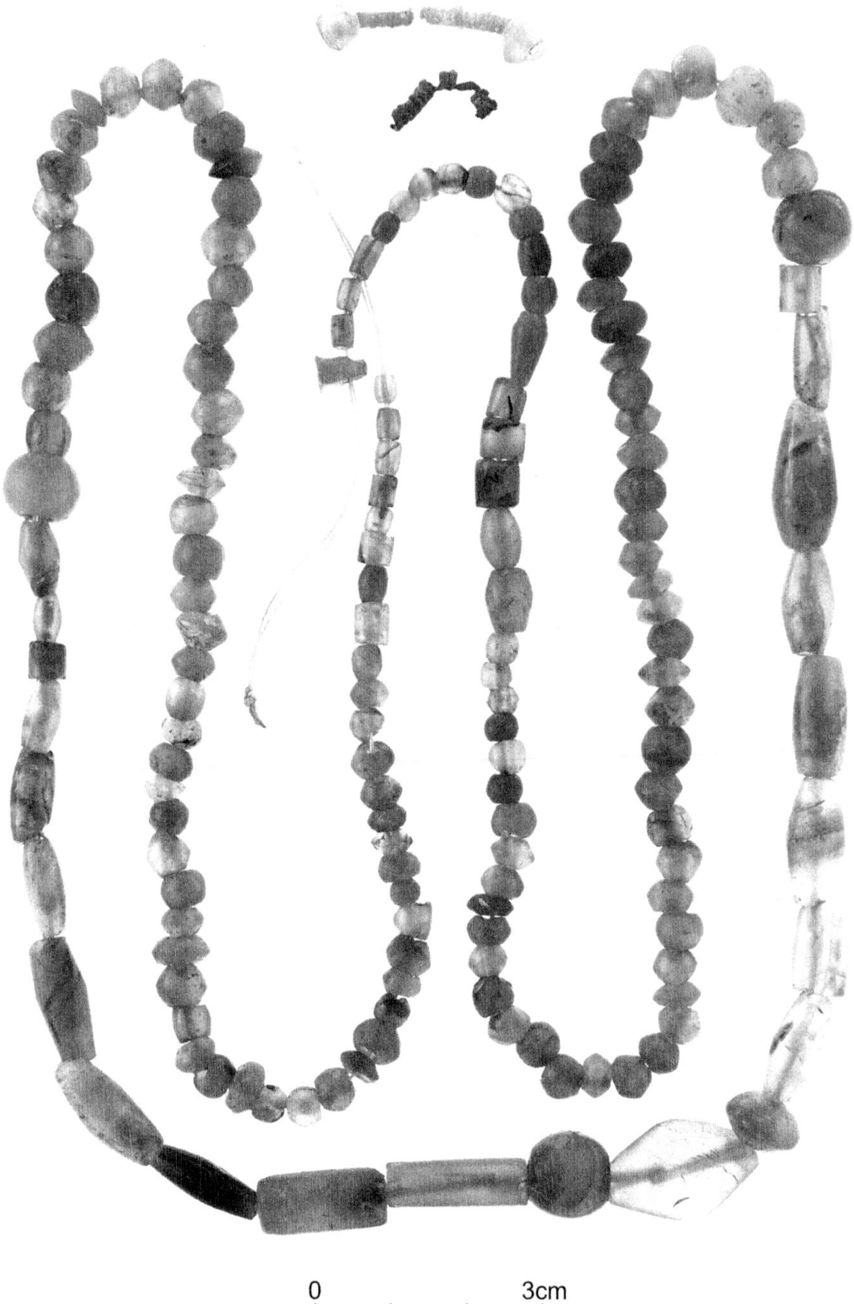

A.12 Necklace of stone and bronze beads from the Megiddo B hoard (Courtesy of the Oriental Institute of the University of Chicago)

zoomorphic weights – one in the form of a ram and one in the form of a squatting monkey.[114] There were no silver objects in the hoard and its weight is unknown.

Bibliography: Yadin 1970a, 77–79; 1970b, 47, pl.1–2; Harrison 2004, 78; Zarzecki-Peleg 2005, 13–14, map 4.

21 MEGIDDO D

In the corner of a paved courtyard of stratum H-11 (area H) of the Tel Aviv University excavations at Tel Megiddo a hoard was found in a beer jug, placed in a bowl and covered by another bowl. Although the find was made at the end of the 2010 season, its contents were only discovered the summer after, when the beer jug was emptied of its contents (Figure A.13). Area H is located adjacent to Chicago area AA, which was the palace area, and many storage vessels were found in the courtyard. The precise dating of stratum H-11 is still under study, but the stratum likely covers the period during and after the retreat of the Egyptians from Megiddo, dating into the early Iron I (Chicago

A.13 Megiddo D hoard (Courtesy of the Megiddo Expedition, Tel Aviv University)

[114] Yadin 1970a, 77–79; 1970b, 47, pl. 1–2.

stratum VII A); the hoard might be dated to ca. 1100 or the early eleventh century.[115] Reports of the hoard and its context were published by E. Arie.[116]

Part of the hoard was wrapped in textile, with two types of cloth preserved one on top of the other around a corroded mass of silver. Several other objects (electrum jewellery and electrum, silver and carnelian beads) were not stuck onto the corroded mass, and it is possible that a bag with jewellery contained a second bag of silver objects. Remains of the textile were radiocarbon dated, but turned out at least a century older than the rest of the stratum, indicating a possible 'old-textile' effect.[117]

With permission of I. Finkelstein and E. Arie, the material was investigated in the framework of the current study. The hoard contained 1,301 beads of electrum, silver and carnelian, some of which were corroded with remains of a necklace wire preserved inside. It also contained ten complete items of electrum jewellery: one worn signet ring with a depiction of a fish, eight lunate earrings and a unique and extraordinary leaf-shaped earring with miniature animals. On the outside of the leaf, there were eight appliques of reposing horned animals, while on the inside a standing bird was fastened to the leaf. The use of miniature animals on jewellery is notably rare and has been compared with four examples from New Kingdom Egypt, one of which is a silver ring from the tomb of Tutankhamun.[118] A large part of the corroded mass of silver was cleaned and consisted of ingots and ornamental objects, most of which were cut and broken. One of these concerns a cut and broken Late Bronze Age earring with a 'mulberry' pendant, known from Middle Assyrian graves at Mari.[119] It is clear that the jewellery in the hoard fits the environment of Late Bronze Age Megiddo under Egyptian rule, and the items were likely antiques at the time of deposition. There was also a complete silver globule, two cut but adjoining pieces of a hammered (hexagonal-sectioned) rod and five pieces that were cut off from a single rod. The total weight of the hoard is currently 236.60 g, of which 89.89 g is silver (including the untreated material but excluding the beads). Not counting the necklace (59.05 g) and the untreated material (25.86), the hoard counted thirty-two objects (gold and silver), with a total weight of 151.68 g.

Bibliography: Arie 2013; Hall 2016, 85–87, 106–107; Arie et al. 2019.

[115] Arie 2013; Toffolo et al. 2014; Arie et al. 2019; personal communication, I. Finkelstein.
[116] Arie 2013; Arie et al 2019.
[117] Toffolo et al. 2014, 228, 233.
[118] Arie 2013, 42; Arie et al. 2019, 93–95.
[119] Maxwell-Hyslop 1971, 178.

Tel Miqne/Ekron

Six hoards were excavated between 1985 and 1995 and reported in various publications.[120] Gitin and Golani provide the most complete overview and offer a breakdown of the hoards in object types and their weights, but, as noted in Chapter 3, they provide no clear description of the categories used.[121]

Samples for LIA have been taken by Stos-Gale and Thompson. Stos-Gale published seven samples, two of which from hoard B (Laurion; Siphnos), four from hoard C (Laurion (2); Chalkidike; Siphnos), and one from hoard D (Chalkidike).[122] Thompson and Skaggs published an additional fifty samples: four from hoard A, twenty-one from hoard B, ten from hoard C, four from hoard D, six from hoard E, and five from hoard F.[123] Their approach, however, has been criticised for failing to address the possibility that silver from different sources was mixed.[124] They claim that thirty-six of the samples are consistent with Laurion ores, but they plot no isotope ratios for the northern Aegean or Siphnos, while several of the values they give appear to fall within the ranges that are known for these sources.[125] No interpretation of the remaining fourteen samples is provided. It has now been argued that part of the Tel Miqne samples represents a mixture of Laurion silver and Iberian silver.[126] We should conclude for now that more work has to be done before the results of these fifty samples can reliably speak for themselves. Preliminary results (i.e., interpretations) are listed by Thompson together with the seven samples published by Stos-Gale: Laurion (42), Siphnos (3), N. Aegean (2), southeast Anatolia (1), Sardinia (8), Spain (1).[127]

22 TEL MIQNE/EKRON A

The first hoard was found in 1985 in a jug under the floor of a room of an auxiliary building south of the Temple Complex in Field IV, and associated with the destruction of stratum IB in 604 BCE.[128]

[120] Gitin 1995; 1997; Golani 1996; Golani and Sass 1998; Gitin and Golani 2001; Kletter 2003; Thompson 2003.
[121] Gitin and Golani 2001.
[122] Stos-Gale 2001, 61–62.
[123] Thompson and Skaggs 2013, fig. 4, tab. 1.
[124] Eshel et al. 2018, 222; 2019; Wood, Montero-Ruiz and Martinón-Torres 2019.
[125] Cf. Gale, Picard and Barrandon 1988; Stos-Gale 2001. N.B.: There is overlap between the isotope-ratio fields of Chalkidike, Thasos, and Laurion (cf. Gale, Picard, and Barrandon 1988; Pernicka 2014, 157–159), and it is possible that some of the values fall in this area of overlap.
[126] Wood, Montero-Ruiz and Martinón-Torres 2019.
[127] Thompson 2007, 44.
[128] Gitin 1995, 69; Golani 1996, 147–148, fig. 29; Golani and Sass 1998, 57, 59, fig. 3; Gitin and Golani 2001, 30–31.

The hoard consists of 330 objects, weighing a total of 33.5 g; 256 of the objects are small beads, and the remaining seventy-four are silver with a weight of 24.5 g. These silver objects consist of cut and/or broken jewellery as well as complete jewellery, and 'silver fragments', supposedly small scrap. The jewellery is described as being worn down, leading Gitin and Golani to infer that 'their value could only lie in their silver content'.[129]

Bibliography: Gitin 1995, 69–70; 1997, 92–93; Golani 1996, 147–148; Golani and Sass 1998, 57–81; Gitin and Golani 2001, 27–48; Kletter 2003, 142; Thompson 2003, 100.

23 TEL MIQNE/EKRON B

In 1988, a hoard was found under mudbrick debris near the wall of a room in an auxiliary building south of the Temple Complex in Field IV (locus 8005, IV NE.8.64), associated with the destruction of stratum IB in 604 BCE. Cloth impressions were preserved on some of the pieces, indicating that the hoard had been kept in a textile bundle.[130]

The hoard consists of sixty-four objects (263.4 g), of which fifty-nine are silver (259.4 g). These are mostly cut or broken ingots and jewellery. Of the jewellery, part is cut or broken, while the rest is complete but worn. There is a single complete rolled-tongue ingot (50.4 g), and at least one of the ingot fragments appears to have a surface comparable to the Ein Gedi ingots, discussed in Section 3.2.4.[131]

Bibliography: Gitin 1995, 69–70; 1997, 92–93; Golani 1996, 148; Golani and Sass 1998, 57–81; Gitin and Golani 2001, 31–33, 37; Kletter 2003, 142; Thompson 2003, 101.

24 TEL MIQNE/EKRON C

This large hoard was found in 1992 in a jug that was placed in a larger jug and buried under a floor of a room in an auxiliary building south of the Temple Complex in Field IV (locus 8035, IV NW.8.167). It is associated with the destruction of stratum IB in 604 BCE.[132]

This hoard consists of eighty-eight objects with a total weight of 956 g. There is one small golden globule, while the remaining objects are all silver ingots, many of which are cut and/or broken. There are several rolled-tongue ingots and several large fragments of rough ingots with a wrinkled surface, similar to the Ein Gedi ingots discussed in Section 3.2.4.

[129] Gitin and Golani 2001, 31.
[130] Golani 1996, 148; Golani and Sass 1998, 57–60; Gitin and Golani 2001, 31.
[131] Cf. Gitin and Golani 2001, 31, pl. 2.4: 3rd column, 3rd row.
[132] Gitin 1995, 69–70; 1997, 92; Gitin and Golani 2001, 32–33.

Bibliography: Gitin 1995, 69–70; 1997, 92; Golani and Sass 1998, n. 3; Gitin and Golani 2001, 32–33, 37; Kletter 2003, 143; Thompson 2003, 101.

25 TEL MIQNE/EKRON D

A second hoard was found in 1992, apparently hidden in a reused perforated weight stone of an oil press (locus 28011; I SW.28.54) in the destruction of stratum IB, in Field I at the upper city.[133]

Of the hoard's thirty objects (102.2 g), twenty-one objects are silver (89.7 g), mostly complete but variously worn pieces of jewellery, such as earrings with basket pendants, Egyptian or Egyptianising rings and an oval medallion pendant with a crude version of a Neo-Assyrian cultic scene.[134] There are also two pieces of *hacksilber* (i.e., cut ingots).

Bibliography: Gitin 1995, 69–70; 1997, 92–93; Golani 1996, 149–150, 152; Golani and Sass 1998, 57–81; Gitin and Golani 2001, 33–34, 37; Kletter 2003, 142–143; Thompson 2003, 101.

26 TEL MIQNE/EKRON E

A fifth hoard was found in 1993 in a small jug beneath a wall of strata IC–IB in Field III (III NE.9.187; object no. 5172), and interpreted as a foundation deposit.[135] Except for its missing neck, the jug was virtually unbroken, and, as we have seen, silver hoards were often placed under the floor, against, in or under a wall as a common place of storage.[136] The interpretation of the excavators need not therefore be correct. Only a full publication of the contents of the hoard can potentially indicate whether the assemblage chronologically fits the construction of stratum IC, or the destruction of IB.

The hoard consists of fifty-three silver and composite silver objects (mounted scarabs or scaraboids), with a weight of 73 g, and 209 non-silver jewellery items, mostly simple beads. The hoard has a total weight of 101.5 g. The silver in the hoard consists of jewellery items, about half of which are cut or broken, and several 'silver fragments'.[137]

Bibliography: Golani 1996, 181, n. 1; Golani and Sass 1998, 76–77, n. 3; Gitin and Golani 2001, 33, 35, 37; Kletter 2003, 143; Thompson 2003, 10; Gitin and Brandl 2018.

[133] Gitin 1995, 69–70; 1997, 92–93; Golani 1996, 149–150, 152; Golani and Sass 1998, 57–81; Gitin and Golani 2001, 33.
[134] Golani and Sass 1998, 62–75; Gitin and Golani 2001, 33–34.
[135] Gitin and Golani 2001, 33, 35; Kletter 2003, 143; Thompson 2003, 101; Gitin and Brandl 2018, 294–295.
[136] Cf. Section 3.3.1.
[137] Gitin and Golani 2001, 33, 37.

27 TEL MIQNE/EKRON F

Found in 1995 on the threshold of a side room of the Temple Complex in Field IV (IV NW.61.131), it was covered by an overturned bowl, suggesting that it fell down from a shelf during the destruction of stratum IB in 604 BCE.[138]

This small hoard consists of twelve objects (20 g), eleven of which were silver (19 g). These are all pieces of jewellery (ten lunate earrings), and seven of these are cut or broken.

Bibliography: Golani and Sass 1998, 76–77, n. 3; Gitin and Golani 2001, 35–37; Kletter 2003, 143; Thompson 2003, 101–102.

28 SHECHEM A

From the first season of excavations at Tell Balata in the summer of 1913, E. Sellin reported the find of 'ein kleiner [Krug], mit einem silbernen Hackfunde (zirka 200 Stückchen und zirka 10 kleine Ringe)'. It was discovered in what he identified as a domestic context in the 'Hellenistic layer' in a long north-south trench on the northern part of the tel.[139] This hoard has been conflated in recent literature with the Shechem B hoard.[140]

Horn attempted to trace the Sellin hoard and other finds from his early excavations and suggested that it would have been sent to Vienna since Sellin worked under Austrian sponsorship.[141] Evidence for these objects and their presence in Vienna prior to the Second World War, Horn noted, is preserved in the form of a series of lantern slides in the collection of F.M.Th. de Liagre Böhl, who excavated with Sellin at Tell Balata after the First World War in the 1920s. These slides, kept today at the Netherlands Institute for the Near East in Leiden, are labelled to have come from Vienna and concern objects from 'Sichem'. One of the slides shows fifteen silver jewellery pieces or fragments thereof, mostly rings (Figure A.14),[142] which Horn assumed were the rings from the hoard, referred to by Sellin. The Kunsthistorisches Museum in Vienna had however been hit during the bombing of the city in the Second World War, and the acute salvage of the objects had understandably left the collection in disorder. Horn reports that in the 1960s, the director of the museum, Dr Komorzynski, had been able to locate most of the objects from

[138] Gitin and Golani 2001, 36.

[139] Sellin 1914, 38, pl. 1; Wright 2002, 24–25, ill. 1.

[140] Golani and Sass 1998, 77; Gitin and Golani 2001, 39–40, 44; Kletter 2003, 145; Thompson 2003, 100. Cf. Balmuth and Thompson 2000, 161.

[141] Horn 1968.

[142] I consulted the slide collection at the NINO in December 2014 and thank D. Gianessi and J. Eidem for their help. The digital scan was kindly provided by W. Waal and C. van Zoest.

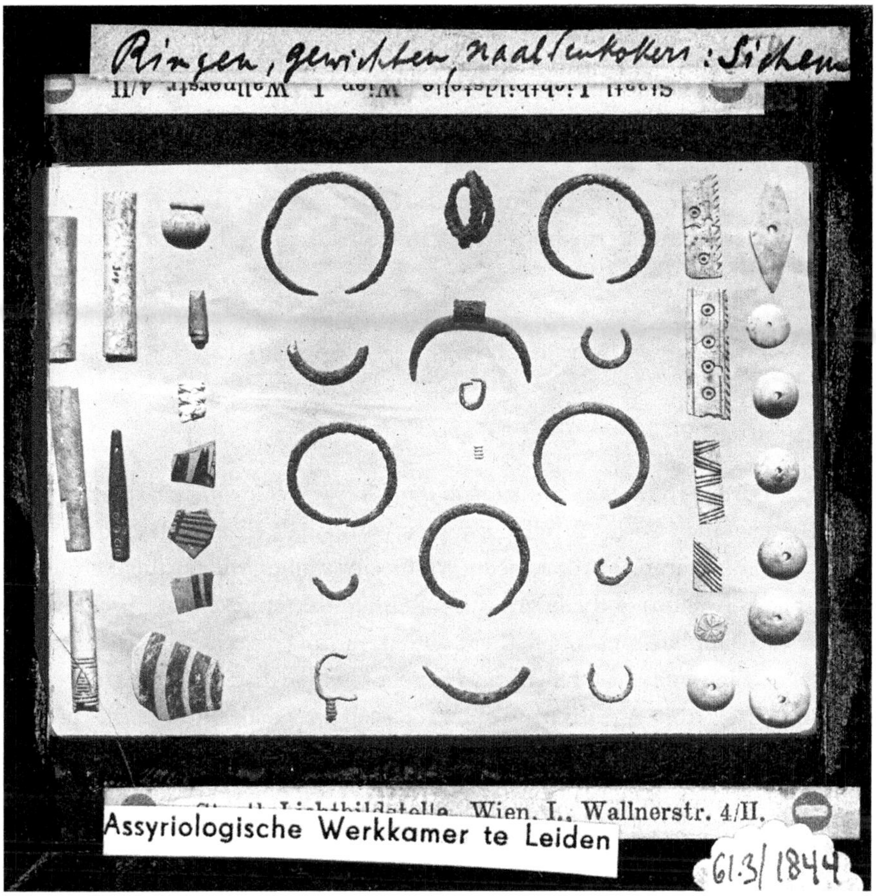

A.14 Silver jewellery items from Tell Balata/Shechem (in the Kunsthistorisches Museum Vienna, now presumed to be lost. From the slide collection of F.M.Th. de Liagre Böhl. Inv. no. NINO 1065-047 [formerly no. 61.3/1844]. Courtesy of the Netherlands Institute for the Near East)

Shechem, recorded on the slides from the collection of de Liagre Böhl. The silver jewellery was however declared lost.[143] In 2015, Dr Regina Hölzl, curator of the museum, was kind enough to check the collection from Shechem at my request, but reported that there were no silver objects among them. She did however confirm that other (bone) objects on the same lantern slide are in Vienna.

The ca. 200 silver objects mentioned by Sellin could have been sent to Istanbul or Vienna, and it is conceivable that they were not recorded on photo, as silver scrap was possibly deemed uninteresting. It is also possible that part of the hoard was on loan from the department of antiquities to Sellin in Berlin, who was studying material from the excavation in preparation of its final

[143] Horn 1968, 71–74.

publication. Objects and excavation notes were all lost when Sellin's house was destroyed during a bombing of Berlin in the fall of 1943.[144]

The lantern slide is thus the only available potential record of the hoard, in addition to Sellin's succinct mention of its discovery. The objects mostly concern penannular rings, a broken earring with what appears like a pendant of globules and an open crescent pendant. If these objects were indeed the rings that were found in the hoard, they suggest a date for the hoard in the MB or LB I at the latest.[145]

Bibliography: Sellin 1914, 38; Wright 1965, 8; Horn 1968, 71–74.

29 SHECHEM B

In 1957, during the second season of the Drew-McCormick Expedition to Tell Balata under G. E. Wright, a juglet with silver objects (B57 Obj. reg. #178) was found in Field III, adjacent to the city wall on the northeastern edge of the tel.[146] A photo of the hoard was published the same year in a preliminary report.[147] Campbell published the context, noting that it was found in a disturbed layer under a Hellenistic house of which the floor was not preserved.[148] No Iron Age strata were preserved in Field III, and the profile drawing shows that the disturbed layer was located directly on top of the LB and MB architectural remains. The jug remains unpublished.

The hoard is currently located in the Museum of the Ancient Near East (formerly Semitic Museum) at Harvard University (Figure A.15), and its curator, Dr Joseph Greene, inspected the material from the hoard at my request, ahead of the publication of this book.[149] In addition to the 102 objects originally assigned a number in the museum, he identified seven additional small objects (displayed in Figure A.15 at the bottom row to the right), which could have broken off other objects or could be remains of sampled fragments. Moreover, one of the original 102 objects is recorded as missing (no. 74). This could concern a large lunate earring: the photo of a selection of the hoard originally published by Kee and Tombs shows three such earrings, while only two of these can be identified on the photo published by Balmuth ten years later.[150]

144 Wright 1965, 30.
145 Cf. Maxwell-Hyslop 1971, 112–116, 149–151; Sass 1997, 241.
146 Wright 2002, 24–26, ill. 1–2.
147 Kee and Tombs 1957, 105, fig. 13.
148 Campbell 2002, 335; Wright 2002, 69–73, ill. 40–42.
149 Inv. no. SM 1976.3.5. I wish to thank Joe Greene for providing the detailed information and various photographs that enabled me to enhance my assessment of the hoard.
150 Balmuth 1967, pl. 1; Balmuth and Thompson 2000, 162, pl. 1, fig. 1. Note that one of the earrings was apparently damaged between 1957 and 1967.

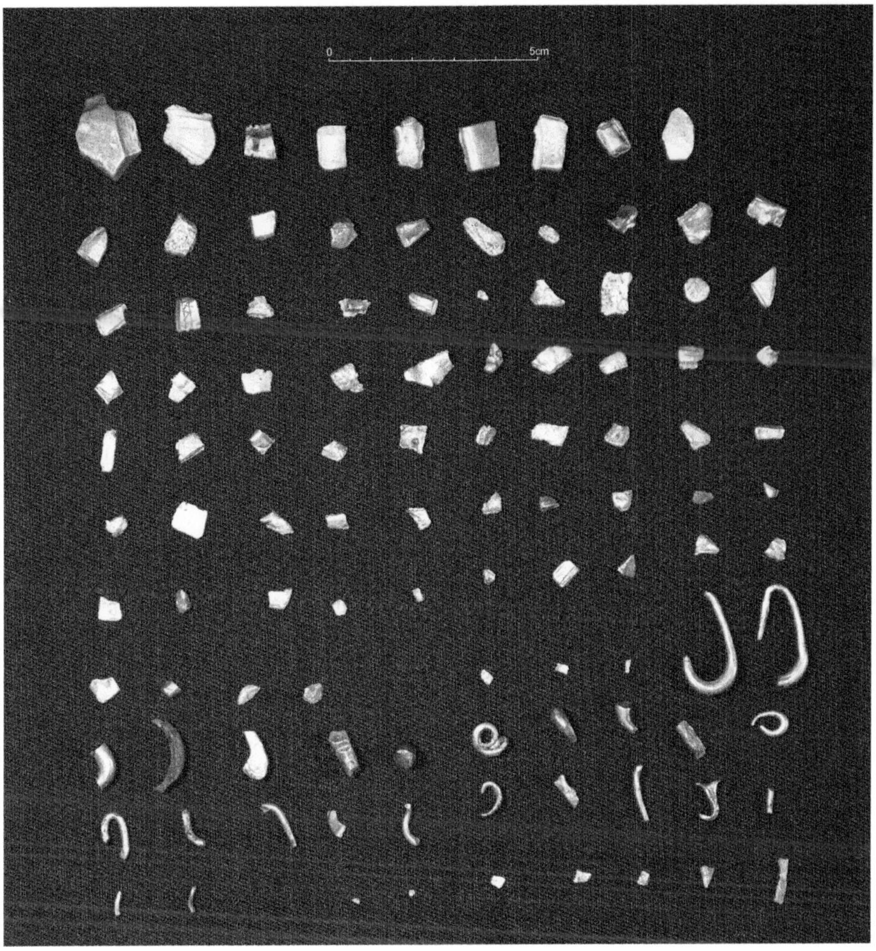

A.15 Shechem Bhoard (Courtesy of the Museum of the Ancient Near East, Harvard University)

In their publication of the hoard, Balmuth and Thompson mention that there had originally been at least 200 pieces[151] but fail to offer any reference for this assertion or information concerning the remaining objects. In the absence of such information, it appears more likely that the supposed original number of at least 200 pieces was perhaps taken from Wright's mention of Sellin's hoard (Shechem A) in the introduction of his 1965 book on Shechem,[152] subsequently conflated by others with the hoard found in his own excavations.[153]

151 Balmuth and Thompson 2000, 163–164; Gitin and Golani 2001, 39.
152 Wright 1965, 8.
153 Golani and Sass 1998, 77; Gitin and Golani 2001, 39; Kletter 2003, 145; Thompson 2003, 100.

The hoard has a total weight of 44.90 g[154] and consists of small cut and broken ingots and ornamental objects, including a large number of sheet fragments. One object is bronze; the remaining 101 objects are silver. Lacking a securely datable archaeological context, the presence of lunate earrings in the hoard could fit any date from the Late Bronze and Iron Age; however, the most likely historical context for the presence of such a hoard in Shechem would be the Iron I to IIB. This is also suggested by the fact that the composition of the hoard is consistent with other hoards from this time frame, most specifically from the Iron I.[155] Stos-Gale published the results of ten LIA samples, pointing to Spain (3) and Iran (7) as the sources of the silver,[156] but additional analyses suggest a mixture of Taurus and Iberian silver.[157]

Bibliography: Kee and Toombs 1957, fig. 13; Balmuth 1967, 28, fig. 1; Balmuth and Thompson 2000; Stos-Gale 2001, 62–66, 71; Campbell 2002, 335; Wright 2002, 69–73, ill. 40–42; Wood, Montero-Ruiz and Martinón-Torres 2019.

30 TAWILAN

A jewellery hoard was found in 1982 outside burial XXV in area II of Tawilan, east of the Arabah valley in Transjordan. The jewellery was located in a corroded copper alloy bowl that was placed on a course sherd and associated with phase V (Persian Period).[158] It consisted of twenty pieces of jewellery, of which twelve were earrings and thirty-four carnelian beads. Ogden, who published the jewellery in great detail (lacking however the object weights), notes that although globules of several earrings were broken off, the jewellery, in particular the tassel earrings, generally had few traces of wear. The four tassel earrings have close parallels from Tell el-Farah (south) and Ogden even suggests that they could have come from the same workshop.[159] He concludes that the hoard must have been significantly older than the associated remains. Following Sass, we can associate the type of jewellery with the end of the Iron I and the early Iron IIA (tenth–ninth century).[160] Kletter suggests a possible lower (i.e., eighth-century) date for the hoard, noting Ogden's comparison with the Eshtemoa hoard,[161] but caution is required here: although long-lived

[154] This was calculated by adding all weights given by Balmuth and Thompson (2000, 169); they list a total weight of 45.163 g. Note that no. 34 is omitted from their list, and no. 74 is listed as missing.

[155] See Section 3.3.

[156] Balmuth and Thompson 2000, 165–168; Stos-Gale 2001, 62–66, 71.

[157] Wood, Montero-Ruiz and Martinón-Torres 2019.

[158] Petocz 1995, 34–35.

[159] Ogden 1995, 75.

[160] Sass 2002a, 23–24, 32.

[161] Kletter 2003, 145.

elements in the Tawilan hoard can be identified also in the Eshtemoa hoard, such as a lunate earring with a knob ('large grain') on the underside,[162] this is no basis to down-date the hoard as such, and several of the objects, such as the tassel earrings, likely represent a distinctly earlier phenomenon.

The hoard contained no ingots or *hacksilber/gold* and is thus a jewellery hoard. Two lunate earrings with a copper-alloy core are furthermore notable.[163]

Bibliography: Maxwell-Hyslop 1984, 22–23; Ogden 1995; Petocz 1995, 34–35; Sass 2002a, 23–24, 32; Kletter 2003, 145.

31 TIMNA

A metal hoard from Timna in the southern Arabah valley was listed by Kletter and is therefore included here for consideration.[164] It was found in locus 101 against wall 1 on the outside (northeast) of the so-called Egyptian Mining Temple at site 200 (box 51 in squares E15–16). The hoard is dated to the end of the Late Bronze Age.[165]

The hoard contained no precious metal, and consisted mainly of copper and bronze objects, mostly jewellery and copper ore nodules, as well as iron bracelets and a large number of faience and shell beads. The hoard has been interpreted as a collection of votive offerings for the temple or a favissa or foundation deposit.[166] As Kletter concludes himself, the hoard does not fit the characteristics of the other precious metal hoards presented.

Bibliography: Rothenberg 1988, 29–32, 147–169, 273; Kletter 2003, 145–146; Avner 2014, 110.

32 WADI EL-MAKKUK

During the exploration of caves in the northern Judean desert in 1993 under Y. Hirschfeld, a hoard was discovered in a cave on the southern side of the upper Wadi el-Makkuk, 2 km northeast of Ma'ale Michmash, directly east of the 458 road and some 15 km northeast of Jerusalem. The hoard was found in an inner chamber or niche in the bedrock (L2) of cave II/3, ca. 0.4 m under

[162] Ogden 1995, no. 13. Cf. Maxwell-Hyslop 1971, 226, pl. 201.
[163] Ogden 1995, 73, nos. 14–15.
[164] Kletter 2003, 145–146.
[165] Rothenberg 1988, 29–32, 273; Avner 2014, 110.
[166] Rothenberg 1988, 273; Kletter 2003, 145–146; Avner 2014, 110.

the surface, using a metal detector.[167] The excavators note the difficulties of excavating in a narrow niche at the end of a cave,[168] and accordingly, it cannot be ruled out that the context is contaminated. In his exemplary publication of the hoard, Sass notes that although some objects could be intrusive (i.e., a bronze buckle, no. 57), the bulk of the finds is chronologically homogenous, and can be dated to the Iron I.[169]

The hoard consists of sixty-nine objects, including four complete gold or electrum earrings, forty-seven silver objects, six bronze implements and one fragment of a bronze earring and eleven non-metal objects (beads and a spindle whorl). The silver objects consist of (cut and/or broken) earrings and pieces of folded sheet, as well as several cut ingots. Excluding the non-metal objects and the six bronze implements, the weight of the metal is 147.92 g (object nos.1–52), of which 3.98 g is gold/electrum and 140.18 g silver.[170]

The close dating of the hoard to the Iron I is based on the Late Bronze to Iron I toggle pins (nos. 53–54) and the dating of the exquisite electrum tassel earring to the Iron I–IIA, following a detailed discussion with reference to the parallels from Tawilan, Timna, Tell el-Farah (south) and Madaba.[171] Although, at our current state of knowledge, this dating remains in place, it is worth pointing out that the Wadi el-Makkuk tassel earring is quite different from the other examples from the southern Levant. While the latter earrings have a tubular tassel,[172] the Wadi el-Makkuk tassel is composed of five cords in a closed formation, with the fifth cord in the centre. Each cord is made up of three strands of four or five globules, suspending from four square platelets that join the stem.[173] Very similar in construction are three earrings from Lori Berd and Horom in Armenia, dated to the ninth–eighth century.[174] They also bring to mind the Middle Assyrian 'mulberry' earrings from Mari[175] and the Late Bronze specimen from the Megiddo D hoard, which were made up of inverted pyramids, or little tetrahedral bunches ('Trauben') of four globules, hanging from larger flattened globules that join the stem. In addition to the potentially exotic tassel earring, the hoard's remote location and deviant

[167] Hirschfeld and Riklin 2002, 6–7. A map of the canyon and drawings of the cave and the pottery can be found in the Hebrew section of 'Atiqot, vol. 41, part 1, p. 7, 12–13; map 2, plan 2, fig. 4.

[168] Hirschfeld and Riklin 2002, 7.

[169] Sass 2002a, 21, 29, 32.

[170] Sass 2002a.

[171] Sass 2002a, 22–24, 26–29.

[172] Cf. Ogden 1995, 70–72, 279–282.

[173] Sass 2002a, 22–23.

[174] Kalantaryan 2007, 402, pl. 56.1–3. I am very grateful to prof. Sass for providing me with these parallels and for his help on the topic. Note that at least grave 29 at Lori Berd contained older finds as well (Kalantaryan 2007, 402, pl. 57). Regretfully, the publication of the earrings is in Armenian, and consequently, I have not been able to review these contexts.

[175] Maxwell-Hyslop 1971, 178.

composition (discussed in Section 3.3) reflect the exceptional nature of this hoard.

Bibliography: Hirschfeld and Riklin 2002, 6–7; Sass 2002a.

33 ERETRIA, GREECE

In 1980, during excavations by the Archaeological Society under P. Themelis in building plot 740, in the northern part of the city, north of the temple of Apollo Daphnephoros, a gold/electrum hoard was found. On the western edge of the building plot two Late Geometric phases were identified, with a curved wall (δ) of an apsidal house belonging to the latest Geometric phase. The hoard was found on the inside of the apse, against or under the foundation wall, in a complete LG II skyphos, covered by a lid from a different vase.[176] The dating of the hoard at the end of the Late Geometric period (late eighth century) is thus secure. Preliminary reports of the archaeological context and the contents of the hoard were published by Themelis.[177]

With the permission of P. Themelis, and with the support of the Swiss School of Archaeology in Greece, the material was reinvestigated in the framework of the current study.[178] The hoard consists of 398 objects[179] and has a total weight of 512.65 g. One large cut tongue-shaped ingot has a weight of 112.41 g; the other objects were generally small. The majority of the objects were cut and/or broken ingots, and a relatively small part of the hoard concerned cut/broken ornamental objects. Notable also was the substantial presence of nuggets (44), testifying to the placer source of the gold. A substantial part of the objects (58; 15 per cent of the total number) was complete. Compositional analyses have yet to be undertaken, but the varying colour of the metal reflects a variation of the gold/silver ratio between objects in the hoard.

Bibliography: Themelis 1981; 1983; Furtwängler 1986, 156; Kopcke 1992, 112; Kroll 2001a, 77–78; 2003, 317; 2008a, 34; 2012, 38; Le Rider and Verdan 2002; Thompson 2003, 91–92; Verdan 2010, 64–71, cat. nos. 47, 59–62; forthcoming; Verdan and Heymans 2021.

176 Themelis 1981, 186–191; 1983, 187–160.
177 Themelis 1981; 1983.
178 The investigation of the material was undertaken in cooperation with S. Verdan and with the help of P. Simon, both of the Swiss School of Archaeology in Greece.
179 In a single instance, ten tiny scraps were inventoried together under one object number.

BIBLIOGRAPHY

Aharoni, M. 1980. 'A Silver Hoard from Arad', *Qadmoniot* 13 (49–50), 39–40 (Hebrew).

Aharoni, Y. 1966. 'The Use of Hieratic Numerals in Hebrew Ostraca and the Shekel Weights', *Bulletin of the American Schools of Oriental Research* 184, 13–19.

1968. 'Tel Arad', *Revue Biblique* 75, 389–392.

Aja, A. J. 2009. 'Philistine Domestic Architecture in the Iron Age I', PhD dissertation, Harvard University, Cambridge, MA.

Akiga Sai, B. [1939] 1965. *Akiga's Story: The Tiv Tribe As Seen by One of Its Members.* Translated and annotated by Rubert East. London.

Akin, D., and Robbins, J. 1999. *Money and Modernity: State and Local Currencies in Melanesia.* ASAO monograph series. Pittsburgh.

Alberti, M. E., Ascalone, E., and Peyronel, L. eds. 2006. *Weights in Context: Bronze Age Weighing Systems of Eastern Mediterranean: Chronology, Typology, Material and Archaeological Contexts. Proceedings of the International colloquium, Roma 22–24 November 2004.* Studi e materiali. Rome.

Alberti, M. E., and Parise, N. 2005. 'Towards an Unification of Mass-Units between the Aegean and the Levant', in Laffineur, R., and Greco, E. eds., *Emporia: Aegeans in the Central and Eastern Mediterranean.* Aegaeum. Liège, 381–391.

Alexandre, Y. 1997. ''En Hofez', *Excavations and Surveys in Israel* 16, 53–54.

2008. ''En Hofez', in Stern, E. ed., *The New Encyclopedia of Archaeological Excavations in the Holy Land.* Vol. 5. Supplementary Volume. Jerusalem, 1728–1730.

2013. 'An Iron II Silver Hoard from 'En Hofez, near Tel Joqne'am', in Guri-Rimon, O. ed., *Hoards and Genizot As Chapters in History.* Haifa, 18–21.

Alroth, B., and Linders, T. eds. 1992. *Economics of Cult in the Ancient Greek World: Proceedings of the Uppsala Symposium 1990.* Acta Universitatis Upsaliensis. Boreas. Uppsala; Stockholm.

Amiran, R., and Van Beek, G. W. 1976. 'Jemmeh, Tell', in Avi-Yonah, M. ed., *Encyclopedia of Archaeological Excavations in the Holy Land.* London, 545–549.

Anderson, G. 2009. 'The Personality of the Greek State', *The Journal of Hellenic Studies* 129, 1–22.

Andreou, S., and Vavelidis, M. 2014. 'So Rich and Yet So Poor: Investigating the Scarcity of Gold Artefacts in Bronze Age Northern Greece', in Meller, H., Risch, R., and Pernicka, E. eds., *Metalle der Macht – Frühes Gold und Silber: 6. Mitteldeutscher Archäologentag vom 17. bis 19. Oktober 2013 in Halle (Saale) [Metals of Power – Early Gold and Silver: 6th Archaeological Conference of Central Germany, October 17–19, 2013 in Halle (Saale)].* Tagungen des Landesmuseums für Vorgeschichte Halle. Halle Saale, 451–465.

Andronikos, M. 1969. *Vergina.* Athens.

Antonova, I., Tolstikow, W., and Treister, M. Y. 1996. *The Gold of Troy: Searching for Homer's Fabled City.* London; New York.

Appadurai, A. 1986a. 'Introduction: Commodities and the Politics of Value', in Appadurai, A. ed., *The Social Life of Things: Commodities in Cultural Perspective.* Cambridge, 3–63.

ed. 1986b. *The Social Life of Things: Commodities in Cultural Perspective.* Cambridge.

Arie, E. 2013. 'A Jewellery Hoard from the Early Iron Age at Megiddo', in Guri-Rimon, O. ed., *Hoards and Genizot As Chapters in History*. Haifa, 38–43 (Hebrew).

Armayor, O. K. 1978. 'Herodotus' Catalogues of the Persian Empire in the Light of the Monuments and the Greek Literary Tradition', *Transactions of the American Philological Association (1974–)* 108, 1–9.

Armstrong, W. E. 1928. *Rossel Island: An Ethnological Study*. Cambridge.

Arnaud, D. 1992. 'Les ports de la 'Phénicie' à la fin de l'âge du Bronze Récent (XIV–XIII siècles) d'après les textes cunéiformes de Syrie', *Studi Micenei ed Egeo-Anatolici* 30, 181–194.

Artzy, M. 1997. 'Nomads of the Sea', in Swiny, S., Hohlfelder, R. L., and Swiny, H. W. eds., *Res maritimae: Cyprus and the Eastern Mediterranean from Prehistory to Late Antiquity: Proceedings of the Second International Symposium 'Cities on the Sea', Nicosia, Cyprus, October 18–22, 1994.* American Schools of Oriental Research Archaeological Reports. Atlanta, 1–16.

1998. 'Routes, Trade, Boats and "Nomads of the Sea"', in Gitin, S., Mazar, A., and Stern, E. eds., *Mediterranean Peoples in Transition: Thirteenth to Early Tenth Centuries BCE.* Jerusalem, 439–448.

Asderaki-Tzoumerkioti, E., Rehren, T., Malakasioti, Z., and Tsiouka, F. In preparation. 'Iron and Steel for Jewellery and Weapons in Early Iron Age Halos'.

Asheri, D. 2007. 'Book III', in Murray, O., and Moreno, A. eds., *A Commentary on Herodotus Books I–IV.* Oxford, 379–542.

Aubet, M. E. 2006. 'On the Organization of the Phoenician Colonial System in Iberia', in Riva, C., and Vella, N. C. eds., *Debating Orientalization: Multidisciplinary Approaches to Change in the Ancient Mediterranean.* Monographs in Mediterranean Archaeology. London, 94–109.

2013. *Commerce and Colonization in the Ancient Near East.* Cambridge.

Austin, M. M., and Vidal-Naquet, P. [1972] 1977. *Economic and Social History of Ancient Greece: An Introduction.* London.

Avner, U. 2014. 'Egyptian Timna – Reconsidered', in Tebes, J. M. ed., *Unearthing the Wilderness: Studies on the History and Archaeology of the Negev and Edom in the Iron Age.* Ancient Near Eastern Studies. Supplement. Leuven, 103–162.

Bachhuber, C. 2011. 'Negotiating Metal and the Metal Form in the Royal Tombs of Alacahöyük in North-Central Anatolia', in Wilkinson, T. C., Sherratt, E. S., and Bennet, J. eds., *Interweaving Worlds: Systemic Interactions in Eurasia, 7th to 1st Millennia BC.* Oxford, 158–174.

2018. 'The Rationality and Mutability of Bullion in Hoard Deposits', in Yalçın, Ü ed., *Anatolian Metal VIII: Eliten–Handwerk–Prestigegüter.* Bochum, 269–279.

Bagg, A. M. 2013. 'Palestine under Assyrian Rule: A New Look at the Assyrian Imperial Policy in the West', *Journal of the American Oriental Society* 133 (1), 119–144.

Baines, J. 1999. 'On Wenamun As a Literary Text', in Assmann, J., and Blumenthal, E. eds., *Literatur und Politik im pharaonischen und ptolemäischen Ägypten: Vorträge der Tagung zum Gedenken an Georges Posener 5.–10. September 1996 in Leipzig.* Cairo, 209–233.

Balmuth, M. S. 1964. 'Forerunners of Coinage: Observations on the Monetary Forerunners of Coinage in the Aegean and the Near East with Special Reference to the Origins of Coinage', PhD dissertation, Harvard University, Cambridge, MA.

1967. 'The Monetary Forerunners of Coinage in Phoenicia and Palestine', in Kindler, A. ed., *International Numismatic Convention: Jerusalem, 27–31 December 1963. The Patterns of Monetary Development in Phoenicia and Palestine in Antiquity. Proceedings.* Tel Aviv, 25–32.

1971. 'Remarks on the Appearance of the Earliest Coins', in Mitten, D. G., Pedley, J. G., and Scott, J. A. eds., *Studies Presented to George M. A. Hanfmann.* Monographs in Art and Archaeology. Mainz, 1–7.

1975. 'The Critical Moment: The Transition from Currency to Coinage in the Eastern Mediterranean', *World Archaeology* 6 (3), 293–298.

1976. 'Jewellers' Hoards and the Development of Early Coinage', in Cahn, H. A., and Le Rider, G. eds., *Proceedings of the 8th International Congress of Numismatics, New York and Washington, September 1973*. Paris, 27–30.

ed. 2001a. *Hacksilber to Coinage: New Insights into the Monetary History of the Near East and Greece. A Collection of Eight Papers Presented at the 99th Annual Meeting of the Archaeological Institute of America*. Numismatic studies no. 24. New York.

2001b. 'Commentary', in Balmuth, M. S. ed., *Hacksilber to Coinage: New Insights into the Monetary History of the Near East and Greece. A Collection of Eight Papers Presented at the 99th Annual Meeting of the Archaeological Institute of America*. Numismatic studies no. 24. New York, 13–17.

Balmuth, M. S., and Thompson, C. M. 2000. 'Hacksilber: Recent Approaches to the Study of Hoards of Uncoined Silver: Laboratory Analyses and Geographical Distribution', in Kluge, B., and Weisser, B. eds., *Akten XII: Internationaler Numismatischer Kongress, Berlin 1997*. Berlin, 159–169.

Barbaro, N. 2018. 'Dedica votiva del mercenario Pedon', *Axon* 2 (1), 19–30.

Bass, G. F. 1967. *Cape Gelidonya: A Bronze Age Shipwreck*. Philadelphia.

2010. 'Cape Gelidonya Shipwreck', in Cline, E. H. ed., *The Oxford Handbook of the Bronze Age Aegean (ca. 3000–1000 BC)*. New York; Oxford, 797–803.

Bassiakos, Y., Nerantzis, N., and Papadopoulos, S. 2019. 'Late Neolithic/Early Bronze Age Metallurgical Practices at Limenaria, Thasos: Evidence for Silver and Copper Production', *Archaeological and Anthropological Sciences* 11 (6), 2743–2757.

Bats, M., and D'Agostino, B. eds. 1998. *Euboica: l'Eubea e la presenza euboica in Calcidica e in Occidente: atti del convegno internazionale di Napoli, 13–16 novembre 1996*. Napoli.

Beazley, J. D., and Payne, H. G. G. 1929. 'Attic Black-Figured Fragments from Naucratis', *The Journal of Hellenic Studies* 49 (2), 253–272.

Bell, M. R. 1986. 'A Hittite Pendant from Amarna', *American Journal of Archaeology* 90 (2), 145–151.

Ben-Dor Evian, S. 2011. 'Egypt and the Levant in the Iron Age I–IIA: The Ceramic Evidence', *Tel Aviv* 38 (1), 94–119.

2017. 'Egypt and Israel: The Never-Ending Story', *Near Eastern Archaeology* 80 (1), 30–39.

Ben-Shlomo, D., and Van Beek, G. W. 2014. 'Introduction', in Ben-Shlomo, D., and Van Beek, G. W. eds., *The Smithsonian Institution Excavation at Tell Jemmeh, Israel, 1970–1990*. Smithsonian contributions to anthropology. Washington, DC, 1–15.

Ben Yosef, E. 2019. 'Archaeological Science Brightens Mediterranean Dark Age', *Proceedings of the National Academy of Science of the United States of America* 116 (13), 5843.

Berlejung, A. 2012. 'The Assyrians in the West: Assyrianization, Colonialism, Indifference, or Development Policy?', in Nissinen, M. ed., *Congress Volume Helsinki 2010*. Leiden, 21–60.

Bessios, M., Tzifopoulos, Y., and Kotsonas, A. 2012. *Methone Pierias I*. Thessaloniki.

Bienkowski, P. 1989. 'Prosperity and Decline in LBA Canaan: A Reply to Liebowitz and Knapp', *Bulletin of the American Schools of Oriental Research* 275, 59–63.

Bienkowski, P., and Steen, E. V. D. 2001. 'Tribes, Trade, and Towns: A New Framework for the Late Iron Age in Southern Jordan and the Negev', *Bulletin of the American Schools of Oriental Research* 323, 21–47.

Bissa, E. M. A. 2009. *Governmental Intervention in Foreign Trade in Archaic and Classical Greece*. Mnemosyne. Supplements. Leiden; Boston.

Bivar, A. D. H. 1971. 'A Hoard of Ingot-Currency of the Median Period from Nūsh-i Jān, near Malayir', *Iran* 9, 97–111.

1982. 'Bent Bars and Straight Bars: An Appendix to the Mir Zakah Hoard', *Studia Iranica* 11, 49–60.

Bjorkman, J. K. 1994. 'Hoards and Deposits in Bronze Age Mesopotamia', PhD dissertation, University of Pennsylvania. University Microfilms International. Ann Arbor.

Blandin, B. 2007. *Eretria XVII. Les pratiques funéraires d'époque géométrique à Érétrie: espace des vivants, demeures des morts*. Gollion.

Bloch, M. 1967. 'Natural Economy or Money Economy: A Pseudo-Dilemma', in J. E. Anderson trans. (from French) and ed., *Land and Work in Medieval Europe*. London, 230–247.

Bloch, M., and Parry, J. 1989. 'Introduction: Money and the Morality of Exchange', in Parry, J., and Bloch, M. eds., *Money and the Morality of Exchange*. Cambridge, 1–32.

Blok, J., and Lardinois, A. P. M. H. 2006. *Solon of Athens: New Historical and Philological Approaches*. Mnemosyne. Supplementum. Leiden.

Boardman, J. 1967. 'The Khaniale Tekke Tombs, II', *The Annual of the British School at Athens* 62, 57–75.

1999. *The Greeks Overseas: Their Early Colonies and Trade*. London.

2005. 'The Knossos Tekke Jewellery Hoards', in Gigli, R. ed., *Megalai Nēsoi: studi dedicati a Giovanni Rizza per il suo ottantesimo compleanno*. Catania, 163–166.

2014. 'Teaching in the West', *Ancient East & West* 13, 213–214.

Bobokhyan, A. 2006. 'Identifying Balance Weights and Weight Systems in Bronze Age Troia: Preliminary ReFlections', in Alberti, M. E., Ascalone, E., and Peyronel, L. eds., *Weights in Context: Bronze Age Weighing Systems of Eastern Mediterranean: Chronology, Typology, Material and Archaeological contexts*. Proceedings of the International colloquium, Roma, 22–24 November 2004. Rome, 71–125.

Bohannan, P. 1955. 'Some Principles of Exchange and Investment among the Tiv', *American Anthropologist* 57 (1), 60–70.

1959. 'The Impact of Money on an African Subsistence Economy', *The Journal of Economic History* 19 (4), 491–503.

Bohannan, P., and Bohannan, L. 1968. *Tiv Economy*. Northwestern University African Studies. Evanston.

Bongenaar, A. C. V. M. 1999. 'Money in the Neo-Babylonian Institutions', in Dercksen, J. G. ed., *Trade and Finance in Ancient Mesopotamia: Proceeding of the First MOS Symposium (Leiden, 1997)*. Leiden, 159–174.

Borek, N. 2020. 'More Than Just Coins: A Metrological Approach to Studying Coin Hoards from the Western Mediterranean c.550–480 BCE', in Heymans, E. D., and Termeer, M. K. eds., *Politics of Value: New Approaches to Early Money and the State – Proceedings of the 19th International Congress of Classical Archaeology, Cologne/Bonn 2018 (panel 5.11)*. Heidelberg, 13–24.

Bourdieu, P. 1970. 'The Berber House or the World Reversed', *Social Science Information* 9 (2), 151–170.

1977. *Outline of a Theory of Practice*. Cambridge Studies in Social Anthropology. Cambridge.

Brandherm, D., Heymans, E. D., and Hofmann, D. 2018. 'Introduction: Comparing Currency and Circulation Systems in Past Societies', in Brandherm, D., Heymans, E. D., and Hofmann, D. eds., *Gifts, Goods and Money – Comparing Currency and Circulation Systems in Past Societies*. Oxford, 1–8.

Brandl, B. 1993. 'Clay, Bone, Metal and Stone Objects', in Finkelstein, I., Bunimovitz, S., and Lederman, Z. eds., *Shiloh: The Archaeology of a Biblical Site*. Tel-Aviv, 223–262.

Bräuning, A., and Kilian-Dirlmeier, I. 2013. *Die eisenzeitlichen Grabhügel von Vergina: Die Ausgrabungen von Photis Petsas 1960–1961*. Monographien des Römisch-germanischen Zentralmuseums. Mainz.

Breniquet, C., and Michel, C. 2014. *Wool Economy in the Ancient Near East and the Aegean*. Ancient Textiles Series. Oxford.

Bresson, A. 2009. 'Electrum Coins, Currency Exchange and Transaction Costs in Archaic and Classical Greece', *Revue Belge de Numismatique* 155, 71–80.

2016. *The Making of the Ancient Greek Economy: Institutions, Markets, and Growth in the City-States*. Princeton.

Briend, J. 1980. 'Les Niveaux 9–11 (Fer I)', in Briend, J., and Humbert, J. eds., *Tell Keisan (1971–1976): Une cite phenicienne en Galilee*. Orbis biblicus et orientalis. Fribourg; Paris, 197–215.

Broshi, M. 1974. 'The Expansion of Jerusalem in the Reigns of Hezekiah and Manasseh', *Israel Exploration Journal* 24 (1), 21–26.

Broshi, M., and Finkelstein, I. 1992. 'The Population of Palestine in Iron Age II', *Bulletin of the American Schools of Oriental Research* 287, 47–60.

Brown, A. 1998. 'Homeric Talents and the Ethics of Exchange', *The Journal of Hellenic Studies* 118, 165–172.

Buchner, G. 1970–1971. 'Recent Work at Pithekoussai (Ischia), 1965–71', *Archaeological Reports* 17, 63–67.

Buchner, G., and Gialanella, C. 1994. *Museo archeologico di Pithecusae, isola d'Ischia*. Rome.

Bunimovitz, S. 1994. 'Socio-Political Transformations in the Central Hill Country in the Late Bronze Iron I Transition', in Finkelstein, I., and Na'aman, N. eds., *From Nomadism to Monarchy: Archaeological and Historical Aspects of Early Israel*. Jerusalem; Washington, DC, 179–202.

Bunimovitz, S., and Finkelstein, I. 1993. 'Pottery', in Finkelstein, I., Bunimovitz, S., and Lederman, Z. eds., *Shiloh: The Archaeology of a Biblical Site*. Tel-Aviv, 81–196.

Bunimovitz, S., and Lederman, Z. 2011. 'Canaanite Resistance: The Philistines and Beth-Shemesh – A Case Study from Iron Age I', *Bulletin of the American Schools of Oriental Research* 364, 37–51.

Byrne, R. 2003. 'Early Assyrian Contacts with Arabs and the Impact on Levantine Vassal Tribute', *Bulletin of the American Schools of Oriental Research* 331, 11–25.

Cahill, N., Hari, J., Önay, B., and Dokumacı, E. 2020. 'Depletion Gilding of Lydian Electrum Coins and the Sources of Lydian Gold', in van Alfen, P., Wartenberg, U., Fischer-Bossert, W., Gitler, H., Konuk, K., and Lorber, C. C. eds., *White Gold: Studies in Early Electrum Coinage*. New York and Jerusalem, 291–336.

Cairns, F. 1984. 'χρέματα δόκιμα: IG XII,9,1273 and 1274 and the Early Coinage of Eretria', *Zeitschrift für Papyrologie und Epigraphik* 54, 145–155.

1991. 'The "Laws of Eretria" ("IG" XII. 9 1273 and 1274): Epigraphic, Legal, Historical, and Political Aspects', *Phoenix* 45 (4), 296–313.

Calder W. M. 1984. 'Gold for Bronze. Iliad 6.232–36', in Rigsby, K. J. ed., *Studies Presented to Sterling Dow on His Eightieth Birthday*. Durham, 31–35.

Campbell, E. F. 2002. *Shechem III: The Stratigraphy and Architecture of Shechem/Tell Balatah. Volume 1: Text*. ASOR Archaeological Reports, no. 6. Boston.

Cantarella, E. 2005. 'Gender, Sexuality, and Law', in Gagarin, M., and Cohen, D. eds., *The Cambridge Companion to Ancient Greek Law*. Cambridge Companions to the Ancient World. Cambridge, 236–253.

Caubet, A., and Yon, M. 2001. 'Une coupe inscrite en chypro-minoen à Ras Shamra et les "trésors" d'Ougarit', in Fischer, P. M. ed., *Contributions to the Archaeology and History of the Bronze and Iron Ages in the Eastern Mediterranean. Studies in Honour of Paul Åström*. Vienna, 149–157.

Černý, J. 1933. 'Fluctuations in Grain Prices during the Twentieth Egyptian Dynasty', *Archív orientalní* 6 (1), 173–178.

1952. *Paper & Books in Ancient Egypt: An Inaugural Lecture Delivered at University College, London, 29 May, 1947*. London.

Childe, V. G. 1942. *What Happened in History*. Harmondsworth.

Chrisomalis, S. 2010. *Numerical Notation: A Comparative History*. Cambridge.

Clay, J. S., Malkin, I., and Tzifopoulos, Y. 2017. *Panhellenes at Methone: Graphê in Late Geometric and Protoarchaic Methone, Macedonia (ca 700 BCE)*. Trends in Classics – Supplementary Volumes. Berlin.

Cline, E. H. 2014. *1177 B.C.: The Year Civilization Collapsed*. Turning Points in Ancient History. Princeton.

Coase, R. 2012. 'Saving Economics from the Economists', *Harvard Business Review* 90 (12), 36.

Codere, H. 1968. 'Money-Exchange Systems and a Theory of Money', *Man* 3 (4), 557–577.

Cogan, M., and Tadmor, H. 1988. *II Kings*. The Anchor Bible. Garden City.

Cohen, D. 2005. 'Theories of Punishment', in Gagarin, M., and Cohen, D. eds., *The Cambridge Companion to Ancient Greek Law*. Cambridge Companions to the Ancient World. Cambridge, 170–190.

Coldstream, J. N. 1983. 'Gift Exchange in the Eighth Century BC', in Hägg, R. ed., *The Greek Renaissance of the Eighth Century B.C.: Tradition and Innovation: Proceedings of the Second International Symposium at the Swedish Institute in Athens, 1–5 June, 1981*. Acta Instituti Atheniensis Regni Sueciae. Stockholm; Lund, 201–228.

1995. 'The Rich Lady of the Areiopagos and Her Contemporaries: A Tribute in Memory of Evelyn Lord Smithson', *Hesperia: The Journal of the American School of Classical Studies at Athens* 64 (4), 391–403.

[1977] 2003. *Geometric Greece, 900–700 B.C.* Classical Archaeology/Ancient History. London.

2008. 'Early Greek Exports to Phoenicia and the East Mediterranean', in Doumet-Serhal, C. ed., *Networking Patterns of the Bronze and Iron Age Levant: The Lebanon and Its Mediterranean Connections*. Beirut, 167–188.

Coldstream, J. N., and Catling, H. W. 1996. *Knossos North Cemetery: Early Greek Tombs*. The British School of Archaeology at Athens: Suppl. vol. London.

Collard, C., and Cropp, M. J. 2008. *Euripides: Fragments. Oedipus-Chrysippus; Other Fragments*. The Loeb Classical Library. Cambridge, MA; London.

Collard, C., Cropp, M. J., and Gibert, J. 2004. *Euripides: Selected Fragmentary Plays*. Vol. 2. The Plays of Euripides. Warminster.

Cook, E. 2004. 'Near Eastern Sources for the Palace of Alkinoos', *American Journal of Archaeology* 108 (1), 43–77.

Cook, R. M. 1958. 'Speculations on the Origins of Coinage', *Historia: Zeitschrift für Alte Geschichte* 7 (3), 257–262.

Coulson, W. D. E. 1983. 'The Architecture', in McDonald, W. A., Coulson, W. D. E., and Rosser, J. eds., *Excavations at Nichoria in Southwest Greece. Vol. 3. Dark Age and Byzantine Occupation*. Minneapolis, 9–60.

Courbin, P. 1983. 'Obéloi d'Argolide et d'allieurs', in Hägg, R. ed., *The Greek Renaissance of the Eighth Century B.C.: Tradition and Innovation: Proceedings of the Second International Symposium at the Swedish Institute in Athens, 1–5 June, 1981*. Acta Instituti Atheniensis Regni Sueciae. Stockholm; Lund, 149–156.

Courtois, J. 1990. 'Poids, prix, taxes et slaires à Ougarit (Syrie) au IIe millénaire', in Gyselen, R. ed., *Res orientales II: Prix, salaires, poids et mesures*. Paris; Leuven, 119–127.

Craddock, P. T. 2000a. 'Reconstruction of the Salt Cementation Process at the Sardis Refinery', in Ramage, A., and Craddock, P. T. eds., *King Croesus' Gold: Excavations at Sardis and the History of Gold Refining*. Monograph/Archaeological Exploration of Sardis. Cambridge, MA, 200–211.

2000b. 'Assaying in Antiquity', in Ramage, A., and Craddock, P. T. eds., *King Croesus' Gold: Excavations at Sardis and the History of Gold Refining*. Monograph/Archaeological Exploration of Sardis. Cambridge, MA, 245–250.

Crawford, M. H. 1985. *Coinage and Money under the Roman Republic: Italy and the Mediterranean Economy*. London.

Crewe, L. 2008. 'Enkomi', in T. Kiely ed., *Ancient Cyprus in the British Museum*. British Museum Online Research Catalogue. www.britishmuseum.org/system_pages/holding_area/ancient_cyprus_british_museum.aspx.

Crump, T. 1990. *The Anthropology of Numbers*. Cambridge Studies in Social Anthropology. Cambridge.

Culican, W. 1966. *The First Merchant Venturers: The Ancient Levant in History and Commerce*. London.

Czichon, R. M., and Werner, P. 1998. *Tall Munbaqa-Ekalte 1: Die Bronzezeitlichen Kleinfunde*. Wissenschaftliche Veröffentlichung der Deutschen Orient-Gesellschaft 97. Saarbrucken.

Dakoronia, F. 1989. 'Krikoi – Pronomismatikes morfes geometrikes epoches', *Archaiologike Ephemeris* 128, 115–120.

Dalton, G. 1965. 'Primitive Money', *American Anthropologist* 67 (1), 44–65.

Davies, G. 2002. *A History of Money: From Ancient Times to the Present Day*. Third edition (first edition, 1994). Cardiff.

Davies, J. K. 2001. 'Temples, Credit, and the Circulation of Money', in Meadows, A., and Shipton, K. M. W. eds., *Money and Its Uses in the Ancient Greek World*. Oxford, 117–128.

2005. 'The Gortyn Laws', in Gagarin, M., and Cohen, D. eds., *The Cambridge Companion to Ancient Greek Law*. Cambridge Companions to the Ancient World. Cambridge, 305–327.

2016. 'Towards a General Model of Long-Distance Trade: Aromatics As a Case Study', in Harris, E. M., Lewis, D. M., and Woolmer, M. eds., *The Ancient Greek Economy: Markets, Households and City-States*. New York, 299–315.

Davis, G. 2011. '*Axones* and *Kurbeis*: A New Answer to an Old Problem', *Historia* 60 (1), 1–35.

2012. 'Dating the Drachmas in Solon's Laws', *Historia* 61 (2), 127–158.

2014. 'Mining Money in Late Archaic Athens', *Historia* 63 (3), 257–277.

Davis, J. 1992. *Exchange*. Concepts in the Social Sciences. Buckingham.

de Jong, I. J. F. 2001. *A Narratological Commentary on the Odyssey*. Cambridge; New York.

Dercksen, J. G. 1996. *The Old Assyrian Copper Trade in Anatolia*. Uitgaven van het Nederlands Historisch-Archaeologisch Instituut te Istanbul. Istanbul.

ed. 1999. *Trade and Finance in Ancient Mesopotamia: Proceedings of the First MOS Symposium (Leiden, 1997)*. Mos Studies 1. Leiden.

Descat, R. 2001. 'Monnaie multiple et monnaie frappée en Grèce archaïque', *Revue numismatique* 6 (157), 69–81.

Descœudres, J.-P. 2008. 'Central Greece on the Eve of the Colonisation Movement', in Tsetskhladze, G. R. ed., *Greek Colonisation: An Account of Greek Colonies and Other Settlements Overseas*. Vol. 2. Mnemosyne, bibliotheca classica Batava. Leiden; Boston, 289–382.

Dever, W. G. 2001. 'The Silver Trail: Response to the Papers of Ephraim Stern and Seymour Gitin', in Balmuth, M. S. ed., *Hacksilber to Coinage: New Insights into the Monetary History of the Near East and Greece. A Collection of Eight Papers Presented at the 99th Annual Meeting of the Archaeological Institute of America*. Numismatic studies no. 24. New York, 49–51.

Dickinson, O. T. P. K. 2006. *The Aegean from Bronze Age to Iron Age: Continuity and Change between the Twelfth and Eighth Centuries BC*. London.

Dignas, B. 2002. *Economy and the Sacred in Hellenistic and Roman Asia Minor*. Oxford Classical Monographs. Oxford.

Dillian, C. D., and White, C. L. 2010. *Trade and Exchange: Archaeological Studies from History and Prehistory*. New York.

Dodd, N. 2014. *The Social Life of Money*. Princeton.

Domínguez Monedero, A. J. 2011. 'The Circulation of Money and Coins in Archaic Greece: The Example of Sanctuaries', in García-Bellido, M. P.,

Callegarin, L., and Diéz, A. J. eds., *Barter, Money and Coinage in the Ancient Mediterranean (10th–1st centuries BC).* Madrid, 43–64.

Donlan, W. 1982. 'Reciprocities in Homer', *The Classical World* 75 (3), 137–175.

1989. 'The Unequal Exchange between Glaucus and Diomedes in Light of the Homeric Gift-Economy', *Phoenix* 43 (1), 1–15.

Dorward, D. C. 1976. 'Precolonial Tiv Trade and Cloth Currency', *The International Journal of African Historical Studies* 9 (4), 576–591.

Dothan, M. 1981. 'Sanctuaries along the Coast of Canaan in the MB Period: Nahariyah', in Biran, A. ed., *Temples and High places in Biblical Times: Proceedings of the Colloquium in Honor of the Centennial of Hebrew Union College-Jewish Institute of Religion, Jerusalem, 14–16 March 1977.* Jerusalem, 74–81.

1992. 'Acco', in Freedman, D. N. ed., *The Anchor Bible Dictionary.* vol. 1. New York, 50–53.

Douglas, M. ed. 1982a. *In the Active Voice.* London.

[1958] 1982b. 'Raffia Cloth Distribution in the Lele Economy', in Douglas, M. ed., *In the Active Voice.* London, 38–56.

[1967] 1982c. 'Primitive Rationing', in Douglas, M. ed., *In the Active Voice.* London, 57–81.

Dressel, H., and Regling, K. 1927. 'Zwei ägyptische Funde altgriechischer Silbermünzen', *Zeitschrift für Numismatik* 37, 1–138.

Earle, T. 2010. 'Exchange Systems in Prehistory', in Dillian, C. D., and White, C. L. eds., *Trade and Exchange: Archaeological Studies from History and Prehistory.* New York, 205–217.

Edel, E. 1997. *Der Vertrag zwischen Ramses II. von Ägypten und Ḫattušili III. von Ḫatti.* Berlin.

Egberts, A. 2001. 'Wenamun', in Redford, D. B. ed., *The Oxford Encyclopedia of Ancient Egypt.* Oxford, 495–496.

Einzig, P. [1949] 1966. *Primitive Money in Its Ethnological, Historical and Economic aspects.* Oxford.

Eissfeldt, O. 1937. 'Eine Einschmelzstelle am Tempel zu Jerusalem', *Forschungen und Forschritte* 13, 163–164.

Elat, M. 1979. 'The Monarchy and the Development of Trade in Ancient Israel', in Lipiński, E. ed., *State and Temple Economy in the Ancient Near East: Proceedings of the International Conference Organized by the Katholieke Universiteit Leuven from the 10th to the 14th of April 1978.* Orientalia Lovaniensia analecta. Leuven, 527–546.

1982. 'The Impact of Tribute and Booty on Countries and People within the Assyrian Empire', *Archiv für Orientforschung, Beiheft* 19, 244–251.

Engelbach, R. 1924. 'The Treasure of Athribis (Benha)', *Annales du service des antiquités de l'Égypt* 24, 181–185.

Engen, D. T. 2005. '"Ancient Greenbacks": Athenian Owls, the Law of Nikophon, and the Greek Economy', *Historia: Zeitschrift für Alte Geschichte* 54 (4), 359–381.

Eran, A. 1990. 'Appendix: A Metrological Consideration of the Eshtemoa Hoard', *'Atiqot (Hebrew Series)* 10, 58–60 (Hebrew).

Eriksen, T. H. [1995] 2001. *Small Places, Large Issues: An Introduction to Social and Cultural Anthropology.* Second edition. Anthropology, Culture and Society. London.

Eshel, T. 2014. 'Four Iron Age Silver Hoards from Northern Israel – Comparative Study.' Unpublished MA thesis, University of Haifa. (Hebrew).

Eshel, T., Erel, Y., Yahalom-Mack, N., Tirosh, O., and Gilboa, A. 2019. 'Lead Isotopes in Silver Reveal Earliest Phoenician Quest for Metals in the West Mediterranean', *Proceedings of the National Academy of Sciences* 116 (13), 6007–6012.

Eshel, T., Yahalom-Mack, N., Shalev, S., Tirosh, O., Erel, Y., and Gilboa, A. 2018. 'Four Iron Age Silver Hoards from Southern Phoenicia: From Bundles to Hacksilber', *Bulletin of the American Schools of Oriental Research* 379, 197–228.

Evans-Pritchard, E. E. 1940. *The Nuer: A Description of the Modes of Livelihood and*

Political Institutions of a Nilotic People. Oxford.

Fantalkin, A. 2001. 'Mezad Hashavyahu: Its Material Culture and Historical Background', *Tel Aviv* 28 (1), 3–165.

2004. 'The Final Destruction of Beth Shemesh and the Pax Assyriaca in the Judahite Shephelah: An Alternative View', *Tel Aviv* 31 (2), 245–261.

2006. 'Identity in the Making: Greeks in the Eastern Mediterranean during the Iron Age', in Villing, A., and Schlotzhauer, U. eds., *Naukratis: Greek Diversity in Egypt. Studies on East Greek Pottery and Exchange in the Eastern Mediterranean.* The British Museum Research Publication. London, 199–208.

2008a. 'Contacts between the Greek World and the Southern Levant during the Seventh-Sixth Centuries BCE', PhD dissertation, Tel Aviv University. (Hebrew).

2008b. 'The Appearance of Rock-Cut Bench Tombs in Iron Age Judah As a Reflection of State Formation', in Fantalkin, A., and Yasur-Landau, A. eds., *Bene Israel: Studies in the Archaeology of Israel and the Levant during the Bronze and Iron Ages in Honour of Israel Finkelstein.* Culture and History of the Ancient Near East. Leiden; Boston, 17–44.

2011. 'Why Did Nebuchadnezzar II Destroy Ashkelon in Kislev 604 BCE', in Finkelstein, I., and Na'aman, N. eds., *The Fire Signals of Lachish: Studies in the Archaeology and History of Israel in the Late Bronze Age, Iron Age, and Persian Period in Honor of David Ussishkin.* Winona Lake, 87–111.

2014. 'Naukratis as a Contact Zone: Revealing the Lydian Connection', in Rollinger, R., and Schnegg, K. eds., *Kulturkontakte in Antiken Welten: Vom Denkmodell zum Fallbeispiel: Proceedings des internationalen Kolloquiums aus Anlass des 60. Geburtstagesvon Christoph Ulf, Innsbruck, 26. bis 30. Januar 2009.* Colloquia antiqua. Leuven, 27–51.

2015. 'Coarse Kitchen and Household Pottery As an Indicator for Egyptian Presence in the Southern Levant: A Diachronic Perspective', in Spataro, M., and Villing, A. eds., *Ceramics, Cuisine and Culture: The Archaeology and Science of Kitchen Pottery in the Ancient Mediterranean World.* Oxford; Philadelphia, 233–241.

Fantalkin, A., and Finkelstein, I. 2006. 'The Sheshonq I Campaign and the 8th-Century BCE Earthquake – More on the Archaeology and History of the South in the Iron I–IIa', *Tel Aviv* 33 (1), 18–42.

Fantalkin, A., and Tal, O. 2009. 'Re-Discovering the Iron Age Fortress at Tell Qudadi in the Context of Neo-Assyrian Imperialistic Policies', *Palestine Exploration Quarterly* 141 (3), 188–206.

Fappas, I. 2012. 'Precious Gifts and the Circulation of Oils in the Ancient Eastern Mediterranean', *Talanta* 44, 157–182.

Faust, A. 2011. 'The Interests of the Assyrian Empire in the West: Olive Oil Production As a Test-Case', *Journal of the Economic and Social History of the Orient* 54 (1), 62–86.

Faust, A., and Weiss, E. 2005. 'Judah, Philistia, and the Mediterranean World: Reconstructing the Economic System of the Seventh Century B.C.E', *Bulletin of the American Schools of Oriental Research* (338), 71–92.

2011. 'Between Assyria and the Mediterranean World: The Prosperity of Judah and Philistia in the Seventh Century BCE in Context', in Wilkinson, T. C., Sherratt, E. S., and Bennet, J. eds., *Interweaving Worlds: Systemic Interactions in Eurasia, 7th to 1st millennia BC.* Oxford, 189–204.

Felsch, R. C., Kienast, H., and Schuler, H. 1980. 'Apollon und Artemis oder Artemis und Apollon? Bericht von den Grabungen im neu entdeckten Heiligtum bei Kalapodi 1973–1977', *Archäologischer Anzeiger*, 38–123.

Felsch, R. C. S. 2007. *Kalapodi II. Ergebnisse der Ausgrabungen im Heiligtum der Artemis und des Apollon von Hyampolis in der antiken Phokis.* Mainz.

Felsch, R. C. S., and Siewert, P. 1987. 'Inschriften aus dem Heiligtum von Hyampolis bei Kalapodi', *Archäologische Anzeiger*, 681–687.

Ferguson, N. 2008. *The Ascent of Money: A Financial History of the World*. London; New York.

Fergusson, A. [1975] 2010. *When Money Dies: The Nightmare of Deficit Spending, Devaluation, and Hyperinflation in Weimar Germany*. New York.

Figueira, T. J. 1981. *Aegina: Society and Politics*. Monographs in Classical Studies. Salem.

Finkelstein, I. 1988. *The Archaeology of the Israelite Settlement*. Jerusalem.

1994. 'The Archaeology of the Days of Manasseh', in Coogan, M. D., Exum, J. C., and Stager, L. E. eds., *Scripture and Other Artifacts: Essays on the Bible and Archaeology in Honor of Philip J. King*. Louisville, 169–187.

1996. 'The Archaeology of the United Monarchy: An Alternative View', *Levant* 28 (1), 177–187.

1999. 'State Formation in Israel and Judah: A Contrast in Context, a Contrast in Trajectory', *Near Eastern Archaeology* 62 (1), 35–52.

2001. 'The Rise of Jerusalem and Judah: The Missing Link', *Levant* 33 (1), 105–115.

2003. 'City-States to States: Polity Dynamics in the 10th–9th Centuries BCE', in Dever, W. G., and Gitin, S. eds., *Symbiosis, Symbolism, and the Power of the Past: Canaan, Ancient Israel, and Their Neighbors from the Late Bronze Age through Roman Palaestina*. Winona Lake, 75–84.

2008. 'The Settlement History of Jerusalem in the Eighth and Seventh Centuries BC', *Revue biblique* 115 (4), 499–515.

2010. 'Kadesh Barnea: A Reevaluation of Its Archaeology and History', *Tel Aviv* 37 (1), 111–125.

2013. *The Forgotten Kingdom: The Archaeology and History of Northern Israel*. Atlanta.

2014a. 'The Archaeology of Tell el-Kheleifeh and the History of Ezion-geber/Elath', *Semitica* 56, 105–136.

2014b. 'The Southern Steppe of the Levant ca. 1050–750 BCE: A Framework for a Territorial History', *Palestine Exploration Quarterly* 146 (2), 89–104.

2015. 'Migration of Israelites into Judah after 720 BCE: An Answer and an Update', *Zeitschrift für die alttestamentliche Wissenschaft* 127, 188–206.

2019. 'First Israel, Core Israel, United (Northern) Israel', *Near Eastern Archaeology* 82 (1), 8–15.

Finkelstein, I., and Brandl, B. 1985. 'A Group of Metal Objects from Shiloh', *Israel Museum Journal* 4, 17–26.

Finkelstein, I., and Fantalkin, A. 2012. 'Khirbet Qeiyafa: An Unsensational Archaeological and Historical Interpretation', *Tel Aviv* 39 (1), 38–63.

Finkelstein, I., and Lederman, Z. 1993. 'Area H-F: Middle Bronze III Fortifications and Storerooms', in Finkelstein, I., Bunimovitz, S., and Lederman, Z. eds., *Shiloh: The Archaeology of a Biblical Site*. Tel Aviv, 49–64.

Finkelstein, I., and Na'aman, N. 2004. 'The Judahite Shephelah in the Late 8th and Early 7th Centuries BCE', *Tel Aviv* 31 (1), 60–79.

Finkelstein, I., and Piasetzky, E. 2008. 'Radiocarbon and the History of Copper Production at Khirbet En-Nahas', *Tel Aviv* 35 (1), 82–95.

2011. 'The Iron Age Chronology Debate: Is the Gap Narrowing?', *Near Eastern Archaeology* 74 (1), 50–54.

Finkelstein, I., and Römer, T. 2014. 'Comments on the Historical Background of the Jacob Narrative in Genesis', *Zeitschrift für die alttestamentliche Wissenschaft* 126 (3), 317–338.

Finkelstein, I., and Sass, B. 2013. 'The West Semitic Alphabetic Inscriptions, Late Bronze II to Iron IIA: Archeological Context, Distribution and Chronology', *Hebrew Bible and Ancient Israel* 2 (2), 149–220.

Finkelstein, I., and Silberman, N. A. 2006. *David and Solomon: In Search of the Bible's Sacred Kings and the Roots of the Western Tradition*. New York; London.

Finkelstein, I., and Singer-Avitz, L. 2009. 'The Pottery of Khirbet En-Nahas: A Rejoinder', *Palestine Exploration Quarterly* 141 (3), 207–218.

Finkelstein, I., Zapassky, E., Gadot, Y., Master, D. M., Stager, L. E., and Benenson, I. 2011. 'Phoenician "Torpedo" Amphoras and Egypt: Standardization of Volume Based on Linear Dimensions', *Ägypten und Levante/Egypt and the Levant* 21, 249–259.

Finley, M. I. 1954. *The World of Odysseus*. New York.

[1973] 1985. *The Ancient Economy*. Sather Classical Lectures. Berkeley.

Firth, R. [1939] 1965. *Primitive Polynesian Economy*. London.

1957. 'The Place of Malinowski in the History of Economic Anthropology', in Firth, R. ed., *Man and Culture: An Evaluation of the Work of Bronislaw Malinowski*. London, 209–228.

Fitzpatrick, S. M. 2002. 'A Massive Undertaking: Examining Stone Money in Its Archaeological Context', *Antiquity* 76 (292), 331–332.

2016. 'The Famous Stone Money of Yap', in Haselgrove, C., and Krmnicek, S. eds., *The Archaeology of Money: Proceedings of the Workshop 'Archaeology of Money', University of Tubingen, October 2013*. Leicester Archaeology Monograph 24. Leicester, 43–66.

Fletcher, R. N. 2012. 'Opening the Mediterranean: Assyria, the Levant and the Transformation of Early Iron Age Rrade', *Antiquity* 86 (331), 211–220.

Forge, A. 1972. 'The Golden Fleece', *Man* 7 (4), 527–540.

Forgeau, A. 1986. 'Scarabées, Scaraboïdes et Cônes', in *Amathonte III, Testimonia 3, L'orfèvrerie (R. Laffineur), avec la contribution d'A. Forgeau, Scarabées, Scaraboïdes et Cônes et A. Hermary, La coupe en argent du British Museum. Éditions Recherche sur les Civilisations – École Française d'Athènes, 'Mémoire' no. 67, Études Chypriotes VII, 1986*. Paris, 135–176.

Frankenstein, S. 1979. 'The Phoenicians in the Far West: A Function of Neo-Assyrian Imperialism', in Larsen, M. T. ed., *Power and Propaganda: A Symposium on Ancient Eempires*. Mesopotamia. Copenhagen, 263–294.

Frankfort, H., and Pendlebury, J. D. S. 1933. *The City of Akhenaten*. Memoir of the Egypt Exploration Society. London.

Furness, W. H. 1910. *The Island of Stone Money, Uap of the Carolines*. Philadelphia.

Furtwängler, A. 1890. *Die Bronzen und die Übrigen kleineren Funde von Olympia*. Olympia: die Ergebnisse der von dem Deutschen Reich veranstalteten ausgrabung, im Auftrage des Königlich Preussischen Ministers der geistlichen, unterrichts- und medicinal-Angelegenheiten. Berlin.

1986. 'Neue Beobachtungen zur frühesten Münzprägung', *Schweizerische Numismatische Rundschau* 65, 153–165.

Gadot, Y. 2008. 'Continuity and Change in the Late Bronze to Iron Age Transition in Israel's Coastal Plain: A Long Term Perspective', in Fantalkin, A., and Yasur-Landau, A. eds., *Bene Israel: Studies in the Archaeology of Israel and the Levant during the Bronze and Iron Ages in Honour of Israel Finkelstein*. Culture and History of the Ancient Near East. Leiden; Boston, 55–73.

Gagarin, M. 1986. *Early Greek Law*. Berkeley; London.

Gagarin, M., and Perlman, P. J. 2016. *The Laws of Ancient Crete c. 650–400 BCE*. Oxford.

Gaimster, M. 2007. 'Viking Economies: Evidence from the Silver Hoards', in Graham-Campbell, J., and Williams, G. eds., *Silver Economy in the Viking Age*. Walnut Creek, 123–133.

Galán, J. M. 2005. *Four Journeys in Ancient Egyptian Literature*. Lingua aegyptia. Studia monographica. Göttingen.

Gale, N. H., Gentner, W., and Wagner, G. A. 1980. 'Mineralogical and Geographical Silver Sources of Archaic Greek Coinage', *Metallurgy in Numismatics* 1, 3–49.

Gale, N. H., Picard, O., and Barrandon, J. N. 1988. 'The Archaic Thasian Silver Coinage', in Wagner, G. A., and

Weisgerber, G. eds., *Antike Edel- und Buntmetallgewinnung auf Thasos*. Der Anschnitt. Beiheft. Bochum, 212–240.

Gale, N. H., and Stos-Gale, Z. A. 1981. 'Cycladic Lead and Silver Metallurgy', *The Annual of the British School at Athens* 76, 169–224.

1984. 'Appendix V. Lead Isotope and Chemical Analyses of Silver, Lead and Copper Artefacts from Pyla-Kokkinokremos', in Karageorghis, V., and Demas, M. eds., *Pyla-Kokkinokremos: A Late 13th-Century B.C. Fortified Settlement in Cyprus*. Nicosia, 96–101.

Gallant, T. W. 1982. 'Agricultural Systems, Land Tenure, and the Reforms of Solon', *The Annual of the British School at Athens* 77, 111–124.

Gangutia, E. 2011. 'Barter, Money and Payment in Archaic Greek Lexicon', in García-Bellido, M. P., Callegarin, L., and Diéz, A. J. eds., *Barter, Money and Coinage in the Ancient Mediterranean (10th–1st centuries BC)*. Madrid, 33–42.

Garfinkel, Y., and Ganor, S. 2009. *Khirbet Qeiyafa*. Jerusalem.

Garfinkel, Y., and Mendel-Geberovich, A. 2016. 'The Administration of Judah in Light of the Geographical Distribution of Epigraphic Finds', *Eretz-Israel: Archaeological, Historical and Geographical Studies* 32, 33–44.

Georganas, I. 2005. 'Weapons and Warfare in Early Iron Age Thessaly', *Mediterranean Archaeology and Archaeometry* 5 (2), 63–74.

Gestoso Singer, G. 2010. 'Forms of Payment in the Amarna Age and in the Uluburun and Cape Gelidonya Shipwrecks', *Ugarit-Forschungen* 42, 261–277.

2013. 'The Gold and Silver Hoard from Tell El-Amarna', *Aula Orientalis* 31 (2), 249–259.

2015. 'Small Ingots and Scrap Metal in the Eastern Mediterranean during the Late Bronze Age', in Mynářová, J., Onderka, P., and Pavúk, P. eds., *There and Back Again: The Crossroads II: Proceedings of an International Conference Held in Prague, September 15–18, 2014*. Prague, 85–127.

Gilbert, E. 2005. 'Common Cents: Situating Money in Time and Place', *Economy and Society* 34 (3), 357–88.

Gilboa, A. 2015. 'Dor and Egypt in the Early Iron Age: An Archaeological Perspective of (Part of) the Wenamun Report', *Ägypten und Levante/Egypt and the Levant* 25, 247–274.

Gilboa, A., and Sharon, I. 2008. 'Between the Carmel and the Sea: Tel Dor's Iron Age Reconsidered', *Near Eastern Archaeology* 71 (3), 146–170.

Gilboa, A., Sharon, I., and Boaretto, E. 2008. 'Tel Dor and the Chronology of Phoenician "Pre-Colonisation Stages"', in Sagona, C. ed., *Beyond the Homeland: Markers in Phoenician Chronology*. Ancient Near Eastern Studies, suppl. 28. Leuven; Paris; Dudley, 113–204.

Gill, C., Postlethwaite, N., and Seaford, R. 1998. *Reciprocity in Ancient Greece*. Oxford.

Gimatzidis, S. 2010. *Die Stadt Sindos: Eine Siedlung von der späten Bronze- bis zur klassischen Zeit am Thermaischen Golf in Makedonien*. Prähistorische Archäologie in Südosteuropa. Rahden.

2011a. 'The Northwest Aegean in the Early Iron Age', in Mazarakis Ainian, A. ed., *The 'Dark Ages' Revisited: Acts of an International Symposium in Memory of William D. E. Coulson, University of Thessaly, Volos, 14–17 June 2007*. Volos, 957–970.

2011b. 'Counting Sherds at Sindos: Pottery Consumption and Construction of Identities in the Iron Age', in Verdan, S., Theurillat, T., and Kenzelmann Pfyffer, A. eds., *Early Iron Age Pottery: A Quantitative Approach: Proceedings of the International Round Table Organized by the Swiss School of Archaeology in Greece (Athens, November 28–30, 2008)*. BAR International Series. Oxford, 97–110.

Gitin, S. 1989. 'Tel Miqne-Ekron: A Type-Site for the Inner Coastal Plain in the Iron Age II Period', in Gitin, S., and Dever, W. G. eds., *Recent Excavations in Israel: Studies in Iron Age Archaeology*. Annual of the

American Schools of Oriental Research. Vol. 49. Winona Lake, 23–58.

1995. 'Tel Miqne-Ekron in the 7th Century BCE: The Impact of Economic Innovation and Foreign Cultural Influences on a Neo-Assyrian Vassal City-State', in Gitin, S. ed., *Recent Excavation in Israel. A View to the West. Reports on Kabri, Nami, Miqne-Ekron, Dor & Ashkelon*. Dubuque, 61–79.

1997. 'The Neo-Assyrian Empire and Its Western Periphery: The Levant, with a Focus on Philistine Ekron', in Parpola, S., and Whiting, R. M. eds., *Assyria 1995. Proceedings of the 10th Anniversary Symposium of the Neo-Assyrian Text Corpus Project. Helsinki, September 7–11, 1995*. Helsinki, 77–103.

2003. 'Neo-Assyrian and Egyptian Hegemony over Ekron in the Seventh Century BCE: A Response to Lawrence E. Stager', *Eretz-Israel: Archaeological, Historical and Geographical Studies* 27, 55*–61*.

Gitin, S., and Brandl, B. 2018. 'An Iron Age II Cache of Phoenician Jewelry from Tel Miqne-Ekron', in Shai, I., Chadwick, J. R., Hitchcock, L., Dagan, A., McKinny, C., and Uziel, J. eds., *Tell It in Gath: Studies in the History and Archaeology of Israel. Essays in Honor of Aren M. Maeir on the Occasion of His Sixtieth Birthday*. Ägypten und Altes Testament 90. Münster, 294–303.

Gitin, S., and Golani, A. 2001. 'The Tel Miqne-Ekron Silver Hoards: The Assyrian and Phoenician Connections', in Balmuth, M. S. ed., *Hacksilber to Coinage: New Insights into the Monetary History of the Near East and Greece. A Collection of Eight Papers Presented at the 99th Annual Meeting of the Archaeological Institute of America*. Numismatic studies no. 24. New York, 27–48.

2004. 'A Silver-Based Monetary Economy in the Seventh Century BCE: A Response to Raz Kletter', *Levant* 36 (1), 203–205.

Gitler, H. 2006. 'A Hacksilber and Cut Athenian Tetradrachm Hoard from the Environs of Samaria: Late Fourth Century BCE', *Israel Numismatic Research* 1, 5–14.

2012. 'Introduction', in Konuk, K., Lorber, C. C., and Gitler, H. eds., *White Gold: Revealing the World's Earliest Coins*. Jerusalem, 7–10.

Gitler, H., and Tal, O. 2019. 'Test Cuts on Philistian *Rb' Sheqels*/Quarters: A Case Study', *Israel Numismatic Research* 14, 3–24.

2020. 'A View from the Near East: The Transition from Metal to Coin Economy in the Southern Levant', in van Alfen, P., Wartenberg, U., Fischer-Bossert, W., Gitler, H., Konuk, K., and Lorber, C. C. eds., *White Gold: Studies in Early Electrum Coinage*. New York and Jerusalem, 35–48.

Goedicke, H. 1975. *The Report of Wenamun*. Baltimore.

Goetzmann, W. N. 2016. *Money Changes Everything: How Finance Made Civilization Possible*. Princeton.

Goffman, E. 1975. *Frame Analysis: An Essay on the Organization of Experience*. Harmondsworth.

Golani, A. 1996. 'The Jewelry and the Jeweler's Craft at Tel Miqne-Ekron during the Iron Age', unpublished MA dissertation, Hebrew University, Jerusalem.

2013. *Jewelry from the Iron Age II Levant*. Orbis biblicus et orientalis. Series archaeologica. Fribourg; Göttingen.

Golani, A., and Galili, E. 2015. 'A Late Bronze Age Canaanite Merchant's Hoard of Gold Artifacts and Hematite Weights from the Yavneh-Yam Anchorage, Israel', *Journal of Ancient Egyptian Interconnections* 7 (2), 16–29.

Golani, A., and Sass, B. 1998. 'Three Seventh-Century B.C.E. Hoards of Silver Jewelry from Tel Miqne-Ekron', *Bulletin of the American Schools of Oriental Research* 311, 57–81.

Goldberg, D. 2005. 'Famous Myths of "Fiat Money"', *Journal of Money, Credit and Banking* 37 (5), 957–967.

Gombrich, E. H. 1979. *The Sense of Order: A Study in the Psychology of Decorative Art*. Wrightsman lectures. Oxford.

Goodenough, J. 2011. 'Exchange, Coin, and the Economy of the Greek Sanctuary', DPhil thesis, University of Oxford.

Gosden, C. 2004. *Archaeology and Colonialism: Cultural Contact from 5000 B.C. to the Present.* Topics in Contemporary Archaeology. Cambridge.

Goudsmit, S. 2004. *The Limits of Money: Three Perceptions of Our Most Comprehensive Value System.* Delft.

Graeber, D. 1996. 'Beads and Money: Notes toward a Theory of Wealth and Power', *American Ethnologist* 23 (1), 4–24.

2001. *Toward an Anthropological Theory of Value: The False Coin of Our Own Dreams.* New York.

2009. 'Debt, Violence, and Impersonal Markets: Polanyian Meditations', in Hann, C. M., and Hart, K. eds., *Market and Society: The Great Transformation Today.* Cambridge, 106–132.

2011. *Debt: The first 5,000 years.* Brooklyn.

Graham, A. J. 1978. 'The Foundation of Thasos', *The Annual of the British School at Athens* 73, 61–98.

[1994] 2001. 'Greek and Roman Settlements on the Black Sea Coasts: Historical Background', in Graham, A. J. ed., *Collected Papers on Greek Colonization.* Leiden, 139–147.

Graham-Campbell, J. 1982. 'Viking Silver Hoards: An Introduction', in Farrell, R. T. ed., *The Vikings.* London, 32–41.

2007. 'Reflections on "Silver Economy in the Viking Age"', in Graham-Campbell, J., and Williams, G. eds., *Silver Economy in the Viking Age.* Walnut Creek, 215–223.

Graham-Campbell, J., and Williams, G. eds. 2007. *Silver Economy in the Viking Age.* Walnut Creek.

Graham-Campbell, J., Sindbæk, S. M., and Williams, G., eds. 2011. *Silver Economies, Monetisation and Society in Scandinavia, AD 800–1100.* Aarhus.

Gray, D. H. F. 1954. 'Metal-Working in Homer', *The Journal of Hellenic Studies* 74, 1–15.

Gray, J. 1970. *I & II Kings: A Commentary.* London.

Grayson, A. K. 1996. *Assyrian Rulers of the Early First Millennium BC.* Royal Inscriptions of Mesopotamia. Assyrian Periods. Toronto; London.

Grayson, A. K., and Novotny, J. R. 2012. *The Royal Inscriptions of Sennacherib, King of Assyria (704–681 BC), Part 1.* The Royal Inscriptions of the Neo-Assyrian Period. Vol. 3/1. Winona Lake.

Green, J. D. M. 2009. 'Forces of Transformation in Death: The Cemetery at Tell es-Sa'idiyeh, Jordan', in Bachhuber, C., and Roberts, R. G. eds., *Forces of Transformation: The End of the Bronze Age in the Mediterranean: Proceedings of an International Symposium Held at St. John's College, University of Oxford, 25–6th March, 2006.* Themes from the Ancient Near East BANEA Publication Series. Oxford; Oakville, 80–91.

Greenfield, J. C. 1985. 'The Meaning of *tkwnh*', in Iwry, S., Kort, A., and Morschauser, S. eds., *Biblical and Related Studies Presented to Samuel Iwry.* Winona Lake, 81–85.

Gregory, C. A. 1982. *Gifts and Commodities.* Studies in Political Economy. London; New York.

1983. 'Kula Gift Exchange and Capitalist Commodity Exchange: A Comparison', in Leach, J. W., and Leach, E. R. eds., *The Kula: New Perspectives on Massim Exchange.* Cambridge, 103–117.

1997. *Savage Money: The Anthropology and Politics of Commodity Exchange.* Studies in Anthropology and History. Amsterdam.

[1982] 2015. *Gifts and Commodities.* Second edition. Chicago.

Grierson P. 1977. *The Origins of Money.* London.

Guarducci, M. 1944–1945. 'Tripodi, lebeti, oboli', *Rivista di Filologia classica* 22–23, 171–180.

Guyer, J. I. 2004. *Marginal Gains: Monetary Transactions in Atlantic Africa.* The Lewis Henry Morgan lectures. Chicago.

2012. 'Soft Currencies, Cash Economies, New Monies: Past and Present', *Proceedings of the National Academy of Sciences* 109 (7), 2214–2221.

Haarer, P. S. 2000. 'Obeloi and Iron in Archaic Greece', DPhil dissertation, University of Oxford.

2001. 'Problematising the Transition from Bronze to Iron', in Shortland, A. J. ed., *The Social Context of Technological Change: Egypt and the Near East, 1650–1550 BC: Proceedings of a Conference Held at St. Edmund Hall, Oxford 12–14 September 2000*. Oxford, 255–273.

Hägg, R. ed. 1983a. *The Greek Renaissance of the Eighth century B.C.: Tradition and Innovation: Proceedings of the Second International Symposium at the Swedish Institute in Athens, 1–5 June, 1981*. Acta Instituti Atheniensis Regni Sueciae. Stockholm; Lund.

1983b. 'Preface', in Hägg, R. ed., *The Greek Renaissance of the Eighth Century B.C.: Rradition and Innovation: Proceedings of the Second International Symposium at the Swedish Institute in Athens, 1–5 June, 1981*. Acta Instituti Atheniensis Regni Sueciae. Stockholm; Lund, 7–8.

Hall, E. 2016. 'Hoarding at Tel Megiddo in the Late Bronze Age and Iron Age I', unpublished MA thesis, Tel Aviv University.

Hall, J. M. 2007. *A History of the Archaic Greek World, ca. 1200–479 BCE*. Blackwell History of the Ancient World. Malden.

Hammond, N. G. L. 1998. 'Eretria's Colonies in the Area of the Thermaic Gulf', *The Annual of the British School at Athens* 93, 393–399.

Hann, C. M., and Hart, K. 2011. *Economic Anthropology: History, Ethnography, Critique*. Cambridge.

Hansen, M. H. 2006. *Polis: An Introduction to the Ancient Greek City-State*. Oxford.

Hansen, M. H., and Nielsen, T. H. 2004. *Inventory of Archaic and Classical Poleis*. Oxford.

Harari, Y. N. 2014. *Sapiens: A Brief History of Humankind*. London.

Hårdh, B. 1996. *Silver in the Viking Age: A Regional-Economic Survey*. Stockholm.

2007. 'Hacksilver and Ingots', in Skre, D. ed., *Means of Exchange: Dealing with Silver in the Viking Age*. Kaupang Excavation Project Publication Series. Aarhus, 95–118.

Harris, D. 1995. *The Treasures of the Parthenon and Erechtheion*. Oxford Monographs on Classical Archaeology. Oxford.

Harris, E. M. 2006. 'Solon and the Spirit of the Laws in Archaic and Classical Greece', in Blok, J., and Lardinois, A. P. M. H. eds., *Solon of Athens: New Historical and Philological Approaches*. Mnemosyne. Supplementum. Leiden, 290–318.

Harris, O. 1989. 'The Earth and the State: The Sources and Meanings of Money in Northern Potosí, Bolivia', in Parry, J., and Bloch, M. eds., *Money and the Morality of Exchange*. Cambridge, 232–268.

Harrison, T. P. 2004. *Megiddo 3: Final Report on the Stratum VI Excavations*. University of Chicago Oriental Institute Publications. Chicago.

Hart, K. 1986. 'Heads or Tails? Two Sides of the Coin', *Man* 21 (4), 637–656.

2005. 'Money: One Anthropologist's View', in Carrier, J. G. ed., *A Handbook of Economic Anthropology*. Cheltenham, 160–175.

2008. 'The Human Economy', *ASAonline* 1 (1), 1–12.

2012. 'In Rousseau's Footsteps: David Graeber and the Anthropology of Unequal Society'. http://thememorybank.co.uk/2012/07/04/in-rousseaus-footsteps-david-graeber-and-the-anthropology-of-unequal-society-2/.

Hart, K., Laville, J., and Cattani, A. D. 2010. *The Human Economy: A Citizen's Guide*. Cambridge; Malden.

Hart, K., and Ortiz, H. 2014. 'The Anthropology of Money and Finance: Between Ethnography and World History', *Annual Review of Anthropology* 43 (1), 465–482.

Haselgrove, C., and Krmnicek, S. 2012. 'The Archaeology of Money*', *Annual Review of Anthropology* 41 (1), 235–250.

Hauptmann, A., Laschimke, R., and Burger, M. 2016. 'On the Making of Copper Oxhide Ingots: Evidence from Metallography and Casting Experiments', *Archaeological and Anthropological Sciences* 8 (4), 751–761.

Hauptmann, A., Maddin, R., and Prange, M. 2002. 'On the Structure and Composition of Copper and Tin Ingots Excavated from the Shipwreck of Uluburun', *Bulletin of the American Schools of Oriental Research* 328, 1–30.

Heady, P. 2005. 'Barter', in Carrier, J. G. ed., *A Handbook of Economic Anthropology*. Cheltenham, 262–274.

Helck, W. 1986. 'Wenamun', *Lexicon der Ägyptologie* 6, 1215–1217.

Helms, M. W. 1988. *Ulysses' Sail: An Ethnographic Odyssey of Power, Knowledge, and Geographical Distance*. Princeton.

Heltzer, M. 1999. 'The Economy of Ugarit', in Watson, W. G. E., and Wyatt, N. eds., *Handbook of Ugaritic Studies*. Handbuch der Orientalistik. Erste Abteilung, Nahe und der Mittlere Osten. Leiden, 423–454.

Helwing, B. 2014. 'Silver in the Early State Societies of Greater Mesopotamia', in Meller, H., Risch, R., and Pernicka, E. eds., *Metalle der Macht – Frühes Gold und Silber: 6. Mitteldeutscher Archäologentag vom 17. bis 19. Oktober 2013 in Halle (Saale) [Metals of power – Early Gold and Silver: 6th Archaeological Conference of Central Germany, October 17–19, 2013 in Halle (Saale)]*. Tagungen des Landesmuseums für Vorgeschichte Halle. Halle Saale, 411–421.

Herbert, E. W. 1984. *Red Gold of Africa: Copper in Precolonial History and Culture*. Madison; London.

Herzog, Z. 1997. 'The Arad Fortresses', in *Arad*. Tel Aviv, 111–292 (Hebrew).

2002. 'The Fortress Mound at Tel Arad an Interim Report', *Tel Aviv* 29 (1), 3–109.

Herzog, Z., and Singer-Avitz, L. 2004. 'Redefining the Centre: The Emergence of State in Judah', *Tel Aviv* 31 (2), 209–244.

Heymans, E. D. 2018a. 'Heads or Tails: Metal Hoards from the Iron Age Southern Levant', in Brandherm, D., Heymans, E. D., and Hofmann, D. eds., *Gifts, Goods and Money – Comparing Currency and Circulation Systems in Past Societies*. Oxford, 85–104.

2018b. 'Argonauts of the Eastern Mediterranean: The Early History of Money in the Eastern Mediterranean Iron Age', PhD dissertation, Tel Aviv University.

2019. 'Pre-Coinage Money in the Grave? The Case of Amathus t.198', *Journal of Archaeological Numismatics* 9, 45–66.

Heymans, E. D., and Termeer, M. K. eds. 2020a. *Politics of Value: New Approaches to Early Money and the State – Proceedings of the 19th International Congress of Classical Archaeology, Cologne/Bonn 2018 (panel 5.11)*. Heidelberg.

2020b. 'Introduction: Rethinking Early Money and the State', in Heymans, E. D., and Termeer, M. K. eds. *Politics of Value: New Approaches to Early Money and the State – Proceedings of the 19th International Congress of Classical Archaeology, Cologne/Bonn 2018 (panel 5.11)*. Heidelberg, 1–12.

Heymans, E. D., and Van Wijngaarden, G. J. 2011. 'Low-Value Manufactured Exotics in the Eastern Mediterranean in the Late Bronze and Early Iron Ages', in Vianello, A. ed., *Exotica in the Prehistoric Mediterranean*. Oakville, 124–136.

Hirschfeld, Y., and Riklin, S. 2002. 'Region II: Survey and Excavations in the Upper Wadi el-Makkuk Caves', *'Atiqot* 41, 5–19.

Hoffman, G. L. 1997. *Imports and Immigrants: Near Eastern Contacts with Iron Age Crete*. Ann Arbor.

Hogendorn, J., and Johnson, M. 1986. *The Shell Money of the Slave Trade*. Cambridge.

Hölkeskamp, K. 1990. 'Review: Early Greek Law by Michael Gagarin', *Gnomon* 62 (2), 116–128.

1999. *Schiedsrichter, Gesetzgeber und Gesetzgebung im archaischen Griechenland*. Historia. Einzelschriften. Stuttgart.

Holladay, J. S. Jr. 1995. 'The Kingdoms of Israel and Judah: Political and Economic Centralization in the Iron IIA–B (ca. 1000–750 BCE)', in Levy, T. E. ed., *The Archaeology of Society in the Holy Land*. New York, 368–398.

2006. 'Hezekiah's Tribute, Long-Distance Trade, and the Wealth of Nations ca. 1000–600 BC: A New Perspective', in Gitin, S., Wright, J. E., and Dessel, J. P. eds., *Confronting the Past: Archaeological and Historical Essays on Ancient Israel in Honor of William G. Dever*. Winona Lake, 311–331.

2009. 'How Much Is That in ...? Monetization, Money, Royal States, and Empires', in Schloen, J. D. ed., *Exploring the Longue Durée: Essays in Honor of Lawrence E. Stager*. Winona Lake, 207–222.

Holloway, R. R. 1971. 'An Archaic Hoard from Crete and the Early Aeginetan Coinage', *Museum Notes (American Numismatic Society)* 17, 1–21.

Hooker, J. T. 1989. 'Gifts in Homer', *Bulletin of the Institute of Classical Studies* 36 (1), 79–90.

Hopkins, K. 1983. 'Introduction', in Garnsey, P., Hopkins, K., and Whittaker, C. R. eds., *Trade in the Ancient Economy*. London, ix–xxv.

Hopper, R. J. 1979. *Trade and Industry in Classical Greece*. Aspects of Greek and Roman life. London.

Horn, S. H. 1968. 'Objects from Shechem: Excavated 1913 and 1914', *Jaarbericht van het Vooraziatisch-Egyptisch Genootschapt Ex Oriente Lux* 20, 71–90.

Houtman, C. 1996. *Exodus*. Commentaar op het Oude Testament. Kampen.

Howgego, C. J. 1995. *Ancient History from Coins*. Approaching the Ancient World. London.

Hudson, M. 2004. 'The Archaeology of Money', in Wray, L. R. ed., *Credit and State Theories of Money*. Cheltenham; Northampton, 99–127.

Hudson, M., and Van de Mieroop, M. eds. 2002. *Debt and Economic Renewal in the Ancient Near East*. Bethesda.

Huizinga, J. 1949. *Homo ludens: A Study of the Play-Element in Culture*. London.

Humphrey, C. 2000. 'An Anthropological View of Barter in Russia', in Seabright, P. ed., *The Vanishing Rouble: Barter Networks and Non-Monetary Transactions in Post-Soviet Societies*. Cambridge, 71–90.

Humphrey, C., and Hugh-Jones, S. 1992. 'Introduction: Barter, Exchange and Value', in Humphrey, C., and Hugh-Jones, S. eds., *Barter, Exchange, and Value: An Anthropological Approach*. Cambridge, 1–20.

Hurowitz, V. 1986. 'Another Fiscal Practice in the Ancient near East: 2 Kings 12: 5–17 and a Letter to Esarhaddon (LAS 277)', *Journal of Near Eastern Studies* 45 (4), 289–294.

Ialongo, N., Vacca, A., and Peyronel, L. 2018. 'Breaking Down the Bullion: The Compliance of Bullion-Currencies with Official Weight-Systems in a Case-Study from the Ancient Near East', *Journal of Archaeological Science* 91, 20–32.

Ialongo, N., Vacca, A., and Vanzetti, A. 2018. 'Indeterminacy and Approximation in Mediterranean Weight Systems, in the 3rd and 2nd millennia BC', in Brandherm, D., Heymans, E. D., and Hofmann, D. eds., *Gifts, Goods and Money – Comparing Currency and Circulation Systems in Past Societies*. Oxford, 9–44.

Ingham, G. K. 2001. 'Fundamentals of a Theory of Money: Untangling Fine, Lapavitsas and Zelizer', *Economy and Society* 30 (3), 304–323.

2004. *The Nature of Money*. Cambridge.

Innes, A. M. 1913. 'What Is Money', *Banking Law Journal* 30, 377–408.

Isaac, B. L. 2005. 'Karl Polanyi', in Carrier, J. G. ed., *A Handbook of Economic Anthropology*. Cheltenham, 14–25.

Isaac, B. H. 1986. *The Greek Settlements in Thrace until the Macedonian Conquest*. Studies of the Dutch Archaeological and Historical Society. Leiden.

James, F. W. 1966. *The Iron Age at Beth Shan: A Study of Levels VI–IV*. Museum Monographs. Philadelphia.

James, P. 2005. 'The Date of the Ekron Temple Inscription: A Note', *Israel Exploration Journal* 55 (1), 90–93.

2006. 'Dating Late Iron Age Ekron (Tel Miqne)', *Palestine Exploration Quarterly* 138 (2), 85–97.

Janes, S. 2010. 'Negotiating Island Interactions: Cyprus the Aegean and the Levant in the Late Bronze to Early Iron Ages', in van Dommelen, P., and Knapp, A. B. eds., *Material Connections in the Ancient Mediterranean: Mobility, Materiality, and Mediterranean Identities*. London, 127–146.

Janssen, J. J. 1975. *Commodity Prices from the Ramessid Period: An Economic Study of the Village of Necropolis Workmen at Thebes*. Leiden.

Jeffery, L. H. 1956. 'The Courts of Justice in Archaic Chios', *The Annual of the British School at Athens* 51, 157–167.

[1961] 1990. *The Local Scripts of Archaic Greece: A Study of the Origin of the Greek Alphabet and Its Development from the Eighth to the Fifth Centuries B.C.* Revised edition. Oxford.

Jevons, W. S. 1875. *Money and the Mechanism of Exchange*. The International Scientific Series. London.

Jones, D. W. 1999. 'The Archaeology and Economy of Homeric Gift Exchange', *Opuscula Atheniensia* 24, 11–24.

Jones, M. R. 2007. 'Oxhide Ingots, Copper Production, and the Mediterranean Trade in Copper and Other Metals in the Bronze Age', PhD dissertation, Texas A&M University.

Joukowsky, M., and Ward, W. A. eds. 1992. *The Crisis Years: The 12th century B.C. from Beyond the Danube to the Tigris*. Dubuque.

Jurman, C. 2015. '"Silver of the Treasury of Herishef": Considering the Origin and Economic Significance of Silver in Egypt during the Third Intermediate Period', in Babbi, A., Bubenheimer-Erhart, F., Marín-Aguilera, B., and Mühl, S. eds., *The Mediterranean Mirror: Cultural Contacts in the Mediterranean Sea between 1200 and 750 B. C. International Post-doc and Young Researcher Conference Heidelberg, 6th–8th October 2012*. Mainz, 51–68.

Jursa, M. 2010. *Aspects of the Economic History of Babylonia in the First Millennium BC: Economic Geography, Economic Mentalities, Agriculture, the Use of Money and the Problem of Economic Growth*. Alter Orient und Altes Testament. Münster.

2013. 'Epistolographic Evidence for Trips to Susa by Borsippean Priests and for the Crisis in Borsippa at the Beginning of Xerxes' Reign', *ARTA* 3, 1–12.

2016. 'Silver and Other Forms of Elite Wealth in Seventh Century BC Babylonia', in Kleber, K., and Pirngruber, R. eds., *Silver, Money and Credit: A Tribute to Robartus J. van der Spek on the Occasion of His 65th Birthday*. PIHANS. Uitgaven van het Nederlands Instituut voor het Nabije Oosten te Leiden. Leiden, 61–71.

Kakavoyannis, E. 2001. 'The Silver Ore-Processing Workshops of the Lavrion Region', *The Annual of the British School at Athens* 96, 365–380.

Kalantaryan, A. A. 2007. *The Gold of Ancient Armenia (III mill. BCE–14 cent. AD)*. Erevan.

Kaminski G. 1991. 'Thesauros: Untersuchungen zum antiken Opferstock', *Jahrbuch des Deutschen Archäologischen Instituts* 106, 63–181.

Karageorghis, V., and Demas, M. 1984. *Pyla-Kokkinokremos: A Late 13th-Century B.C. Fortified Settlement in Cyprus*. Nicosia.

Karo, G. 1930a. *Die Schachtgräber von Mykenai*. München.

1930b. 'Schatz von Tiryns', *Athenische Mitteilungen* 55, 119–140.

Kasseri, A. 2012. 'Foinikikoi emporikoi amforeis apo te Methone Pierias', in Kephalidou, E., and Tsiafaki, D. eds., *Kerameos Paides*. Thessaloniki, 299–308.

Kassianidou, V. 2012. 'The Origin and Use of Metals in Iron Age Cyprus', in Iacovou, M. ed., *Cyprus and the Aegean in the Early Iron Age: The Legacy of Nicolas Coldstream*. Nicosia, 229–259.

Kee, H. C., and Toombs, L. E. 1957. 'The Second Season of Excavation at Biblical Shechem', *The Biblical Archaeologist* 20 (4), 81–105.

Keel, O. 1980. 'La Glyptique', in Briend, J., and Humbert, J. eds., *Tell Keisan (1971–1976):*

Une cite phenicienne en Galilee. Orbis biblicus et orientalis. Fribourg; Paris, 257–295.

Kemp, B. J. 2006. *Ancient Egypt: Anatomy of a Civilization*. London.

Kenzelmann Pfyffer, A., Theurillat, T., and Verdan, S. 2005. 'Graffiti d'époque géométrique provenant du sanctuaire d'Apollon Daphnéphoros à Erétrie', *Zeitschrift für Papyrologie und Epigraphik* 151, 51–83.

Kershaw, J. 2017. 'An early Medieval Dual-Currency Economy: Bullion and Coin in the Danelaw', *Antiquity* 91 (355), 173–190.

Keynes, J. M. 1982. 'Keynes and Ancient Currencies', in Moggridge, D. ed., *The Collected Writings of John Maynard Keynes. Volume XXVIII. Social, Political and Literary Writings*. London, 223–294.

Keyser, P. T., and Clark, D. D. 2001. 'Analyzing and Interpreting the Metallurgy of Early Electrum Coins', in Balmuth, M. S. ed., *Hacksilber to Coinage: New Insights into the Monetary History of the Near East and Greece. A Collection of Eight Papers Presented at the 99th Annual Meeting of the Archaeological Institute of America*. Numismatic studies no. 24. New York, 105–126.

Kienast, B. 1979. 'Rechtsurkunden in ugaritischer Sprache', *Ugarit-Forschungen* 11, 431–452.

Kilger, C. 2007. 'Wholeness and Holiness: Counting, Weighing and Valuing Silver in the Early Viking Period', in Skre, D. ed., *Means of Exchange: Dealing with Silver in the Viking Age*. Kaupang Excavation Project publication series. Aarhus, 253–326.

Kilian, K. 1975. *Fibeln in Thessalien von der mykenischen bis zur archaischen Zeit*. Prähistorische Bronzefunde. Abteilung XIV. München.

Kilian-Dirlmeier, I. 1985. 'Fremde Weihungen in griechischen Heiligtümern vom 8. bis zum Beginn des 7. Jahrhunderts v. Chr.', *Jahrbuch des römisch-germanischen Zentralmuseums Mainz* 32, 215–254.

Kim, H. S. 2001. 'Archaic Coinage As Evidence for the Use of Money', in Meadows, A., and Shipton, K. M. W. eds., *Money and Its Uses in the Ancient Greek World*. Oxford, 7–21.

2002. 'Small Change and the Moneyed Economy', in Cartledge, P., Cohen, E. E., and Foxhall, L. eds., *Money, Labour and Land: Approaches to the Economies of Ancient Greece*. London; New York, 44–51.

2004. 'Electrum Ingot Hoard (2002): A Proto-Monetary Hoard?', *Schweizerische Numismatische Rundschau* 83, 5–16.

Kim, H. S., and Kroll, J. H. 2008. 'A Hoard of Archaic Coins of Colophon and Unminted Silver (CH I. 3)', *American Journal of Numismatics* 20, 53–104.

Klaffenbach, G. 1953. 'Archaische Weihinschrift aus Samos', *Mitteilungen des Deutschen Archäologischen Instituts* 6, 16–20.

Kleber, K. 2016. 'The Kassite Gold and the Post-Kassite Silver Standards Revisited', in Kleber, K., and Pirngruber, R. eds., *Silver, Money and Credit: A Tribute to Robartus J. van der Spek on the Occasion of His 65th Birthday*. PIHANS. Uitgaven van het Nederlands Instituut voor het Nabije Oosten te Leiden. Leiden, 39–60.

Kleiman, A. 2017. 'A North Israelite Royal Administrative System and Its Impact on Late-Monarchic Judah', *Hebrew Bible and Ancient Israel* 6 (3), 354–371.

Kletter, R. 1998. *Economic Keystones: The Weight System of the Kingdom of Judah*. Journal for the study of the Old Testament. Supplement series. Sheffield.

2003. 'Iron Age Hoards of Precious Metals in Palestine – an "Underground Economy"?', *Levant* 35 (1), 139–152.

2004. 'Coinage before Coins? A Response', *Levant* 36 (1), 207–210.

2013. 'Hoards and Hoarders BCE', in *Hoards and Genizot As Chapters in History*. Haifa, 6–13.

Kletter, R., and Brand, E. 1998. 'A New Look at the Iron Age Silver Hoard from Eshtemoa', *Zeitschrift des Deutschen Palästina-Vereins* 114 (2), 139–154.

Kletter, R., and De Groot, A. 2007. 'The Iron Age Hoard of "Hacksilber" from En-Gedi', in Stern, E. ed., *En-Gedi Excavations I: Final report (1961–1965)*. Jerusalem, 367–375.

Knapp, A. B. 1989. 'Response: Independence, Imperialism, and the Egyptian Factor', *Bulletin of the American Schools of Oriental Research* 275, 64–68.

Knapp, A. B., and Manning, S. W. 2016. 'Crisis in Context: The End of the Late Bronze Age in the Eastern Mediterranean', *American Journal of Archaeology* 120 (1), 99–149.

Knapp, A. B., Muhly, J. D., and Muhly, P. M. 1988. 'To Hoard Is Human: Late Bronze Age Metal Deposits in Cyprus and the Aegean', *Report of the Department of Antiquities, Cyprus* 1, 233–262.

Knapp, G. F. [1905] 1924. *The State Theory of Money*. London.

Koehler, L., Baumgartner, W., Richardson, M. E. J., and Stamm, J. J. 1996. *The Hebrew and Aramaic lexicon of the Old Testament*. Leiden.

Koerner, R. 1993. *Inschriftliche Gesetzestexte der frühen griechischen Polis*. Akten der Gesellschaft für Griechische und Hellenistische Rechtsgeschichte. Cologne.

Konuk, K. 2012. 'Asia Minor to the Ionian Revolt', in Metcalf, W. E. ed., *The Oxford Handbook of Greek and Roman Coinage*. Oxford, 43–60.

Konuk, K., Lorber, C. C., and Gitler, H. 2012. *White Gold: Revealing the World's Earliest Coins*. Catalogue. Jerusalem.

Kopcke, G. 1992. 'What Role for Phoenicians?', in Kopcke, G., and Tokumaru, I. eds., *Greece between East and West: 10th–8th centuries B.C.: Papers of the Meeting at the Institute of Fine Arts, New York University, March 15–16th, 1990*. Mainz, 103–113.

Kopytoff, I. 1986. 'The Cultural Biography of Things: Commoditization As Process', in Appadurai, A. ed., *The Social Life of Things: Commodities in Cultural Perspective*. Cambridge, 64–91.

Kotsonas, A. 2006. 'Wealth and Status in Iron Age Knossos', *Oxford Journal of Archaeology* 25 (2), 149–172.

2012. 'What Makes a Euboean Colony or Trading Station? Zagora in the Cyclades, Methone in the Thermaic Gulf, and Aeagean Networks in the 8th Century BC', *Mediterranean Archaeology* 25, 243–257.

Kraay, C. M. 1964. 'Hoards, Small Change and the Origin of Coinage', *The Journal of Hellenic Studies* 84, 76–91.

1976. *Archaic and Classical Greek Coins*. London.

Kraay, C. M., and Moorey, P. R. S. 1968. 'Two Fifth Century Hoards from the Near East', *Revue numismatique* 6 (10), 181–235.

Kramer-Hajos, M. T. 2016. *Mycenaean Greece and the Aegean world: Palace and Province in the Late Bronze Age*. Cambridge.

Kroll, J. H. 1998. 'Silver in Solon's Laws', in Ashton, R., and Hurter, S. eds., *Studies in Greek Numismatics in Memory of Martin Jessop Price*. London, 225–232.

2000. 'Review: Coins, Bodies, Games, and Gold: The Politics of Meaning in Archaic Greece by Leslie Kurke', *The Classical Journal* 96 (1), 85–90.

2001a. 'Observations on Monetary Instruments in Pre-Coinage Greece', in Balmuth, M. S. ed., *Hacksilber to Coinage: New Insights into the Monetary History of the Near East and Greece. A Collection of Eight Papers Presented at the 99th Annual Meeting of the Archaeological Institute of America*. Numismatic studies no. 24. New York, 77–91.

2001b. 'A Small Find of Silver Bullion from Egypt', *American Journal of Numismatics (1989–)* 13, 1–20.

2003. 'Weights, Bullion Currency, Coinage', in Stampolidis, N. C., and Karageorghis, V. eds., *Ploes – Sea Routes: Interconnections in the Mediterranean, 16th–6th c. BC: Proceedings of the International Symposium Held at Rethymnon, Crete, September 29th–October 2nd, 2002*. Athens, 313–323.

2008a. 'The Monetary Use of Weighted Bullion in Archaic Greece', in Harris, W. V. ed., *The Monetary Systems of the Greeks and Romans*. Oxford, 12–37.

2008b. 'Early Iron Age Balance Weights at Lefkandi, Euboea', *Oxford Journal of Archaeology* 27 (1), 37–48.

2011. 'Minting for Export: Athens, Aegina and Others', in Faucher, T., Marcellesi, M., and Picard, O. eds., *Nomisma: La circulation monétaire dans le monde grec antique. Actes du colloque international, Athènes, 14–17 avril 2010*. BCH Supplément 57. Athens, 27–38.

2012. 'The Monetary Background of Early Coinage', in Metcalf, W. E. ed., *The Oxford Handbook of Greek and Roman Coinage*. Oxford, 33–42.

2013a. 'Finds of Hacksilber in the Ancient Near East and Greece: A Survey', in Hunter, F., and Painter, K. S. eds., *Late Roman Silver: The Traprain Treasure in Context*. Edinburgh, 375–380.

2013b. 'Review: Véronique Van Driessche, Des étalons pré-monétaires au monnayage en bronze; Charles Doyen. Étalons de l.'argent et du bronze en Grèce hellénistique', *The Numismatic Chronicle and Journal of the Royal Numismatic Society* 173, 531–536.

2020a. 'The Inscribed Account on Lead from the Ephesian Artemisium', in van Alfen, P., Wartenberg, U., Fischer-Bossert, W., Gitler, H., Konuk, K., and Lorber, C. C. eds., *White Gold: Studies in Early Electrum Coinage*. New York and Jerusalem, 49–64.

2020b. 'Issue Identification, *Dynastai*, and the Plethora of Types in Early Electrum Coinage', in van Alfen, P., Wartenberg, U., Fischer-Bossert, W., Gitler, H., Konuk, K., and Lorber, C. C. eds., *White Gold: Studies in Early Electrum Coinage*. New York and Jerusalem, 537–546.

Kroll, J. H., and Waggoner, N. M. 1984. 'Dating the Earliest Coins of Athens, Corinth and Aegina', *American Journal of Archaeology* 88 (3), 325–340.

Krugman, P. R. 1994. *Peddling Prosperity: Economic Sense and Nonsense in the Age of Diminished Expectations*. New York; London.

Kruse, S. E. 1988. 'Ingots and Weight Units in Viking Age Silver Hoards', *World Archaeology* 20 (2, Hoards and Hoarding), 285–301.

Kurke, L. 1999. *Coins, Bodies, Games, and Gold: The Politics of Meaning in Archaic Greece*. Classics/Ancient history. Princeton.

Kyrieleis, H. 1996. *Der grosse Kuros von Samos*. Samos 10. Bonn.

Laffineur, R. 1986. *Amathonte III, Testimonia 3, L'orfèvrerie (R. Laffineur), avec la contribution d'A. Forgeau, Scarabées, Scaraboïdes et Cônes et A. Hermary, La coupe en argent du British Museum. Éditions Recherche sur les Civilisations – École Française d'Athènes, 'Mémoire' no. 67, Études Chypriotes VII, 1986*. Paris.

2010. 'Thorikos', in Cline, E. H. ed., *The Oxford Handbook of the Bronze Age Aegean (ca. 3000–1000 BC)*. New York; Oxford, 712–721.

Lambert, S. D. 2002. 'The Sacrificial Calendar of Athens', *The Annual of the British School at Athens* 97, 353–399.

Langdon, S. 1987. 'Gift Exchange in the Geometric Sanctuaries', in Linders, T., and Nordquist, G. eds., *Gifts to the Gods: Proceedings of the Uppsala Symposium 1985*. Acta Universitatis Upsaliensis. Uppsala; Stockholm, 107–113.

Langgut, D., Finkelstein, I., and Litt, T. 2013. 'Climate and the Late Bronze Collapse: New Evidence from the Southern Levant', *Tel Aviv* 40 (2), 149–175.

Laum, B. 1924. *Heiliges Geld: eine historische Untersuchung über den sakralen Ursprung des Geldes*. Tübingen.

Lavelle, B. M. 2005. *Fame, Money, and Power: The Rise of Peisistratos and 'Democratic' Tyranny at Athens*. Ann Arbor.

Le Rider, G. 2001. *La naissance de la monnaie: pratiques monétaires de l'Orient ancien*. Histoires. Paris.

Le Rider, G., and Verdan, S. 2002. 'La Trouvaille d'Érétrie: Réserve d'un Orfèvre ou Dépôt Monétaire?', *Antike Kunst* 45, 133–152.

Leach, J. W. 1983. 'Introduction', in Leach, J. W., and Leach, E. R. eds., *The Kula: New*

Perspectives on Massim Exchange. Cambridge, 1–26.

Leach, J. W., and Leach, E. 1983. *The Kula: New Perspectives on Massim Exchange*. Cambridge.

Leão, D. F., and Rhodes, P. J. 2015. *The Laws of Solon: A New Edition with Introduction, Translation and Commentary*. Library of Classical Studies 7. London.

Lemos, I. S. 1998. 'Euboea and Its Aegean Koine', in Bats, M., and D'Agostino, B. eds., *Euboica: L'Eubea e la presenza euboica in Calcidica e in Occidente: Atti del convegno internazionale di Napoli, 13–16 novembre 1996*. Napoli, 45–58.

2002. *The Protogeometric Aegean: The Archaeology of the Late Eleventh and Tenth Centuries BC*. Oxford.

Leone, B. 2012. 'A Trade Route between Euboea and the Northern Aegean', *Mediterranean Archaeology* 25, 229–241.

2017. 'Leggi di Eretria', *Axon* 1 (1), 63–74.

Levy, J. 1924. *Worterbuch uber die Talmudim und Midraschim*. Berlin.

Levy, T. E., Adams, R. B., Najjar, M., Hauptmann, A., Anderson, J. D., Brandl, B., Robinson, M. A., and Higham, T. 2004. 'Reassessing the Chronology of Biblical Edom: New Excavations and 14C dates from Khirbat en-Nahas (Jordan)', *Antiquity* 78 (302), 865–879.

Lie, A. G. 1929. *The Inscriptions of Sargon II, King of Assyria*. Paris.

Liebowitz, H. 1987. 'Late Bronze II Ivory Work in Palestine: Evidence of a Cultural Highpoint', *Bulletin of the American Schools of Oriental Research* 265, 3–24.

Liep, J. 1983. 'Ranked Exchange in Yela (Rossel Island)', in Leach, J. W., and Leach, E. R. eds., *The Kula: New Perspectives on Massim Exchange*. Cambridge, 503–525.

1999. 'Pecuniary Schismogenesis in the Massim', in Akin, D., and Robbins, J. eds., *Money and Modernity: State and Local Currencies in Melanesia*. ASAO Monograph Series. Pittsburgh, 131–150.

Lilyquist, C. 1996. 'Stone Vessels at Kamid el-Loz, Lebanon: Egyptian, Egyptianizing, or Non-Egyptian? A Question at Sites from the Sudan to Iraq to the Greek Mainland', in Hachmann, R. ed., *Kamid el-Loz. 16. Schatzhaus Studien*. Bonn, 133–173.

2012. 'Treasures from Tell Basta: Goddesses, Officials, and Artists in an International Age', *Metropolitan Museum Journal* 47 (1), 9–72.

Lindenlauf, A. 2006. 'Recycling of Votive Offerings in Greek Sanctuaries: Epigraphical and Archaeological Evidence.', in Mattusch, C. C., Donohue, A. A., and Brauer, A. eds., *Proceedings of the XVIth International Congress of Classical Archaeology, Boston, August 23–26, 2003. Common Ground: Archaeology, Art, Science, and Humanities*. Oxford, 30–32.

Linders, T. 1987. 'Gods, Gifts, Society', in Linders, T., and Nordquist, G. eds., *Gifts to the Gods: Proceedings of the Uppsala Symposium 1985*. Acta Universitatis Upsaliensis. Uppsala; Stockholm, 115–122.

Lipiński, E. 1978. 'The Elegy on the Fall of Sidon in Isaiah 23', *Eretz-Israel: Archaeological, Historical and Geographical Studies* 14, 79*–88*.

1979. 'Les Temples Néo-Assyriens et les Origines du Monnayage', in Lipiński, E. ed., *State and Temple Economy in the Ancient Near East: Proceedings of the International Conference Organized by the Katholieke Universiteit Leuven from the 10th to the 14th of April 1978*. Orientalia Lovaniensia analecta. Leuven, 564–588.

1988. 'In Search of the Etymology of Some Semitic Loan-Words', in Arbeitman, Y. L. ed., *Fucus: A Semitic/Afrasian Gathering in Remembrance of Albert Ehrman*. Amsterdam Studies in the Theory and History of Linguistic Science. Series IV, Current Issues in Linguistic Theory. Amsterdam; Philadelphia, 325–333.

Lipschits, O. 2006. 'On Cash-Boxes and Finding or Not Finding Books: Jehoash's and Josiah's Decisions to Repair the Temple', in Amit, Y., Ben-Zvi, E., Finkelstein, I., and Lipschits, O. eds., *Essays on Ancient Israel in Its Near Eastern Context: A Tribute to Nadav Na'aman*. Winona Lake, 239–254.

Lipschits, O., Sergi, O., and Koch, I. 2010. 'Royal Judahite Jar Handles: Reconsidering the Chronology of the lmlk Stamp Impressions', *Tel Aviv* 37 (1), 3–32.

2011. 'Judahite Stamped and Incised Jar Handles: A Tool for Studying the History of Late Monarchic Judah', *Tel Aviv* 38 (1), 5–41.

Liverani, M. 1992. *Studies on the Annals of Ashurnasirpal II.* Quaderni di Geografia storica/Universita di Roma 'la Sapienza', Dipartimento di scienze storiche, archeologiche e antropologiche dell'antichita. Roma.

2003. 'The Influence of Political Institutions on Trade in the Ancient Near East (Late Bronze to Early Iron Age)', in Zaccagnini, C. ed., *Mercanti e politica nel mondo antico.* Saggi di Storia Antica, 22. Rome, 119–137.

Lloyd, A. 2007. 'Book II', in Murray, O., and Moreno, A. eds., *A Commentary on Herodotus books I–IV.* Oxford, 219–378.

Lordkipanidze, O. 2001. 'The Golden Fleece: Myth, Euhemeristic Explanation and Archaeology', *Oxford Journal of Archaeology* 20 (1), 1–38.

Loud, G. 1948. *Megiddo II: Seasons of 1935–39.* Chicago.

Luckenbill, D. D. 1924. *The Annals of Sennacherib.* The University of Chicago Oriental Institute Publications. Chicago.

Luke, J. 2003. *Ports of Trade, Al Mina, and Geometric Greek Pottery in the Levant.* Oxford.

Macalister, R. A. S. 1912. *The Excavation of Gezer, 1902–1905 and 1907–1909.* Vol. 2. London.

Malinowski, B. 1920. 'Kula: The Circulating Exchange of Valuables in the Archipelagoes of Eastern New Guinea', *Man* 20, 97–105.

1921. 'The Primitive Economics of the Trobriand Islanders', *The Economic Journal* 31 (121), 1–16.

1922. *Argonauts of the Western Pacific: An Account of Native Enterprise and Adventure in the Archipelagoes of Melanesian New Guinea.* London; New York.

Malkin, I. 1998. *The Returns of Odysseus: Colonization and Ethnicity.* Berkeley; London.

2011. *A Small Greek World: Networks in the Ancient Mediterranean.* Greeks overseas. Oxford.

Mankiw, N. G. 2004. *Principles of Economics.* Mason.

Maran, J. 2006. 'Coming to Terms with the Past: Ideology and Power in Late Helladic IIIC', in Deger-Jalkotzy, S., and Lemos, I. S. eds., *Ancient Greece: From the Mycenaean Palaces to the Age of Homer.* Edinburgh, 123–150.

2012. 'Ceremonial Feasting Equipment, Social Space and Interculturality in Post-Palatial Tiryns', in Maran, J., and Stockhammer, P. eds., *Materiality and Social Practice: Transformative Capacities of Intercultural Encounters.* Oxford, 121–136.

Marinatos, S. 1960. 'Lausitzer Goldschmuck in Tiryns', in Eckstein, F. ed., *Theoria: Festschrift für W.-H.Schuchhardt.* Deutsche Beiträge zur Altertumswissenschaft. Doppelband 12/13. Baden-Baden, 151–157.

Markoe, G. 2000. *The Phoenicians.* Peoples of the Past. Berkeley.

Marshall, F. H. 1911. *Catalogue of the Jewellery, Greek, Etruscan, and Roman, in the Departments of Antiquities, British Museum.* London.

Martin Pruvot, C., Reber, K., Theurillat, T., and Ecole suisse d'archeologie en Grece, Antikenmuseum Basel und Sammlung Ludwig and Ethnikon Archaiologikon Mouseion 2010. *Ausgegraben! Schweizer Archäologen erforschen die griechische Stadt Eretria: Eine Ausstellung der Schweizerischen Archäologischen Schule in Griechenland in Zusammenarbeit mit dem Antikenmuseum Basel und Sammlung Ludwig.* Basel; Gollion.

Marx, K. 1970. *A Contribution to the Critique of Political Economy.* Moscow.

1976. *Capital: A Critique of Political Economy.* Vol. I. Penguin Classics. London.

Master, D. M. 2001. 'State Formation Theory and the Kingdom of Ancient Israel', *Journal of Near Eastern Studies* 60 (2), 117–131.

2010. 'Institutions of Trade in 1 And 2 Kings', *The Books of Kings*, 501–516.

2014. 'Economy and Exchange in the Iron Age Kingdoms of the Southern Levant', *Bulletin of the American Schools of Oriental Research* 372, 81–97.

Matthäus, H. 2001. 'Studies on the Interrelations of Cyprus and Italy during the 11th to 9th Centuries B.C.: A Pan-Mediterranean Perspective', in Bonfante, L., and Karageorghis, V. eds., *Italy and Cyprus in Antiquity 1500–450 B.C.: Proceedings of an International Symposium Held at the Italian Academy for Advanced Studies in America at Columbia University, November 16–18, 2000*. Nicosia, 153–214.

Matthews, R. 1994. 'Imperial Catastrophe or Local Incident? An Akkadian Hoard from Tell Brak, Syria', *Cambridge Archaeological Journal* 4 (2), 290–302.

Maurer, B. 2006. 'The Anthropology of Money', *Annual Review of Anthropology* 35 (1), 15–36.

Mauss, M. 1970. *The Gift: Forms and Functions of Exchange in Archaic Societies*. London.

Maxwell-Hyslop, K. R. 1971. *Western Asiatic Jewellery c.3000–612 B.C.* Methuen's Handbooks of Archaeology. London.

1984. 'Appendix B: The Gold Jewellery, in Excavations at Tawilan in Southern Jordan, 1982. By C.-M. Bennett', *Levant* 16 (1), 22–23.

Mazar, A. 1993. 'Beth Shean in the Iron Age: Preliminary Report and Conclusions of the 1990–1991 Excavations', *Israel Exploration Journal* 43 (4), 201–229.

1997. 'Iron Age Chronology: A Reply to I. Finkelstein', *Levant* 29 (1), 157–167.

2006. 'Beth-Shean from the Late Bronze Age IIB to the Medieval Period: A Summary', in Mazar, A. ed., *Excavations at Tel Beth-Shean, 1989–1996. Vol. I. From the Late Bronze Age IIB to the Medieval Period*. The Hebrew University of Jerusalem, the Institute of Archaeology. Jerusalem, 26–47.

2009. 'Introduction and Overview', in Panitz-Cohen, N., and Mazar, A. eds., *Excavations at Tel Beth-Shean 1989–1996. Vol. III. The 13th–11th Century BCE Strata in Areas N and S*. The Hebrew University of Jerusalem, the Institute of Archaeology. Jerusalem, 1–32.

2010. 'Tel Beth-Shean: History and Archaeology', in Kratz, R. G., and Spieckermann, H. eds., *One God, One Cult, One Nation: Archaeological and Biblical Perspectives*. Beihefte zur Zeitschrift für die alttestamentliche Wissenschaft 405. Berlin; New York, 239–271.

2011. 'The Iron Age Chronology Debate: Is the Gap Narrowing? Another Viewpoint', *Near Eastern Archaeology* 74 (2), 105–111.

Mazar, B. 1963. 'Excavations at the Oasis of Engedi', *Archaeology* 16, 99–107.

Mazar, E. 2004. *The Phoenician Family Tomb N.1 at the Northern Cemetery of Achziv (10th–6th centuries BCE): Sam Turner Expedition, Final Report of the Excavations*. Cuadernos de arqueología mediterránea. Vol. 10. Barcelona.

Mazarakis Ainian, A. 1997. *From Rulers' Dwellings to Temples: Architecture, Religion and Society in Early Iron Age Greece (1100–700 B.C.)*. Studies in Mediterranean Archaeology. Jonsered.

McDonald, W. A., and Coulson, W. D. E. 1983. 'The Dark Age at Nichoria: A Perspective', in McDonald, W. A., Coulson, W. D. E., and Rosser, J. eds., *Excavations at Nichoria in Southwest Greece. Vol. 3. Dark Age and Byzantine Occupation*. Minneapolis, 316–329.

McGeough, K. M. 2007. *Exchange Relationships at Ugarit*. Ancient Near Eastern Studies Supplement. Leuven; Dudley.

McInerney, J. 2010. *The Cattle of the Sun: Cows and Culture in the World of the Ancient Greeks*. Princeton.

Meadows, A. 2008. 'Part 2: Coinage', in Oleson, J. P. ed., *The Oxford Handbook of Engineering and Technology in the Classical World*. Oxford, 769–777.

2009. 'Money in an Ideal World: *Plato's Laws* and the Dual Nature of Coinage' *Κερματια φιλιας. Τιμητικός τόμος για τον Ιωάννη Τουράτσογλου*. Athens, 25–31.

Meeks, N. D., and Craddock, P. T. 2013. 'Annexe 4: Scientific Examination of Two Sherds with Gold Particles', in Verdan, S. ed., *Eretria XXII. Le sanctuaire d'Apollon Daphnéphoros à l'époque géométrique*. Gollion; Lausanne, 271–273.

Meiggs, R. 1982. *Trees and Timber in the Ancient Mediterranean World*. Oxford.

Mele, A. 1979. *Il commercio Greco arcaico: Prexis ed emporie*. Publications du Centre Jean Bérard. Rome.

Melis, M. G. 2014. 'Silver in the Neolithic and Eneolithic Sardinia', in Meller, H., Risch, R., and Pernicka, E. eds., *Metalle der Macht – Frühes Gold und Silber: 6. Mitteldeutscher Archäologentag vom 17. bis 19. Oktober 2013 in Halle (Saale) [Metals of Power – Early Gold and Silver: 6th Archaeological Conference of Central Germany, October 17–19, 2013 in Halle (Saale)]*. Tagungen des Landesmuseums für Vorgeschichte Halle. Halle Saale, 483–494.

Melitz, J. 1970. 'The Polanyi School of Anthropology on Money: An Economist's View', *American Anthropologist* 72 (5), 1020–1040.

Merkel, S. W. 2016. *Silver and the Silver Economy at Hedeby*. Der Anschnitt. Beiheft 33. Bochum.

Merrillees, R. S. 2003. 'Egyptian Foreign Relations (Late Bronze Age and Iron Age)', in Stampolidis, N. C., and Karageorghis, V. eds., *Ploes – Sea Routes: Interconnections in the Mediterranean, 16th–6th c. BC: Proceedings of the International Symposium Held at Rethymnon, Crete, September 29th–October 2nd, 2002*. Athens, 35–39.

Metcalf, D. M. 2007. 'Regions around the North Sea with a Monetised Economy in the Pre-Viking and Viking Ages', in Graham-Campbell, J., and Williams, G. eds., *Silver Economy in the Viking Age*. Walnut Creek, 1–11.

Michailidou, A. 2010. 'Measuring by Weight in the Late Bronze Age Aegean: The People Behind the Measuring Tools', in Morley, I., and Renfrew, C. eds., *The Archaeology of Measurement: Comprehending Heaven, Earth and Time in Ancient Societies*. Cambridge; New York, 71–87.

Michel, C. 2001. *Correspondance des marchands de Kanis au début du IIe millénaire avant J.-C.* Paris.

Millard, A. 2011. 'Are There Anachronisms in the Books of Samuel?', in Khan, G., and Lipton, D. eds., *Studies on the Text and Versions of the Hebrew Bible in Honour of Robert Gordon*. Vetus Testamentum, Supplements. Leiden, 39–48.

Miller, D. 1987. *Material Culture and Mass Consumption*. Oxford.

2010. *Stuff*. Cambridge.

Misailidou-Despotidou, V. 2011. *Chalkina kosmēmata archaïkēn chronēn apo tē Makedonia: Ereuna sta chalkina kosmēmata tēn nekrotapheīen tēs Agias Paraskeuēs kai tēs Neas Philadelpheias*. Dēmosieumata Archaiologikou Institoutou Makedonikōn kai Thrakikōn Spoudōn. Thessaloniki.

Mitchiner, M. 2004. *Ancient Trade and Early Coinage*. London.

Monroe, C. M. 2005. 'Money and Trade', in Snell, D. C. ed., *A Companion to the Ancient Near East*. Malden; Oxford, 155–168.

2009. *Scales of Fate: Trade, Tradition, and Transformation in the Eastern Mediterranean, ca. 1350–1175 BCE*. Alter Orient und Altes Testament. Münster.

Montgomery, J. A. 1951. *A Critical and Exegetical Commentary on the Books of Kings*. International Critical Commentary. Edinburgh.

Moran, W. L. 1992. *The Amarna Letters*. Baltimore; London.

Moreno García, J. C. ed. 2016a. *Dynamics of Production in the Ancient Near East: 1300–500 BC*. Oxford.

2016b. 'Economies in Transition: Trade, "Money", Labour and Nomads at the Turn of the 1st Millennium BC', in Moreno García, J. C. ed., *Dynamics of Production in the Ancient Near East: 1300–500 BC*. Oxford, 1–39.

Morgan, C. 1990. *Athletes and Oracles. The Transformation of Olympia and Delphi in the Eighth Century B.C.* Cambridge.

1993. 'The Origins of Pan-Hellenism', in Marinatos, N., and Hägg, R. eds., *Greek Sanctuaries: New Approaches*. London, 14–33.

1999. *Isthmia VIII: Excavations by the University of Chicago under the Auspices of the American School of Classical Studies. The Late Bronze Age Settlement and Early Iron Age Sanctuary*. Princeton.

2003. *Early Greek States beyond the Polis*. London.

2009. 'The Early Iron Age', in Raaflaub, K. A., and van Wees, H. eds., *A Companion to Archaic Greece*. Malden; Oxford, 43–63.

Morris, I. 1986a. 'Gift and Commodity in Archaic Greece', *Man* 21 (1), 1–17.

1986b. 'The Use and Abuse of Homer', *Classical Antiquity* 5 (1), 81–138.

1987. *Burial and Ancient Society: The Rise of the Greek City-State*. New Studies in Archaeology. Cambridge.

1989. 'Circulation, Deposition and the Formation of the Greek Iron Age', *Man* 24 (3), 502–519.

1994. 'Review Article: The Athenian Economy Twenty Years after the Ancient Economy', *Classical Philology* 89 (4), 351–366.

2000. *Archaeology As Cultural History: Words and Things in Iron Age Greece*. Social Archaeology (Series). Malden; Oxford.

2003. 'Mediterraneanization', *Mediterranean Historical Review* 18 (2), 30–55.

2007. 'Early Iron Age Greece', in Scheidel, W., Morris, I., and Saller, R. P. eds., *The Cambridge Economic History of the Greco-Roman World*. Cambridge; New York, 211–241.

2009. 'The Eighth-Century Revolution', in Raaflaub, K. A., and van Wees, H. eds., *A Companion to Archaic Greece*. Malden; Oxford, 64–80.

Morris, S. P. 1984. *The Black and White Style: Athens and Aigina in the Orientalizing Period*. New Haven.

1992a. *Daidalos and the Origins of Greek Art*. Princeton.

1992b. 'Introduction', in Kopcke, G., and Tokumaru, I. eds., *Greece between East and West: 10th–8th Centuries B.C.: Papers of the Meeting at the Institute of Fine Arts, New York University, March 15–16th, 1990*. Mainz, xiii–xviii.

Moschonissioti, S. 1998. 'Excavations at Ancient Mende', in Bats, M., and D'Agostino, B. eds., *Euboica: L'Eubea e la presenza euboica in Calcidica e in Occidente: atti del convegno internazionale di Napoli, 13–16 novembre 1996*. Napoli, 255–271.

2017. 'The City of Mende during the Late Eighth and Seventh Centuries BC', in Charalambidou, X., and Morgan, C. eds., *Interpreting the Seventh Century BC: Tradition and Innovation*. Oxford, 355–363.

Muhly, J. D. 1992. 'The Crisis Years in the Mediterranean World: Transition or Cultural Disintegration?', in Joukowsky, M., and Ward, W. A. eds., *The Crisis Years: The 12th century B.C. from Beyond the Danube to the Tigris*. Dubuque, 10–26.

2011. 'Silver', in Finkelberg, M. ed., *The Homer Encyclopedia*. Chichester; Malden, 799–801.

Müller, G. G. W. 1997. 'Gedanken zur neuassyrischen "Geldwirtschaft"', in Waetzoldt, H., and Hauptmann, H. eds., *Assyrien im wandel der zeiten: XXXIXe Rencontre Assyriologique Internationale, Heidelberg 6.–10. Juli 1992*. Heidelberger Studien zum alten Orient 6. Heidelberg, 115–121.

Mullins, R. A. 2012. 'The Late Bronze and Iron Age Temples at Beth-Shean', in Kamlah, J. ed., *Temple Building and Temple Cult: Architecture and Cultic Paraphernalia of Temples in the Levant (2.–1. Mill. BCE); Proceedings of a Conference on the Occasion of the 50th Anniversary of the Institute of Biblical Archaeology at the University of Tübingen (28th–30th of May 2010)*. Wiesbaden, 127–157.

Münger, S., and Levy, T. E. 2014. 'The Iron Age Egyptian Amulet Assemblage', in Levy, T. E., Najjar, M., and Ben-Yosef, E. eds., *New Insights into the Iron Age Archaeology of Edom, Southern Jordan: Surveys, Excavations, and*

Research from the University of California, San Diego – Department of Antiquities of Jordan, Edom Lowlands Regional Archaeology Project (ELRAP). Monumenta archaeological: vol. 35. Los Angeles, 741–765.

Munn, N. D. 1983. 'Gawan Kula: Spatiotemporal Control and the Symbolism of Influence', in Leach, J. W., and Leach, E. R. eds., *The Kula: New Perspectives on Massim Exchange.* Cambridge, 277–308.

Murgan, A. M., and Kemmers, F. 2016. 'Temples, Hoards and Pre(?)Monetary Practices – Case Studies from Mainland Italy and Sicily in the 1st Millennium B.C.', in Baitinger, H. ed., *Materielle Kultur und Identität im Spannungsfeld zwischen mediterraner Welt und Mitteleuropa: Akten der internationalen Tagung am Römisch-Germanischen Zentralmuseum Mainz, 22.–24. Oktober 2014: Abschlusstagung des DFG-Projekts 'Metallfunde als Zeugnis für die Interaktion zwischen Griechen und Indigenen auf Sizilien zwischen dem 8. und 5. Jahrhundert v. Chr.' [Material Culture and Identity between the Mediterranean World and Central Europe].* RGZM-Tagungen. Mainz, 277–290.

Murray, A. S., Smith, A. H., and Walters, H. B. 1900. *Excavations in Cyprus, Bequest of Miss E. T. Turner to the British Museum.* London.

Murray, O. [1980] 1993. *Early Greece.* Second edition. Fontana History of the Ancient World. London.

Mussche, H. F. 1967. *Thorikos 1965: Rapport préliiminaire sur la troisième campagne de fouilles [voorlopig verslag over de derde opgravingscampagne].* Bruxelles.

Na'aman, N. 1981. 'Economic Aspects of the Egyptian Occupation of Canaan', *Israel Exploration Journal* 31 (3), 172–185.

1986. 'Historical and Chronological Notes on the Kingdoms of Israel and Judah in the Eighth Century B.C.', *Vetus Testamentum* 36 (1), 71–92.

1991. 'The Kingdom of Judah under Josiah', *Tel Aviv* 18 (1), 3–71.

1994. 'The "Conquest of Canaan" in the Book of Joshua and in History', in Finkelstein, I., and Na'aman, N. eds., *From Nomadism to Monarchy: Archaeological and Historical Aspects of Early Israel.* Jerusalem; Washington, DC, 218–281.

1998. 'Royal Inscriptions and the Histories of Joash and Ahaz, Kings of Judah', *Vetus Testamentum* 48 (3), 333–349.

2003. 'Ekron under the Assyrian and Egyptian Empires', *Bulletin of the American Schools of Oriental Research* 332, 81–91.

2007. 'When and How Did Jerusalem Become a Great City? The Rise of Jerusalem As Judah's Premier City in the Eighth-Seventh Centuries B.C.E.', *Bulletin of the American Schools of Oriental Research* 347, 21–56.

2010. 'The Date of the List of Towns That Received the Spoil of Amalek (1 Sam 30:26–31)', *Tel Aviv* 37 (2), 175–187.

2013. 'The Kingdom of Judah in the 9th Century BCE: Text Analysis versus Archaeological Research', *Tel Aviv* 40 (2), 247–276.

2014. 'Dismissing the Myth of a Flood of Israelite Refugees in the Late Eighth Century BCE', *Zeitschrift für die alttestamentliche Wissenschaft* 126 (1), 1–14.

Nam, R. S. 2012. *Portrayals of Economic Exchange in the Book of Kings.* Leiden.

Neeft, C. W. 2012. 'Corinthian Pottery in Thasos and Argilos: Preliminary Observations', in Tiverios, M. A., Arvanitakē, A., Misaēlidou-Despotidou, V., and Manakidou, H. P. eds., *Hē keramikē tēs archaikēs epoches sto Voreio Aigaio kai tēn peripheréia tou (700–480 p.Ch.): Praktika archaiologikēs synantēsēs, Thessalonikē, 19–22 Maiou 2011.* Dēmosieumata Archaiologikou Institoutou Makedonikōn kai Thrakikōn Spoudōn. Thessalonikē, 189–196.

2020. *Argilos 1: The Corinthian Pottery.* Thessaloniki.

Negbi, O. 1970. *The Hoards of Goldwork from Tell El-'Ajjul.* Göteborg.

Nerantzis, N., and Papadopoulos, S. 2013. 'Reassessment and New Data on the

Diachronic Relationship of Thassos Island with Its Indigenous Metal Resources: A Review', *Archaeological and Anthropological Sciences* 5 (3), 183–196.

Netz, R. 2002. 'Counter Culture: Towards a History of Greek Numeracy', *History of Science* 40, 321–352.

Nezafati, N., and Pernicka, E. 2012. 'Early Silver Production in Iran', *Iranian Archaeology* 3, 38–45.

Nicolet-Pierre, H. 2006. 'Les talents d'Homère', in van Alfen, P. G. ed., *Agoranomia: Studies in Money and Exchange Presented to John H. Kroll*. New York, 1–20.

Nijboer, A. J. 2008. 'A Phoenician Family Tomb, Lefkandi, Huelva and the Tenth Century BC in the Mediterranean', in Sagona, C. ed., *Beyond the Homeland: Markers in Phoenician Chronology*. Ancient Near Eastern Studies, suppl. 28. Leuven; Paris; Dudley, 365–377.

Nodet, É. 1980. 'Objets en métal', in Briend, J., and Humbert, J. eds., *Tell Keisan (1971–1976): Une cite phenicienne en Galilee*. Fribourg; Paris, 323–326.

Noeske, H.-Chr. 1991. 'Ein Hacksilberfund aus Elephantine', in Noeske, H.-Chr., and Schubert, H. eds. *Die Münze: Bild – Botschaft – Bedeutung. Festschrift für Maria R.-Alföldi*. Frankfurt, 342–351.

1993. 'Prämonetäre Wertmesser und Münzfunde aus Elephantine', *Mitteilungen des Deutschen Archäologischen Instituts. Abteilung Kairo* 49, 203–209.

Nriagu, J. O. 1985. 'Cupellation: The Oldest Quantitative Chemical Process', *Journal of Chemical Education* 62 (8), 668–674.

Oddy, A. 1983. 'Assaying in Antiquity', *Gold Bulletin* 16 (2), 52–59.

Ofer, A. 1994. '"All the Hill Country of Judah": From a Settlement Fringe to a Prosperous Monarchy', in Finkelstein, I., and Na'aman, N. eds., *From Nomadism to Monarchy: Archaeological and Historical Aspects of Early Israel*. Jerusalem; Washington, DC, 92–121.

Ogden, J. 1982. *Jewellery of the Ancient World*. London.

1990/1991. 'Gold in a Time of Bronze and Iron', *Journal of the Ancient Chronology Forum* 4, 6–14.

1995. 'The Gold Jewellery', in Bennett, C. M., and Bienkowski, P. eds., *Excavations at Tawilan in Southern Jordan*. Oxford, 69–78.

Oppenheim, A. L. 1947. 'A Fiscal Practice of the Ancient Near East', *Journal of Near Eastern Studies* 6 (2), 116–120.

1957. 'A Bird's-Eye View of Mesapotamian Economic History', in Polanyi, K., Arensberg, C. M., and Pearson, H. W. eds., *Trade and Market in the Early Empires: Economies in History and Theory*. Glencoe, 27–37.

1977. *Ancient Mesopotamia: Portrait of a Dead Civilization*. Chicago.

Osborne, R. 1996. 'Pots, Trade and the Archaic Greek Economy', *Antiquity* 70 (267), 31–44.

2007. 'Archaic Greece', in Scheidel, W., Morris, I., and Saller, R. P. eds., *The Cambridge Economic History of the Greco-Roman World*. Cambridge; New York, 277–301.

[1996] 2009. *Greece in the Making, 1200–479 B.C.* Second edition. Routledge History of the Ancient World. London.

Pafford, I. A. 2006. 'Cult Fees and the Ritual of Money in Greek Sanctuaries of the Classical and Hellenistic Period', PhD dissertation, University of California, Berkeley.

2013. 'Priestly Portion vs. Cult Fees – The Finances of Greek Sanctuaries', in Horster, M. ed., *Cities and Priests: Cult Personnel in Asia Minor and the Aegean Islands from the Hellenistic to the Imperial Period*. Religionsgeschichtliche Versuche und Vorarbeiten. Boston, 49–64.

Painter, K. S., with an appendix by Hunter, F. 2013. 'Hacksilber: A Means of Exchange?', in Hunter, F., and Painter, K. S. eds., *Late Roman Silver: The Traprain Treasure in Context*. Edinburgh, 215–242.

Panagiotopoulos, D. 2006. 'Foreigners in Egypt in the Time of Hatshepsut and Thutmose III', in Cline, E. H., and O'Connor, D. B.

eds., *Thutmose III: A New Biography*. Ann Arbor, 370–412.

Panitz-Cohen, N., and Mazar, A. 2009. 'Chapter 4: Area S: Stratigraphy and Architecture', in Panitz-Cohen, N., and Mazar, A. eds., *Excavations at Tel Beth-Shean 1989–1996. Vol. III. The 13th–11th Century BCE Strata in Areas N and S*. The Hebrew University of Jerusalem, the Institute of Archaeology. Jerusalem, 94–194.

Panitz-Cohen, N., Mullins, R. A., and Bonfil, R. 2013. 'Northern Exposure: Launching Excavations at Tell Abil el-Qameḥ (Abel Beth Maacah)', *STRATA: Bulletin of the Anglo-Israel Archaeological Society* 31, 27–42.

2015. 'Second Preliminary Report of the Excavations at Tell Abil el Qameḥ (Abel Beth Maacah)', *STRATA: Bulletin of the Anglo-Israel Archaeological Society* 33, 35–59.

Panitz-Cohen, N., Mullins, R. A., Yahalom-Mack, N., and Lavi, M. 2016. 'A Silver Lining at Abel Beth Maacah', *Biblical Archaeology Review* July/August, 22–23.

Papadopoulos, J. K. 1994. 'Early Iron Age Potters' Marks in the Aegean', *Hesperia: The Journal of the American School of Classical Studies at Athens* 63 (4), 437–507.

1996. 'Euboians in Macedonia? A Closer Look', *Oxford Journal of Archaeology* 15 (2), 151–181.

1997. 'Phantom Euboians', *Journal of Mediterranean Archaeology* 10 (2), 191–219.

2002. 'Minting Identity: Coinage, Ideology and the Economics of Colonization in Akhaian Magna Graecia', *Cambridge Archaeological Journal* 12 (1), 21–55.

2011. '"Phantom Euboians" – A Decade On', in Rupp, D. W., and Tomlinson, J. E. eds., *Euboea and Athens: Proceedings of a Colloquium in Memory of Malcolm B. Wallace: Athens 26–27 June 2009*. Publications of the Canadian Institute in Greece. Toronto, 113–133.

2012. 'Money, Art, and the Construction of Value in the Ancient Mediterranean', in Papadopoulos, J. K., and Urton, G. eds., *The Construction of Value in the Ancient World*. Cotsen Advanced Seminar Series. Los Angeles, 261–287.

2016. 'The Early History of the Greek Alphabet: New Evidence from Eretria and Methone', *Antiquity* 90 (353), 1238–1254.

2017. 'To Write and to Paint: More Early Iron Age Potters' Marks in the Aegean', in Clay, J. S., Malkin, I., and Tzifopoulos, Y. eds., *Panhellenes at Methone: Graphê in Late Geometric and Protoarchaic Methone, Macedonia (ca 700 BCE)*. Berlin; Boston, 36–104.

Parker, R. 1998. 'Pleasing Thighs: Reciprocity in Greek Religion', in Gill, C., Postlethwaite, N., and Seaford, R. eds., *Reciprocity in Ancient Greece*. Oxford, 105–126.

Parry, J., and Bloch, M. eds. 1989. *Money and the Morality of Exchange*. Cambridge.

Peacock, M. S. 2011a. 'The Political Economy of Homeric Society and the Origins of Money', *Contributions to Political Economy* 30 (1), 47–65.

2011b. 'Rehabilitating Homer's Phoenicians: On Some Ancient and Modern Prejudices against Trade', *Ancient Society* 41, 1–29.

Pelloso, C. 2013. 'The Myth of the Priority of Procedure over Substance in the Light of Early Greek Epos', *Rivista di Diritto Ellenico/Review of Hellenic Law* 3, 223–275.

Pendlebury, J. D. S. 1931. 'Preliminary Report of Excavations at Tell el-'Amarnah 1930–1', *The Journal of Egyptian Archaeology* 17 (3), 233–244.

Perreault, J. Y., and Bonias, Z. 2012. 'After Zagora – Andrian Colonization in the Northern Aegean: The Case of Argilos', *Mediterranean Archaeology* 25, 259–271.

Pernicka, E. 2014. 'Possibilities and Limitations of Provenance Studies of Ancient Silver and Gold', in Meller, H., Risch, R., and Pernicka, E. eds., *Metalle der Macht – Frühes Gold und Silber: 6. Mitteldeutscher Archäologentag vom 17. bis 19. Oktober 2013 in Halle (Saale) [Metals of Power – Early Gold and Silver: 6th Archaeological Conference of Central Germany, October 17–19, 2013 in Halle (Saale)]*. Tagungen des

Landesmuseums für Vorgeschichte Halle. Halle Saale, 153–164.

Pernicka, E., Rehren, T., and Schmitt-Strecker, S. 1998. 'Late Uruk Silver Production by Cupellation at Habuba Kabira, Syria', *Metallurgica Antiqua, der Anschnitt,* 8, 123–134.

Pernicka, E., and Wagner, G. A. 1985. 'Die metallurgische Bedeutung von Sifnos im Altertum', in Wagner, G., and Weisgerber, G. eds., *Silber, Blei und Gold auf Sifnos: Prähistorische und antike Metallproduktion.* Der Anschnitt. Beiheft. Bochum, 200–211.

Petocz, D. 1995. 'Area II', in Bennett, C. M., and Bienkowski, P. eds., *Excavations at Tawilan in Southern Jordan.* Oxford, 23–38.

Petrie, W. M. F. 1928. *Gerar.* Publications of the Egyptian Research Account and British School of Archaeology in Egypt. London.

1934. *Ancient Gaza IV: Tell el Ajjul.* Publications of the Egyptian Research Account. London.

Pettegrew, D. K. 2011. 'The *Diolkos* of Corinth', in *American Journal of Archaeology* 115 (4), 549–574.

Peyronel, L. 2010. 'Ancient Near Eastern Economics: The Silver Question between Methodology and Archaeological Data', in Matthiae, P., Pinnock, F., Nigro, L., and Marchetti, N. eds., *Proceedings of the 6th International Congress on the Archaeology of the Ancient Near East.* Vol. 1. Wiesbaden, 925–948.

2014. 'Between the Archaic Market and Gift Exchange: The Role of Silver in the Embedded Economies of the Ancient Near East during the Bronze Age', in Carlà, F., and Gori, M. eds., *Gift Giving and the 'Embedded' Economies in the Ancient World.* Heidelberg, 355–376.

Pfeiffer, S. 2013. 'Egypt and Greece before Alexander', in Grajetzki, W., and Wendrich, W. eds., *UCLA Encyclopedia of Egyptology.* Los Angeles. http://digital2.library.ucla.edu/viewItem.do?ark=21198/zz002hj251.

Philipp, H. 1981. *Olympische Forschungen, Vol. 13. Bronzeschmuck aus Olympia.* Berlin.

Polanyi, K. 1944. *The Great Transformation.* New York.

1968a. 'The Economy As Instituted Process', in Dalton, G. ed., *Primitive, Archaic, and Modern Economies: Essays of Karl Polanyi.* Boston, 139–174.

1968b. 'The Semantics of Money-Uses', in Dalton, G. ed., *Primitive, Archaic, and Modern Economies: Essays of Karl Polanyi.* Boston, 175–203.

Polanyi, K., Arensberg, C. M., and Pearson, H. W. eds. 1957. *Trade and Market in the Early Empires: Economies in History and Theory.* Glencoe.

Polignac, F. de [1984] 1995. *Cults, Territory, and the Origins of the Greek City-State.* Chicago.

Popham, M. R., and Lemos, I. S. 1995. 'A Euboian Warrior Trader', in *Oxford Journal of Archaeology* 14 (2), 151–157.

1996. *Lefkandi III: The Toumba Cemetery: The Excavations of 1981, 1984, 1986 and 1992–4. Plates.* Supplementary volume 29, British School at Athens. London.

Popham, M. R., Calligas, P. G., and Sackett, L. H. eds. 1993. *Lefkandi II: The Protogeometric Building at Toumba. Part 2. The Excavation, Architecture and Finds.* Supplementary volume 23, British School at Athens. London.

Popham, M. R., Sackett, L. H., and Themelis, P. G. eds. 1980. *Lefkandi I: The Iron Age. The Settlement, the Cemeteries.* Supplementary volume 11, British School of Archaeology at Athens. London.

Postgate, J. N. 1973. *The Governor's Palace Archive.* Cuneiform Texts from Nimrud. London.

1974. *Taxation and Conscription in the Assyrian Empire.* Studia Pohl. Series maior. Rome.

1979. 'The Economic Structure of the Assyrian Empire', in Larsen, M. T. ed., *Power and Propaganda: A Symposium on Ancient Empires.* Mesopotamia. Copenhagen, 193–221.

Powell, M. A. 1978. 'A Contribution to the History of Money in Mesopotamia Prior to the Invention of Coinage', in Hrouška,

B., and Komoróczy, G. eds., *Festschrift Lubor Matouš*. Vol. II. Budapest, 211–243.

1992. 'Weights and Measures', in Freedman, D. N. ed., *The Anchor Bible Dictionary*. Vol. 6. New York, 897–908.

1996. 'Money in Mesopotamia', *Journal of the Economic and Social History of the Orient* 39 (3, Money in the Orient), 224–242.

1999. '*Wir müssen alle unsere Nische nutzen*: Monies, Motives, and Methods in Babylonian Economics', in Dercksen, J. G. ed., *Trade and Finance in Ancient Mesopotamia: Proceeding of the First MOS symposium (Leiden, 1997)*. Leiden, 5–24.

Price, M. J. 1983. 'Thoughts on the Beginnings of Coinage', in Brooke, C. N. L., Stewart, B. H. I. H., Pollard, J. G., and Volk, T. R. eds., *Studies in Numismatic Method, Presented to Philip Grierson*. Cambridge, 1–10.

Price, M., and Waggoner, N. 1975. *Archaic Greek Coinage: The Asyut Hoard*. London.

Pritchett, W. K. 1971. *Ancient Greek Military Practices: Part I*. University of California Publications. Classical Studies. Berkeley.

Propp, W. H. 2006. *Exodus 19–40: A New Translation with Introduction and Commentary*. The Anchor Bible. New York; London.

Pryor, F. L. 1977. *The Origins of the Economy: A Comparative Study of Distribution in Primitive and Peasant Economies*. New York.

Psoma, S. E. 2011. 'The Law of Nicophon (*SEG* 26.72) and Athenian Imitations', *Revue Belge de Numismatique et de Sillographie* 157, 27–36.

2015. 'Did the So-Called Thraco-Macedonian Standard Exist?', in Wartenberg, U., and Amandry, M. eds., *Kairos: Contributions to Numismatics in Honor of Basil Demetriadi*. New York, 167–190.

2016. 'Choosing and Changing Monetary Standards in the Greek World during the Archaic and the Classical Periods', in Harris, E. M., Lewis, D. M., and Woolmer, M. eds., *The Ancient Greek Economy: Markets, Households and City-States*. New York, 90–115.

Pulak, C. 1988. 'The Bronze Age Shipwreck at Ulu Burun, Turkey: 1985 Campaign', *American Journal of Archaeology* 92 (1), 1–37.

1996. 'Analysis of the Weight Assemblages from the Late Bronze Age Shipwrecks at Uluburun and Cape Gelidonya, Turkey', PhD dissertation, Texas A&M University.

2000. 'The Balance Weights from the Late Bronze Age Shipwreck at Uluburun', in Pare, C. F. E. ed., *Metals Make the World Go Round: The Supply and Circulation of Metals in Bronze Age Europe: Proceedings of a Conference Held at the University of Birmingham in June 1997*. Oxford, 247–266.

2001. 'The Cargo of the Uluburun Ship and Evidence for Trade with the Aegean and Beyond', in Bonfante, L., and Karageorghis, V. eds., *Italy and Cyprus in Antiquity 1500–450 B.C.: Proceedings of an International Symposium Held at the Italian Academy for Advanced Studies in America at Columbia University, November 16–18, 2000*. Nicosia, 13–60.

2006. 'The Balance Weights from the Uluburun and Cape Gelidonya Shipwrecks (*Abstract*)', in Alberti, M. E., Ascalone, E., and Peyronel, L. eds., *Weights in Context: Bronze Age Weighing Systems of Eastern Mediterranean: Chronology, Typology, Material and Archaeological Contexts: Proceedings of the International Colloquium, Roma 22nd–24th November 2004*. Studi e materiali (Rome, Italy). Roma, 47–48.

2008. 'The Uluburun Shipwreck and Late Bronze Age Trade', in Aruz, J., Benzel, K., and Evans, J. M. eds., *Beyond Babylon: Art, Trade, and Diplomacy in the Second Millennium B.C.* New York; London, 289–385.

Pye, M. 2014. *The Edge of the World: How the North Sea Made Us Who We Are*. London.

Quiggin, A. H. 1949. *A Survey of Primitive Money: The Beginning of Currency*. New York; London.

Qviller, B. 1981. 'The Dynamics of the Homeric Society', *Symbolae Osloenses* 56 (1), 109–155.

Raaflaub, K. A. 1998. 'A Historian's Headache: How to Read "Homeric Society"?', in Fisher, N. R. E., and van Wees, H. eds., *Archaic Greece: New Approaches and New Evidence*. London, 169–193.

2008. 'Homeric Warriors and Battles: Trying to Resolve Old Problems', *Classical World* 101 (4), 469–483.

Radford, R. A. 1945. 'The Economic Organisation of a P.O.W. Camp', *Economica* 12 (48), 189–201.

Radner, K. 1999. 'Money in the Neo-Assyrian Empire', in Dercksen, J. G. ed., *Trade and Finance in Ancient Mesopotamia: Proceeding of the First MOS Symposium (Leiden, 1997)*. Leiden, 127–157.

Rahmstorf, L. 2010. 'The Concept of Weighing during the Bronze Age in the Aegean, the Near East and Europe', in Morley, I., and Renfrew, C. eds., *The Archaeology of Measurement: Comprehending Heaven, Earth and time in Ancient Societies*. Cambridge; New York, 88–105.

2015. 'The Aegean before and after c. 2200 BC between Europe and Asia: Trade As a Prime Mover of Cultural Change', in Meller, H., Arz, H. W., Jung, R., and Risch, R. eds., *2200 BC: Ein Klimasturz als Ursache für den Zerfall der Alten Welt?: 7. Mitteldeutscher Archäologentag, vom 23. bis 26. Oktober 2014 in Halle (Saale) [2200 BC: A Climatic Breakdown As a Cause for the Collapse of the Old World?: 7th Archaeological Conference of Central Germany, October 23–26, 2014 in Halle (Saale)*. Tagungen des Landesmuseums für Vorgeschichte Halle. Halle Saale, 149–180.

2016a. 'From "Value Ascription" to Coinage: A Sketch of Monetary Developments in Western Eurasia from the Stone to the Iron Age', in Haselgrove, C., and Krmnicek, S. eds., *The Archaeology of Money: Proceedings of the Workshop 'Archaeology of Money', University of Tubingen, October 2013*. Leicester, 19–42.

2016b. 'Emerging Economic Complexity in the Aegean and Western Anatolia during the Earlier Third Millennium BC', in Molloy, B. ed., *Of Odysseys and Oddities: Scales and Modes of Interaction between Prehistoric Aegean Societies and Their Neighbors*. Oxford, 225–276.

Ramage, A. 2000. 'The Excavation and Finds', in Ramage, A., and Craddock, P. T. eds., *King Croesus' Gold: Excavations at Sardis and the History of Gold Refining*. Monograph/ Archaeological Exploration of Sardis. Cambridge, MA, 72–98.

Ramage, A., and Craddock, P. T. 2000. *King Croesus' Gold: Excavations at Sardis and the History of Gold Refining*. Monograph/ Archaeological Exploration of Sardis. Cambridge, MA.

Reade, J. 1986. 'A Hoard of Silver Currency from Achaemenid Babylon', *Iran* 24, 79–89.

Redford, D. B. 1992. *Egypt, Canaan, and Israel in Ancient Times*. Princeton.

Rehren, T., and Klappauf, L. 1995. '... ut oleum aquis: Vom Schwimmen des Silbers auf Bleiglätte', *Metalla (Bochum)* 2, 19–28.

Rhodes, P. J. 1975. 'Solon and the Numismatists', *The Numismatic Chronicle (1966–)* 15, 1–11.

1981. *A Commentary on the Aristotelian 'Athenaion politeia'*. Oxford.

Rhodes, P. J., and Osborne, R. 2003. *Greek Historical Inscriptions, 404–323 BC*. Oxford.

Richardson, N. J. 1993. *The Iliad: A Commentary. Volume VI: Books 21–24*. Cambridge.

Richter, S. L. 2017. 'The Question of Provenance and the Economics of Deuteronomy', *Journal for the Study of the Old Testament* 42 (1), 23–50.

Ridgeway, W. 1892. *The Origin of Metallic Currency and Weight Standards*. Cambridge.

Risberg, C. 1992. 'Metal-Working in Greek Sanctuaries', in Alroth, B., and Linders, T. eds., *Economics of Cult in the Ancient Greek World: Proceedings of the Uppsala Symposium 1990*. Acta Universitatis Upsaliensis. Boreas. Uppsala; Stockholm, 33–40.

1997. 'Evidence of Metal Working in Early Greek Sanctuaries', in Gillis, C., Risberg, C., and Sjöberg, B. eds., *Trade and Production in Premonetary Greece: Production and the Craftman. Proceedings of the 4th and 5th International Workshops, Athens 1994 and 1995.* Jonsered, 185–196.

Robbins, J., and Akin, D. 1999. 'An Introduction to Melanesian Currencies. Agency, Identity, and Social Reproduction', in Akin, D., and Robbins, J. eds., *Money and Modernity: State and Local Currencies in Melanesia.* ASAO Monograph Series. Pittsburgh, 1–40.

Robinson, E. S. G. 1937. 'A Hoard from "Sidon" [Beni-Hassan]', *The Numismatic Chronicle and Journal of the Royal Numismatic Society* 17 (67), 197–199.

1950. 'A "Silversmith's Hoard" from Mesopotamia', *Iraq* 12 (1), 44–51.

Rosa, D. F. 2011. 'Argento, annaku e il problema della moneta e del denaro nel periodo Medio Assiro (XIV-XI sec. a.C.)', *Rivista di Storia Economica* 27 (1), 111–130.

Rothenberg, B. 1988. *The Egyptian Mining Temple at Timna.* Researches in the Arabah, 1959–1984. London.

Röthlin, G., and le Roux, M. 2013. 'Hezekiah and the Assyrian Tribute', *Verbum et Ecclesia* 34 (2), 1–8.

Routledge, B. E. 2004. *Moab in the Iron Age: Hegemony, Polity, Archaeology.* Archaeology, Culture, and Society. Philadelphia.

Routledge, B. E., and McGeough, K. M. 2009. 'Just What Collapsed? A Network Perspective on "Palatial" and "Private" Trade at Ugarit', in Bachhuber, C., and Roberts, R. G. eds., *Forces of Transformation: The End of the Bronze Age in the Mediterranean: Proceedings of an International Symposium Held at St. John's College, University of Oxford, 25–6th March, 2006.* Themes from the Ancient Near East BANEA Publication Series. Oxford; Oakville, 22–29.

Rowe, A. 1930. *The Topography and History of Beth-Shan: With Details of the Egyptian and Other Inscriptions Found on the Site.* Beth-Shan I. Philadelphia.

1940. *The Four Canaanite Temples of Beth-Shan.* Publications of the Palestine Section of the University Museum, University of Pennsylvania. Philadelphia.

Ruschenbusch, E. 1966. *Solonos Nomoi: Die Fragmente des Solonischen Gesetzeswerkes, mit einer Text- und Überlieferungsgeschichte.* Historia Einzelschriften. Wiesbaden.

2010. *Solon: Das Gesetzeswerk – Fragmente: Übersetzung und Kommentar. hrsg. K. Bringmann.* Historia. Einzelschriften. Stuttgart.

Rutter, N. K. 1981. 'Early Coinage and the Influence of the Athenian State', in Cunliffe, B. W. ed., *Coinage and Society in Britain and Gaul: Some Current Problems.* Research Report; Council for British Archaeology. London, 1–9.

1997. *The Greek Coinages of Southern Italy and Sicily.* London.

Sahlins, M. D. [1972] 2004. *Stone Age Economics.* Second edition. Routledge Classic Ethnographies. London.

[1993] 2002. *Waiting for Foucault, Still.* Chicago.

Salmon, J. 1984. *Wealthy Corinth: A History of the City to 338 BC.* Oxford.

Sass, B. 1997. 'Jewelry', in Meyers, E. M. ed., *The Oxford Encyclopedia of Archaeology in the Near East.* Vol. 3. New York, 238–246.

2002a. 'An Iron Age I Jewelry Hoard from Cave II/3 in Wadi El-Makkuk', *'Atiqot* 41, 21–33.

2002b. 'Wenamun and His Levant – 1075 BC or 925 BC?', *Ägypten und Levante/Egypt and the Levant* 12, 247–55.

2005. *The Alphabet at the Turn of the Millennium: The West Semitic Alphabet ca. 1150–850 BCE: The Antiquity of the Arabian, Greek and Phrygian Alphabets.* Tel Aviv. Occasional Publications. Tel-Aviv.

Schaeffer, C. F.-A. 1932. 'Les Fouilles de Minet-el-Beida et de Ras-Shamra Troisième campagne (Printemps 1931): Rapport sommaire', *Syria* 13 (1), 1–27.

1935. 'Les fouilles de Ras Shamra-Ugarit. Sixième campagne (Printemps 1934). Rapport sommaire', *Syria* 16 (2), 141–176.

1937. 'Les Fouilles de Ras Shamra-Ugarit Huitième Campagne (Printemps 1936): Rapport sommaire', *Syria* 18 (2), 125–154.

1939. *Ugaritica: Études relatives aux découvertes de Ras Shamra.* Mission de Ras Shamra. Paris.

1963. 'Ausgrabungen und Forschungsreisen. Neue Entdeckungen in Ugarit', *Archiv für Orientforschung* 20, 206–215.

Schaps, D. M. 1997. 'The Monetization of the Marketplace in Athens', in Andreau, J., Briant, P., and Descat, R. eds. *Économie Antique: Prix et formation des rrix dans les économies antiques*. Saint-Bertrand-de-Comminges, 91–104.

2001. 'The Conceptual Prehistory of Money and Its Impact on the Greek Economy', in Balmuth, M. S. ed., *Hacksilber to Soinage: New Insights into the Monetary History of the Near East and Greece. A Collection of Eight Papers Presented at the 99th Annual Meeting of the Archaeological Institute of America*. Numismatic studies no. 24. New York, 93–103.

2004. *The Invention of Coinage and the Monetization of Ancient Greece*. Ann Arbor.

2007. 'The Invention of Coinage in Lydia, in India, and in China', *Bulletin du Cercle d'Études Numismatiques* 44, 313–322.

2008. 'What Was Money in Ancient Greece?', in Harris, W. V. ed., *The Monetary Systems of the Greeks and Romans*. Oxford, 38–48.

Scheidel, W. 2007. 'Demography', in Scheidel, W., Morris, I., and Saller, R. P. eds., *The Cambridge Economic History of the Greco-Roman World*. Cambridge; New York, 38–86.

2010. 'The Divergent Evolution of Coinage in Eastern and Western Eurasia', in Harris, W. V. ed., *The Monetary Systems of the Greeks and Romans*. Oxford, 267–286.

Schipper, B. U. 2005. *Die Erzahlung des Wenamun: ein Literaturwerk im Spannungsfeld von Politic, Geschichte und Religion*. Orbis biblicus et orientalis. Fribourg; Gottingen.

Schliemann, H. 1881. *Ilios, Stadt und Land der Trojaner. Forschungen und Entdeckungen in der Troas und besonders auf der Baustelle von Troja*. Leipzig.

Schloen, J. D. 2001. *The House of the Father As Fact and Symbol: Patrimonialism in Ugarit and the Ancient Near East*. Studies in the Archaeology and History of the Levant. Winona Lake.

Schmid, K. 2014. 'The Monetization and Demonetization of the Human Body: The Case of Compensatory Payments for Bodily Injuries and Homicide in Ancient Near Eastern and Ancient Israelite Law Books', in Hagen, J. V., and Welker, M. eds., *Money As God? The Monetization of the Market and Its Impact on Religion, Politics, Law, and Ethics*. Cambridge, 259–281.

Schon, R. 2015. 'Weight Sets: Identification and Analysis', *Cambridge Archaeological Journal* 25 (2), 477–494.

Scott, R. B. Y. 1965. 'The Scale-Weights from Ophel, 1963–64', *Palestine Exploration Quarterly* 97 (2), 128–139.

Seabright, P. ed. 2000. *The Vanishing Rouble: Barter Networks and Non-Monetary Transactions in Post-Soviet Societies*. Cambridge.

Seaford, R. 2004. *Money and the Early Greek Mind: Homer, Philosophy, Tragedy*. Cambridge.

2011. 'Exchange', in Finkelberg, M. ed., *The Homer Encyclopedia*. Chichester; Malden, 281–284.

Seger, J. D. 1976. 'Reflections on the Gold Hoard from Gezer', *Bulletin of the American Schools of Oriental Research* 221, Memorial Issue: Essays in Honor of George Ernest Wright, 133–140.

Sellin, E. 1914. 'Vorläufiger kurzer Bericht über die Ergebnisse seiner Ausgrabungen in Balata-Sichem (Wortlaut des Berichtes)', Anzeiger der Kaiserlichen Akademie der Wissenschaften, *Wien. Phil.-Hist. Klasse* 51 (7), 35–40.

Sergi, O., Karasik, A., Gadot, Y., and Lipschits, O. 2012. 'The Royal Judahite Storage Jar: A Computer-Generated Typology and Its Archaeological and Historical Implications', *Tel Aviv* 39 (1), 64–92.

Shalev, S., Shechtman, D., and Shilstein, S. S. 2014. 'A Study of the Composition and Microstructure of Silver Hoards from Tel Beth-Shean, Tel Dor, and Tel Miqne,

Israel', *Archaeological and Anthropological Sciences* 6 (3), 221–225.

Shea, W. H. 1978. 'Menahem and Tiglath-Pileser III', *Journal of Near Eastern Studies* 37 (1), 43–49.

Sheedy, K. 2012. 'Aegina, the Cyclades, and Crete', in Metcalf, W. E. ed., *The Oxford Handbook of Greek and Roman Coinage*. Oxford, 105–127.

Sheehan, J. 2007. 'The Form and Structure of Viking-Age Silver Hoards: The Evidence from Ireland', in Graham-Campbell, J., and Williams, G. eds., *Silver Economy in the Viking Age*. Walnut Creek, 149–162.

Sherratt, A. G. and Sherratt, E. S. 1991. 'From Luxuries to Commodities: The Nature of Mediterranean Bronze Age Trading Systems', in Gale, N. H. ed., *Bronze Age Trade in the Mediterranean: Papers Presented at the Conference Held at Rewley House, Oxford, in December 1989*. Studies in Mediterranean Archaeology. Jonsered, 351–386.

Sherratt, E. S. 1990. '"Reading the Texts": Archaeology and the Homeric Question', *Antiquity* 64 (245), 807–824.

1998. '"Sea Peoples" and the Economic Structure of the Late Second Millennium in the Eastern Mediterranean', in Gitin, S., Mazar, A., and Stern, E. eds., *Mediterranean Peoples in Transition: Thirteenth to Early Tenth Centuries BCE*. Jerusalem, 292–313.

2000. 'Circulation of Metals and the End of the Bronze Age in the Eastern Mediterranean', in Pare, C. F. E. ed., *Metals Make the World Go Round: The Supply and Circulation of Metals in Bronze Age Europe: Proceedings of a Conference Held at the University of Birmingham in June 1997*. Oxford, 82–98.

2010. 'Greeks and Phoenicians: Perceptions of Trade and Traders in the Early First Millennium BC', in Bauer, A. A., and Agbe-Davies, A. S. eds., *Social Archaeologies of Trade and Exchange: Exploring Relationships among People, Places, and Things*. Walnut Creek, 119–142.

Sherratt, E. S., and Sherratt, A. G. 1993. 'The Growth of the Mediterranean Economy in the Early First Millennium BC', *World Archaeology* 24 (3), 361–378.

Shipley, G. 1987. *A History of Samos, 800–188 BC*. Oxford.

Sigrist, R. M. 1982. 'Une tablette cunéiforme de Tell Keisan', *Israel Exploration Journal* 32 (1), 32–35.

Sillitoe, P. 2006. 'Why Spheres of Exchange?', *Ethnology* 45 (1), 1–23.

Silver, M. 2006. '"Coinage before Coins?": A Further Response to Raz Kletter', *Levant* 38 (1), 187–189.

Simmel, G. 1900. *Philosophie des Geldes*. Leipzig.

Sindbæk, S. M. 2008. 'Local and Long Distance exchange', in Brink, S., and Price, N. eds., *The Viking World*. London, 150–158.

2011. 'Silver Economies and Social Ties: Long-Distance Interaction, Long-Term Investments – and Why the Viking Age Happened', in Graham-Campbell, J., Sindbæk, S. M., and Williams, G., eds., *Silver Economies, Monetisation and Society in Scandinavia, AD 800–1100*. Aarhus, 41–65.

Singer, I. 1988–1989. 'The Political Status of Megiddo VIIA', *Tel Aviv* 15–16 (1), 101–112.

1994. 'Egyptians, Canaanites, and Philistines in the Period of the Emergence of Israel', in Finkelstein, I., and Na'aman, N. eds., *From Nomadism to Monarchy: Archaeological and Historical Aspects of Early Israel*. Jerusalem; Washington, DC, 282–338.

1999. 'A Political History of Ugarit', in Watson, W. G .E., and Wyatt, N. eds., *Handbook of Ugaritic Studies*. Handbuch der Orientalistik. Erste Abteilung, Nahe und der Mittlere Osten. Leiden, 603–733.

2006. 'Ships Bound for Lukka: A New Interpretation of the Companion Letters RS 94.2530 and RS 94.2523', *Altorientalische Forschungen* 33, 242–262.

Singer-Avitz, L. 2002. 'Arad: The Iron Age Pottery Assemblages', *Tel Aviv* 29 (1), 110–214.

Sismanidis, K. 2003. *Ancient Stageira: Birthplace of Aristotle*. Athens.

Skre, D. ed. 2007. *Means of Exchange: Dealing with Silver in the Viking Age*. Kaupang

Excavation Project publication series. Vol. 2. Aarhus.

Smith, A. 1776. *An Inquiry into the Nature and Causes of the Wealth of Nations*. Vol. 1. Dublin.

Snodgrass, A. M. 1964. *Early Greek Armour and Weapons: From the End of the Bronze Age to 600 B.C.* Edinburgh.

1971. *The Dark Age of Greece: An Archaeological Survey of the Eleventh to Eighth Centuries B.C.* Edinburgh.

1974. 'An Historical Homeric Society?', *The Journal of Hellenic Studies* 94, 114–125.

1980. *Archaic Greece: The Age of Experiment*. Berkeley.

Söderberg, A. 2004. 'Metallurgic Ceramics As a Key to Viking Age Workshop Organisation', *Journal of Nordic Archaeological Science* 14, 115–124.

Sokolowski, F. 1954. 'Fees and Taxes in the Greek Cults', *Harvard Theological Review* 47 (3), 153–164.

Sommerfeld, C. 1994. *Gerätegeld Sichel: Studien zur monetären Struktur bronzezeitlicher Horte im nördlichen Mitteleuropa*. Vorgeschichtliche Forschungen. Berlin.

Stager, L. E. 1996. 'Ashkelon and the Archaeology of Destruction: Kislev 604 BCE', *Eretz-Israel: Archaeological, Historical and Geographical Studies* 25, 61*–74*.

2003. 'Phoenician Shipwrecks in the Deep Sea', in Stampolidis, N. C., and Karageorghis, V. eds., *Ploes – Sea Routes: Interconnections in the Mediterranean, 16th–6th c. BC: Proceedings of the International Symposium Held at Rethymnon, Crete, September 29th–October 2nd, 2002*. Athens, 233–247.

Stager, L. E., Schloen, J. D., Master, D. M., Press, M. D., and Aja, A. 2008. 'Part Four: Stratigraphic Overview', in Stager, L. E., Schloen, J. D., and Master, D. M. eds., *Ashkelon 1: Introduction and Overview (1985–2006)*. Harvard Semitic Museum Publications. Winona Lake, 215–323.

Stanley, P. V. 1986. 'The Function of Trade in Homeric Society', *Münstersche Beiträge zur antiken Handelsgeschichte* 5 (2), 5–19.

Stefanakis, M. I. 1999. 'The Introduction of Coinage in Crete and the Beginning of Local Minting', in Chaniotis, A. ed., *From Minoan Farmers to Roman Traders: Sidelights on the Economy of Ancient Crete*. Heidelberger althistorische Beiträge und epigraphische Studien. Stuttgart, 247–268.

Stern, E. 1998. 'Buried Treasure: The Silver Hoard from Dor', *Biblical Archaeology Review* 24 (4), 46–62.

2001. 'The Silver Hoard from Tel Dor', in Balmuth, M. S. ed., *Hacksilber to Coinage: New Insights into the Monetary History of the Near East and Greece. A Collection of Eight Papers Presented at the 99th Annual Meeting of the Archaeological Institute of America*. Numismatic studies no. 24. New York, 19–26.

2007. *En-Gedi Excavations I: Final Report (1961–1965)*. Jerusalem.

2008. 'Dor', in Stern, E. ed., *The New Encyclopedia of Archaeological Excavations in the Holy Land*. Vol. 5. Supplementary Volume. Jerusalem, 1695–1703.

Stevens, M. E. 2006. *Temples, Tithes, and Taxes: The Temple and the Economic Life of Ancient Israel*. Peabody.

Stork, L. 2015. 'Systems of Value and the Changing Perception of Metal Commodities, ca. 4000–2600 BC', *Journal of Near Eastern Studies* 74 (1), 115–132.

Stos-Gale, Z. A. 2001. 'The Impact of the Natural Sciences on Studies of *Hacksilber* and Early Silver Coinage', in Balmuth, M. S. ed., *Hacksilber to Coinage: New Insights into the Monetary History of the Near East and Greece. A Collection of Eight Papers Presented at the 99th Annual Meeting of the Archaeological Institute of America*. Numismatic studies no. 24. New York, 53–76.

Stos-Gale, Z. A., and Macdonald, C. F. 1991. 'Sources of Metal and Trade in the Bronze Age', in Gale, N. H. ed., *Bronze Age Trade in the Mediterranean: Papers Presented at the Conference Held at Rewley House, Oxford, in December 1989*. Studies in Mediterranean archaeology. Jonsered, 249–284.

Stos-Gale, Z. A., and Gale, N. H. 2010. 'Bronze Age Metal Artefacts Found on Cyprus – Metal from Anatolia and the Western Mediterranean', *Trabajos de Prehistoria* 67 (2), 389–403.

Strøm, I. 1992. 'Obeloi of Pre- or Proto-Monetary Value in the Greek Sanctuaries', in Alroth, B., and Linders, T. eds., *Economics of Cult in the Ancient Greek World: Proceedings of the Uppsala Symposium 1990*. Acta Universitatis Upsaliensis. Boreas. Uppsala; Stockholm, 41–51.

Stroud, R. S. 1974. 'An Athenian Law on Silver Coinage', *Hesperia: The Journal of the American School of Classical Studies at Athens* 43 (2), 157–188.

1979. *The axones and kyrbeis of Drakon and Solon*. University of California Publications: Classical Studies. Berkeley.

Sweeney, J., and Sweeney, R. J. 1977. 'Monetary Theory and the Great Capitol Hill Baby Sitting Co-op Crisis: Comment', *Journal of Money, Credit and Banking* 9 (1, Part 1), 86–89.

Tandy, D. W. 1997. *Warriors into Traders: The Power of the Market in Early Greece*. Classics and Contemporary Thought. Berkeley.

2011. 'Economy', in Finkelberg, M. ed., *The Homer Encyclopedia*. Chichester; Malden, 226–228.

Tartaron, T. F. 2013. *Maritime Networks in the Mycenaean World*. New York.

Tebes, J. M. 2016. 'The Kingdom of Edom? A Critical Reappraisal of the Edomite State Model', in Milevski, I., and Levy, T. E. eds., *Framing Archaeology in the Near East: The Application of Social Theory to Fieldwork*. New Directions in Anthropological Archaeology. Sheffield; Bristol, 113–122.

Temin, P. 2006. 'Mediterranean Trade in Biblical Times', in Findlay, R., Henriksson, R. G. H., Lindgren, H., and Lundahl, M. eds., *Eli Heckscher, International Trade, and Economic History*. Cambridge, MA; London, 141–156.

Termeer, M. K. 2016. 'Roman Colonial Coinages beyond the City-State: A View from the Samnite World', *Journal of Ancient History* 4, 158–190.

Terrenato, N. 2020. 'Discussion', in Heymans, E. D., and Termeer, M. K. eds. *Politics of Value: New Approaches to Early Money and the State – Proceedings of the 19th International Congress of Classical Archaeology, Cologne/Bonn 2018 (panel 5.11)*. Heidelberg, 63–69.

Thareani, Y. 2016. 'The Empire and the "Upper Sea": Assyrian Control Strategies along the Southern Levantine Coast', *Bulletin of the American Schools of Oriental Research* 375, 77–102.

Themelis, P. G. 1981. 'Εργαστήριο χρυσοχόϊας του 8ου π.Χ. αι. στην Ερέτρια', *AAA* 14, 185–208.

1983. 'An 8th Century Goldsmith's Workshop at Eretria', in Hägg, R. ed., *The Greek Renaissance of the Eighth century B.C.: Tradition and Innovation: Proceedings of the Second International Symposium at the Swedish Institute in Athens, 1–5 June, 1981*. Acta Instituti Atheniensis Regni Sueciae. Stockholm; Lund, 158–165.

Thomas, C. G. 2009. 'The Mediterranean World in the Early Iron Age', in Raaflaub, K. A., and van Wees, H. eds., *A Companion to Archaic Greece*. Malden; Oxford, 22–40.

Thomas, R. 2005. 'Writing, Law, and Written Law', in Gagarin, M., and Cohen, D. eds., *The Cambridge Companion to Ancient Greek Law*. Cambridge Companions to the Ancient World. Cambridge, 41–60.

Thompson, C. M. 1999. 'A New Look at Barrekub's Treasure: Silver from Zinjirli', *Minerva* 10 (2), 48–50.

2003. 'Sealed Silver in Iron Age Cisjordan and the "Invention" of Coinage', *Oxford Journal of Archaeology* 22 (1), 67–107.

2007. 'Silver in the Age of Iron and the Orientalizing Economies of Archaic Greece', PhD dissertation, University of California, Los Angeles.

2009. 'Precious Metals and Jewelry. Chapter 11A: Three 20th Dynasty Silver Hoards from the Egyptian Garrison', in Panitz-Cohen, N., and Mazar, A. eds.,

Excavations at Tel Beth-Shean 1989–1996. Vol. III. The 13th–11th Century BCE Strata in Areas N and S. The Hebrew University of Jerusalem, The Institute of Archaeology. Jerusalem, 597–611.

2020. 'Two Bundles of *Hacksilber*', in Stager, L. E., Master, D. M., and Aja, A. J. eds., *Ashkelon 7: The Iron Age I.* University Park, 597–604.

Thompson, C. M., and Skaggs, S. 2013. 'King Solomon's Silver? Southern Phoenician Hacksilber Hoards and the Location of Tarshish', *Internet Archaeology* 35. doi.org/10.11141/ia.35.6.

Tiverios, M. A. 1998. 'The Ancient Settlement in the Anchialos-Sindos Double Trapeza. Seven Years (1990–1996) of Archaeological Research', in Bats, M., and D'Agostino, B. eds., *Euboica: l'Eubea e la presenza euboica in Calcidica e in Occidente : atti del convegno internazionale di Napoli, 13–16 novembre 1996.* Napoli, 243–253.

2008. 'Greek Colonization of the Northern Aegean', in Tsetskhladze, G. R. ed., *Greek Colonisation: An Account of Greek Colonies and Other Settlements Overseas.* Volume Two. Mnemosyne, bibliotheca classica Batava. Leiden; Boston, 1–154.

2012. 'Andros and Its Colonies', *Mediterranean Archaeology* 25, 273–281.

Toffolo, M., Arie, E., Martin, M., Boaretto, E., and Finkelstein, I. 2014. 'Absolute Chronology of Megiddo, Israel, in the Late Bronze and Iron Ages: High-Resolution Radiocarbon Dating', *Radiocarbon* 56 (1), 221–244.

Torrey, C. C. 1936. 'The Foundry of the Second Temple at Jerusalem', *Journal of Biblical Literature* 55 (4), 247–260.

1943. 'The Evolution of a Financier in the Ancient Near East', *Journal of Near Eastern Studies* 2 (4), 295–301.

Treister, M. Y. 1996a. 'The Trojan Treasures: Description, Chronology, Historical Context', in Antonova, I., Tolstikow, W., and Treister, M. Y. eds., *The Gold of Troy: Searching for Homer's Fabled City.* London; New York, 197–234.

1996b. *The Role of Metals in Ancient Greek History.* Mnemosyne, bibliotheca classica Batava. Supplementum. Leiden.

Tsetskhladze, G. R. 1994. 'Greek Penetration of the Black Sea', in Tsetskhladze, G. R., and De Angelis, F. eds., *The Archaeology of Greek Colonization.* Oxford University School of Archaeology Monograph. Oxford, 111–135.

1995. 'Did the Greeks Go to Colchis for Metals?', *Oxford Journal of Archaeology* 14 (3), 307–331.

1998. 'Trade at the Black Sea in the Archaic and Classical Periods: Some Observations', in Parkins, H. M., and Smith, C. J. eds., *Trade, Traders and the Ancient City.* London, 52–74.

Tsigarida, B. 2011. 'Chalcidice', in Lane Fox, R. ed., *Brill's Companion to Ancient Macedon: Studies in the Archaeology and History of Macedon, 650 BC–300 AD.* Leiden, 137–158.

Tyldesley, J. A. 1996. *Hatchepsut: The Female Pharaoh.* London.

Ulf, C. 2009. 'The World of Homer and Hesiod', in Raaflaub, K. A., and van Wees, H. eds., *A Companion to Archaic Greece.* Malden; Oxford, 81–99.

Ussishkin, D. 1995. 'The Destruction of Megiddo at the End of the Late Bronze Age and Its Historical Significance', *Tel Aviv* 22 (2), 240–267.

Vanschoonwinkel, J. 2006. 'Mycenaean Expansion', in Tsetskhladze, G. R. ed., *Greek Colonisation: An Account of Greek Colonies and Other Settlements Overseas.* Volume One. Mnemosyne, bibliotheca classica Batava. Leiden; Boston, 41–113.

van Alfen, P. 2016. 'Aegean-Levantine Trade, 600–300 BCE – Commodities, Consumers, and the Problem of Autarkeia', in Harris, E. M., Lewis, D. M., and Woolmer, M. eds., *The Ancient Greek Economy: Markets, Households and City-States.* New York, 277–298.

2020. 'The Role of "The State" in Early Electrum Coinage', in van Alfen, P., Wartenberg, U., Fischer-Bossert, W., Gitler, H., Konuk, K., and Lorber, C. C.

eds., *White Gold: Studies in Early Electrum Coinage*. New York and Jerusalem, 547–568.

van Alfen, P., Wartenberg, U., Fischer-Bossert, W., Gitler, H., Konuk, K., and Lorber, C. C. eds. 2020. *White Gold: Studies in Early Electrum Coinage*. New York and Jerusalem.

Van Beek, G. W. 1993. 'Tell Jemmeh', in Stern, E., Lewinson-Gilboa, A., and Aviram, J. eds., *The New Encyclopedia of Archaeological Excavations in the Holy Land*. Jerusalem, 667–674.

Van de Mieroop, M. 2002. 'A History of Near Eastern Debt?', in Hudson, M., and Van de Mieroop, M. eds., *Debt and Economic Renewal in the Ancient Near East*. Bethesda, 59–94.

2004. *A History of the Ancient Near East, ca. 3000–323 BC*. Blackwell History of the Ancient World. Malden.

2011. *A History of Ancient Egypt*. Blackwell History of the Ancient World. Chichester.

van der Brugge, C. 2017. 'Of Production, Trade, Profit and Destruction: An Economic Interpretation of Sennacherib's Third Campaign', *Journal of the Economic and Social History of the Orient* 60 (3), 292–335.

van Wees, H. 1998. 'The Law of Gratitude: Reciprocity in Anthropological Theory', in Gill, C., Postlethwaite, N., and Seaford, R. eds., *Reciprocity in Ancient Greece*. Oxford, 13–49.

2009. 'The Economy', in Raaflaub, K. A., and van Wees, H. eds., *A Companion to Archaic Greece*. Malden; Oxford, 444–467.

2013. *Ships and Silver, Taxes and Tribute: A Fiscal History of Archaic Athens*. London.

van Wijngaarden, G. J. 2017. 'Shifts in Value? Exotica in the 13th–12th Centuries BCE Mediterranean', in Fischer, P. M., and Bürge, T. eds., *'Sea Peoples' Up-to-Date: New Research on Transformations in the Eastern Mediterranean in the 13th–11th Centuries BCE: Proceedings of the ESF-Workshop Held at the Austrian Academy of Sciences, Vienna, 3–4 November 2014*. Österreichische Akademie der Wissenschaften. Denkschriften der Gesamtakademie. Vienna, 401–412.

Vargyas, P. 2007. 'Fakes before Coins?: On the Gold and Silver Hoards from Level V at Beth-Shean', in Crawford, S. W., Ben-Tor, A., Dessel, J. P., Dever, W. G., Mazar, A., and Aviram, J. eds., *'Up to the Gates of Ekron': Essays on the Archaeology and History of the Eastern Mediterranean in Honor of Seymour Gitin*. Jerusalem, 295–304.

2010. 'The Amarna Treasure and the Thief', in Csabai, Z. ed., *From Elephantine to Babylon: Selected Studies of Péter Vargyas on Ancient Near Eastern Economy*. Ancient Near Eastern and Mediterranean Studies. Budapest, 147–156.

Vaux, R. de 1961. *Ancient Israel: Its Life and Institutions*. London.

Vavelidis, M., and Andreou, S. 2008. 'Gold and Gold Working in Late Bronze Age Northern Greece', *Naturwissenschaften* 95 (4), 361–366.

Velde, F. R. 2020. 'A Quantitative Approach to the Beginnings of Coinage', in van Alfen, P., Wartenberg, U., Fischer-Bossert, W., Gitler, H., Konuk, K., and Lorber, C. C. eds., *White Gold: Studies in Early Electrum Coinage*. New York and Jerusalem, 497–516.

Venit, M. S. 1984. 'Early Attic Black Figure Vases in Egypt', *Journal of the American Research Center in Egypt* 21, 141–154.

Verdan, S. 2010. 'Die Einstehung der Stadt', in Martin Pruvot, C., Reber, K., and Theurillat, T. eds., *Ausgegraben! Schweizer Archäologen erforschen die griechische Stadt Eretria : Eine Ausstellung der Schweizerischen Archäologischen Schule in Griechenland in Zusammenarbeit mit dem Antikenmuseum Basel und Sammlung Ludwig*. Basel; Gollion, 64–71.

2013. *Eretria XXII. Le sanctuaire d'Apollon Daphnéphoros à l'époque géométrique*. Gollion; Lausanne.

2017. 'Counting on Pots? Reflections on Numerical Notations in Early Iron Age Greece', in Clay, J. S., Malkin, I., and Tzifopoulos, Y. eds., *Panhellenes at*

Methone: Graphê in Late Geometric and Protoarchaic Methone, Macedonia (ca 700 BCE). Berlin; Boston, 105–122.

forthcoming. 'Metallurgical Ceramics from the Hypogeion at Methone' in Morris, S. P., and Papadopoulos, J. K. eds., *Excavations at Ancient Methone, 2003–2011*. Los Angeles.

Verdan, S., and Heymans, E. D. forthcoming. 'Men and Metals on the Move: The Case of 'Euboean' Gold', in Cinquantaquattro, T. E., and D'Acunto, M. eds. *Pithecusa and Euboea between East and West (Euboica II)*. Proceedings of the International Colloquium in Lacco Ameno (Ischia), 14–17 May, 2018.

Villing, A. 2015. 'Naukratis, Egypt and Mediterranean World: Greek-Egyptian Relations in the 7th to 6th centuries BC.' www.britishmuseum.org/PDF/Naukratis_ORC_Greek_Egyptian_Relations_Villing.pdf.

Villing, A., and Schlotzhauer, U. 2006a. *Naukratis: Greek Diversity in Egypt: Studies on East Greek Pottery and Exchange in the Eastern Mediterranean*. British Museum Research Publication. London.

2006b. 'Naukratis and the Eastern Mediterranean: Past, Present and Future', in Villing, A., and Schlotzhauer, U. eds., *Naukratis: Greek Diversity in Egypt. Studies on East Greek Pottery and Exchange in the Eastern Mediterranean*. The British Museum Research Publication. London, 1–10.

Vittmann, G. 2003. *Ägypten und die Fremden im ersten vorchristlichen Jahrtausend*. Mainz.

von Luschan, F., and Andrae, W. E. 1943. *Ausgrabungen in Sendschirli V. Die Kleinfunde von Sendschirli*. Mitteilungen aus den orientalischen Sammlungen. Berlin.

von Reden, S. 1995. *Exchange in Ancient Greece*. London.

1997. 'Money, Law and Exchange: Coinage in the Greek Polis', *The Journal of Hellenic Studies* 117, 154–176.

2002. 'Money in the Ancient Economy: A Survey of Recent Research', *Klio* 84 (1), 141–174.

2010. *Money in Classical Antiquity*. Key Themes in Ancient History. New York.

Voutsaki, S., and Killen, J. T. eds. 2001. *Economy and Politics in the Mycenaean Palace States: Proceedings of a Conference Held on 1–3 July 1999 in the Faculty of Classics, Cambridge*. Supplementary Volume/Cambridge Philological Society. Cambridge.

Wagner, G. A., Pernicka, E., Gialoglou, G., and Vavelidis, M. 1981. 'Ancient Gold Mines on Thasos', *Naturwissenschaften* 68 (5), 263–264.

Wagner, G. A., Pernicka, E., Vavelidis, M., Baranyi, I., and Bassiakos, Y. 1986. 'Archaeometallurgische Untersuchungen auf Chalkidike', *Der Anschnitt* 5–6, 166–186.

Wagner, G., and Weisgerber, G. eds. 1985. *Silber, Blei und Gold auf Sifnos: Prähistorische und antike Metallproduktion*. Der Anschnitt. Beiheft. Bochum.

Waiman-Barak, P., Gilboa, A., and Goren, Y. 2014. 'A Stratified Sequence of Early Iron Age Egyptian Ceramics at Tel Dor, Israel', *Ägypten und Levante/Egypt and the Levant* 24, 315–342.

Waldstein, C. 1902. *The Argive Heraeum, Vol. 1: General Introduction, Geology, Architecture, Marble Statuary and Inscriptions*. Boston; New York.

1905. *The Argive Heraeum, Vol. 2: Terra-Cotta Figurines, Terra-Cotta Reliefs, Vases and Vase Fragments, Bronzes, Engraved Stones, Gems, and Ivories, Coins, Egyptian or Graeco-Egyptian, Objects*. Boston; New York.

Wallace, R. W. 1983. 'The Date of Solon's Reforms', *American Journal of Ancient History* 8, 81–95.

1987. 'The Origin of Electrum Coinage', *American Journal of Archaeology* 91 (3), 385–397.

2016. 'Redating Croesus: Herodotean Chronologies, and the Dates of the Earliest Coinages', *The Journal of Hellenic Studies* 136, 168–181.

Walton, J. T. 2015. 'The Regional Economy of the Southern Levant in the 8th–7th Centuries BCE', PhD dissertation, Harvard University.

Warburton, D. A. 2009. 'Economics, Anthropological Models and the Ancient Near East', *Anthropology of the Middle East* 4 (1), 65–90.

Watts, J. W. 2011. 'Aaron and the Golden Calf in the Rhetoric of the Pentateuch', *Journal of Biblical Literature* 130 (3), 417–430.

Weatherford, J. M. 1997. *The History of Money: From Sandstone to Cyberspace*. New York.

Weiner, A. B. 1992. *Inalienable Possessions: The Paradox of Keeping-While-Giving*. Berkeley; Oxford.

Weinstein, J. M. 1981. 'The Egyptian Empire in Palestine: A Reassessment', *Bulletin of the American Schools of Oriental Research* 241, 1–28.

1992. 'The Collapse of the Egyptian Empire in the Southern Levant', in Joukowsky, M., and Ward, W. A. eds., *The Crisis Years: the 12th Century B.C. from Beyond the Danube to the Tigris*. Dubuque, 142–163.

Weiss, E., and Kislev, M .E. 2004. 'Plant Remains As Indicators for Economic Activity: A Case Study from Iron Age Ashkelon', *Journal of Archaeological Science* 31 (1), 1–13.

Wengrow, D. 2011. '" Archival" and "Sacrificial" Economies in Bronze Age Eurasia: An Interactionist Approach to the Hoarding of Metals', in Wilkinson, T. C., Sherratt, E. S., and Bennet, J. eds., *Interweaving Worlds: Systemic Interactions in Eurasia, 7th to 1st millennia BC*. Oxford, 135–144.

Wente, E. F. 1990. *Letters from Ancient Egypt*. Atlanta.

2003. 'The Report of Wenamon', in Simpson, W. K. ed., *The Literature of Ancient Egypt: An Anthology of Stories, Instructions, Stelae, Autobiographies, and Poetry*. New Haven, 116–124.

Wertime, T. A. 1973. 'The Beginnings of Metallurgy: A New Look: Arguments over Diffusion and Independent Invention Ignore the Complex Metallurgic Crafts Leading to Iron', *Science (New York)* 182 (4115), 875–887.

West, M. L. 1997. *The East Face of Helicon: West Asiatic Elements in Early Poetry and Myth*. Oxford.

2005. '"Odyssey" and "Argonautica"', *The Classical Quarterly* 55 (1), 39–64.

2011. *Hellenica: Selected Papers on Greek Literature and Thought*. Oxford.

2014. *The Making of the Odyssey*. New York.

Whitley, J. 1991. 'Social Diversity in Dark Age Greece', *The Annual of the British School at Athens* 86, 341–365.

2001. *The Archaeology of Ancient Greece*. Cambridge World Archaeology. Cambridge.

2002. 'Objects with Attitude: Biographical Facts and Fallacies in the Study of Late Bronze Age and Early Iron Age Warrior Graves', *Cambridge Archaeological Journal* 12 (2), 217–232.

Wigg-Wolf, D. 2011. 'The Function of Celtic Coinages in Northern Gaul', in García-Bellido, M. P., Callegarin, L., and Diéz, A. J. eds., *Barter, Money and Coinage in the Ancient Mediterranean (10th–1st centuries BC)*, 301–314.

Williams, G. 2007. 'Kingship, Christianity and Coinage: Monetary and Political Perspectives on Silver Economy in the Viking Age', in Graham-Campbell, J., and Williams, G. eds., *Silver Economy in the Viking Age*. Walnut Creek, 177–214.

Williamson, G. C. 1894. *The Money of the Bible: Illustrated by Numerous Woodcuts and Facsimile Representations*. By-paths of Bible Knowledge. London.

Wilson, D. F. 2002. *Ransom, Revenge, and Heroic Edentity in the Iliad*. Cambridge.

Winand, J. 2011. 'The *Report of Wenamun*: A Journey in Ancient Egyptian Literature', in Collier, M., and Snape, S. R. eds., *Ramesside Studies in Honour of K. A. Kitchen*. Bolton, 541–559.

Winter, I. J. 1995. 'Homer's Phoenicians: History, Ethnography, or Literary Trope? A Perspective on Early Orientalism', in Carter, J. B., and Morris, S. P. eds., *The Ages of Homer: A Tribute to Emily Townsend Vermeule*. Austin, 247–271.

Wiseman, R. 2018. 'Random Accumulation and Breaking: The Formation of Bronze Age Scrap Hoards in England and Wales', *Journal of Archaeological Science* 90, 39–49.

Wood, J. R., Montero-Ruiz, I., and Martinón-Torres, M. 2019. 'From Iberia to the Southern Levant: The Movement of Silver across the Mediterranean in the Early Iron Age', *Journal of World Prehistory* 32 (1), 1–31.

Wolf, E. R. 1982. *Europe and the People without History*. Berkeley; Los Angeles; London.

Wray, L. R. ed. 2004. *Credit and State Theories of Money: The Contributions of A. Mitchell Innes*. Cheltenham.

Wright, G. E. 1965. *Shechem: The Biography of a Biblical City*. The Norton Lectures of the Southern Baptist Theological Seminary. New York.

Wright, G. R. H. 2002. *Shechem III: The Stratigraphy and Architecture of Shechem/Tell Balatah. Volume 2: The Illustrations*. ASOR Archaeological Reports no. 6. Boston.

Wright, L. S. 1989. '*MKR* in 2 Kings XII 5–17 and Deuteronomy XVIII 8', *Vetus Testamentum* 39 (4), 438–448.

Yadin, Y. 1970a. 'Megiddo of the Kings of Israel', *The Biblical Archaeologist* 33 (3), 65–96.

1970b. 'The Megiddo of the Kings of Israel', *Qadmoniot* 10, 38–56 (Hebrew).

Yahalom-Mack, N., Langgut, D., Dvir, O., Tirosh, O., Eliyahu-Behar, A., Erel, Y., Langford, B., Frumkin, A., Ullman, M., and Davidovich, U. 2015. 'The Earliest Lead Object in the Levant', *PLOS ONE* 10 (12), e0142948.

Yahalom-Mack, N., Panitz-Cohen, N., Eshel, T., and Mullins, R. 2019. 'A Late Bronze IIB Silver Hoard from Tel Abel Beth Maacah', *Israel Exploration Journal* 69 (2), 129–153.

Yan, Y. 2005. 'The Gift and Gift Economy', in Carrier, J. G. ed., *A Handbook of Economic Anthropology*. Cheltenham, 246–261.

Yannai, E. 1996. 'A New Approach to Levels VI–V at Tel Beth-Shan', *Tel Aviv* 23 (2), 185–194.

Yeivin, Z. 1971a. 'Eshtemoa', *Hadashot Archeologiot* 37, 24 (Hebrew).

1971b. 'Es-Samo'a (As-Samu')', *Israel Exploration Journal* 21 (2/3), 174–175.

1972. 'The Silver Hoard from Eshtemoa', *Qadmoniot* 18, 45–46 (Hebrew).

1987. 'The Mysterious Silver Hoard from Eshtemoa', *Biblical Archaeology Review* 13 (6), 38–44.

1990. 'The Silver Hoard from Eshtemoa', *'Atiqot (Hebrew Series)* 10, 43–57 (Hebrew).

1993. 'Eshtemoa', in Stern, E., Lewinson-Gilboa, A., and Aviram, J. eds., *The New Encyclopedia of Archaeological Excavations in the Holy Land*. Vol. 2. Jerusalem, 423–426.

Yellen, J. E. 1990. 'The Transformation of the Kalahari !Kung', *Scientific American* 262 (4), 96–105.

Yon, M. 1992. 'The End of the Kingdom of Ugarit', in Joukowsky, M., and Ward, W. A. eds., *The Crisis Years: The 12th Century B.C. from Beyond the Danube to the Tigris*. Dubuque, 111–122.

Younger, K. L. Jr. 2000a. 'Black Obelisk (2.113F)', in Hallo, W. W., and Younger K. L. Jr. eds., *The Context of Scripture. Vol. II. Monumental Inscriptions from the Biblical World*. Leiden, 269–270.

Younger, K. L. 2000b. 'The Calah Annals (2.117A)', in Hallo, W. W., and Younger, K. L. Jr. eds., *The Context of Scripture. Vol. II. Monumental Inscriptions from the Biblical World*. Leiden, 284–286.

2000c. 'The Iran stela (2.117B)', in Hallo, W. W., and Younger, K. L. Jr. eds., *The Context of Scripture. Vol. II. Monumental Inscriptions from the Biblical World*. Leiden, 287.

2000d. 'Summary Inscription 4 (2.117C)', in Hallo, W. W., and Younger, K. L. Jr. eds., *The Context of Scripture. Vol. II. Monumental Inscriptions from the Biblical World*. Leiden, 287–289.

2000e. 'Summary Inscription 7 (2.117D)', in Hallo, W. W., and Younger, K. L. Jr. eds., *The Context of Scripture. Vol. II. Monumental Inscriptions from the Biblical World*. Leiden, 289–290.

2015. 'The Assyrian Economic Impact on the Southern Levant in the Light of Recent Study', *Israel Exploration Journal* 65 (2), 179–204.

Zaccagnini, C. 1973. *Lo scambio dei doni nel Vicino Oriente durante i secoli XV–XIII*. Orientis antiqui collectio. Rome, 224.

1991. 'Ancora sulle coppe d'oro e d'argento nel Vicino Oriente del Tardo Bronzo', *Scienze dell'antichità* 5, 369–379.

1999–2001. 'The Mina of Karkemiš and Other Minas', *State Archives of Assyria Bulletin* 13, 39–56.

Zangani, F. 2016. 'Amarna and Uluburun: Reconsidering Patterns of Exchange in the Late Bronze Age', *Palestine Exploration Quarterly* 148 (4), 230–244.

Zapassky, E., Gadot, Y., Finkelstein, I., and Benenson, I. 2012. 'An Ancient Relation between Units of Length and Volume Based on a Sphere', *PLOS ONE* 7 (3), e33895.

Zarzecki-Peleg, A. 2005. 'Tel Megiddo during the Iron Age I and IIA–IIB. The Excavations of the Yadin Expedition at Megiddo and their Contribution for Comprehending the History of this Site and other Contemporary Sites in Northern Israel', PhD dissertation, Hebrew University (Hebrew).

Zelizer, V. A. R. 1994. *The social meaning of money*. New York.

Zertal, A. 2007. *The Manasseh Hill Country Survey. Volume II: The Eastern Valleys and the Fringes of the Desert*. Leiden.

Zertal, A., and Mirkam, N. 2016. *The Manasseh Hill Country Survey. Volume III: From Nahal 'Iron to Nahal Shechem*. Leiden.

Zurbach, J. 2017. 'Esclaves, dette, monnaie en Grèce mycénienne', in Nosch, M., and Landenius Enegren, H. eds., *Aegean Scripts: Proceedings of the 14th International Colloquium on Mycenaean Studies, Copenhagen, 2–5 September 2015*. Incunabula Graeca. Rome, 659–672.

2018. 'New Perspectives on Money in the Late Bronze to Iron Age Aegean', in Tekin, O. ed., *Second International Congress on the of History of Money and Numismatics in the Mediterranean World, 5–8 January 2017, Antalya. Proceedings*. Istanbul, 1–13.

INDEX OF ANCIENT SOURCES

This index is limited to ancient Greek, Roman and biblical sources.

Literary texts

Inscriptions

Hebrew Bible/Old Testament

GENERAL INDEX